The Essays of
Virginia Woolf

The Essays of Virginia Woolf

VOLUME II

1912–1918

EDITED BY
ANDREW McNEILLIE

A Harvest/HBJ Book

Harcourt Brace Jovanovich, Publishers

San Diego   New York   London

Requests for permission to make copies of any part of the work should be mailed to:
Permissions Department,
Harcourt Brace Jovanovich, Publishers,
Orlando, Florida 32887.

Library of Congress Cataloging-in-Publication Data
(Revised for vol. 2)
Woolf, Virginia, 1882-1941.
The essays of Virginia Woolf.
Bibliography: v. 1, p.
Includes index.
Contents: v. 1. 1904-1912—v. 2. 1912-1918.
1. McNeillie, Andrew. I. Title.
PR6045.O72.A6 1987   824'.912   86-29520
ISBN 0-15-129056-3
ISBN 0-15-629055-3 (pbk.)

Printed in the United States of America

First Harvest/HBJ edition 1990

A B C D E

Contents

Introduction

The marriage of Virginia Stephen and Leonard Woolf in August 1912 marked the beginning of one of the most notable collaborations in our recent cultural history. She was thirty; he would be thirty-two in November; and so they were not conspicuously young. Nor were they exactly untried in the world. Virginia Woolf had already displayed evidence of her genius, as those familiar with the first volume of this edition of her essays, with her early shorter fiction,[1] and who have read her first novel *The Voyage Out*, will know. On leaving Trinity College, Cambridge, in 1904, Leonard Woolf had 'spent 7 years in Ceylon, governing natives, inventing ploughs, shooting tigers'.[2] The Colonial Service had recently offered him 'a very high place' but he chose instead to resign: 'gave up his entire career' on the chance that Virginia Stephen might agree to marry him.[3] On his return, he had also begun his first novel, *The Village in the Jungle*, which was to appear in 1913. But at the same time, neither of the Woolfs could be described as being established in life. Indeed, Leonard Woolf ('He has no money of his own'[4]) was now positively disestablished. They resolved to live as inexpensively as they could, to write – their novels, and journalism – and also, in Leonard's case, 'to find out about labour and factories and to keep outside Government and do things on his own account'.[5] But during at least the first three years of their marriage, the question of how the Woolfs might live turned out to be a far more fundamental one, a matter, in fact, of Virginia Woolf's personal survival. For she suffered in that period two prolonged bouts of severe mental illness: first in 1913, when an attempted suicide brought her close to death, and then again in 1915, the year in which *The Voyage Out* was published.

These tragic circumstances are reflected in the composition of this volume, which contains no articles for the years 1914 and 1915 and three only for 1913. (The years 1910–12 were also relatively poor in journalistic output. But, although she certainly was ill in 1912 and required periods of seclusion and rest, this poverty had more to do with the fact that she was at that time almost exclusively occupied in writing and rewriting *The Voyage Out*, the completed manuscript of which she was to deliver to Duckworth & Co. in March 1913.)

The Woolfs lived first in rooms at Clifford's Inn in London and then in October 1914 removed to Richmond. There they remained, until the following March, amid extraordinary domestic turmoil at 17 The Green ('this House of Trouble'[6]), a number of Belgian refugees, compatriots of Mrs Le Grys, the landlady, among their fellow lodgers. From the diary Virginia Woolf briefly kept in January–February 1915, we may catch sight of the Woolfs in the interlude between the nightmare periods of her derangement: '. . . the evenings reading by the fire . . . reading Michelet & The Idiot & smoking & talking to L. in what stands for slippers & dressing gown',[7] the days spent 'scribbling',[8] reading, walking, attending concerts, house-hunting, going to the 'picture palace'[9] and the music hall, visiting libraries, seeing friends and in-laws, discussing the war, declaring oneself a Fabian.[10] Leonard Woolf wrote reviews for the *New Statesman, New Weekly, Co-operative News* and the *TLS*, lectured on co-operation and international subjects, worked at his highly influential book on *International Government* (1916) and at *Co-operation and the Future of Industry* (1919), a work begun in 1914. (In which year was published his second, and last, novel *The Wise Virgins* – 'very bad in parts; first rate in others'.)[11]

By March 1915 Virginia Woolf's condition was desperate. She seemed altogether to have lost her balance of mind. The Woolfs that month acquired Hogarth House, in Richmond, and Leonard took possession of it on the 25th. On the 26th *The Voyage Out* was published and in general the reviewers, discerning its distinction, received it with enthusiasm. But it was to be a long time before its author could fully appreciate her success. Not until the end of the year can she really be said to have emerged from her ordeal. Her association with the *TLS* recommenced in January 1916 with the appearance of her first review ('Queen Adelaide') in that journal, or, as far as we know, in any other journal, since she had reviewed *Les Copains* by Jules Romains in August 1913. By the end of 1916, as Quentin Bell has said, the Woolfs had 'evolved a pattern of life at Hogarth House to which they adhered more or less all their lives. They wrote in the morning, they walked in the afternoon, they read in the evening . . . once or twice a week Virginia would accompany Leonard to London and visit libraries, shops, concerts or friends'.[12] To this it should be added that they also divided their time between town and country (again, part of a lifelong pattern), migrating from Richmond periodically to stay in Sussex, at Asheham House, which Virginia had rented since before her marriage.

In April 1917 the Woolfs obtained a printing press and in July issued their first publication, *Two Stories*. This contained 'The Mark on the Wall' by Virginia Woolf and Leonard Woolf's 'Three Jews', and four woodcuts by Dora Carrington. They found the fascination of printing 'something extreme'[13] and at moments it seemed the press would completely take over their lives. But it did not quite do that. A year was to pass before the appearance of their second listed publication: *Prelude* by Katherine Mansfield. (They had also issued for private circulation, in about May or June 1918, *Poems* by Cecil Woolf, Leonard's brother, who had been killed in November 1917.) In the meantime, Virginia Woolf worked at her second novel, *Night and Day* (1919), which she had first conceived in July 1916. She also wrote a great amount of journalism, almost all for the *TLS*. (In the period covered by this volume only one of her articles appeared elsewhere, and that, 'Heard on the Downs', was published in *The Times* itself, 15 August 1916.) She was in great demand. Hardly had she time to declare herself 'rejected' by the *TLS*, than she must turn round and announce the revocation of her dismissal.[14] On occasion the *TLS* would 'shower'[15] her with books, and there is no doubt but that she thoroughly enjoyed it:

When I have to review at command of a telegram, & Mr Geal has to ride off in a shower to fetch the book at Glynde [a mile or so from Asheham House], & comes & taps at the window about 10 at night to receive his shilling & hand in the parcel, I feel pressed & important & even excited a little.[16]

She might receive '2 or even 3 books weekly':

& thus breast one short choppy wave after another. It fills up the time while Night & Day lies dormant; it gives me distinct pleasure I own to formulate rapid views of Henry James & Mr Hergesheimer; chiefly because I slip in some ancient crank of mine.[17]

And again we may see how by now she flourished, as she had not quite always done earlier in her career, when driven by the spur of the newspaper deadline:

... this sort of writing is always done against time; however much time I may have ... I write & write; I am rung up & told to stop writing till the messenger from the Times appears; I correct the pages in my bedroom with him sitting over the fire here.

'A Christmas number not at all to Mr [Bruce] Richmond [Editor to the *TLS*]'s taste, he said. Very unlike the supplement style.'

'Gift books, I suppose?' I suggested.

'Oh no. Mrs Woolf, its [sic] for the advertisers.'[18]

If Virginia's mental illness overshadowed the Woolfs' lives for a great part of the period spanned by this volume, their lives were also darkened by another lunacy: the war.

The war, and in particular the introduction of conscription in the spring of 1916, brought certain members of Bloomsbury into the public arena. Clive Bell, for one, knew his mind on the issue sooner than most of his friends. In 1915 he voiced his opposition to the confrontation in a pamphlet, calling for *Peace at Once*, a publication destroyed by order of the authorities. Maynard Keynes, although now a Treasury official actively engaged in organising war finance, became involved in the affairs of the No-Conscription Fellowship, as more directly did Virginia's brother Adrian Stephen, giving evidence on behalf of friends who had, as Conscientious Objectors, to appear before the Military and Appeal Tribunals. The 'private nightmare' of Virginia's illness prevented Leonard Woolf from considering, for some time, his own 'personal relation' to the war.[19] But when he did consider it, although convinced that the war was 'senseless and useless', he found that he could not be 'a complete pacifist'.[20] He was, however, exempted from military service, in June 1916, and again in October 1917. (He suffered from a congenital tremor of the hands.)

To Virginia Woolf the war was, artistically and otherwise, a subject almost unspeakable. She felt, as far as fiction was concerned, 'that the vast events now shaping across the channel are towering over us too closely and too tremendously to be worked [in] without a painful jolt in the perspective'[21] (and even in her later novels she treated it obliquely). She reported these and other events that brought the war closer to home, cursorily, in her diary. There she recorded incidents: casualties, ships sunk, air raids, the progress (or otherwise) at the Front. Patriotism she held to be, if not the last refuge of a scoundrel, a 'base emotion'.[22] On hearing the national anthem and a hymn at a Queen's Hall concert in 1915, all she could feel was 'the entire absence of emotion in myself & everyone else'.[23] For the non-participant, at least, life went on, and the inhumanity of war itself passed so far beyond common reality as to seem impossible to relate to. (Upon this point see the distinctly odd piece of writing 'Heard on the Downs'.) Relating to the war was perhaps especially difficult for one whose mental equilibrium had recently proved to be so disastrously unstable under even the most pacific external conditions.

The war, to propagate itself, also made away with the most ordinary kinds of truth. The 'peculiar irony' of Rupert Brooke's 'canonisation'[24] was for Virginia Woolf a supreme, personal example of this process. She remarked upon it when concluding her review ('The New Crusade', *TLS*, 27 December 1917) of John Drinkwater's *Prose Papers*. In this book Drinkwater had written on Brooke (who had died on active service in the Aegean in 1915), and, in recalling 'that volatile, irreverent, and extremely vivacious spirit before the romantic public took possession of his fame',[25] earned her gratitude. (She had known Brooke as a child on holiday at St Ives and in later years they were to enjoy a period of intimate acquaintance and to have many friends in common.) If she appreciated Drinkwater's account of Brooke, she failed to feel the same some eight months later about that by Edward Marsh. His memoir published with Brooke's *Collected Poems* she dismissed in the privacy of her diary as 'a disgraceful sloppy sentimental rhapsody'.[26] In the *TLS* ('Rupert Brooke', 8 August 1918), she necessarily tempered her feelings and, in her own words, 'trod out my 2 columns as decorously as possible'.[27] She agreed with the prefatory observations of the poet's mother that, as the work of someone not at all of Brooke's generation, Marsh's memoir was inevitably incomplete. His was more the Brooke of halcyon legend, who had 'died in the glory of public gratitude'.[28] Of Brooke's charming, ebullient, but also strangely flawed character, Virginia Woolf knew far more than she could begin to state in public. Her article, more an *éloge* than a review, nonetheless sought to provide, from her 'tantalising fund of memories',[29] a rounder picture of the man. She mentions the war directly only once, in asserting the inevitability of his prompt enlistment. On the subject of his famous war sonnets she is silent. (For other writings related to the war and its literature, see also 'A Cambridge V.A.D.', 'Two Irish Poets', 'War in the Village'.)

This is the period when, although engaged in writing the very traditional *Night and Day* (the likes of which Katherine Mansfield was to protest 'we had not thought to look upon . . . again'),[30] Virginia Woolf was evolving, with gathering momentum, her modernist aesthetic. It is interesting to observe how, in speculating about Brooke, had he lived to fulfil his promise, she fancied that 'he would in the end have framed a speech that came very close to the modern point of view – a subtle analytic poetry, or prose perhaps, full of intellect, and full of his keen unsentimental curiosity'.[31]

She had already engaged in speculations as to the future promise of Siegfried Sassoon's poetry ('Mr Sassoon's Poems', *TLS*, 31 May 1917; see also the more muted appreciation in 'Two Soldier-Poets', *TLS*, 11 July 1918). But she also saw, immediately, how Sassoon had struck the authentic note in his war poems. Here she discerned 'realism of the right, of the poetic kind', saw how 'Yes, this [war] is going on; and we are sitting here watching it', and did so 'with a new shock of surprise, with an uneasy desire to leave [her] place in the audience . . .'[32] Her preoccupations in this article and some of her expressions (among them: 'moments of vision', 'shocks of emotion', 'moments of emotion') are those of her mature criticism. 'As it is the poet's gift', she begins, 'to give expression to the moments of insight and experience that come to him now and then, so in following him we have to sketch for ourselves a map of those submerged lands which lie between one pinnacle and the next'.[33] The language here, of 'moments' and concealed transitions, is concerned with what she refers to elsewhere as the artist's 'power to omit'.[34] It is also about the directness of vision which makes us unable to think of Sassoon 'putting down [his] thoughts in any form save the one he has chosen'.[35] To very few recent and still fewer contemporary English writers was she prepared to grant such accomplishment. (The most important native exception is Thomas Hardy, from whose poem and volume of poems – published in 1917 – the phrase 'moments of vision' derives. But she does not write on Hardy here. Samuel Butler is another significant exception – see 'A Man With a View'.)

Only to the Russians did she turn with similar applause to that bestowed upon Sassoon. The Russians were now, in an expression she applies to Dostoevsky ('More Dostoevsky', *TLS*, 22 February 1917), beginning to 'permeate'[36] the lives of English readers, above all in the steady stream of translations from Constance Garnett's pen. There was 'even something humiliating'[37] in the experience. The English nineteenth-century novel especially paled beside the Russian classics. They seemed to reduce such a writer as George Meredith ('On Re-reading Meredith', *TLS*, 25 July 1918) to the status of 'an insular hero bred and cherished for the delight of connoisseurs in some sheltered corner of a Victorian hothouse'.[38] But it was not just the Victorians. It was felt to be an open question whether any English novel could 'survive in the furnace of that overpowering sincerity'[39] of the Russians.

The Russian example had a profound influence upon the formulation of her later fictional method. We see this clearly in 'On Re-reading Meredith', and also in 'More Dostoevsky'. The latter, predating the piece on Sassoon by some three months, uses the same kind of critical language we find in the later article, only more extensively and in relation to fiction:

> ... if we try to construct our mental processes later [having stopped reading], we find that the links between one thought and another are submerged. The chain is sunk out of sight and only the leading points emerge to mark the course. Alone among writers Dostoevsky has the power of reconstructing these most swift and complicated states of mind, of rethinking the whole train of thought in all its speed, now as it flashes into light, now as it lapses into darkness; for he is able to follow not only the vivid streak of achieved thought, but to suggest the dim and populous underworld of the mind's consciousness where desires and impulses are moving blindly beneath the sod.[40]

We may be prompted by this to remember the tunnelling process Virginia Woolf described in writing about her approach to *Mrs Dalloway* (1925), at a time when 'the old post-Dostoevsky argument'[41] was very much in her mind. She was prompted to reflect upon the English and the method of 'most of our novelists' who 'reproduce all the external appearance – tricks of manner, landscape, dress, and the effect of the hero upon his friends – but very rarely, and only for an instant, penetrate to the tumult of thought which rages within his own mind'.[42] Such criticism, echoed in 'On Re-reading Meredith', recalls her later famous attack on Arnold Bennett and the 'Edwardians' in 'Character in Fiction' (*III VW Essays*) – which is more genially anticipated here in 'Books and Persons'.

Virginia Woolf took a more comprehensive view of the Russians than is represented by the classics – Tolstoy, Dostoevsky, Chekhov, Aksakoff (see 'Tolstoy's *The Cossacks*', 'More Dostoevsky', 'A Minor Dostoevsky', 'A Russian Schoolboy', 'Tchehov's Questions'; and see also 'Mr Hudson's Childhood'). Of course to a large extent a reviewer's reading is determined by fashion and contingency, but Virginia Woolf was always keenly interested in uncanonised authors (contemporary or otherwise), and sought to see her literature, whether English, French, Russian or Greek, as a whole. A quotation for which she gives no source, in 'A

Russian Schoolboy', reveals that she read, or used, Prince Kropotkin's survey of *Russian Literature* – a kind of literary guide – which Duckworth & Co. published in 1905. Her *Common Reader* essay 'The Russian Point of View' (*IV VW Essays*) derives in part from her review of *The Village Priest and Other Stories* by Elena Militsina and Mikhail Saltikov (see 'The Russian View'), the former a figure of considerable obscurity, the latter a relatively minor author and editor.

She first conceived her plan for *The Common Reader* (1st series: 1925) in 1921, its provisional title being 'Reading' or 'Reading & Writing'. The articles she drew upon directly in creating that book belong chiefly to the period 1919–24 (see *III VW Essays*). The two exceptions in this volume are 'The Russian View', already remarked upon, and 'Charlotte Brontë' (*TLS*, 13 April 1916), part of which is included in the essay '*Jane Eyre* and *Wuthering Heights*'. If the remainder of her articles here do not themselves surface in *The Common Reader*, a great many of them relate closely, in subject and argument, to the essays in both series of that work, and hence to Virginia Woolf's abiding literary interests. The essay 'Hours in a Library' (*TLS*, 30 November 1916), with its reader's-eye and exploratory view of literature, its emphasis upon 'pure and disinterested reading',[43] upon 'how it strikes a contemporary',[44] may be taken as a kind of condensed prototype for the later *Common Reader* volumes. The *Common Reader* essay 'How It Strikes a Contemporary' itself is again recalled in 'Mr Howells on Form' (*TLS*, 14 November 1918), not least in the review's deferential reference to the coming 'great critic'.[45] Here Virginia Woolf, ostensibly reviewing a novel by her contemporary Leonard Merrick (see also 'Mr Merrick's Novels'), uses the book's introduction by W. D. Howells as a springboard for an extended flight upon the subject of form, the problems and value of contemporary criticism, and the important historical function the reader may perform by continuing 'to frame tentative outlines of belief'.[46]

Among the contemporaries upon whom she writes, formulating her 'rapid views',[47] in this volume are: Gilbert Cannan ('*Mummery*'); Joseph Conrad ('*Lord Jim*'; 'Mr Conrad's "Youth" ', 'Mr Conrad's Crisis', all in a sense groundwork for her *Common Reader* essay 'Joseph Conrad'); John Galsworthy ('Mr Galsworthy's Novel'); Joseph Hergesheimer ('*The Three Black Pennys*'); L. P. Jacks ('Philosophy in Fiction'); Compton Mackenzie ('The "Movie" Novel'); Viola Meynell ('*Second Marriage*'); Elinor Mordaunt ('*The Park Wall*', '*Before Midnight*');

Frank Swinnerton ('Honest Fiction'); H. G. Wells ('The Rights of Youth', a review of *Joan and Peter* in which there occurs what proves to be an interesting 'Edwardian' diversion on Post-Impressionism and the Omega Workshops – see also 'Books and Persons'). 'Women Novelists', an account of a contemporary work of criticism, is additionally interesting in being germane to *The Common Reader*.

About as far away from the contemporary as, literary-historically, it is possible to be, we have Virginia Woolf's devotion to the 'peculiar magic'[48] of the Greeks. The *Common Reader* article 'On Not Knowing Greek' is obviously anticipated here in 'The Perfect Language' (*TLS*, 24 May 1917). In this piece she takes an almost Platonic view of Greek as the perfect linguistic form, 'the type of literature . . . the supreme example of what can be done with words'.[49] It is clearly an important essay, especially for readers interested in her aestheticism, and has not previously been collected.

Her similarly enduring interest in Richard Hakluyt's writings, and in the contents of 'The Elizabethan Lumber Room'[50] in general, is evidenced in 'Trafficks and Discoveries', as it was by the article of the same title in *I VW Essays*. Hakluyt turned out 'on mature inspection', as she observed in her diary on 7 December 1918, 'to justify over & over again my youthful discrimination'. She delighted in the 'great wealth of good reading' he provided, reciprocating in her own more utilitarian prose the 'sense of wonder unexhausted' of the Elizabethans.[51] Both her Elizabethan and wider historical curiosity may also be traced in '*The House of Lyme*' – *TLS*, 29 March 1917 – wherein she places something approaching a Yeatsean value on the 'great house' and its tradition, in time of war and strife. (See also '*Sir Walter Raleigh*'.)

Such an account as this, while drawing out certain unifying strands in her journalistic output, can only begin to suggest the diversity and range of the pieces in this volume or the speed with which she must have read and written to produce them. (Consider as a further indicator of her industry the joint occurrence in the *TLS*, 21 December 1916, of '*Social Life in England*' and 'Mr Symons's Essays'; in the *TLS*, 12 April 1917, of 'A Talker' and '*In Good Company*'; in the *TLS*, 10 October 1918, of 'Adventurers All' and 'Honest Fiction'.) There are, in addition to the pieces already mentioned, important essays here on a number of Americans: Edgar Allan Poe ('*Poe's Helen*'), Henry David Thoreau ('Thoreau'), Walt Whitman ('Visits to Walt Whitman'), and Henry James ('*The Method of Henry James*').

Most of the articles were produced in intervals while *Night and Day* lay dormant. Their vivacity is nonetheless undiluted. Perhaps we should expect nothing less from one who saw that 'Whether you are writing a review or a love letter the great thing is to be confronted with a very vivid idea of your subject'.[52] Her ideas are invariably vivid, and her memorable expressions abound: 'So queer and topsy-turvy is the atmosphere of these little stories that one feels . . . much as if one had been trying to walk over the bridge in a willow pattern plate' ('Chinese Stories'); 'to be always in love and always a governess is to go through the world with blinkers on one's eyes' ('Charlotte Brontë'); 'But, after reading . . . [*The Way of All Flesh*], we hardly dare inspect some of the masterpieces of English fiction; it would be as unkind as to let in the cold light of day upon a dowager in a ball dress' ('A Man With a View'); 'one native frog is of more importance than a whole grove of sham nightingales' ('A Talker'); 'A branch of learning suggests a withered stick with a few dead leaves attached to it. But Greek is the golden bough; it crowns its lovers with garlands of fresh and sparkling leaves' ('The Perfect Language'); 'when you do not read him he ceases to exist' ('*John Davidson*'); and so on.

By 12 March 1918 Virginia Woolf had written over 100,000 words of *Night and Day*. She completed it in the following November – the month of the Armistice – and it would be published by Duckworth & Co. in October 1919. In that same November The Hogarth Press began printing *Kew Gardens* (published in May 1919), and a start was made to the writing of the story 'Solid Objects' (first published in the *Athenaeum*, 22 October 1920). In 1917 Leonard Woolf had become a member of the editorial board of *War and Peace*, a political journal that evolved to become the *International Review*, of which he was appointed editor in September 1918. At the same time he was engaged in completing *Empire and Commerce in Africa. A Study in Imperialism* (1920). As proprietors of The Hogarth Press, the Woolfs had by now made the acquaintance of Katherine Mansfield, and of T. S. Eliot, whose *Poems* they published in May 1919. In 1918, Harriet Weaver approached them with a request that they consider publishing James Joyce's *Ulysses* (1922) – a task for which their small press was regrettably hardly adequate, even if it had been legally advisable to proceed. They were thus, whether they wished to do so or not, beginning to emerge upon the metropolitan cultural scene.

Elsewhere and earlier in Bloomsbury, the Second Post-Impressionist

Exhibition, with Leonard Woolf its secretary, had been organised by Roger Fry in October–December 1912. In the following July, the Omega Workshops opened at 33 Fitzroy Square. Clive Bell's book *Art*, in which he expounded the doctrine of 'significant form', was published in 1914; in May 1918 appeared a collection of his journalism, *Potboilers*. Vanessa Bell and Duncan Grant took up residence in 1916 at Charleston, a farmhouse under the Downs near the village of Firle, in Sussex, and there continued their lifelong collaboration as decorative artists. In 1918 was published Desmond MacCarthy's *Remnants*, a volume of journalism, and, far more momentously, Lytton Strachey's *Eminent Victorians* (both authors sought to have Virginia Woolf review their books in the *TLS*, but, for a variety of reasons, she did not do so).

The next decade would see a marked proliferation in the books and artefacts to come from the hands of Bloomsbury. Maynard Keynes would appear upon the literary and political stage. But no one in that illustrious group of friends stood, in relation to his or her life, quite as did Virginia Woolf at the close of 1918, upon the brink of the richest era in her authorial career.

1 – *The Complete Shorter Fiction of Virginia Woolf* (Hogarth Press, 1985), ed. Susan Dick.
2 – *I VW Letters*, no. 628, to Madge Vaughan, June 1912.
3 – *Ibid.*
4 – *Ibid.*
5 – *Ibid.*
6 – *I VW Diary*, 22 January 1915.
7 – *Ibid.*, 6 January 1915
8 – *Ibid.*, 2 January 1915.
9 – *Ibid.*, 25 January 1915.
10 – *Ibid.*, 23 January 1915.
11 – *Ibid.*, 31 January 1915.
12 – *II QB*, ch. ii, p. 35.
13 – *II VW Letters*, no. 840, to Vanessa Bell, 8 June 1917.
14 – *I VW Diary*, 12 and 14 March 1918.
15 – *Ibid.*, 23 September 1918.
16 – *Ibid.*
17 – *Ibid.*, 7 December 1918.
18 – *Ibid.*
19 – *II LW*, ch. iii, p. 127.
20 – *Ibid.*
21 – *'Before Midnight'*, p. 87.
22 – *I VW Diary*, 3 January 1915.

23 – *Ibid.*
24 – 'The New Crusade', p. 203.
25 – *Ibid.*
26 – *I VW Diary*, 23 July 1918.
27 – *II VW Letters*, no. 959, to Katherine Cox, 13 August 1918.
28 – 'Rupert Brooke', p. 278.
29 – *Ibid.*
30 – *Athenaeum*, 21 November 1919.
31 – 'Rupert Brooke', p. 281.
32 – 'Mr Sassoon's Poems', p. 120.
33 – *Ibid.*, p. 119.
34 – 'Mr Howells on Form' p. 324.
35 – 'Mr Sassoon's Poems', p. 119.
36 – 'More Dostoevsky', p. 83.
37 – 'Tolstoy's *The Cossacks*', p. 77
38 – 'On Re-reading Meredith', p. 273
39 – *Ibid.*
40 – 'More Dostoevsky', p. 85.
41 – *II VW Diary*, 19 June 1923.
42 – 'More Dostoevsky', p. 85.
43 – 'Hours in a Library', p. 55.
44 – The title of the last essay in *CR1*.
45 – 'Mr Howells on Form', p. 324; and *CR1*, 'How It Strikes a Contemporary', pp. 232–5.
46 – 'Mr Howells on Form', p. 324.
47 – *I VW Diary*, 7 December 1918.
48 – 'The Perfect Language', p. 116.
49 – *Ibid.*, p. 118.
50 – The title of the third essay in *CR1*.
51 – Appendix I, 'Reading Notes', p. 357, and p. 358.
52 – 'Poe's Helen' p. 104.

Editorial Note

The first article in this volume, '*Frances Willard*', was published in the *Times Literary Supplement* on 28 November 1912, and is the earliest piece of journalism Virginia Woolf is known to have published following her marriage in the previous August (Volume I of these essays spanning the years 1904–1912 contains all of the articles up to her marriage). The final article in this volume, '*The Method of Henry James*', appeared in the *TLS*, 26 December 1918. In all, 98 articles are reprinted here, in chronological order, each, with the exception of 'Heard on the Downs' (*The Times*, 15 August 1916), from the pages of the *TLS*. Of these, 58 have not been collected before.

Annotations and other editorial interventions have been effected upon the same principles as those outlined in the Editorial Note to Volume I.

Two sets of Virginia Woolf's reading notes, relating to her essays 'Coleridge as Critic' and 'Trafficks and Discoveries' – the only such notes known to have survived from this period – have been transcribed from manuscripts in the Berg Collection, New York Public Library, and the Monks House Papers, Sussex University Library, and are reproduced in Appendix I.

Acknowledgements

I remáin especially indebted to the directors of The Hogarth Press and to Professor Quentin Bell and Angelica Garnett, administrators of Virginia Woolf's Literary Estate, for retaining me to prepare this edition, and to the Leverhulme Trustees for the renewal of their original Research Grant. For her stalwart support throughout and for sharing in a large part of the reading required to annotate the essays, I owe a very great debt of gratitude to my wife, Diana McNeillie. I am also very grateful to Nicola Edwards, who, for no reward but the work itself has undertaken an immense amount of reading and researching for this volume. Christine Carswell of The Hogarth Press has again curbed my excesses, with great rigour and tact, for which I wish to thank her. I must also thank, once more, Professor S. P. Rosenbaum, for reading my introduction in its original draft, and for innumerable facts, words of advice, and other kindnesses conducive to the volume's completion. In addition, I wish to acknowledge the help and support of Professor Elizabeth Steele, Professor Quentin Bell, Anne Olivier Bell, Elizabeth Inglis, and of Colin Masters, Director and Secretary of the Thomas Coram Foundation for Children. I remain indebted to London University's Librarian and to the staff of the Library's periodicals department.

For permission to publish the material in Appendix I, I have to thank Professor Quentin Bell and Angelica Garnett, Sussex University Library, and the Henry W. and Albert A. Berg Collection, the New York Public Library, Astor, Lenox and Tilden Foundations.

Abbreviations

B&P	*Books and Portraits*, ed. Mary Lyon (Hogarth Press, London, 1977; Harcourt Brace Jovanovich, New York, 1978)
CE	*Collected Essays*, 4 vols ed. Leonard Woolf (vols 1–2, Hogarth Press, London, 1966, Harcourt Brace & World Inc., New York, 1967; vols 3–4, Hogarth Press, London, and Harcourt Brace & World Inc., New York, 1967)
CR	*The Common Reader*: 1st series (Hogarth Press, London, and Harcourt Brace & Co., New York, 1925; annotated edition, 1984) 2nd series (Hogarth Press, London, and Harcourt, Brace & Co., New York, 1932; annotated edition, 1986)
CW	*Contemporary Writers*, with a Preface by Jean Guiget (Hogarth Press, London, 1965; Harcourt Brace & World Inc., New York, 1966)
DNB	*Dictionary of National Biography*
DoM	*The Death of the Moth and Other Essays*, ed. Leonard Woolf (Hogarth Press, London, and Harcourt Brace & Co., New York, 1942)
G&R	*Granite and Rainbow*, ed. Leonard Woolf (Hogarth Press, London, and Harcourt Brace & Co., New York, 1958)
Kp	B. J. Kirkpatrick, *A Bibliography of Virginia Woolf* (third ed., Oxford University Press, Oxford, 1980)
LW	Leonard Woolf, *An Autobiography*, 2 vols (Oxford University Press, Oxford, 1980)
MoB	Virginia Woolf, *Moments of Being*, ed. Jeanne Schulkind

	(2nd ed., Hogarth Press, London, 1985; Harcourt Brace Jovanovich, New York, 1985)
QB	Quentin Bell, *Virginia Woolf. A Biography. Volume One. Virginia Stephen, 1882–1912. Volume Two. Mrs Woolf, 1912–1941.* (Hogarth Press, London, and Harcourt Brace Jovanovich Inc., New York, 1972)
TLS	*Times Literary Supplement*
VW Diary	*The Diary of Virgina Woolf,* ed. Anne Olivier Bell (5 vols. Hogarth Press, London, and Harcourt Brace Jovanovich, New York, 1977–84)
VW Essays	*The Essays of Virginia Woolf,* 6 vols
VW Letters	*The Letters of Virginia Woolf,* ed. Nigel Nicolson (6 vols, Hogarth Press, London, and Harcourt Brace Jovanovich, New York, 1975–80)
W&W	*Women & Writing,* ed. Michèle Barrett (Women's Press, London, 1979; Harcourt Brace Jovanovich, New York, 1980)

The Essays of
Virginia Woolf

The Essays

1912

'Frances Willard'

The great merits of Mrs Strachey's life of Miss Willard,[2] its directness and candour and complete lack of padding, produce a very interesting picture of the famous philanthropist. They make one ask questions about her and her life which the ordinary biographer usually contrives to stifle, because his subject is dead. To begin with, Miss Willard was once young and very imperfect. Brought up in the West when the West was an untamed land, she loved shooting, climbing trees, and would rather saddle a cow than not ride at all; she hated housework, and had a passion for horse-racing. Very vivid is the account of their life in the middle of the last century at Janesville:

We see the hard work of the farm; the fencing and ploughing, the cutting of trees and rearing of cattle, the growing of the precious crops, and all the daily difficulties; how the house was banked up for fear of the winter hurricanes, and how the prairie fires were fought with fire; how the hogs escaped down the road, the gophers ate up the corn, and the rats got among the potatoes; how the apple trees died and the oxen were lost, and the milk froze in the churn by the fire and the blue-jays were caught in the quail traps.[3]

In those days she was no more interested in temperance than clever girls usually are. Her own culture was the object of her greatest enthusiasm. Although she loved her home, she insisted upon getting away from it to make experiments and have experiences of her own. Because the man[4] she loved and was to marry proved also a prig, though a worthy one, she broke off her engagement and lived the rest of her life independently. She

3

was, in short, a delightful and spirited American girl, and Mrs Strachey has surely done well to concentrate upon this period of her life and to devote less space to the years of immense success and celebrity. For Miss Willard did not remain, as she had become, a great schoolmistress.[5] The merest accident, a heavy fall of snow, induced a certain Dr Dio Lewis, who was lecturing about the country in 1873, to stay over the night and deliver another lecture upon temperance. It started a crusade which 'spread with the violence of a prairie fire'.[6] Women were the crusaders.

It must have been very strange ⟨writes Mrs Strachey⟩ to see the lines of women marching out from the churches into the snowy streets, singing their gentle hymns to warlike tunes, and strange to watch them halt before the saloons to kneel on the pavement to weep and 'pray for the soul of the proprietor that he might see the error of his ways'. And it must have been stranger still when these proprietors surrendered and rolled out their barrels into the streets to pour the 'poison' into the gutter, confessing their sins with tears, while the church bells rang, and the women wept for joy, and the roughs scooped up the rum-soaked snow and cursed the praying women.[7]

But the strangest thing of all was that Miss Willard gave up the profession which she loved to kneel upon the floors of public houses, too. She formed the women into a society, with herself for their leader. The story of the growth of that society is told briefly and competently by Mrs Strachey. Beginning with two or three women in a dingy little office, it spread over America, reached to England, rose in distant countries, India, China, Japan, culminating in a world society, with 'Do Everything'[8] for its motto, and world conventions with Miss Willard at their head. It is a wonderful story, and yet this part of the book is the least vivid. When one begins dealing with figures one is apt to be paralysed by them. Three hundred and sixty-five meetings a year – ten thousand letters – those facts are so startling that we forget to ask, What were they about? It is strange how little we know what Miss Willard believed, how vague her own creed was. Perhaps it is summed up as well in the message that her sister left her when she died as in other words: 'Tell everybody to be good.'[9] Miss Willard spent the best years of her life in doing that; in telling them, that is, not to drink, to be pure, to love each other, to enfranchise women, to help the poor. There is nothing very profound in that teaching, but consider the scale on which she did it. In 1881 she sent out ten thousand letters; 'forty different branches of work were carried on'; 'she averaged 365 meetings and many thousand miles of travel every year';[10] thirty million pages of literature were issued yearly from her office. So prolific was she that she put together 650,000 words of autobiography in three weeks.[11] It is all very American, but it is also very philanthropic. The modern philanthropist must also be an amazingly efficient machine. The reason is not far to seek. Their mission is not to create new ideas – Johnson, Shelley, Rousseau were not philanthropists – but to popularise, to make people practise as far as practicable the ideas of others, old ideas for the most part, ideas that have become rather dull and rather vague to most people. Of course their books, as Mrs Strachey says that Miss Willard knew her own to be, are 'horrible'.[12] Could they fulfil their mission if they were not? You must have bold phrases to slip in under people's doors, to force into their hands, to bawl into their faces. They must be phrases, too, about the most private of emotions. You must be ready to share all with crowds in the streets. Thus Miss Willard, when she heard of the death of her only brother, went to her meeting, told the audience 'all about it, and they cried together, praying, and talking of the heavenly life'.[13]

She shared everything; she died of sharing things, worn out, and glad to die long before she was an old woman. And the result? The result is as difficult to estimate as the number of letters she wrote is easy, for what things make people good, and what being good consists in are questions not easy to answer. Only no one who has read Mrs Strachey's book can doubt that Miss Willard was one of those rare beings, true, single-minded and courageous, above all of immeasurable powers of love, who may be said to be good, and therefore to do good whether we hold that telling people to be good on any possible scale of vastness is valuable or merely a kind of friction on the surface.

1 – A review in the *TLS*, 28 November 1912, (Kp C49) of *Frances Willard. Her Life and Work. With an introduction by Lady Henry Somerset. And eight illustrations* (Fisher Unwin, 1912) by Ray Strachey.
2 – Ray (Rachel Conn) Strachey, *née* Costelloe (1887–1940), pioneering feminist, married Oliver Strachey – an older brother of Lytton – in 1911. (Her sister Karin married VW's brother Adrian Stephen three years later.) Frances Willard (1839–98) was from 1879 president of the Women's Christian Temperance Union, which she had helped to found in 1874.
Lady Henry Somerset (1851–1921), who introduces the biography, was a daughter of Virginia Pattle, and so a relation of VW. Her friendship with Frances Willard, discussed in ch. XI, began when the two women met in Boston in 1891.
3 – Strachey, ch. I, p. 6, which has: 'the farm, the fencing', and 'and blue-jays'. The Willard family settled to farm on the banks of the Rock River in Wisconsin, near the then village of Janesville, in 1847.

4 – Rev. Charles H. Fowler (1837–1908), Methodist bishop, president of Northwestern University, 1873–6; see also next note.

5 – Frances Willard was president of Evanston College for Ladies when, in 1873, it became part of Northwestern University. She resigned from her new post as dean of women and professor of aesthetics in the following year, having been outmanoeuvred in a struggle for authority by the Rev. Fowler.

6 – Strachey, ch. VII, p. 173; Dr Dio (Dioclesian) Lewis (1823–86), author of *New Gymnastics* (1862) who from 1871 campaigned in aid of the Women's Christian Temperance Union.

7 – *Ibid.*, p. 177, which has: 'warlike tunes; and strange to watch', and ' "praying women"'.

8 – *Ibid.*, ch. IX, p. 211.

9 – *Ibid.*, ch. III, p. 108; Mary Willard died of consumption in 1862.

10 – For these two quotations, *ibid.*, ch. X, p. 252, and ch. IX, p. 228.

11 – *Glimpses of Fifty Years* (1889).

12 – Strachey, ch. III, p. 113.

13 – *Ibid.*, ch. VIII, pp. 206–7; Oliver Willard died in 1878.

1913

Chinese Stories

According to Mr George Soulié, the translator of these stories, we seriously mistake the nature of the ordinary Chinaman if we imagine him any more exclusively occupied with the great classics of his literature than we are with ours. If we see him with a book in his hand it is likely to be 'a novel like the *History of the Three Kingdoms* or a selection of ghost stories'.[2] Like us they have a hunger for novels and stories, which they read over and over again, so that, although in the West nothing is known about it, the influence of such light literature upon the Chinese mind 'is much greater than the whole bulk of the classics'.[3] They may resemble us in their craving for something lighter, nearer to the life they know than the old and famous books, but in all else how different they are! The twenty-five stories in *Strange Stories from the Lodge of Leisure*, translated from the Chinese by George Soulié, were written in the second half of the eighteenth century by P'ou Song-Lin, at a time, that is, when with Fielding and Richardson[4] our fiction was becoming increasingly robust and realistic. To give any idea of the slightness and queerness of these stories one must compare them to dreams, or the airy, fantastic, and inconsequent flight of a butterfly. They skim from world to world, from life to death. The people they describe may kill each other and die, but we cannot believe either in their blood or in their dissolution. The barriers against which we in the West beat our hands in vain are for them almost as transparent as glass.

Some people ⟨one of the stories begins⟩ remember every incident of their former existences; it is a fact which many examples can prove. Other people do not forget what they learned before they died and were born again, but remember only confusedly what they were in a precedent life. Wang, the acceptable of the yellow peach-blossom city, when people discussed such questions before him used to narrate the experience he had had with his first son.[5]

And the story which occupies three little pages tells how a boy had once been born a student, then a donkey, and then a boy again. Very often these stories are like the stories a child will tell of a sight which has touched its imagination for no reason that we can discover, lacking in point where we expect the point to come, suddenly breaking off and done with, but somehow memorable. Or it may be they are extravagantly sensational, or of the nature of fairy stories, where all is miraculously set right in the end, or again purposeless and callous as a child's stories, the good man being killed merely to make an end. But they all alike have a quality of fantasy and spirituality which sometimes, as in 'The Spirit of the River' or 'The River of Sorrows',[6] becomes of real beauty, and is greatly enhanced by the unfamiliar surroundings and exquisite dress. Take, for example, the following description of a Chinese ghost:

He went farther and farther: the moving lights were rarer; ere long he only saw before him the fire of a white lantern decorated with two red peonies. The paper globe was swinging to the steps of a tiny girl clothed in the blue linen that only slaves wore. The light behind showed the elegant silhouette of another woman, this one covered with a long jacket made in a rich pink silk edged with purple. As the student drew nearer the belated walker turned round, showing an oval face and big long eyes wherein shone a bright speck cruel and mysterious.[7]

So queer and topsy-turvy is the atmosphere of these little stories that one feels, when one has read a number of them, much as if one had been trying to walk over the bridge in a willow pattern plate.

1 – A review in the TLS, 1 May 1913, (Kp C49.1) of *Strange Stories from the Lodge of Leisures. Translated from the Chinese by George Soulié of the French Consular Service in China* (Constable & Co. Ltd, 1913).

2 – Soulié, Pref., p. v; *The History of the Three Kingdoms* or *San Kuo Chih yen-i*, an adventurous novel of the thirteenth century, set in the period 220–65, following the collapse of the Han dynasty.

3 – *Ibid.*, p. vi, which has: 'These works . . . have on the Chinese mind an influence much greater . . .'

4 – P'ou Song-Lin or P'u Sung-ling (1640–1715), whose stories and legends,

originally entitled *Liao-chaochih-i* and numbering more than three hundred, are usually attributed to actual localities, sometimes with a basis in fact; an edition of them was first published in 1766. Henry Fielding (1707–54), whose *Tom Jones* appeared in 1749, and Samuel Richardson (1689–1761), whose *Clarissa* was published in 1747–8.

5 – Soulié, 'Through Many Lives', p. 110, which has 'Wang The-acceptable of the Yellow-peach-blossom city, . . .'

6 – *Ibid.*, pp. 114–19; pp. 125–30.

7 – *Ibid.*, 'The Ghost in Love', pp. 2–3.

'Jane Austen'

In many ways Jane Austen must be considered singularly blessed. The manner in which from generation to generation her descendants respect her memory is, we imagine, precisely that which she would have chosen for herself – and she would have been hard to please. In 1870 the *Memoir* by her nephew[2] gave us not only the facts of her life, but reproduced the atmosphere in which that life was lived so instinctively that his book can never be superseded; and now once more the son and grandson of that nephew show themselves possessed to the full of the family taste and modesty. In this final biography, for surely no other will be possible, they have brought together all that is known about Jane Austen, basing their narrative, of course, upon the original memoir but completing it with the letters which appeared in Lord Brabourne's two volumes,[3] and adding certain other letters, traditions, and family histories. By doing so they have given depth and perspective to the figure which we see in our mind's eye; to say that they have told us anything fresh about her would not be true. Miss Cassandra Austen[4] put that effectively beyond their power. To her alone did Jane Austen write freely and impulsively; to her she must have expressed the hopes and, if the rumour is true, the one keen disappointment of her life; but when Miss Cassandra Austen grew old and suspected that a time might come when strangers would be curious about her sister's private affairs, she burnt, at great cost to herself, every letter which could gratify their curiosity. The letters which remain exist simply because she thought that no one, not even the nephews and nieces, would be sufficiently interested in Jane Austen to disturb them. Had she guessed that they would not only be read but published, that many thousands would enjoy the wit and ransack every sentence for revelations, we may be sure that she would have flung them also on to the flames with one sweep of her arm.

This being so, we are aware that it is a confession which is made when we say that we are sufficiently interested in Jane Austen to wish to know everything that it is possible to know about her. We are grateful to little Philadelphia Austen, who describes Jane 'not at all pretty and very prim, unlike a girl of twelve . . . Jane is whimsical and affected';[5] and to old Mrs Mitford, who remembered the Austens as girls and knew Jane as 'the prettiest, silliest, most affected, husband-hunting butterfly she ever remembers',[6] and to Miss Mitford's properly anonymous friend who

visits her now and says that she has stiffened into the most perpendicular, precise, taciturn piece of 'single blessedness' that ever existed, and that, until *Pride and Prejudice* showed what a precious gem was hidden in that unbending case, she was no more regarded in society than a poker or a firescreen . . . The case is very different now; she is still a poker – but a poker of whom everybody is afraid . . . A wit ⟨the good lady exclaims, and we cannot help hoping with more reason than she knew of at the time⟩, a delineator of character, who does not talk, is terrific indeed![7]

Of course these critics are wrong, but it is amusing to see as clearly as we do why they went wrong. Finally we are ready to bless Marianne Knight[8] perpetually for having recalled not very many years ago how 'Aunt Jane would sit very quietly at work beside the fire in the Godmersham library, then suddenly burst out laughing, jump up, cross the room to a distant table with papers lying on it, write something down, returning presently and sitting down quietly to her work again.'[9] Was it then that Mrs Norris gave William 'something considerable', or Lady Bertram had the happy idea of sending Chapman to help Miss Fanny?[10] We are grateful for trifles, in short, for it is by means of such trifles that we draw a little closer to the charm, the brilliance, the strength and sincerity of character that lay behind the novels. For the rest, we cannot grudge Jane and Cassandra the glance of satisfaction which they must cast at each other as after fresh scrutiny of that serene and smiling face we turn away baffled, and they know that their secrets are their own for ever. We need not be surprised that even the jealous Cassandra had no inkling of the curiosity of the generations to come. So lately as 1870 there was only one complete edition of the novels,[11] and the taste for them was a gift that ran in families and was a mark of rather peculiar culture. Today things have changed so far that the present biography is the third work about Jane Austen that has been published in the course of the year.[12] One, by Miss Brinton, takes the original form of continuing the fortunes of the characters and devising marriages between them – a work of great love and great ingenuity which, if taken not as fiction but as talk about Jane Austen's characters, will please that select public which is never tired of discussing them.

But the time has come, surely, when there is no need to bring witnesses to prove Jane Austen's fame. Arrange the great English novelists as one will, it does not seem possible to bring them out in any order where she is not first, or second, or third, whoever her companions may be. Unlike other great writers in almost every way, she is unlike them, too, in the very slow and very steady rise of her reputation: it has been steady because there is probably no novelist of the nineteenth century who requires us to make so little excuse for her, and it has been slow because she has limitations of a kind particularly likely to cramp a writer's popularity. The mere sight of her six neat volumes suggests something of the reason, for when we look at them we do not remember any page or passage which so burnt itself into our minds when we read it first that from time to time we take the book down, read that sentence again, and are again exalted. We doubt whether one of her novels was ever a long toil and stumble to any reader with a splendid view at the end. She was never a revelation to the young, a stern comrade, a brilliant and extravagantly admired friend, a writer whose sentences sang in one's brain and were half absorbed into one's blood. And directly one has set down any of the above phrases one is conscious of the irony with which she would have disclaimed any such wish or intention. We can hear it in the words addressed to the nephew who had lost two chapters of his novel. 'How could I possibly join them on to the little bit (two inches wide) of ivory on which I work with so fine a brush, as produces little effect after much labour?';[13] and again in the famous, 'Let other pens dwell on guilt and misery. I quit such odious subjects as soon as I can.'[14]

But however modest and conscious of her own defects she may be, the defects are there and must be recognised by readers who are as candid as Jane Austen herself would wish them to be. The chief reason why she does not appeal to us as some inferior writers do is that she has too little of the rebel in her composition, too little discontent, and of the vision which is the cause and the reward of discontent. She seems at times to have accepted life too calmly as she found it, and to any one who reads her biography or letters it is plain that life showed her a great deal that was smug, commonplace, and, in a bad sense of the word, artificial. It showed her a world made up of big houses and little houses, of gentry inhabiting them who were keenly conscious of their grades of gentility, while life itself consisted of an interchange of tea parties, picnics, and dances, which eventually, if the connection was respectable and the income on each side satisfactory, led to a thoroughly suitable marriage. It happens very seldom, but still it does happen, that we feel that the play of her spirit has been hampered by such obstacles; that she believes in them as well as laughs at them, and that she is debarred from the most profound insight into human nature by the respect which she pays to some unnatural convention. There are characters such as the characters of Elinor Dashwood[15] and Fanny Price which bore us frankly; there are pages which, though written in excellent English, have to be skipped; and these defects are due to the fact that she is content to take it for granted that such characters and conduct are good without trying to see them in a fresh light for herself.

But the chief damage which this conservative spirit has inflicted on her art is that it tied her hands together when she dealt with men. Her heroes were less the equals of her heroines than should have been the case, making allowance for the fact that so it must always be when a woman writes of men or a man of women. It is where the power of the man has to be conveyed that her novels are always at their weakest; and the heroines themselves lose something of their life because in moments of crisis they have for partners men who are inferior to them in vitality and character. A clergyman's daughter in those days was, no doubt, very carefully brought up, and in no other age, we imagine, were men and women less at their ease together; still, it rests with the novelists to break down the barriers; it is they who should imagine what they cannot know even at the risk of making themselves superbly ridiculous. Miss Austen, however, was so fastidious, so conscious of her own limitations, that when she found out that hedges do not grow in Northamptonshire she eliminated her hedge rather than run the risk of inventing one which could not exist. This is the more annoying because we are inclined to think that she could have run almost all the risks and triumphed. In proof of this we might quote two passages from *Mansfield Park* (the first is quoted by Professor Bradley in his lecture to the English Association),[16] where, forsaking her usual method, she suddenly hazards herself in a strange new atmosphere and breathes into her work a spirit of beauty and romance. Fanny Price standing at a window with Edmund breaks into a strange rhapsody, which begins, 'Here's harmony! here's repose! here's what may leave all painting and all music behind, and what poetry only can attempt to describe!'[17] &c. And, again, she throws a curious atmosphere of symbolism over the whole scene where Maria and Henry Crawford refuse to wait for Rushworth, who is bringing the key of the gate. 'But unluckily', Maria exclaims, 'that iron gate, that ha-ha gives me a feeling of restraint and hardship. I cannot get out, as the starling said.'[18]

But these limitations are noticeable only when Jane Austen is committing herself to saying seriously that such things and such people are good, which in the works of any writer is a dangerous moment, leading us to hold our breath; when she is pointing out where they are bad, weak, faulty, exquisitely absurd she is winged and inapproachable. Her heroes may be insipid, but think of her fools! Think of Mr Collins, Mr Woodhouse, Miss Bates, Mrs Norris, Mrs Bennet, and in a lesser degree of Mrs Allen, Lady Bertram, Sir William Lucas![19] What a light the thought of them will cast on the wettest day! How various and individual is their folly! For they are no more consistently foolish than people in real life. It is only that they have a peculiar point of view, and that when health, or economy, or ladies of title are mentioned, as must frequently happen in the world we live in, they give vent to their views to our eternal delight; but there are a great many circumstances in which they do not behave foolishly at all. Indeed, we are inclined to think that the most painful incident in any of the novels is when Miss Bates's feelings are hurt at the picnic, and, turning to Mr Knightley, she says, 'I must have made myself very disagreeable or she would not have said such a thing to an old friend.'[20] Again, when they are discussing the study of human nature and Darcy remarks, 'But people themselves alter so much that there is something to be observed in them for ever,' Mrs Bennet's reply is surely a stroke of genius. 'Yes, indeed,' cried Mrs Bennet, offended by his manner of mentioning a country neighbourhood, 'I assure you there is quite as much of that going on in the country as in town.'[21] Such is the light it throws upon the muddled vacuity of the poor lady's mind that she ceases to be ridiculous and becomes almost tragic in her folly.

It came so naturally to Jane Austen to describe people by means of their faults that had there been a drop of bitterness in her spirit her novels would have given us the most consistently satirical picture of life that exists. Open them where you will, you are almost certain to light upon some passage exquisitely satirising the absurdities of life – satirising them, but without bitterness, partly no doubt because she was happy in her life, partly because she had no wish that things should be other than they are. People could never be too absurd, life never too full of humours and singularities for her taste, and as for telling people how they ought to live, which is the satiric motive, she would have held up her hands in amazement at the thought. Life itself – that was the object of her love, of her absorbed study; that was the pursuit which filled those unrecorded years and drew out the 'quiet intensity of her nature', making her appear to the outer world a little critical and aloof, and 'at times very grave'.[22] More than any other novelist she fills every inch of her canvas with observation, fashions every sentence into meaning, stuffs up every chink and cranny of the fabric until each novel is a little living world, from which you cannot break off a scene or even a sentence without bleeding it of some of its life. Her characters are so rounded and substantial that they have the power to move out of the scenes in which she placed them into other moods and circumstances. Thus, if someone begins to talk about Emma Woodhouse or Elizabeth Bennet voices from different parts of the room begin saying which they prefer and why, and how they differ, and how they might have acted if one had been at Box Hill and the other at Rosings,[23] and where they live, and how their houses are disposed, as if they were living people. It is a world, in short, with houses, roads, carriages, hedgerows, copses, and with human beings.

All this was done by a quiet maiden lady who had merely paper and ink at her disposal; all this is conveyed by little sentences between inverted commas and smooth paragraphs of print. Only those who have realised for themselves the ridiculous inadequacy of a straight stick dipped in ink when brought in contact with the rich and tumultuous glow of life can appreciate to the full the wonder of her achievement, the imagination, the penetration, the insight, the courage, the sincerity which are required to bring before us one of those perfectly normal and simple incidents of average human life. Besides all these gifts and more wonderful than any of them, for without it they are apt to run to waste, she possessed in a greater degree perhaps than any other English woman the sense of the significance of life apart from any personal liking or disliking; of the beauty and continuity which underlies its trivial stream. A little aloof, a little inscrutable and mysterious, she will always remain, but serene and beautiful also because of her greatness as an artist.

1 – A review in the TLS, 8 May 1913, (Kp C49.2) of *Jane Austen [1775–1817]. Her Life and Letters. A Family Record. With a Portrait* (Smith, Elder & Co., 1913) by

William Austen-Leigh, and of *Old Friends and New Faces* (Holden and Hardingham, 1913) by Sybil G. Brinton. 'Jane Austen was received,' VW wrote in late May to Violet Dickinson (*II VW Letters*, no. 670), 'with pleasure by some, hatred by others. It has won for me the friendship of a tawny bitch in South Kensington, Edith Sichel [1862–1914, writer on French history and culture, who lived at 42 Onslow Gdns] who is black to the 3rd finger joint in ink.' The other recipients of the article referred to are not identified. The same letter also announced the far more momentous news that Gerald Duckworth had accepted for publication *The Voyage Out* (1915).

See also 'Jane Austen and the Geese', 'Jane Austen Practising' and 'Jane Austen at Sixty', *III VW Essays*; and 'Jane Austen', *IV VW Essays* and CR1.

2 – J. E. Austen-Leigh, *A Memoir of Jane Austen* (Richard Bentley, 1870).

3 – Edward, Lord Brabourne, *Letters of Jane Austen. Ed with an introduction and critical remarks* . . . (2 vols, Richard Bentley & Son, 1884).

4 – Cassandra Austen (1772–1845), only sister of Jane Austen.

5 – *Life and Letters*, ch. IV, p. 58, Philadelphia Walter writing to her brother James, July 1788.

6 – *Ibid.*, ch. VI, p. 84, Mary Russell Mitford (1787–1855), writing to Sir William Elford, 3 April 1815.

7 – *Ibid.*, which has: 'a poker of whom everybody is afraid', and 'But a wit'.

8 – Jane Austen's niece. She was the daughter of Jane's brother Edward, who took the name Knight after a second cousin.

9 – *Life and Letters*, ch. XVI, p. 290.

10 – For the 'something considerable' given by Mrs Norris to William Price, *Mansfield Park* (1814), ch. 31 (ed. Tony Tanner, Penguin, 1966, p. 308); and for Lady Bertram's happy idea to send her own maid Mrs Chapman ('too late of course to be of any use') to help Fanny Price, *ibid.*, ch. 27, p. 277.

11 – I.e., *Novels by Miss Jane Austen* (5 vols, Richard Bentley, 1833; reissued, 1856).

12 – The other work referred to, published in February 1913, was *Jane Austen. A Criticism and Appreciation* by Percy Fitzgerald. A fourth work, *Jane Austen* by Francis W. Cornish, appeared the following October.

13 – *Life and Letters*, ch. XX, p. 378, from a letter to Edward Austen, 16 December 1816.

14 – *Mansfield Park*, ch. 48, p. 446, which continues: 'as soon as I can, impatient to restore every body, not greatly in fault themselves, to tolerable comfort, and to have done with all the rest.'

15 – In *Sense and Sensibility* (1811).

16 – A. C. Bradley, 'Jane Austen. A Lecture' in H. C. Beeching (coll.), *Essays and Studies by Members of the English Association*, vol. II (O.U.P., 1911), p. 35, fn. 2.

17 – *Mansfield Park*, ch. 11, p. 139, which has: '"Here's harmony!" said she.'

18 – *Ibid.*, ch. 10, p. 127.

19 – Of the characters listed here and not previously identified in either text or notes: Mr Collins, Mrs Bennet and Sir William Lucas appear in *Pride and Prejudice* (1813); Mr Woodhouse and Miss Bates in *Emma* (1816); Mrs Allen in *Northanger Abbey* (1818).

20 – *Emma* (1816), ch. 43 (ed. Ronald Blythe, Penguin, 1966, p. 364).
21 – *Pride and Prejudice* (1813), ch. 9 (ed. Tony Tanner, Penguin, 1972, p. 88).
22 – *Life and Letters*, ch. XIV, p. 240, which has: 'She was not only shy: she was also at times very grave. Her niece Anna is inclined to think that Cassandra was the more equably cheerful of the two sisters. There was, undoubtedly, a quiet intensity of nature in Jane for which some critics have not given her credit.'
23 – Box Hill, scene of the famous picnic in *Emma*; Rosings, seat of Lady Catherine de Bourgh, in *Pride and Prejudice*.

'Les Copains'

It is doubtful whether it would be possible to recall the names of half a dozen living novelists in England and France and honestly say to oneself in the case of each, 'He has not brought it off yet, but really his next book *might* be a masterpiece.' When M. Jules Romains[2] two years ago published *Mort de Quelqu'un*, for some people he certainly entered into this select and honourable band. The book was not only a good book, but it had that particular type of goodness which does not kill the hope that the author may produce one infinitely better; and a novel infinitely better than *Mort de Quelqu'un* would undoubtedly deserve some consideration from posterity. M. Romains has this year published *Les Copains*, and he would probably himself agree that, as far as posterity is concerned, his last book leaves him in the position he occupied in 1911. He has not attempted to fulfil the promise of two years ago; he has, in a sense, begun again. It would be impossible to imagine a more serious book than *Mort de Quelqu'un* or a less serious one than *Les Copains*. The former belonged to that class of modern French *roman* of which there is scarcely an equivalent in English fiction, in which there are no 'characters', no humour, no plot, only a few dramatised psychological and metaphysical theories. The latter is a farce – for the most part a broad-humoured, rather knockabout, and sometimes salacious farce.

There is, of course, no reason why a farce should not be a masterpiece, although the literature of all countries seems to show that it is easier to weep or preach or mock or even revile with genius than to fool with genius. It is rather refreshing, therefore, to find in a French novel so much honest fun as there is in M. Romains's book. It recalls in an odd way the extravaganzas of Mr Chesterton.[3] No two writers have less in common in style, feelings, opinions; and yet one can imagine a Latin Mr Chesterton telling with the same genial gusto the story of the adventures of the seven copains who set out to revenge themselves upon the two provincial towns, Issoire and Ambert, for looking as they did upon the map of the eighty-six departments of France. And, as in Mr Chesterton's books, though there is plenty of fun for fun's sake, some of the best things in Les Copains point a moral or possess a sting which take them out of the province of farce into that of satire. M. Romains knows that it is pleasant to laugh, but still pleasanter to laugh at someone. He does so in the Rabelaisian sermon which Bénin preaches in the church at Ambert. Sometimes his irony has the lightness and effectiveness of the best French tradition. The copain Broudier is going to play a practical joke upon the garrison of Ambert by pretending to be a cabinet minister; he dresses up his three companions in full finery and decorates them with orders to represent his 'commandant', 'mon cher directeur', and 'mon secrétaire particulier';[4] then he addresses them as follows:

Quant à moi, vous le voyez, j'ai la mise savamment negligée et la bonhomie autoritaire qui convient aux premiers serviteurs d'une démocratie. Vous êtes là pour me garnir. Je porte moi-même ma puissance; mais c'est vous qui portez mon décorum, comme un larbin mon pardessus.[5]

In France they are at present fond of labels for writers as well as for painters, and M. Romains's label is, of course, *Unanimisme*. There is not, perhaps, at first sight a very great deal of the doctrine in *Les Copains*; it does not dominate the book as it did *Mort de Quelqu'un*; but the important thing which lies behind the label and the doctrine is always with M. Romains. What really interests him is the feelings of persons, not as individual characters, but as members of groups; what he delights and excels in doing is to trace the mysterious growth, where two or three are gathered together, of a kind of consciousness of the group in addition to that of each individual of the group. It is probable that M. Romains intended *Les Copains* to be the farce of *Unanimisme*; but it is important, as showing where his powers and his future lie, that the best things in the book are to be found, not where he is laughing at anything, even his own doctrines, but where he makes us feel in subtle language those kinds of feelings which peculiarly interest him. The following passage could only have been written by the author of *Mort de Quelqu'un*, and it makes one hope that M. Romains believes, as we do, that he may write a much better book than *Les Copains*, but that it will not be a farce:

Le Saint-Péret mousseux débarbouilia les esprits. Il accrut l'ardeur, mais en l'épurant.

Les copains étaient envahis par un sentiment singulier, qui n'avait pas de nom, mais qui leur donnait des ordres, qui exigeait d'eux une satisfaction soudaine: on ne sait quoi qui ressemblait à un besoin d'unité absolue et de conscience absolue.

Ils en arrivèrent à comprendre qu'ils voulaient certaines paroles, qu'ils seraient assouvis par une voix.

Si plusieurs choses n'étaient pas dites, cette nuit même, il serait à jamais trop tard pour les dire.

Si plusieurs choses n'étaient pas constatées et manifestées, elles seraient à jamais perdues.[6]

1 – A review in the *TLS*, 7 August 1913, (Kp C49.3) of *Les Copains* (Eugène Figuière et Cie, 1913) by Jules Romains.

2 – Jules Romains (Louis Farigoule, 1885–1972), whose works at this date included the collection of poems *La Vie unanime* (1908) and the novel *Mort de quelqu'un* (1911), a translation of which, *The Death of a Nobody*, by Desmond MacCarthy and Sydney Waterlow, was to appear in 1914.

3 – G. K. Chesterton (1874–1936), among whose most recent works were *The Innocence of Father Brown* (1911) and *Manalive* (1912).

4 – For the first two companions, Romains, ch. v, p. 153; and for the last, *ibid.*, p. 154.

5 – *Ibid.*, p. 154.

6 – *Ibid.*, ch. VIII, p. 243, which has: 'Si plusieurs choses réelles'.

1916

Queen Adelaide

'I request not to be dissected nor embalmed, and desire to give as little trouble as possible,' wrote Queen Adelaide[2] characteristically when she was considering the disposition of her dead body; and all the industry of Miss Sandars has not been able to violate the privacy of her spirit. For if Queen Anne[3] is dead, we must invent some more absolute form of annihilation for Queen Adelaide. We cannot boldly affirm, after reading 289 pages about her, that she never existed; but we feel much as though we had been to visit someone in a large handsome house, and after wandering through all the state rooms and up the grand staircase and through the attics had heard only the swishing of a skirt and once – that was the most vivid moment of all – caught a glimpse of a 'wonderful red and grey parrot',[4] but never met the owner of the house, or heard more than the murmur of her voice in the next room. It is not Miss Sandars's fault. She has done her best to produce the Queen for us, and, as the Queen is dumb, has imagined what her feelings must have been on several very important occasions, as for example when she landed in England to marry a husband she had never seen.

The sea was rough . . . and the Princess Adelaide's spirits were doubtless at a low ebb . . . Nothing is reported of the interview between him and his future bride, and we can only guess the feelings of the Princess when, at the end of what must have been for one of her delicate physique a most exhausting fortnight, she was introduced to her middle-aged, garrulous, unpolished bridegroom. We may guess, however, that even were her agitation great, nothing of it appeared on the surface. Her manners were good, she was possessed of much reticence and self-control, and she doubtless behaved suitably and with the sense of propriety natural to her.[5]

That is the style of the volume. We are made to feel that it is not permitted in the case of a great lady so recently dead to impute to her any feelings save those that she might show to the public through the windows of her crystal coach on her way down the Mall when, although in constant fear of assassination, she made a point of sitting rather forward and very upright. She was always on her guard with the English, who disliked her, and she never lost the traces of her long girlhood in the pious secluded Court of Meiningen, where a paternal government issued decrees about coffins, and begging, and dancing on Sundays and wrestled, unsuccessfully it appears, with the problem of geese who stray from the flock. The Princess was well suited to pet and bully a state of devoted retainers, but only the arbitrary exigencies of politics could have forced a woman so trained to become the bride of William the Fourth, with his large family of illegitimate children, and given her the most corrupt court and the least reputable royal family in Europe for her circle and surroundings.

As fate would have it she became Queen Consort when England was struggling for reform. The mere thought of reform, were it merely the introduction of gas in a palace,[6] affected Queen Adelaide like an explosion of gunpowder, and suggested immediate death on a scaffold. She would accept William and George the Fourth, and a large impertinent family of FitzClarences with angelical sweetness and sub-mission, as part of the lot of womanhood, but the idea of giving power to the people stiffened her into something like self-assertion. All the influence she had she brought to bear on the King against the Reform Bill,[7] and drew on herself such hatred from the people that William paced the room anxiously if she were late home from the opera, and the newspapers bespattered her with names which nowadays would not be applied to any woman in the land.

But the Reform Bill passed and there was no martyrdom for Adelaide. Her head, that is, remained on her shoulders; but the discomforts of her lot surely amount in sum of agony to a beheading if it were possible to extract them and compute them. Doubtless, to borrow a very useful phrase from Miss Sandars, the manners of the Royal Family afflicted her considerably. They remind us of those astounding scenes in Dickens and George Eliot[8] when uncles and aunts behave in such a manner at the dinner table that we are inclined to think it is put on for the reader's benefit; but William the Fourth had exactly the same method. At a birthday dinner he took the occasion to jump up and abuse the Duchess of Kent, who was sitting next to him: 'I have no hesitation in saying that I have been insulted – grossly and continually insulted – by that person now near me'[9] upon which the Princess Victoria burst into tears, and the Duchess ordered her carriage. At another dinner party, to annoy the same lady's brother, he pretended to be deaf; and we have an appalling picture of the scene after dinner, when the chairs were placed in such a way that conversation was impossible, and the only diversion apparently for that silent company was to listen to the snores of the Duke of Somerset happily sleeping behind a pillar. But the domestic evenings of calm were no less trying, according to poor Lady Grey,[10] who hoped that she might never see a mahogany table again after sitting for two evenings round the one at Windsor, while the Queen netted a purse, and the King slept, 'occasionally waking for the purpose of saying, "Exactly so, Ma'am" and then sleeping again'. When he kept awake for any length of time, the King would pull out a 'curiosity'[11] for the company to look at, and then wander about signing papers, which a Princess blotted for him, while the Queen beckoned a small society of intimate friends into a corner and handed round her sketches. The nearest approach to the hypnotised boredom of that assembly is to imagine thirty people gathered nightly in a dentist's waiting room, with its round tables, and albums, its horsehair chairs, and diamond spotted carpet, and without even the excitement of the anticipated summons. This dreary scene dragged on until 1837, when the Queen found herself a widow, with an income of £100,000 a year. But her perpetual colds in the head and other indispositions had now developed into chronic ill-health, which made her 'rather fidgety about due attention being shown her',[12] and her chief interest seems to have lain in seeking health, in suppressing dissent and providing colonial bishops, in smiling graciously upon assembled multitudes and, let us hope, in admiring the gifts and cherishing the plumage of that remarkable bird, the red and grey parrot.

1 – A review in the *TLS*, 13 January 1916, (Kp C50) of *The Life and Times of Queen Adelaide* (Stanley Paul & Co., 1915) by Mary F. Sandars. Reprinted: *B&P*.
2 – Sandars, ch. xv, p. 285; Amelia Adelaide Louisa Theresa Caroline (1792–1849), Dowager Queen, was the eldest child of the Duke and Duchess of Saxe-Coburg

Meiningen. In 1818, she married William Henry, Duke of Clarence (1765–1837), who became William IV following the death of George IV in 1830.

3 – Queen Anne (1665–1714).

4 – Sandars, ch. xv, p. 279.

5 – For the matter before the second ellipsis, *ibid.*, ch. III, p. 46; and for the remainder, pp. 47–8.

6 – *Ibid.*, ch. VIII, p. 130; gas had been installed at Windsor but was cut off on the instructions of Queen Adelaide, who thought it a dangerous innovation.

7 – Introduced by Lord John Russell in 1831, to extend the franchise and bring about other electoral reforms, and passed by parliament in 1832.

8 – Charles Dickens (1812–70); George Eliot (1819–80).

9 – Sandars, ch. xiv, p. 258, slightly adapted; Victoria Mary Louisa, Duchess of Kent (1786–1861), daughter of the Prince and Princess of Saxe-Saalfield-Coburg. She married Edward, Duke of Kent (1767–1820), in 1818, and was the mother of the future Queen Victoria, who came to the throne on William IV's death in 1837.

10 – Henry Somerset, 7th Duke of Beaufort (1792–1853), sometime soldier, M.P., and, more famously, huntsman. Mary Elizabeth, *née* Ponsonby, Lady Grey (d. 1824), wife of the Whig statesman Charles, 2nd Earl Grey, Viscount Howick (1764–1845).

11 – For the king on waking, Sandars, ch. XIII, p. 229, quoting *Creevey Papers* (John Murray, 1903), p. 262; and for his 'curiosities' [sic], *ibid.*, ch. X, p. 162.

12 – *Ibid.*, ch. xv, p. 280.

A Scribbling Dame

There are in the Natural History Museum certain little insects so small that they have to be gummed to the cardboard with the lightest of fingers, but each of them, as one observes with constant surprise, has its fine Latin name spreading far to the right and left of the miniature body. We have often speculated upon the capture of these insects and the christening of them, and marvelled at the labours of the humble, indefatigable men who thus extend our knowledge. But their toil, though comparable in its nature, seems light and certainly agreeable compared with that of Mr Whicher in the book before us. It was not for him to wander through airy forests with a butterfly net in his hand; he had to search out dusty books from desolate museums, and in the end to pin down this faded and antique specimen of the domestic house fly with all her seventy volumes in orderly array around her. But it appears to the Department of English and Comparative Literature in Columbia

University that Mrs Haywood has never been classified, and they approve therefore of the publication of this book on her as 'a contribution to knowledge worthy of publication'.[2] It does not matter, presumably, that she was a writer of no importance, that no one reads her for pleasure, and that nothing is known of her life. She is dead, she is old, she wrote books, and nobody has yet written a book about her.

Mr Whicher accordingly has supplied not merely an article, or a few lines in a history of literature, but a careful, studious, detailed account of all her works regarded from every point of view, together with a bibliography which occupies 204 pages of print. It is but fair to him to add that he has few illusions as to the merits of his authoress, and only claims for her that her 'domestic novels' foreshadowed the work of Miss Burney and Miss Austen,[3] and that she helped to open a new profession for her sex. Whatever help he can afford us by calling Pope 'Mr' Pope or Pope Alexander, and alluding to Mrs Haywood as 'the scribbling dame',[4] he proffers generously enough. But it is scarcely sufficient. If he had been able to throw any light upon the circumstances of her life we should make no complaint. A woman who married a clergyman and ran away from him, who supported herself and possibly two children, it is thought without gallantry, entirely by her pen in the early years of the eighteenth century, was striking out a new line of life and must have been a person of character. But nobody knows anything about her, save that she was born in 1693 and died in 1756; it is not known where she lived or how she got her work; what friends she had, or even, which is strange in the case of a woman, whether she was plain or handsome. 'The apprehensive dame', as Mr Whicher calls her, warned, we can imagine, by the disgusting stanzas in *The Dunciad*,[5] took care that the facts of her life should be concealed, and, withdrawing silently, left behind her a mass of unreadable journalism which both by its form and by the inferiority of the writer's talent throws no light upon her age or upon herself. Anyone who has looked into the works of the Duchess of Newcastle and Mrs Behn[6] knows how easily the rich prose style of the Restoration tends to fall languid and suffocate even writers of considerable force and originality. The names alone of Mrs Haywood's romances[7] make us droop, and in the mazes of her plots we swoon away. We have to imagine how Emilia wandering in Andalusia meets Berinthus in a masquerade. Now Berinthus was really Henriquez her brother . . . Don Jaque di Morella determines to marry his daughter Clementine to a certain cardinal . . . In Montelupe Clementina meets the funeral of a young woman who has been torn to pieces by wolves . . . The young and gay Dorante is tempted to expose himself to the charms of the beautiful Kesiah . . . The doting Baron de Tortillés marries the extravagant and lascivious Mademoiselle la Motte . . . Melliora, Placentia, Montrano, Miramillia, and a thousand more swarm over all the countries of the South and of the East, climbing ropes, dropping letters, overhearing secrets, plunging daggers, languishing and dying, fighting and conquering, but loving, always loving, for, as Mr Whicher puts it, to Mrs Haywood 'love was the force that motivated all the world'.[8]

These stories found certain idle people very ready to read them, and were generally successful. Mrs Haywood was evidently a born journalist. As long as romances of the heart were in fashion she turned out romance after romance; when Richardson and Fielding[9] brought the novel into closer touch with life she followed suit with her *Miss Betsy Thoughtless* and her *Jemmy and Jenny Jessamy*. In the interval she turned publisher, edited a newspaper called *The Parrot*[10] and produced secret histories and scandal novels rather in the style of our gossip in the illustrated papers about the aristocracy. In none of these departments was she a pioneer, or even a very distinguished disciple; and it is more for her steady industry with the pen than for the product of it that she is remarkable. Reading when Mrs Haywood wrote was beginning to come into fashion, and readers demanded books which they could read 'with a tea-cup in one hand without danger of spilling the tea'.[11] But that class, as Mr Gosse indicates when he compares Mrs Haywood to Ouida,[12] has not been improved away nor lessened in numbers. There is the same desire to escape from the familiar look of life by the easiest way, and the difference is really that we find our romance in accumulated motor-cars and marquises rather than in foreign parts and strange-sounding names. But the heart which suffered in the pages of the early romancers beats today upon the railway bookstall beneath the shiny coloured cover which depicts Lord Belcour parting from the Lady Belinda Fitzurse, or the Duchess of Ormonde clasping the family diamonds and bathed in her own blood at the bottom of the marble staircase.

In what sense Mr Whicher can claim that Mrs Haywood 'prepared the way for . . . quiet Jane Austen'[13] it is difficult to see, save that one lady was undeniably born some eighty years in advance of the other. For it would be hard to imagine a less professional woman of letters than the lady who wrote on little slips of paper, hid them when anyone was near, and kept her novels shut up in her desk, and refused to write a romance about the august House of Coburg at the suggestion of Prince Leopold's librarian[14] – behaviour that must have made Mrs Haywood lift her hands in amazement in the grave. And in that long and very intricate process of living and reading and writing which so mysteriously alters the form of literature, so that Jane Austen, born in 1775, wrote novels, while Jane Austen born a hundred years earlier would probably have written not novels but a few exquisite lost letters, Mrs Haywood plays no perceptible part, save that of swelling the chorus of sound. For people who write books do not necessarily add anything to the history of literature, even when those books are little old volumes, stained with age, that have crossed the Atlantic; nor can we see that the students of Columbia University will love English literature the better for knowing how very dull it can be, although the University may claim that this is a 'contribution to knowledge'.

1 – A review in the *TLS*, 17 February 1916, (Kp C51) of *The Life and Romances of Mrs Eliza Haywood* [1693?–1756] (Columbia University Press, 1915) by George Frisbie Whicher, Ph.D., Instructor in the University of Illinois. Reprinted: *B&P*.
2 – Whicher, preliminary pages, from a declaration by A. H. Thorndike, Executive Officer, Columbia University Press.
3 – *Ibid.*, Pref., p. vii; Frances Burney (1752–1840); Jane Austen (1775–1817).
4 – *Ibid.*, ch. IV, p. 106; Alexander Pope (1688–1744) is referred to throughout by Whicher as Mr Pope, except at ch. I, p. 21, where the full name is used.
5 – For the 'apprehensive dame', *ibid.*, ch. I, p. 1, quoting David Erskine Baker's *Companion to the Play House* (1764); and for the 'disgusting stanzas', *ibid.*, ch. v, 'The Heroine of the "Dunciad"'; and see 'Eliza .../ ... yon Juno of majestic size,/ With cow-like udders, and with ox-like eyes', Alexander Pope, *The Dunciad*, 1728, bk ii, ll.149ff; and 1743, bk ii, ll.157ff.
6 – Margaret Cavendish, Duchess of Newcastle (1624?–74), on whom VW wrote in 'The Duke and Duchess of Newcastle' (*I VW Essays*) and 'The Duchess of Newcastle' (*IV VW Essays* and *CR1*); and Aphra Behn (1640–89), author of plays, poems and novels, including *Oroonoko, or the History of the Royal Slave (c. 1678)*.
7 – E.g., *Memoirs of a Certain Island adjacent to Utopia, written by a celebrated author of that country. Now translated into English* (1725), and a similar work, also with a key identifying the characters with well-known living persons, *The Secret History of the Present Intrigues of the Court of Caramania* (1727) – works which directly inspired Pope's attack on their author in *The Dunciad*.
8 – Whicher, ch. II, p. 76; the characters Berinthus, Emilia and Henriques occur in *The Lucky Rape* (1727); Don Jacques [sic] di Dorante and Kesiah in *The Fair Hebrew* (1729); Baron de Tortillee [sic] and Mlle la Motte in *The Injur'd Husband* (1723); Melliora in *Love in Excess* (1720); Placentia in *Philidore and Placentia: or L'Amour trop Delicat* (1727); Montrano and Miramillia in *The Fruitless Enquiry* (1727).

9 – Samuel Richardson (1689–1761); Henry Fielding (1707–54).

10 – *The History of Betsy Thoughtless* (1751); *The History of Jemmy and Jenny Jessamy* (1753); *The Parrot, with a Compendium of the Times*, 2 August–14 October 1746, which had been preceded by a similar publication, *The Female Spectator*, 1744–6.

11 – Whicher, ch. VII, p. 162.

12 – For the comparison by Edmund Gosse (1849–1928), *ibid.*, ch. I, p. 26; Ouida (Marie Louise de la Ramée, 1839–1908), whose works include *Under Two Flags* (1867), *Tricortin* (1869), *Two Little Wooden Shoes* (1874) and *A Village Commune* (1881).

13 – *Ibid.*, ch. VIII, p. 175, which has: 'preparing the way'; the ellipsis marks the omission of 'modest Fanny Burney and'.

14 – This suggestion was put to Jane Austen in 1816 by J. S. Clarke, librarian to Prince Leopold of the House of Coburg, the future king of the Belgians who that year had married Princess Charlotte, daughter of the Prince Regent. See *A Memoir of Jane Austen* (1870) by J. E. Austen-Leigh (ed. D. W. Harding, Penguin, 1965, p. 353).

Charlotte Brontë

The hundredth anniversary of the birth of Charlotte Brontë will strike, we believe, with peculiar force upon the minds of a very large number of people. Of those hundred years she lived but thirty-nine, and it is strange to reflect what a different image we might have of her if her life had been a long one. She might have become, like other writers who were her contemporaries, a figure familiarly met with in London and elsewhere, the subject of anecdotes and pictures innumerable, removed from us well within the memory of the middle-aged, in all the splendour of established fame. But it is not so. When we think of her we have to imagine someone who had no lot in our modern world; we have to cast our minds back to the fifties of the last century, to a remote parsonage upon the wild Yorkshire moors. Very few now are those who saw her and spoke to her; and her posthumous reputation has not been pro-longed by any circle of friends whose memories so often keep alive for a new generation the most vivid and most perishable characteristics of a dead man.

Nevertheless, when her name is mentioned, there starts up before our eyes a picture of Charlotte Brontë, which is as definite as that of a living person, and one may venture to say that to place her name at the head of a page will cause a more genuine interest than almost any other inscription that might be placed there. What new thing, one may well ask, is to be said of so strange and famous a being? How can we add anything about her life or her work which is not already part of the consciousness of the educated man and woman of today? We have seen Haworth, either in fact or in picture; long ago Mrs Gaskell[2] stamped our minds with an ineffaceable impression; and the devotion of later students has swept together every trifle that may render back the echoes of that short and circumscribed life.

But there is one peculiarity which real works of art possess in common. At each fresh reading one notices some change in them, as if the sap of life ran in their leaves, and with skies and plants they had the power to alter their shape and colour from season to season. To write down one's impressions of *Hamlet* as one reads it year after year, would be virtually to record one's own autobiography, for as we know more of life, so Shakespeare comments upon what we know. In their degree, the novels of Charlotte Brontë must be placed within the same class of living and changing creations, which, so far as we can guess, will serve a generation yet unborn with a glass in which to measure its varying stature. In their turn they will say how she has changed to them, and what she has given them. If we collect a few of our impressions today, it is not with any hope of assigning her to her final position, or of drawing her portrait afresh; we offer merely our little hoard of observations, which other readers may like to set, for a moment, beside their own.

So many novels once held great have gone out of fashion, or are pronounced unreadable, that we may justly feel a little anxiety when the time comes to make trial of *Jane Eyre*[3] and the rest. We have suggested that a book, in order to live, must have the power of changing as we change, and we have to ask ourselves whether it is possible that Charlotte Brontë can have kept pace with us. Shall we not go back to her world of the fifties and find that it is a place only to be visited by the learned, only to be preserved for the curious? A novelist, we reflect, is bound to build up his structure with much very perishable material, which begins by lending it reality, and ends by cumbering its form. The mid-Victorian world, moreover, is the last that we of the present moment wish to see resuscitated. One opens *Jane Eyre* with all these half-conscious premonitions and excuses, and in ten minutes one finds the whole of them dispersed and the light shining and the wind blowing upon a wild and bracing prospect.

Folds of scarlet drapery shut in my view to the right hand; to the left were the clear panes of glass, protecting, but not separating, me from the drear November day. At intervals while turning over the leaves of my book, I studied the aspects of that winter afternoon. Afar, it offered a pale blank of mist and cloud; near, a scene of wet lawn and storm-beat shrub, with ceaseless rain sweeping away wildly before a long and lamentable blast.[4]

As a room full of people makes one who enters suddenly conscious of heightened existence, so the opening passages of this book make us glow and shiver as though we stood out in the storm and saw the rain drive across the moor. There is nothing here that seems more perishable than the moor itself, or more subject to the sway of fashion than the 'long and lamentable blast'. Nor is this exhilaration short-lived; it rushes us through the entire volume and scarcely gives us time to ask what is happening to us, nor in the end are we able to make out a very clear account of our adventures. We may reflect that this is exactly the opposite of our experience with certain other books justly numbered among the great. When we have finished *The Idiot*, or *Jude the Obscure*,[5] and even in the course of reading them, the plethoric state of mind which they induce is to be traced in a head resting on the hands, and oblivious eyes fixed upon the fire. We brood and ponder and drift away from the text in trains of thought which build up round the characters an atmosphere of question and suggestion in which they move, but of which they are unconscious. But it is not possible, when you are reading Charlotte Brontë, to lift your eyes from the page. She has you by the hand and forces you along her road, seeing the things she sees and as she sees them. She is never absent for a moment, nor does she attempt to conceal herself or to disguise her voice. At the conclusion of *Jane Eyre* we do not feel so much that we have read a book, as that we have parted from a most singular and eloquent woman, met by chance upon a Yorkshire hillside, who has gone with us for a time and told us the whole of her life history. So strong is the impression that if we are disturbed while we are reading the disturbance seems to take place in the novel and not in the room.

There are two reasons for this astonishing closeness and sense of personality – that she is herself the heroine of her own novels, and (if we may divide people into those who think and those who feel) that she is primarily the recorder of feelings and not of thoughts. Her characters are linked together by their passions as by a train of gunpowder. One of these small, pale, volcanic women, be she Jane Eyre or Lucy Snowe,[6] has but to come upon the scene, and wherever she looks there start up round her characters of extreme individuality and intensity who are branded for ever with the features she discerns in them. There are novelists, like Tolstoy and Jane Austen, who persuade us that their characters live and are complex by means of their effect upon many different people, who mirror them in the round. They move hither and thither whether their creator watches them or not. But we cannot imagine Rochester when he is apart from Jane Eyre, or rather we can only see him in different situations as she would have seen him in them, and to be always in love and always a governess is to go through the world with blinkers on one's eyes.

These are serious limitations, perhaps, and it may be true that they give her work a look of crudeness and violence beside that of more impersonal and more experienced artists. At the same time it is by reason of this marvellous gift of vision that she takes her place with the greatest novelists we have. No writer, that is to say, surpasses her in the power of making what she describes immediately visible to us. She seems to sit down to write from compulsion. The scenes in her mind are painted so boldly and in such strong colours that her hand (so we feel) drives rapidly across the paper, and trembles with the intensity of her thought. It is not surprising to hear that she did not enjoy writing her books, and yet that writing was the only occupation that could lift her up when the burden of sorrow and shame which life laid on her weighted her to the ground. Every one of her books seems to be a superb gesture of defiance, bidding her torturers depart and leave her queen of a splendid island of imagination. Like some hard-pressed captain, she summoned her powers together and proudly annihilated the enemy.

But although much has been said of her habit of describing actual people, and introducing scenes which had happened to her, the vividness of the result is not so easy to analyse. She had both an abnormal sensibility which made every figure and incident strike its pattern upon her mind, and also an extraordinary tenacity and toughness of purpose which drove her to test and investigate these impressions to the last ounce of them. 'I could never,' she writes, 'rest in communication with strong discreet and refined minds, whether male or female, till I had passed the outworks of conventional reserve and crossed the threshold of confidence, and won a place by their hearts' very hearthstone.'[8] It is by the 'heart's very hearthstone' that she begins her writing, with the light of it glowing on her page. Indeed, her production, whatever its faults, always seems to issue from a deep place where the fire is eternal. The peculiar virtues of her style, its character, its speed, its colour and strength, seem all of her own forging and to owe nothing to literary instruction or to the reading of many books. The smoothness of the professional writer, his ability to stuff out and sway his language as he chooses, was never learnt by her. She remains always unsophisticated, but with a power through sheer force of meaning of creating the word she needs and winging her way with a rhythm of her own. This mastery over language grew as she gained maturity as an artist; and in *Villette*, the last and greatest of her works, she is mistress not only of a strong and individual style, but of a style that is both variable and splendid. We are made to remember, too, her long toil with brush and pencil, for she has a strange gift, rare in a writer, of rendering the quality of colour and of texture in words, and thus investing many of her scenes with a curious brilliance and solidity.

Yet it was merely a very pretty drawing room, and within it a boudoir, both spread with white carpets, on which seemed laid brilliant garlands of flowers; both ceiled with snowy moulding of white grapes and vine leaves, beneath which glowed in rich contrast crimson couches and ottomans; while the ornaments on the pale Parian mantelpiece were of sparkling Bohemia glass, ruby red; and between the windows large mirrors repeated the general blending of snow and fire.[9]

We not only see that, we can almost touch it. She never heaps her colours, but lays a blue or a purple or her favourite crimson so rightly on the page that they paint the sentence as with actual pigment. Naturally, therefore, we should expect to find her a great landscape painter, a great lover of the air and the sky and all the pageant that lies between earth and heaven; nor may a student of hers tell whether he cares more for her people or for the keen air and the scent of the moor and the 'plumes of the storm'[10] which surround them with such light and atmosphere, and such overwhelming poetry. Her descriptions, too, are not separate visions, as they tend to be so often with writers of less powerful gift, but work themselves into the heart of the book.

It was a mile from Thornfield, in a lane noted for wild roses in summer, for nuts and blackberries in autumn, and even now possessing a few coral treasures in hips and haws, but whose best winter delight lay in its utter solitude and leafless repose. If a breath of air stirred, it made no sound here; for there was not a holly, not an evergreen to rustle, and the stripped hawthorn and hazel bushes were as still as the white worn stones which causewayed the middle of the path. Far and wide on each side there were only fields where no cattle now browsed, and the little brown birds which stirred occasionally looked like single russet leaves that had forgotten to drop.[11]

How beautifully that spreads the mood of the moment over the face of the land!

But these are the details of a great literary gift. We go back to her books, and sometimes this quality strikes us and sometimes that. But all the while we are conscious of something that is greater than one gift or another and is perhaps the quality that attaches us to books as to people – the quality, that is, of the writer's mind and personality. With their limitations and their great beauty these are stamped upon every page that Charlotte Brontë wrote. We do not need to know her story, or to have climbed the steep hill and gazed upon the stone house among the graves to feel her tremendous honesty and courage, and to know that she loved liberty and independence and the splendour of wild country, and men and women who are above all things passionate and true-minded. These are part of her as her imagination and genius are part of her; and they add to our admiration of her as a writer some peculiar warmth of feeling which makes us desire, when there is any question of doing her honour, to rise and salute her not only as a writer of genius, but as a very noble human being.

1 – An essay in the *TLS*, 13 April 1916, (Kp C52) commemorating the centenary of the birth, on 21 April 1816, of Charlotte Brontë (d. 1855), and which VW later incorporated in '"Jane Eyre" and "Wuthering Heights"', *IV VW Essays* and *CR1*. See also 'Charlotte Brontë' below, and 'Haworth, November, 1904', *I VW Essays*.
2 – Elizabeth Gaskell, *The Life of Charlotte Brontë* (1857). VW saw Haworth 'in fact' in 1904.
3 – *Jane Eyre* (1847).
4 – *Ibid.*, ch. 1 (ed. Q. D. Leavis, Penguin, 1966, pp. 39–40).
5 – Fyodor Dostoevsky (1821–81), *The Idiot* (1866); Thomas Hardy (1840–1928), *Jude the Obscure* (1895).
6 – Lucy Snowe, the heroine-narrator in *Villette* (1853).
7 – L. N. Tolstoy (1828–1910); Jane Austen (1775–1817).
8 – *Jane Eyre*, ch. 32, p. 400.
9 – *Ibid.*, ch. 11, p. 135.
10 – Apparently adapted from *Villette*, ch. 42 (ed. Mark Lilly, Penguin, 1979, p. 596): 'Not till the destroying angel of tempest had achieved his perfect work, would he fold the wings whose waft was thunder – the tremor of whose plumes was storm.'
11 – *Jane Eyre*, ch. 12, p. 142, which has: 'I was a mile'.

'Past and Present at the English Lakes'

We all know the charm of the country newspaper, in which columns are devoted to the flower show, or the trial of a poacher, or the wedding of the mayor's daughter, while the speeches of the Prime Minister and the agitations of the Empire are dismissed in very small type in some obscure corner. In reading Canon Rawnsley's book we feel something of this delightful change of proportion, as if a magnifying glass had been laid over the fells and dales of the north, and everything that happened beyond the rim of his glass had no existence at all.

Moreover, it is not the present time that his glass magnifies, but the summers of a century ago. We hear Hartley Coleridge murmur as he stops before each portrait in a friend's dining room, 'I wish you could give me a glass of beer.'[2] We see Wordsworth and Coleridge, De Quincey and Scott;[3] and so steeped is Canon Rawnsley in their thought that, though he travels in a motor-car, the landscape comes before him still as it was when Wordsworth looked at it. Shall we ever, we cannot help wondering, see these famous hills with our own eyes as though Wordsworth had never lived? And why is it that the art of describing places and skies in words is so seldom successfully accomplished? When Canon Rawnsley paints directly from the scene before him his sunsets and sunrises tend to remain merely an assembly of the names of colours – purple and gold, fawn and amber – without enough coherence in them to stir our imaginations into activity. But, on the other hand, in a charming paper called 'Crossing the Sands'[4] his method is different and far more successful. It is the narrative of a summer day's walk across the sand of Morecambe Bay. There are a great many facts, a certain amount of history, and a straightforward itinerary; but it is told in such a manner that we feel ourselves to be walking, too, upon the hard-baked sand with its wave-like ridges, fording the rivers and talking to the guide, and getting hot and blistered, and suddenly seeing the beauty of the whole, much as though we were there in the flesh. Perhaps then if you are not a Ruskin[5] or a Wordsworth, it is best not to look straight into the sunset but to rub along with humble facts until the mind at last is all of a glow and sees the sunset without its being described.

But the most interesting paper in the book is that on Gough and his dog.[6] Everyone remembers the story of the young man who was killed on Helvellyn and of the dog who watched beside his body until the shepherds found it three months later, for both Scott and Wordsworth have told the story in famous poems.[7] Canon Rawnsley desired to commemorate the event by placing a tablet on the spot. But almost by accident he was led to inquire into the facts, and now there came to him and to us a most cruel disillusionment. To us, living at a distance, it does not very much matter whether Gough fell at Striding Edge or at Swirrel Edge, so long as fall he did; but to read the heartless statement of a contemporary that the dog was found 'uncommonly fat' by her master's side, 'and the flesh of the latter was mostly consumed',[8] was of the nature of a catastrophe. For how many years, we exclaim, has not this impious creature robbed us of our sympathy!

But Canon Rawnsley's energy and faith were boundless, although at every step he was met by fresh disillusionments. For when once the story was examined each fact became doubtful, or was variously reported by different witnesses. Gough was certainly killed; but whether he fell or perished of starvation, whether he was fishing or making scientific observations, whether he was accompanied by two dogs or by one, nobody seemed to know. The breed of the dog varied as much as its character. Was it a spaniel or a terrier, a Dandie Dinmont or a 'laal yallow short-haired tarrier dog'?[9] The artists were consulted, but to no purpose. One has painted a huge white mongrel, another a black and tan collie, another a retriever, and another a small white terrier. Wordsworth would only say that it was not of mountain breed and barked like a fox. In his perplexity Canon Rawnsley sought out the descendant of the young man, and established the fact that he often went out with a dog and a walking-stick, and was fond of reciting poetry in the evening. Aged nurses and peasants tottering on the edge of the grave were consulted. The more anxious point of the dog's behaviour was submitted to a series of shepherds versed in the nature of dogs. Canon Rawnsley finds them unanimously of opinion that 'a dog wad nivver dea sic a thing; and he kenned dogs, t' naatur o' t' animal. But they did say that ravens had picked at him a bit.'[10] Still, as Canon Rawnsley says, 'better far does it seem that the poor traveller should have fallen a prey to the fowls of the air, those natural scavengers of the mountain side, than that the honour and fidelity of his faithful four-footed friend and mourner should be called in question'.[11] In the end it is pretty well established that Mr Gough was accompanied by two dogs, one of which left him, while the other remained, giving birth to puppies, and maintaining herself respectably upon the bodies of sheep, until she was discovered much emaciated and so wild that the hounds had to be set upon her before she could be taken. She was an Irish terrier, and her name was Foxey. But those who like to see the way in which the artist's mind works upon a subject cannot do better than compare the versions of the same story which have been given by a journalist, by Scott, by Wordsworth, and by De Quincey.[12]

1 – A review in the TLS, 29 June 1916, (Kp C52.1) of *Past and Present at the English Lakes* (James MacLehose & Sons, 1916) by the Rev. H. D. Rawnsley (1851–1920), honorary canon of Carlisle, author of numerous books on the Lake District. See also 'Wordsworth and the Lakes', *I VW Essays*.

2 – Rawnsley, 'Reminiscences of Hartley Coleridge', p. 19, which has: 'stopping before each picture and saying *sotto voce* to the picture, as if it were a living person, "I wish .."' Hartley Coleridge (1796–1849), the brilliant but tragically feckless eldest son of S. T. Coleridge.

3 – William Wordsworth (1770–1850); S. T. Coleridge (1772–1834); Thomas De Quincey (1785–1859); Sir Walter Scott (1771–1832).

4 – Rawnsley, pp. 230–69.

5 – John Ruskin (1819–1900), who settled at Coniston in 1871.

6 – *Ibid.*, 'Gough and His Dog', pp. 153–208; the remains of Charles Gough were found on Helvellyn in July 1805.

7 – *Ibid.*, pp. 154–5; Sir Walter Scott, 'Helvellyn' (1805); William Wordsworth, 'Fidelity' (1805).

8 – *Ibid.*, p. 167, from an account in the *Cumberland Pacquet*, 30 July 1805.

9 – *Ibid.*, p. 187. Dandy Dinmont, terrier-breeder in Scott's *Guy Mannering* (1815).

10 – *Ibid.*, p. 194.

11 – *Ibid.*, p. 174.

12 – *Ibid.*, pp. 174–8, which quotes De Quincey's extensive footnote on 'The case of Mr Gough' in 'Early Memorials of Grasmere', *Selections Grave and Gay* (1854).

A Man With a View

It is probable that any one who reads Samuel Butler[2] will wish to know more about him. He is one of those rare spirits among the dead whom we like, or it may be dislike, as we do the living, so strong is their individuality and so clearly can we make up our minds about their manners and opinions. Johnson[3] is of this company, and we can each add others according to our private tastes; but the number of people who will put Samuel Butler upon their list must be increasing every day. For this reason we would give a good deal to have a life of Butler, with plenty of letters and anecdotes and reports of those private sayings and doings in which surely he must have excelled. Mr Harris has had access apparently to no more information than is already before the public, so that he cannot gratify us in this respect; and at first there may seem little reason for another study of Butler's works when Mr Cannan's book[4] is scarcely a year old. But Mr Harris is quite strong enough to dispel our doubts. He writes clearly and with considerable force; he generates in us a desire to contradict him flatly, and again he makes us sigh, half with relief and half with annoyance, when he says something so true that we have always been on the point of saying it ourselves. His work has the merit, in particular the very clear chapter on the scientific books, of bringing out the main lines of thought which unite all Butler's work, so that instead of thinking him an eccentric who took up subjects much at random, we have a more serious picture of a man who built up solidly a house with many storeys. But the justification of Mr Harris's volume is that directly we have finished it we take down Butler to see what the change in our conception of him amounts to.

All this writing and disputing on his account is, of course, much what Butler himself expected of an intelligent posterity. But why is it that his lamp not only still shines among the living, but with a light that positively grows brighter and seems altogether more friendly and more kindling as the years go by? Perhaps it is that the other lights are going out. Certainly Mr Harris paints a very depressing picture of the great Victorians. There was George Eliot with her philosophic tea parties; and Tennyson declaiming pompously before the statues in the British Museum; and Pater with a style that Butler likened to the face of an enamelled old woman; and Arnold's 'odour which was as the faint sickliness of hawthorn'.[5] It was an age, according to Mr Harris, 'of false values and misplaced enthusiasms, unaccountable prejudices, astonishing deficiency in artistic perception, and yet with it a bewildering lack of real practical efficiency'.[6] Whether this is true or not, it represents very fairly Butler's own point of view. Further on, however, Mr Harris points out more suggestively that Butler was singular in being the spectator of his age, an amateur, 'a non-professional worker . . . as well as a lover'.[7] These words seem to us to indicate the most vital distinction that there was between Butler and his contemporaries. The Victorian age, to hazard another generalisation, was the age of the professional man. The biographies of the time have a depressing similarity; very much over-worked, very serious, very joyless, the eminent men appear to us to be, and already strangely formal and remote from us in their likes and dislikes. Butler, of course, hated nothing more than the professional spirit; and this may account for the startling freshness of his books, as if they had been laid up all these years in sweet-scented roots and pungent spices. Naturally his fellow men owed him a grudge (though we should like more evidence of what Mr Harris calls 'the conspiracy' against him),[8] as schoolboys set to do their sums in a dreary schoolroom have a grudge against a boy who passes the window with a butterfly net in his hand and nothing to do but enjoy himself.

But why, if they were imprisoned, was Butler free? Had the achievement been an easy one, we should not owe him the enormous debt of thanks which is his due. To free himself from the fetters which he found so galling it was not enough by a long way merely to refuse to be a clergyman. He had to preserve that kind of honesty, originality, or sensibility which asserts itself whether you are about to baptise a child or go to an evening party, and asks, 'Now why am I doing this? Is it because other people do it? Is it right? Do I enjoy doing it?' and is always preventing its possessor from falling into step with the throng. In Butler's day, at any rate, such a disposition was fatal to success. He failed in everything he took up – music and science, painting and literature; and lived the most secluded of lives, without need of dress clothes, in a set of rooms in Clifford's Inn, where he cooked his own breakfast and fetched his own water. But his triumph lay not in being a failure, but in achieving the kind of success he thought worth while, in being the master of his life, and in selecting the right things to do with it. Never, we imagine, did Butler have to plead that he was too busy for some pleasant thing, such as a concert or a play, or a visit to a friend. Every summer found him with sufficient pocket money to afford a trip to Italy; his week-end jaunts to the country were conducted with extreme regularity, and we should guess that he seldom put himself out to catch a train. But, above all, he had achieved a freedom of soul which he expressed in one book after another. In his obscurity he had wrought out a very clear notion of 'the Kingdom of Heaven'[9] and of the qualities needed by those who seek it; of the people who are the 'only people worth troubling about',[10] and of the things 'which nobody doubts who is worth talking to'.[11] He had, of course, a splendid collection of hatreds, just as he worshipped Handel and Shakespeare, Homer and the authoress of the

Odyssey, Tabachetti and Bellini,[12] so as to make him rather suspicious of other worshippers. In his isolation and idiosyncrasies he sometimes recalls Edward FitzGerald,[13] but with the great difference that whereas FitzGerald early realised the vanity of fighting the monster, Butler was always busy planting his darts in the flanks of his age, always pugnacious and always full of self-confidence. And against neglect and disapproval he had a private supply of most satisfactory consolations. It was much better fun, he said, to write fearlessly for posterity than to write, 'like, we will say, George Eliot, and make a lot of money by it'.[14] These reflections certainly kept his temper cooler than is usual in the case of a man who has so much to satirise, and also preserved in all its vigour his most uncompromising individuality. But perhaps his greatest fault as a writer springs from this irresponsibility, his determination, that is, to humour his own ideas in season and out of season, whether they serve to clog the story to stagnation, as sometimes happens in *The Way of All Flesh*, or to give it shade and depth. Very occasionally he reminds one of those eccentric and insistent people who persist in bathing daily in the Serpentine, or in wearing a greatcoat all the year round, and proclaim that such is the only road to salvation. But that trifling defect is the one drawback of the solitude to which he was condemned.

His many-sided training in art and music, sheep-farming[15] and literature, by exposing so many different sides of his mind to the light, kept him amazingly fresh to the end of life; but he achieved this freshness quite consciously also by treating life as an art. It was a perpetual experiment which he was for ever watching and manipulating and recording in his note-books; and if today we are less ambitious, less apt to be solemn and sentimental, and display without shame a keener appetite for happiness, we owe this very largely to Butler's example. But in this, too, he differed very much from his contemporaries.

All these qualities and a thousand more – for Butler is a very complex personality, and, like all great writers, finally inscrutable – are to be found in his books. Of these the most remarkable, perhaps, are *The Way of All Flesh*, and *The Note-books*. He had worked upon both for many years, and the novel he would have written yet again had he lived. As it is, it has all the qualities of work done almost as a hobby, from sheer love of it, taken up and laid down at pleasure, and receiving the very impress of the maker's hand. And yet it is easy to understand why it did not arouse enthusiasm when it first appeared – why it yields more upon the third reading than upon the first. It is a book of conviction, which goes its own way, passing the conventional turnings without looking at them. But, after reading it, we hardly care to inspect some of the masterpieces of English fiction; it would be as unkind as to let in the cold light of day upon a dowager in a ball dress. It would be easy to enumerate many important and splendid gifts in which Butler as a novelist was deficient; but his deficiency serves to lay bare one gift in which he excelled, and that is his point of view. To have by nature a point of view, to stick to it, to follow it where it leads, is the rarest of possessions, and lends value even to trifles. This gift Butler had in the highest degree; he gives a turn or a twist to the most ordinary matter, so that it bores its way to the depths of our minds, there to stay when more important things have crumbled to dust. If proof of this is wanted, read his account of buying new-laid eggs in *The Note-books*, or the story of 'The Aunt, the Nieces, and the Dog', or the anecdote of the old lady and her parrot in *The Humour of Homer*.[16] These *Note-books* of Butler's will certainly beget many other note-books, which will be a source of profound disappointment to their owners. It seems so simple a thing to have a note-book and to have ideas; but what if the ideas refuse to come, or lodge in the same place instead of ranging from earth to Heaven? We shall, at any rate, learn to respect Butler more highly. The truth is that despite his homeliness and his seeming accessibility, no one has ever succeeded in imitating Butler; to do so one would have to unscrew one's head and put it on altogether differently. At one time we think it is his humour that eludes us, that strange, unlaughing, overwhelming gift which compresses his stories at one grasp into their eternal shape; at another the peculiar accent and power of his style; but in the end we cease to dissect, and give ourselves up to delight in a structure which seems to us so entire and all of a piece; so typically English, we would like to think, remembering his force of character, his humanity, and his great love of beauty.

1 – A review in the *TLS*, 20 July 1916, (Kp C53) of *Samuel Butler: Author of Erewhon, the Man and His Work* (Grant Richards, 1916) by John F. Harris. VW wrote to Violet Dickinson, 26 May 1916 (*II VW Letters*, no. 759): 'Did you know old Samuel Butler? I have got to write about him. I wish I'd known him.' See also 'The Way of All Flesh', *III VW Essays*, and 'The Two Samuel Butlers', *IV VW Essays*. Reprinted: *CW*.
2 – Samuel Butler (1835–1902), author of *Erewhon* (1872), *The Authoress of the Odyssey* (1897), *Erewhon Revisited* (1901) and *The Way of All Flesh* (1903).
3 – Dr Samuel Johnson (1709–84).
4 – Gilbert Cannan (1884–1955), *Samuel Butler. A Critical Study* (1915).

5 – For George Eliot (1819–80), Harris, intro., p. 12; for Alfred, Lord Tennyson (1809–92), *ibid.*, 'Conclusion', p. 273: 'Tennyson stood "bare-headed" and "imperial-looking". At length the party moved on to look at the sculpture. Tennyson led. "But the only remark," says Mr Gosse [in *Portraits and Sketches*, 1912], "which my memory has retained was made before the famous black bust of Antinous. Tennyson bent forward a little, and said, in his deep, slow voice: 'Ah! This is the inscrutable Bithynian!' There was a pause, and then he added, gazing into the eyes of the bust: 'If we knew what he knew, we should understand the ancient world'"'; for Walter Pater (1839–94) and for Matthew Arnold (1822–88), *The Note-Books of Samuel Butler*, ed. Henry Festing Jones (A. C. Fifield, 1912), p. 184: 'Mr Walter Pater's style is, to me, like the face of some old woman who has been to Madame Rachel and had herself enamelled. The bloom is nothing but powder and paint and the odour is cherry-blossom. Mr Matthew Arnold's odour is as the faint sickliness of hawthorn' (not quoted in Harris).

6 – Harris, intro., p. 16.

7 – *Ibid.*, ch. VIII, p. 257.

8 – *Ibid.*, intro., p. 17.

9 – Butler makes several allusions to 'The Kingdom of Heaven' and has one note so entitled in *Note-Books*, pp. 168–9.

10 – *Ibid.*, 'Art and Usefulness', p. 174, which has: 'Briefly, the world resolves itself into two great classes – those who hold that honour after death is better worth having than any honour a man can get and know anything about, and those who doubt this; to my mind, those who hold it, and hold it firmly, are the only people worth thinking about.'

11 – *Ibid.*, 'The Kingdom of Heaven,' p. 169, which has: 'Nobody who doubts any of this is worth talking with.'

12 – For Handel and Shakespeare, *ibid.*, 'Preparation for Death', p. 363; for Homer and the authoress, see n. 2 above, and *ibid.*, 'My Work', p. 376; for Tabachetti (the Flemish sculptor Jean de Wespin, so known in Italy) and for Giovanni and Gentile Bellini, *ibid.*, p. 376.

13 – Edward Fitzgerald (1809–83), author of *The Rubáiyát of Omar Khayyám* (1859).

14 – Harris, intro., p. 20, quoting Butler, *Note-Books*, 'Myself and My Books', p. 160.

15 – Having taken a first in classics at St John's College, Cambridge, in 1858, Butler emigrated the following year to New Zealand and made a very profitable living there as a sheep-farmer until his return to England in 1864–5.

16 – See *Note-Books*, 'New Laid Eggs', p. 249; Butler, *Essays on Life Art and Science* (1904), 'The Aunt, the Nieces and the Dog'; *The Humour of Homer* (1892), a lecture delivered at the Working Men's College, Great Ormond St, London, 30 January 1892.

Heard on the Downs: The Genesis of Myth

Two well-known writers were describing the sound of the guns in France, as they heard it from the top of the South Downs. One likened it to 'the hammer stroke of Fate'; the other heard in it 'the pulse of Destiny'.

More prosaically, it sounds like the beating of gigantic carpets by gigantic women, at a distance. You may almost see them holding the carpets in their strong arms by the four corners, tossing them into the air, and bringing them down with a thud while the dust rises in a cloud about their heads. All walks on the Downs this summer are accompanied by this sinister sound of far-off beating, which is sometimes as faint as the ghost of an echo, and sometimes rises almost from the next fold of grey land. At all times strange volumes of sound roll across the bare uplands, and reverberate in those hollows in the Downside which seem to await the spectators of some Titanic drama. Often walking alone, with neither man nor animal in sight, you turn sharply to see who it is that gallops behind you. But there is no one. The phantom horseman dashes by with a thunder of hoofs, and suddenly his ride is over and the sound lapses, and you only hear the grasshoppers and the larks in the sky.[2]

Such tricks of sound may easily be accounted for by the curious planes of curve and smoothness into which these Downs have been shaped, but for hundreds of years they must have peopled the villages and the solitary farmhouses in the folds with stories of ghostly riders and unhappy ladies forever seeking their lost treasure. These ghosts have rambled about for so many centuries that they are now old inhabitants with family histories attached to them; but at the present moment one may find many phantoms hovering on the borderland of belief and scepticism – not yet believed in, but not properly accounted for. Human vanity, it may be, embodies them in the first place. The desire to be somehow impossibly, and therefore all the more mysteriously, concerned in secret affairs of national importance is very strong at the present moment. It is none of our business to supply reasons; only to notice queer signs, draw conclusions, and shake our heads. Each village has its wiseacre, who knows already more than he will say; and in a year or two who shall limit the circumstantial narratives which will be current in the neighbourhood, and possibly masquerade in solemn histories for the instruction of the future!

In this district, for instance, there are curious ridges or shelves in the hillside, which the local antiquaries variously declare to have been caused by ice-pressure, or by the pickaxes of prehistoric man. But since the war we have made far better use of them. Not so very long ago, we say a hundred years at most, England was invaded, and, the enemy landing on the Down at the back of our village, we dug trenches to withstand him, much like those in use in Flanders now. You may see them with your own eyes. And this, somehow, is proof that if the Germans land they will land here, which, although terrifying, also gratifies our sense of our own importance.[3]

But these historical speculations are for the contemplative mind of the shepherd, or of the old cottager, who can almost carry back to the days of the great invasion. His daughter has evidence of the supernatural state of things now existing without going farther than the shed in which her hens are sitting. When she came to hatch out her eggs, she will tell you, only five of the dozen had live chicks in them, and the rest were addled. This she attributes unhesitatingly to vibrations in the earth caused by the shock of the great guns in Flanders. If you express a doubt she will overwhelm you with evidence from all the country round. But no one here limits the action of the guns to the addling of a few hen's eggs; the very sun in the sky, they assert, has been somehow deranged in his mechanism by our thunder on earth. The dark spell of cloudy weather which spoilt July was directly due to these turmoils, and the weather-wise at the cottage laid it down as a fact that we should see no more sun all summer. None could rightly divine the reason; but to offer a reason for such sublime transactions would be almost to cast a doubt upon them. The sun has shone fiercely since then and is shining still, and local wisdom has fastened with renewed hope upon the behaviour of the church bell. The bell belongs to a church which stands solitary upon a hill in the midst of wild marshes, and is gifted with the power of foretelling the return of peace by dropping from the belfry exactly three months before peace is declared. Thus, at least, did it testify to the advent of peace after the Boer War; and once again, on 3 May last, to the delight of all beholders, the rope broke and the bell fell to earth.

August is well on its way, but you may still hear the guns from the top of the Downs; the sun blazes in a cloudless sky, and the eggs are no longer addled; but we are by no means downcast, and merely turn our minds to the next riddle, with a deeper conviction than before that we live in a world full of mysteries.

1 – An article, 'from a correspondent', in *The Times*, 15 August 1916, (Kp C54). The Woolfs had spent most of the previous month, and were to spend the whole of August and up to 16 September at Asheham House, on the edge of the Downs, a short distance from Itford, near Lewes, in Sussex. The genesis of VW's article is not documented.
2 – Followed in *The Times* by the sub-heading: 'Borderland of Mystery'.
3 – Followed in *The Times* by the sub-heading: 'Portents at Home'.

'The Park Wall'

The Park Wall confirms us in our belief that Elinor Mordaunt takes a very high place among living novelists and also a very honourable one. The book, indeed, is good enough to make us cast our eyes back to the old novels of great reputation, not merely to make the old comparisons and declare that here at last we have a writer worthy, &c., &c.; but to see how far we have travelled and in what respects we differ. Mrs Mordaunt's books appear to us sufficiently original and therefore emphatic to serve as a landmark. She writes in her way, and they in theirs; and one writer may be more richly gifted than another: but that sometimes seems to be of less importance than to have, as only true artists have, a world of one's own; and we begin to think that, whether big or small, Mrs Mordaunt's world is certainly her own.

The Park Wall is a wall of solid bricks, for Alice Ingpen, the heroine, lives in a substantial country house, but it is also a wall of tough though immaterial prejudice. Although she is by nature very slow and diffident, Alice soon finds herself amazingly further outside her park wall than most young women of her station. In the first place, her marriage takes her to live at Terracine, an island which lies 'a species of blister on the hot face of the Indian Ocean'; and then her husband turns out to be 'a common low cad',[2] a speculator, a gambler, and, naturally, a completely unfaithful husband. By means of a stratagem he sends her back to England on the same ship with a man to whom she has no tie save that of friendship; and directly they land he proceeds to divorce her. Her family shut their park gates against her. A child is born to her, and she goes to live in the south of London, where eventually she finds work in a factory for making cheap dresses. We may add that the story, after many more complications than we have described, ends happily; but the story is not the important thing.

If it were the important thing there would be faults to find with it – the husband's stratagem, to begin with, is not a very convincing one; nor can we believe that a respectable family of country gentlefolk would bring themselves to desert their daughter, as the Ingpens deserted Alice. But does it very much matter? So long as the writer moves from point to point as one who follows the lead of his mind fearlessly, it does not seem to matter at all. Mrs Mordaunt's mind is an extremely honest one, and where it points, she follows. She takes us with her, therefore, our intelligence on the alert, uncertain what is to happen, but with an increasing consciousness that all that happens is part of a genuine design. The writer is sufficiently mistress of her art to hold this out firmly before us, without any of those sudden immersions in this character or that incident which overcome the ill-equipped writer and destroy his composition. Her mastery of her subject allows her to enrich it with reflections of real profundity:

In the romance of young lovers there is the bud; in marriage there is the real fruit, sweet or bitter, as the case may be. Those who have their teeth in the rind may be slow to discover its flavour, for there is a sort of shock of the taste which for a while conceals taste. But while they are still uncertain the onlookers know all about it; wait, with some interest, for the inevitable grimace, and then go away. The man or woman who thinks to keep them amused by going on grimacing is mistaken.[3]

This ability to withdraw slightly and see the picture as a whole and reflect upon it is very rare; it generally implies, as we think it does in the case of Mrs Mordaunt, a power to strike out characters with solid bodies and clear-cut features. Her men (unless we are merely hypnotised to think so by a woman's name on the title page) are less good than her women; but even they fill their spaces in the design satisfactorily, and Alice herself is extraordinarily successful. We feel ourselves thinking so closely with her that, as in the case of a living person, we almost anticipate her words. Mrs Mordaunt treats her without any of the self-consciousness and the random boldness which mark her portraits of men, and makes us wonder whether the most successful work in fiction is not done almost instinctively. Again, we find ourselves glancing back at the classics. But if anyone seeks proof that the moderns are attempting and achieving something different from the great dead, let him read the scene in the Bloomsbury hotel,[4] when the family spirit utters itself in scarcely articulate cries and curses, with a curious effect as of angry parrots fluttering in a cage round some mute dove with folded wings. Surely Mrs Mordaunt is here attempting something that the Victorians never thought of, feeling and finding expression for an emotion that escaped them entirely. But whether this is so or not, the fact remains that *The Park Wall* is separate and individual enough to be studied for itself.

1 – A review in the *TLS*, 31 August 1916, (Kp C55) of *The Park Wall* (Cassell & Co. Ltd., 1916) by Elinor Mordaunt (pseudonym for Evelyn May Mordaunt, *née* Clowes, 1877–1942), prolific author of fiction and travel books. 'I've just read Mrs Mordaunts latest novel "The Park Wall",' VW wrote to Molly MacCarthy on 26 August 1916, 'very good, I think, and if it weren't for you, I should again attempt to write to her.' (*II VW Letters*, no. 782; the reference to a previous attempt to write to Mrs Mordaunt is unexplained.) See also *'Before Midnight'* below. Reprinted: *CW*.
2 – Mordaunt, ch. VI, p. 54; ch. XVI, p. 153.
3 – *Ibid.*, ch. XI, p. 107; which has: 'cancels taste'.
4 – *Ibid.*, ch. XVII, pp. 174–88.

The Fighting Nineties

As the title indicates, this is not an autobiography or a book of ordinary recollections so much as the selection of a few memories dear to the writer. Mrs Pennell has never made notes – never, as it seems, had the time to stop and comment when life pressed such a succession of duties and delights upon her. She tells few anecdotes even of the dead, and leaves a wide space between herself and those living celebrities who are, she hints, ready to spring out with all their claws displayed at the least rattle upon the bars of their privacy. But her memories are much too personal and spontaneous to need such artificial ornaments. If 'Arnold at Venice'[2] catches your eye, you will read of a gentleman who 'found the café as comfortable a place to sleep in as any other', and 'the one thing that roused him was baseball',[3] from which we may deduce that he was not even related to Arnold the poet.

Mrs Pennell's day was one of strenuous bicycling and journalism; but this she cuts off and dwells almost exclusively upon a long series of nights in Rome and Venice, London and Paris, when the gilt mirrors of innumerable restaurants reflected little parties of very youthful artists discussing all things in life and art, until the proprietor had to produce candles for them to go home with. Mrs Pennell conveys very charmingly the impression of the wonderfully gifted beings who drifted round the table on those nights, with their eccentric adventures, and their casual way of upsetting all the traditions current in Spruce Street, Philadelphia, where she was brought up. At first she was continually surprised; they never mentioned 'history, dates, periods, schools', took no account of Ruskin, and considered living artists more interesting than dead ones. 'The vital questions were treatment, colour values, tone, mediums ... There were nights when I went away believing that nothing mattered in the world except the ground on a copper plate or the grain of a canvas, or the paint in a tube.'[4] And they all believed consistently that in the whole world the only thing that matters is art.

Nights when the little tables in a café attract all the artists in a quarter have never flourished in London, although Mrs Pennell's pages give the lie once more to the notion that English people refuse to congregate and talk if they are given a comfortable private room, whisky and soda and a hospitable hostess. To judge by names, the best of all the nights, so far as brilliance of talk goes, must have been those in the Buckingham Street rooms overlooking the river. Henley came there, and R. A. M. Stevenson, Henry Harland, Whistler, Aubrey Beardsley[5] – all the stars, in short, of the last years of the nineteenth century. The rooms shook with Henley's robust roar, which drove timid spirits to seek far corners; or there was heard the 'Ha, ha!'[6] of Whistler, which also made certain guests thankful that the room was provided with many doors.

And here we must make what appears to be a confession. The little shelf of books bequeathed to us by the writers of that age has always seemed the fruit of an evening time after the hot blaze of day, when swift, moth-like spirits were abroad; a time of graceful talent and thin little volumes whose authors had done with life long before they were old. Nothing annoys Mrs Pennell more than such a description of her incomparable age. They were days above all of fighting and clamour. What they despised they called 'bleat'; what they loved they called 'human'.[7] 'The Fighting Nineties' she calls them in preference to any other description – fighting, it seems, 'Victorian sham prudery and respectability'.[8] Whether the historian will agree with her hardly matters. To the people who lived in them they were, mercifully enough, the one tolerable season of recorded time. If fortune has given us a different period, we may think Mrs Pennell mistaken, but we can sympathise. The difficulty is to sympathise with her in the later chapters, when she becomes so drastically exclusive that ninety-nine out of a hundred of her readers must feel themselves included in the vast herd of 'tourists', 'outsiders', or 'average Englishmen',[9] who, as they flounder about in cafés and galleries, have to be avoided, or, if they cannot be avoided, to be shocked. And from this artistic exclusiveness the step is very short to the worst exclusiveness of all – that which shuts itself up against youth and decries and belittles its work. The change from intense enjoyment of her own youth to disparagement of the youth of others is really surprising. What, one wonders, would Mrs Pennell have said if anyone had addressed her group as she addresses the artists of today?

I have watched with sympathetic amusement these late years one new movement, one new revolt after another, started and led by little men who have not the strength to move anything, or the independence to revolt against anything, except in their boast of it.[10]

Or again:

Their inability to take themselves with gaiety is what makes the young men of the twentieth century so hopelessly different from the young men of the eighteen-nineties. Their high moral ideal and concern with social problems would not permit them to see anything to laugh at in the experiment of feeding a peacock on cake steeped in absinthe.[11]

If such is the toll that time exacts from those who have tasted the best of life, one may surely be content to dine at all the wrong places and be shocked by all the right things.

1 – A review in the *TLS*, 12 October 1916, (Kp C55.1) of *Nights. Rome, Venice in the Aesthetic Eighties. London, Paris in the Fighting Nineties … With sixteen illustrations* (William Heinemann, 1916) by Elizabeth Robins Pennell (1855–1936), art critic and writer on cookery, wife of the eminent American etcher and illustrator Joseph Pennell (1860–1926), several of whose pictures are reproduced in *Nights*; the Pennells collaborated on a number of books, including the authorised *Life of James McNeill Whistler* (1908).

2 – Pennell, an entry in the index.

3 – *Ibid.*, p. 86; p. 87.

4 – *Ibid.*, p. 46; John Ruskin (1819–1900), whose *Stones of Venice* was published in 1851–3.

5 – William Ernest Henley (1849–1903), poet, dramatist, critic and editor; Robert Alan Mowbray Stevenson (1847–1900), painter and art critic, champion of Impressionism, a cousin of R. L. Stevenson; Henry Harland (1861–1905), American novelist, who settled in England in the early nineties and became literary editor of the

Yellow Book; James McNeill Whistler (1834–1903), painter; Aubrey Vincent Beardsley (1872–98), artist, art editor of the *Yellow Book*.

6 – Pennell, p. 142.

7 – *Ibid.*, p. 136: 'Pretence of any kind was as the red rag; "bleat" was the unpardonable sin; the man who was "human" was the man to be praised. I would not pretend to say who invented this meaning for the word "human". Perhaps Robert Louis Stevenson . . . But however that may have been, "bleat" and "human" were the two words ever recurring like a refrain in the columns of the *National Observer* [ed. W. E. Henley] . . .'

8 – *Ibid.*, p. 118; p. 190.

9 – The terms 'tourist' and 'outsider' occur regularly *passim*, as do Englishmen; for the only reference to 'the average Englishman', *ibid.*, p. 284.

10 – *Ibid.*, p. 235.

11 – *Ibid.*, p. 265.

Among the Poets

On the face of it there is a great deal to be said in favour of such a book as this. For it is very pleasant to think of literature rather informally sometimes, and to be led about a library by some enthusiast who is always pulling out a volume and saying 'Listen to this'. And there is a real service to be performed by people who are not professors or specialists, but merely know good writing when they see it. The mass of new poetry is vast; every year hundreds of poems must sink to the depths and be lost for ever. We need, therefore, watchers with trained eyes who will go through book after book and extract what is worth keeping. And who, after all, is better qualified than Mr Coleridge to discharge the duties of an examiner or warden of letters? 'I have lived all my life in libraries,' he writes, 'first in my father's, which was magnificent, and afterwards in my own, which is precious.'[2] And, then, he is a Coleridge.

He begins with sufficient spirit to raise our hopes very high. Here, he says, taking down a book of poems by a young American, called Charles Henry Luders, 'is one of the most lovely things in the world'.[3] Naturally after hearing that we are disappointed by the poem itself. We are immediately prepared to cap it with something just as good by someone as little known. Next we have an extract from a prize poem on the Apollo Belvedere by Dean Milman;[4] and then, after a little discourse upon the value of classical study, a famous sonnet of Wordsworth's.[5]

What are the principles that guide Mr Coleridge in choosing selections for our improvement and delight? It is not difficult to discover them. The prize always goes to the poet of finish and scholarship, who observes the laws of prosody and elevates and refines the passions, which is, Mr Coleridge observes, the 'true function of the poet'.[6] And with this for his standard he moves his poets up and down like boys in a class. Walt Whitman and his admirers go to the very bottom. '. . . it is as impossible to argue with persons who admire tnis kind of flux from a dictionary ⟨The Song of the Broad Axe⟩ as it is to discuss principles of beauty in art with an admirer of the Cubists . . .';[7] and so on. There is more to be said for Lowell,[8] but Mr Coleridge pauses in his remarks upon him to observe rather plaintively that he wore a beard. On the other hand, Miss Anne Reeves Aldritch and Miss Lucy Larcom[9] get almost full marks. But Mr Coleridge's range is very wide and purposely haphazard. Here, for instance, he opens Swinburne, and remarks, 'In the later years of the nineteenth century Swinburne enjoyed a very considerable reputation.'[10] We may possibly be aware of that already; but other comments are more disputable and should make Mr Coleridge's library ring with argument. Pope, he says, 'never attains the grand style';[11] 'it is remarkable that even the finest work of Wordsworth appears to be generally quite uninspired';[12] 'the finest work is always perfectly simple';[13] of Walter Savage Landor, 'his excursions into poetry do nothing to enhance his fame'.[14] To all of which we can only reply that we do not agree with a word of it.

Living writers as a rule are not well represented in Mr Coleridge's library; or, if he admits them, there must be labels attached to them to warn off the public. Both Mr Masefield and Mr Bernard Shaw have 'projected upon the public the foul expletive which never passes the lips of any decent person'.[15] And Mr Yeats is by no means safe reading. He encourages a loose habit of mind – a confusion between beauty and vagueness. There is a line of his about evening which has been much admired by the young:

> And evening, full of the linnet's wings,

whereas the truth is that linnets 'go to roost no later than any other birds'.[16]

But these quotations show Mr Coleridge with the birch in his hand, driving intruders out of the sanctuary; and, that done, he falls down and worships with the most devout and thankful of hearts. His god – one need hardly say it – is Tennyson. And his final exhortation is to read through *In Memoriam* once a year at least; then he quotes 'Tears, Idle Tears',[17] and the beauty of it is so much greater than we remembered that we take down Tennyson at once. Enough has been said, perhaps, to show that, though we should not allow Mr Coleridge to choose our new poets for us, he is a very vigilant guardian of the old.

1 – A review in the *TLS*, 2 November 1916, (Kp c56) of *An Evening in my Library Among the English Poets* (John Lane, The Bodley Head, 1916) by the Hon. Stephen Coleridge.

2 – Coleridge, Preface, p. vii; Stephen William Buchanan Coleridge (1854–1936), clerk of assize, author, son of John Duke Coleridge (1st Baron Coleridge), the lord chief justice, and a graduate of Trinity College, Cambridge. His numerous publications include *New Poems* (1911), *Memories* (1913) and *A Morning in my Library* (1914).

3 – *Ibid.*, p. 4, referring to a poem, 'Wind of the North, wind of the norland snows', 'written by a young American over the grave of a beautiful girl that he had loved and lost and whom he soon followed'. Charles Henry Luders (1858–91), author of *The Dead Nymph and Other Poems* (1892) and *A Garden God* (1893).

4 – *Ibid.*, p. 5; Henry Hart Milman (1791–1868), dean of St Paul's, from 1849, had won the Newdigate Prize in 1812 with an English poem on the 'Apollo Belvidere' (sic); he was later to write historical dramas and religious histories.

5 – *Ibid.*, p. 8: the famous sonnet referred to is that beginning 'The world is too much with us . . .' William Wordsworth (1770–1850).

6 – *Ibid.*, p. 31, which has: 'It may be conceded that the chief function of the poet is to communicate pleasure, as that of the man of science is to communicate truth, but one of the poet's functions is to express in a perfect and soul-satisfying form the sorrows and losses that visit us all, and by clothing them with beauty, rob them of some of their crushing weight.'

7 – *Ibid.*, pp. 36–7; Walt Whitman (1819–92), *The Song of the Broad Axe* (1856).

8 – *Ibid.*, pp. 41–2; James Russell Lowell (1819–91).

9 – For Anne Reeve Aldritch (1866–92), author of *The Rose of Flame and Other Poems of Love* (1889), *Songs About Life, Love and Death* (1892), *ibid.*, p. 164; for Lucy Larcom (1824–93), author of *As It Is In Heaven* (1891), *At the Beautiful Gate and Other Songs of Faith* (1892), *ibid.*, p. 166.

10 – *Ibid.*, p. 180; Algernon Charles Swinburne (1837–1909).

11 – *Ibid.*, p. 144; Alexander Pope (1688–1744).

12 – *Ibid.*, p. 172.

13 – *Ibid.*, p. 135.

14 – *Ibid.*, p. 170; Walter Savage Landor (1775–1864).

15 – *Ibid.*, p. 163; John Masefield (1878–1967); George Bernard Shaw (1856–1950).

16 – *Ibid.*, p. 188, quoting from 'The Lake Isle of Innisfree' by W. B. Yeats (1865–1939).

17 – *Ibid.*, pp. 210–11; Alfred, Lord Tennyson (1809–92), *In Memoriam A.H.H.* (1850); 'Tears, Idle Tears', a song from *The Princess* (1847).

'London Revisited'

It is rather difficult to decide what section of the public ought to be advised to lay out six shillings upon Mr Lucas's book. If you want to look up information about a church or a building as you look up a train in the A B C, you will find nine times out of ten that there is no mention of that church or building. If, again, you want to contemplate London philosophically, humorously, or aesthetically, the lists of pictures, statues, and historic houses, delivered in the impersonal manner of a cathedral guide, will grate upon your teeth rather dryly. But if you belong to what is evidently no small section of the human race – that is, the public which reads whatever Mr Lucas writes[2] – the book may be recommended as a good example of his manner. He displays his neat, trim style, his love of old books, odd characters, cricket, Charles Lamb, collections, antiquities, water-colour paintings, curiosities, quotations – but the list threatens to be a long one; and the dominant interest in the present book is certainly London.

But if Mr Lucas had a million interests he could safely find pegs for them all in the streets of London. Personally, we should be willing to read one volume about every street in the city, and should still ask for more. From the bones of extinct monsters and the coins of Roman emperors in the cellars to the name of the shopman over the door, the whole story is fascinating and the material endless. Perhaps cockneys are a prejudiced race, but certainly this inexhaustible richness seems to belong to London more than to any other great city. By side of her Paris is small and frivolous; and, though all Continental cities have copied Paris, for Londoners, at any rate, there is only one real example of a town in the world – compared with her the rest are country villages. But each Londoner has a London in his mind which is the real London, some denying the right of Bayswater to be included, others of Kensington; and each feels for London as he feels for his family, quietly but deeply, and with a quick eye for affront.

Many of us, for instance, have never quite reconciled ourselves to the attempt which has been made of late to comb out her huddle of little streets and substitute military-looking avenues with enormous symbolical mounds of statuary placed exactly at the wrong spot – for we have no sense, like the French, for the outdoor dramatic. And the lavish use of white stone, though commended by Mr Lucas (it is, he says, 'the only true building material for London'),[3] lends itself too much in the hands of modern architects to scrolls and festoons, fit for the white sugar of a wedding cake rather than for the streets of a great city. But in the last two winters many of us must have realised the beauty of the white church spires for the first time; as they lie against the blue of the night in their ethereal ghostliness. There is room for all diversion of opinion about London; and, however often you may walk her streets, you are always picking up new facts about her. How many of us know two facts mentioned by Mr Lucas – that in St Giles's-in-the-Fields off the Charing Cross Road lie buried Marvell and Chapman, James Shirley and Lord Herbert of Cherbury?[4] and that all the lampposts in the parish of St Martin-in-the-Fields bear a relief of St Martin giving his cloak to the beggar?[5] The list of open-air statues which Mr Lucas has compiled is far longer than we should have expected. We own to finding ourselves completely outdone by Mr Lucas in appreciation of these works. But even the statues of London are lovable; and the sparrows find the top hats of statesmen good lodging for their nests. Finally, if Cleopatra's Needle is to count as a statue, why is there no mention of one of the few pieces of sculpture in the streets of London that is pleasing to the eye – the woman with an urn which fronts the gates of the Foundling Hospital?[6] In future editions of this book we hope that Mr Lucas will spare her a word of praise; and reveal the name of the sculptor.

1 – A review in the *TLS*, 9 November 1916, (Kp C57) of *London Revisited. With sixteen drawings in colour by H. M. Livens and sixteen other illustrations* (Methuen & Co. Ltd., 1916) by E. V. Lucas. (The book was issued as a companion to Lucas's *A Wanderer in London*, 1906.)

2 – Edward Verrall Lucas (1868–1938), journalist and critic, was a prolific author of light essays – of which he published about thirty collections – in the manner of Charles Lamb (1775–1834), of whom Lucas was both an editor and biographer, and whose essay 'Valentine's Day' (*Elia*, 1823), he discusses and quotes from at length in ch. II here.

3 – *Ibid.*, ch. I, p. 5.

4 – For the burial place of Andrew Marvell (1621–78), George Chapman (1559?–1634?), James Shirley (1596–1666) and Lord Herbert of Cherbury (1583–1648), *ibid.*, ch. III, pp. 51–3.

5 – *Ibid.*, ch. XXIII, p. 271.

6 – Lucas refers to the statue opposite the Foundling Hospital, at the end of Lamb's Conduit, of the philanthropist founder of the hospital Captain Thomas Coram (1668–1751) – see *ibid.*, ch. XIV, p. 163. The statue of 'the woman with an urn' which he neglected to mention is known as the Water Bearer and listed in A. Byron, *London Statues* (Constable, 1981), p. 272, as the Francis Whiting Fountain, 1870.

In a Library

We hope that the modesty of Professor Hudson's[2] preface will not mislead many of his readers into thinking that it is quite a simple matter to write such a book themselves. It is, he says, a by-product of 'more serious work in literature',[3] and unless we are much mistaken, behind each of the essays lies a background of extremely wide and serious reading. The learning is suppressed rather than obtruded; but it raises Professor Hudson to an eminence from which he can see his subject in the right proportions, and makes his treatment at once light and authoritative.

Anyone who chances to read an essay now and again upon such forgotten writers as Henry Carey and George Lillo[4] is aware how earnestly the essayist strains to prove the importance of his subject. Either he was the unacknowledged father of the novel or the forgotten originator of the essay – a claim we would willingly concede, for the most part, if by so doing we might escape the proofs of it. Professor Hudson, on the other hand, frankly acknowledges the obscurity of his heroes, and, by demonstrating that their writing was often extremely dull, persuades us to find a good deal of amusement in it. But, having all the facts at his fingers' ends, he can do what is more to the point – he can show us why it is that men like Carey and Lillo, while themselves unimportant, are yet interesting figures in the history of literature.

Carey, we all know, wrote 'Sally in our Alley'. But we do not know that he wrote it after 'dodging' a shoemaker's 'prentice who was taking his sweetheart to a 'sight of Bedlam, the Puppet-Shows, the Flying Chairs, and all the elegancies of Moorfields'.[5] We do not perhaps know that he was one of the first writers in that aristocratic age to see the 'beauty of a chaste and disinterested passion, even in the lowest class of human life'.[6] Before his time, chaste and disinterested passions were considered to be the monopoly of the peerage. It was only when you wrote a comedy or wanted to provide some comic relief that you could introduce the lower classes with propriety. This interesting theory is discussed at greater length in the paper upon George Lillo, whose play, *The London Merchant*, did much to bring middle-class men and women upon the stage not as butts, but as heroes and heroines – a piece of presumption which much offended 'the Town', although the play has been acted from 1731 down to our own time, when Sir Henry Irving used to play it in the provinces.[7] As a stout democrat Professor Hudson asserts that the prejudice which made an aristocratic hero essential is nowadays 'in the last degree unintelligible'.[8] But is that so? Considering the rarity of coronets, the number of lords and ladies in modern fiction is really notable, and must be supported by some demand on the part of the public. And the tendency is not quite so unintelligible or so vicious as Professor Hudson would have it. Without saying that certain kinds of emotion are actually made more dignified by the fact that they are felt by a king or a queen it is far easier to make them seem dignified. The associations are on the side of the peerage. And who shall say that a line like

Queens have died young and fair[9]

would have the same charm if it were merely girls, or maids, who had died young and fair?

The question, however, is not one of title or no title so much as the more interesting question of realism or romance. It is in this respect that Lillo was a great innovator. His heroes and heroines were not only merchants and clerks, but they felt like merchants and clerks. Their virtues were decency, honesty and thrift; and, however tragic they might be, they spoke in prose. And so, as Professor Hudson observes, we descend to the plays of Ibsen[10] and the modern development of prose fiction. But have we made things any easier for the novelist or the dramatist by widening their scope? Naturally not; for where everything may be written about, the difficulty is to know what to leave out. Our modern problem is that we want to preserve the beauty and romance of the heroic together with what is called character-drawing and likeness to life; and the peerage, if it tempts, tempts because it puts our characters a little further from us and invests them with a softer light. The whole subject of the middle-class drama and the growth of realism is a very interesting one, and we are glad to see that Professor Hudson proposes to treat it at length in a forthcoming book.[11]

1 – A review in the *TLS*, 23 November 1916, (Kp C58) of *A Quiet Corner in a Library* (G. G. Harrap & Co., 1916) by W. H. Hudson. Reprinted: *CW*.

2 – William Henry Hudson (1862–1918), an extension lecturer in English literature at London University. In the period 1897–1903, he had held professorial appointments in America at the universities of Stanford and Chicago.

3 – Hudson, Pref., p. vii.

4 – Henry Carey (d. 1743), poet and musician, author of burlesques, including, notably, *Chrononhotonthologos . . . the most tragical tragedy ever yet tragedised* (1734), and of 'Sally in Our Alley' and 'Namby Pamby' (*Poems*, 1729), verses written in ridicule of Ambrose Philips. George Lillo (1693–1739), dramatist, author of *The London Merchant, or the History of George Barnwell* (1731), *The Christian Hero* (1735), *Fatal Curiosity* (1736), *Elmerick, or Justice Triumphant* (1740). Hudson's other chapters are devoted to Thomas Hood (1799–1845) and to Samuel Richardson (1689–1761).

5 – Hudson, p. 68, quoting Carey's prefatory note to the poem.

6 – *Ibid.*

7 – *Ibid.*, p. 122: '. . . strange as it may seem to those of us who remember him only in his later years, Sir Henry Irving [1838–1905] frequently performed in the character of Barnwell when a member of the Manchester Theatre Royal'.

8 – *Ibid.*, pp. 126–7.

9 – Thomas Nashe (1567–1601), 'In Time of Pestilence':

> Brightness falls from the air;
> Queens have died young and fair;
> Dust hath closed Helen's eye.
> I am sick, I must die.
> Lord have mercy on us.

10 – Henrik Ibsen (1838–1906). And see Hudson, pp. 132–3, where it is argued that 'To us today, fresh from the perusal . . . of *Ghosts* [1881] or *Rosmersholm* [1886]', the idea that the impressiveness of tragedy, and its moral force, depend ultimately upon the rank and dignity of the characters seems monstrous and 'obviously . . . has no basis in fact'. And see p. 162 where Lillo's work is described as the forerunner of both melodrama and, 'more important than this, of that social play of realistic character and serious purpose which is so prominent a feature of our modern stage'.

11 – *Ibid.*, Pref., p. vii: 'a volume on George Lillo and the Middle Class Drama of the Eighteenth Century, now nearing completion', but which was not published.

Hours in a Library

Let us begin by clearing up the old confusion between the man who loves learning and the man who loves reading, and point out that there is no connection whatever between the two. A learned man is a sedentary, concentrated solitary enthusiast, who searches through books to discover some particular grain of truth upon which he has set his heart. If the passion for reading conquers him, his gains dwindle and vanish between his fingers. A reader, on the other hand, must check the desire for learning at the outset; if knowledge sticks to him well and good, but to go in pursuit of it, to read on a system, to become a specialist or an authority, is very apt to kill what it suits us to consider the more humane passion for pure and disinterested reading.

In spite of all this we can easily conjure up a picture which does service for the bookish man and raises a smile at his expense. We conceive a pale, attenuated figure in a dressing-gown, lost in speculation, unable to lift a kettle from the hob, or address a lady without blushing, ignorant of the daily news, though versed in the catalogues of the second-hand booksellers, in whose dark premises he spends the hours of sunlight – a delightful character, no doubt, in his crabbed simplicity, but not in the least resembling that other to whom we would direct attention. For the true reader is essentially young. He is a man of intense curiosity; of ideas; open-minded and communicative, to whom reading is more of the nature of brisk exercise in the open air than of sheltered study; he trudges the high road, he climbs higher and higher upon the hills until the atmosphere is almost too fine to breathe in; to him it is not a sedentary pursuit at all.

But, apart from general statements, it would not be hard to prove by an assembly of facts that the great season for reading is the season between the ages of eighteen and twenty-four. The bare list of what is read then fills the heart of older people with despair. It is not only that we read so many books, but that we had such books to read. If we wish to refresh our memories, let us take down one of those old note-books which we have all, at one time or another, had a passion for beginning. Most of the pages are blank, it is true; but at the beginning we shall find a certain number very beautifully covered with a strikingly legible hand-writing. Here we have written down the names of great writers in their order of merit; here we have copied out fine passages from the classics; here are lists of books to be read; and here, most interesting of all, lists of books that have actually been read, as the reader testifies with some youthful vanity by a dash of red ink. We will quote a list of the books that someone read in a past January at the age of twenty, most of them probably for the first time. 1. *Rhoda Fleming*. 2. *The Shaving of Shagpat*. 3. *Tom Jones*. 4. *The Laodicean*. 5. Dewey's *Psychology*. 6. *The Book of Job*. 7. Webbe's *Discourse of Poesie*. 8. *The Duchess of Malfi*. 9. *The Revenger's Tragedy*.[2] And so he goes on from month to month, until, as such lists will, it suddenly stops in the month of June. But if we follow the reader through his months it is clear that he can have done practically nothing but read. Elizabethan literature is gone through with some thoroughness; he read a great deal of Webster, Browning, Shelley, Spenser, and Congreve; Peacock he read from start to finish; and most of Jane Austen's novels two or three times over. He read the whole of Meredith, the whole of Ibsen, and a little of Bernard Shaw. We may be fairly certain, too, that the time not spent in reading was spent in some stupendous arguments in which the Greeks were pitted against the moderns, romance against realism, Racine against Shakespeare,[3] until the lights were seen to have grown pale in the dawn.

The old lists are there to make us smile and perhaps to sigh a little, but we would give much to recall also the mood in which this orgy of reading was done. Happily, this reader was no prodigy, and with a little thought we can most of us recall the stages at least of our own initiation. The books we read in childhood, having purloined them from some shelf supposed to be inaccessible, have something of the unreality and awfulness of a stolen sight of the dawn coming over quiet fields when the household is asleep. Peeping between the curtains we see strange shapes of misty trees which we hardly recognise, though we may remember them all our lives; for children have a strange premonition of what is to come. But the later reading of which the above list is an example is quite a different matter. For the first time, perhaps, all restrictions have been removed, we can read what we like; libraries are at our command, and, best of all, friends who find themselves in the same position. For days upon end we do nothing but read. It is a time of extraordinary excitement and exaltation. We seem to rush about recognising heroes. There is a sort of wonderment in our minds that we ourselves are really doing this, and mixed with it an absurd arrogance and desire to show our familiarity with the greatest human beings who have ever lived in the world. The passion for knowledge is then at its keenest, or at least most confident, and we have, too, an intense singleness of mind which the great writers gratify by making it appear that they are at one with us in their estimate of what is good in life. And as it is necessary to hold one's own against someone who has adopted Pope, let us say, instead of Sir Thomas Browne,[4] for a hero, we conceive a deep affection for these men, and feel that we know them not as other people know them, but privately by ourselves. We are fighting under their leadership, and almost in the light of their eyes. So we haunt the old bookshops and drag home folios and quartos, Euripides in wooden boards, and Voltaire in eighty-nine volumes octavo.[5]

But these lists are curious documents, in that they seem to include scarcely any of the contemporary writers. Meredith and Hardy and Henry James were of course alive when this reader came to them, but they were already accepted among the classics. There is no man of his own generation who influences him as Carlyle, or Tennyson, or Ruskin[6] influenced the young of their day. And this we believe to be very characteristic of youth, for unless there is some admitted giant he will have nothing to do with the smaller men, although they deal with the world he lives in. He will rather go back to the classics, and consort entirely with minds of the very first order. For the time being he holds himself aloof from all the activities of men, and, looking at them from a distance, judges them with superb severity.

Indeed, one of the signs of passing youth is the birth of a sense of fellowship with other human beings as we take our place among them. We should like to think that we keep our standard as high as ever; but we certainly take more interest in the writings of our contemporaries and pardon their lack of inspiration for the sake of something that brings them nearer to us. It is even arguable that we get actually more from the living, although they may be much inferior, than from the dead. In the first place there can be no secret vanity in reading our contemporaries, and the kind of admiration which they inspire is extremely warm and genuine because in order to give way to our belief in them we have often to sacrifice some very respectable prejudice which does us credit. We have also to find our own reasons for what we like and dislike, which acts as a spur to our attention, and is the best way of proving that we have read the classics with understanding.

Thus to stand in a great bookshop crammed with books so new that their pages almost stick together, and the gilt on their backs is still fresh, has an excitement no less delightful than the old excitement of the second-hand bookstall. It is not perhaps so exalted. But the old hunger to know what the immortals thought has given place to a far more tolerant curiosity to know what our own generation is thinking. What do living men and women feel, what are their houses like and what clothes do they wear, what money have they and what food do they eat, what do they love and hate, what do they see of the surrounding world, and what is the dream that fills the spaces of their active lives? They tell us all these things in their books. In them we can see as much both of the mind and of the body of our time as we have eyes for seeing.

When such a spirit of curiosity has fully taken hold of us, the dust will soon lie thick upon the classics unless some necessity forces us to read them. For the living voices are, after all, the ones we understand the best. We can treat them as we treat our equals; they are guessing our riddles, and, what is perhaps more important, we understand their jokes. And we soon develop another taste, unsatisfied by the great – not a valuable taste, perhaps, but certainly a very pleasant possession – the taste for bad books. Without committing the indiscretion of naming names we know which authors can be trusted to produce yearly (for happily they are prolific) a novel, a book of poems or essays, which affords us indescribable pleasure. We owe a great deal to bad books; indeed, we come to count their authors and their heroes among those figures who play so large a part in our silent life. Something of the same sort happens in the case of the memoir writers and autobiographers, who have created almost a fresh branch of literature in our age. They are not all of them important people, but strangely enough, only the most important, the dukes and the statesmen, are ever really dull. The men and women who set out, with no excuse except perhaps that they saw the Duke of Wellington once, to confide to us their opinions, their quarrels, their aspirations, and their diseases, generally end by becoming, for the time at least, actors in those private dramas with which we beguile our solitary walks and our sleepless hours. Refine all this out of our consciousness and we should be poor indeed. And then there are the books of facts and history, books about bees and wasps and industries and gold mines and empresses and diplomatic intrigues, about rivers and savages, trade unions, and Acts of Parliament, which we always read and always, alas! forget. Perhaps we are not making out a good case for a bookshop when we have to confess that it gratifies so many desires which have apparently nothing to do with literature. But let us remember that here we have a literature in the making. From these new books our children will select the one or two by which we shall be known for ever. Here, if we could recognise it, lies some poem, or novel, or history which will stand up and speak with other ages about our age when we lie prone and silent as the crowd of Shakespeare's day is silent and lives for us only in the pages of his poetry.

This we believe to be true; and yet it is oddly difficult in the case of new books to know which are the real books and what it is that they are telling us, and which are the stuffed books which will come to pieces when they have lain about for a year or two. We can see that there are many books, and we are frequently told that everyone can write nowadays. That may be true; yet we do not doubt that at the heart of this immense volubility, this flood and foam of language, this irreticence and vulgarity and triviality, there lies the heat of some great passion which only needs the accident of a brain more happily turned than the rest to issue in a shape which will last from age to age. It should be our delight to watch this turmoil, to do battle with the ideas and visions of our own time, to seize what we can use, to kill what we consider worthless, and above all to realise that we must be generous to the people who are giving shape as best they can to the ideas within them. No age of literature is so little submissive to authority as ours, so free from the dominion of the great; none seems so wayward with its gift of reverence, or so volatile in its experiments. It may well seem, even to the attentive, that there is no trace of school or aim in the work of our poets and novelists. But the pessimist is inevitable, and he shall not persuade us that our literature is dead, or prevent us from feeling how true and vivid a beauty flashes out as the young writers draw together to form their new vision, the ancient words of the most beautiful of living languages. Whatever we may have learnt from reading the classics we need now in order to judge the work of our contemporaries, for whenever there is life in them they will be casting their net out over some unknown abyss to snare new shapes, and we must throw our imaginations after them if we are to accept with understanding the strange gifts they bring back to us.

But if we need all our knowledge of the old writers in order to follow what the new writers are attempting, it is certainly true that we come from adventuring among new books with a far keener eye for the old. It seems that we should now be able to surprise their secrets; to look deep down into their work and see the parts come together, because we have watched the making of new books, and with eyes clear of prejudice can judge more truly what it is that they are doing, and what is good and what bad. We shall find, probably, that some of the great are less venerable than we thought them. Indeed, they are not so accomplished or so profound as some of our own time. But if in one or two cases this seems to be true, a kind of humiliation mixed with joy overcomes us in front of others. Take Shakespeare, or Milton,[7] or Sir Thomas Browne. Our little knowledge of how things are done does not avail us much here, but it does lend an added zest to our enjoyment. Did we ever in our youngest days feel such amazement at their achievement as that which fills us now that we have sifted myriads of words and gone along uncharted ways in search of new forms for our new sensations? New books may be more stimulating and in some ways more suggestive than the old, but they do not give us that absolute certainty of delight which breathes through us when we come back again to *Comus*, or 'Lycidas', 'Urn Burial' or *Antony and Cleopatra*.[8] Far be it from us to hazard any theory as to the nature of art. It may be that we shall never know more about it than we know by nature, and our longer experience of it teaches us this only – that of all our pleasures those we get from the great artists are indisputably among the best; and more we may not know. But, advancing no theory, we shall find one or two qualities in such works as these which we can hardly expect to find in books made within the span of our lifetime. Age itself may have an alchemy of its own. But this is true: you can read them as often as you will without finding that they have yielded any virtue and left a meaningless husk of words; and there is a complete finality about them. No cloud of suggestions hangs about them teasing us with a multitude of irrelevant ideas. But all our faculties are summoned to the task, as in the great moments of our own experience; and some consecration descends upon us from their hands which we return to life, feeling it more keenly and understanding it more deeply than before.

1 – An essay in the *TLS*, 30 November 1916, (Kp c59). The title was used by Leslie Stephen for his collections of critical essays originally published in 1874 and 1876. Reprinted: *G&R, CE*.
2 – George Meredith (1828–1909), *Rhoda Fleming* (1865), *The Shaving of Shagpat: an Arabian Entertainment* (1856). Henry Fielding (1707–54), *Tom Jones, a Foundling* (1749). Thomas Hardy (1840–1928), *A Laodicean* (1881). John Dewey (1859–1952), *Psychology* (1887). William Webbe (fl. 1568–91), *A Discourse of English Poetrie* (1586). John Webster (1580?–1625?), *The Duchess of Malfi* (c. 1614). Cyril Tourneur (1575?–1626), *The Revenger's Tragedy* (1607).

3 – Robert Browning (1812–89); Percy Bysshe Shelley (1792–1822); Edmund Spenser (1552?–99); William Congreve (1670–1729); Thomas Love Peacock (1785–1866); Jane Austen (1775–1817); Henrik Ibsen (1828–1906); George Bernard Shaw (1856–1950); Jean Racine (1639–99); William Shakespeare (1564–1616).

4 – Alexander Pope (1688–1744); Sir Thomas Browne (1605–82).

5 – No volume of 'Euripides in wooden boards' is catalogued as having been owned by VW. The edition of the works of Voltaire (1694–1778) is probably that listed in Holleyman: *Oeuvres complètes de Voltaire,* ed. Caron de Beaumarchais, *et al* (70 vols, 1785–89), a set of which belonged to LW and which in 1904 he took to Ceylon – see *ILW,* p. 130.

6 – Henry James (1843–1916); Thomas Carlyle (1795–1881); Alfred, Lord Tennyson (1809–92); John Ruskin (1819–1900).

7 – John Milton (1608–74).

8 – Milton, *Comus, A Masque* (1634, published 1637), 'Lycidas' (1637); Sir Thomas Browne, 'Urn Burial' (1658); Shakespeare, *Antony and Cleopatra* (c. 1606–7).

Old and Young

We have one reason, not the only one by any means, for thinking highly of this book of essays: it makes us wish to write an essay of our own, for the old people. We believe that if they were treated to their share of sermons, in which youth reasoned with them and defined their temptations as frankly as Mr Paget has done it for the young in the present volume, the ordinary life of the household would be much improved. No doubt we have improved it already. The child who calls his mother Mary and his father John is not going to be tongue-tied with false reverence when he grows up; those parents may hope never to stiffen into tyrants living in a sacred, and presumably unhappy, isolation. But as things are the old are as mysterious as idols in a temple; we take off our shoes before we approach them. The whole of our tradition is against unpremeditated intercourse with them; before we speak we sort out what it is proper to say to them as if they were newly made acquaintances, although in fact they may be related to us by the closest ties.

Whether this tradition rests on some truth or is the relic of an age of ancestor worship we do not know; but the effect of such treatment is that we are curiously cut off from communication with the old. They are for the most part mute and scarcely ever the subject of imaginative speculation. And when they do emerge the result is strange. Three or four years ago there was an exhibition of Post-Impressionist pictures,[2] which acted, oddly enough, as a trumpet call to the elderly and consolidated their forces into one opaque block. Everyone of both sexes who was over sixty felt apparently that not only were the principles of art attacked, but also the sanctity of old age. The virulence of the grey-headed was a revelation of the passion that was, and no doubt still is, in them. It was not less puzzling than the pictures themselves. At that time some textbook dealing with the psychology of the old would have been of great assistance; and we suggest that Mr Paget should consider the composition of one. We would ask him to examine particularly the change of mind which takes place between the ages of fifty and sixty. It is when they reach that age, we note, that we begin to treat our elders with respect. Losing the stimulus of contradiction, and relaxing their minds now that they have climbed their ladders, they develop a strange jealousy, a pontifical attitude of mind, so that a celebrated surgeon thinks nothing of dictating laws to a painter, and a successful barrister defines the province of realism in music. Indirectly, Mr Paget's book throws some light on these problems; and his complete immunity from these vices at once makes us desire to qualify any suspicion of harshness in the above remarks. For the old, after all, are the deep mirrors of life, in whose depths we may see all the processions of the past, closely surrounded by the unknown, as the day by the darkness of night.

Mr Paget's book, however, is compact of so many things that we cannot pretend to lasso either it or him with one fling of the rope. We do not know that we can even prove him old as years go; fifty years ago, he tells us, he was a small boy learning Euclid; so that at the most he can lay claim to sixty years only. We accept his word that he is about to become a fossil, and also that his book contains sermons; our experience of the pulpit would not have suggested that particular word. And at the very start he amply proves his own contention that fossils 'are aggressive, contradictious creatures, always spoiling for a fight'.[3] Put him in a Devonshire garden in April and instead of fixing his eyes upon the nearest hedge with a critical stare which suggests the decadence of evergreens, he is off at once upon the beauty of nature and the kindness of his friends. No clergyman could wish for clearer signposts for a sermon; but as Mr Paget treats them they point many different ways. We never know what we may meet at the turn of the page. 'No need here for guide-book talk,' he says; and, indeed, we had settled down to expect something of the kind from him. 'If you want to pay a compliment to the beauty of nature . . . just say *Oh, my*! and expire.' And if Mr Paget talks about himself, he bids us not be offended, because 'every library is full of the beauty of nature and the loving-kindness of man. But so many of these descriptions are impersonal,' he adds, 'they look outside self, not into self.'[4] One more quotation we may take from this essay:

We do feel, all of us, when we think steadily about it, that there must be some sort of limit to what is bad; some level of reality where it leaves off, some purpose which it does not prevent. In our common talk, our stock phrases, we admit this feeling. We explain away, as if we were in eternity – where, indeed, we are – the misconduct not only of ourselves but of others. *He didn't realise what he was doing, we say* . . . or, again, *One of his uncles is in a lunatic asylum*. [. . .] And I say these feelings are not only sane; they are as near the truth as we can get them.[5]

Now all this, we think, throws a little light upon the problems of old age. We see at once that the essayist is wonderfully at his ease, careless of what people may think of him, and convinced that any pretence is waste of time. All these good qualities spring from familiarity with life. But there are two other qualities which are present and which are even more significant. One is the happiness of old age, and the other is the certainty of the old as to what is right and what wrong. This happiness is quite consistent with a belief that things are very much worse than they were fifty years ago; that, indeed, may be one of the causes of it, though certainly it is not so in the case of Mr Paget. But the content of the old is much greater than their discontent, partly because they are for the most part irresponsible; and partly because they do not look ahead, but into the past and into the present. When we come to consider their certainty as to what is right and what wrong, however, we enter into the mystery of age.

It is clear that Mr Paget collects these essays in the hope that they will make young people in some way better. That, we think, is certain to be the result of so charming a book, but would anyone under sixty cherish such an aim? Until we reach that age those of us who are not moralists by profession have not made up our minds about our own lives, let alone the lives of other people. After that age we become, if we have a turn for thinking at all, full of concern for the soul. We lose the sense of separateness from others, and it becomes of great moment to us that people should understand the value of goodness. For evidently some kind of simplification takes place in the minds of the old. The soul rids itself of a multitude of cares and desires, and attaches itself with the greatest devotion to the one or two beliefs which survive. We think that for the most part these are beliefs in the goodness and badness of conduct, and that this is so is certainly confirmed by every one of Mr Paget's essays. Very active of mind, and having that mind stored with a great variety of knowledge, still the main question for him is always the moral question, whether he is discussing 'Moving Pictures', 'Hand-writing', or 'The Beauty of Words'. He has no doubt at all that this is the important aspect of each subject, and therefore he calls us to consider it with an authority which is more impressive than any other of his gifts. By what combination of simplicity, sympathy and absolute sincerity he brings us to an attitude of open-mouthed attention we do not know. But though we cannot define it exactly this we take to be the peculiar gift of the old, which forbids us to be quite at our ease with them, but invests them with mystery and compels our reverence for a knowledge which we ourselves have not.

1 – A review in the *TLS*, 14 December 1916, (Kp C60) of *I Sometimes Think. Essays for the Young People* (Macmillan & Co., 1916) by Stephen Paget (1855–1926), surgeon, propagandist for modern medicine, and man of letters, author of works of biography and of several collections of essays for the young.
2 – The First and Second Post-Impressionist Exhibitions, 1910 and 1912, organised by Roger Fry at the Grafton Galleries.
3 – Paget, Pref., p. vii.
4 – For the three quotations, *ibid.*, 'The World, Myself and Thee', p. 2; p. 3; p. 6.
5 – *Ibid.*, p. 14, which has: 'And I say that'.

'Social Life in England'

These eight lectures were delivered in March 1916, by Dr Foakes Jackson before the Lowell Institute in Boston.[2] The audience apparently received them graciously, and the lecturer has now printed them for a wider audience under a title and inside a cover which seem to us both a little misleading. Dark blue books are not, it is true, necessarily pro-found; but the title seems to promise something more solid than we have here. That particular century[3] was a momentous one in our social history. The industrial revolution, which turned England from an aristocracy to a democracy, which drove the country people into the factories and raised a large and politically powerful middle class, and the passing of the Reform Bill[4] – to mention the most obvious events alone –

moulded England into a new shape. If Shakespeare had come to life again in the middle of the eighteenth century, he would very soon have understood his position; but if Shakespeare were to awake now! The thought of what he would see in the sky and on the earth is at once appalling and fascinating.

No one could expect an exhaustive account of such a transformation in eight lectures lasting presumably one hour each; but we might look for some grouping or emphasis which would bring a general theory to our attention. That is the kind of service which lectures, with all their disadvantages, tend to perform; and it is a real one. But in this readable little book with its amusing assembly of quotations from Creevey and Dickens, Trollope and Surtees,[5] the reader slips from one picture to another, and is left for the most part to make up his mind as to the kind of world they illustrate for himself. If he looks for guidance to Dr Foakes Jackson he will receive it, but that will not help him materially, because the lecturer does not seem to be altogether sure of his own opinion. In one place he seems to suggest that the society of the Regency was far more exclusive than the society of the present day; in another he asserts that the 'rift between classes'[6] is deeper in our own age than in any other. Now he is of opinion 'that the passions of men are much the same as formerly, and that, if the advantage is on either side, it is with the present rather than with the past'; and later he declares that we are living under a plutocracy which tends to 'substitute prudery and respectability for real Christianity'.[7] But there is no reason to be downcast; if we find these statements either contradictory or depressing we must lay the blame, if blame it is, upon the audience.

To Americans, we suppose, England is always something of an old curiosity shop; they rummage in our past with inquisitive affection, and even, one might suggest, with an eye for bargains. Dr Foakes Jackson dips here and there in our annals to provide his hearers with quaint tokens of the past, old rings, and bits of brocade; and he is careful not to go beyond the curiosity shop. He must not fatigue them with dates and details; he must not harrow their feelings, or offend their morals; he must, if possible, introduce some personal flavour into his discourse by informing them that his great grandparents entertained Crabbe,[8] and that he had a very bad cold when he went to Aldeburgh to prepare his lecture. All this is done very neatly and with a gentlemanly modesty which disarms criticism by advancing only the most temperate opinions and supporting them almost invariably by the authority of others. And so, very naturally, we have an account of the trial of Queen Caroline, taken from the pages of Mr Creevey, a sketch of John Wesley, the narrative of Margaret Catchpole,[9] and so on. There is no need to tell our own public that Mr Creevey and John Wesley and Charles Dickens are all very good reading. But what Dr Foakes Jackson has given us, oddly enough, is not a picture of ourselves, but a picture of a cultivated American audience. They are, we gather, exquisitely urbane; they do not like outspoken criticism even of the poet Crabbe; the best way to lead them across the desert of the lecture hour is to bring a pocketful of sweetmeats and produce them one after another until the minutes are consumed. Read by this light, one of Dr Foakes Jackson's sentences has a pathetic ring in it. 'I hope,' he says, 'you will pardon the flippancy of the subject I am about to introduce; but I may say that it is not possible to understand English life without studying it.'[10] Sweeping as the pronouncement is, we are inclined to agree with him.

1 – A review in the TLS, 21 December 1916, (Kp c61) of Social Life in England 1750–1850 (Macmillan & Co., 1916) by F. J. Foakes Jackson.

2 – Frederick John Foakes Jackson (1855–1941), divine and author, Fellow of Jesus College, Cambridge, from 1886, honorary canon of Peterborough, 1910–27. During his visit to lecture at the Lowell Institute, Jackson was offered and accepted a professorship of Christian institutions at the Union Theological Seminary, New York, which he held until 1934.

3 – I.e. 1750–1850.

4 – Jackson, 'Creevey Papers – The Regency', p. 212: 'The Reform Bill of 1832 was the answer of the English middle class to the Bill of Pains and Penalties of 1820'; and 'Mid-Victorianism. W. M. Thackeray [1811–63]', p. 270: 'The ruling aristocracy came to an end when the Reform Bill was passed in 1832, but their prestige remained'.

5 – Thomas Creevey (1768–1838); Charles Dickens (1812–70), see ibid., 'Social Abuses Exposed by Charles Dickens'; Anthony Trollope (1815–82); Robert Smith Surtees (1805–64), see ibid., 'Sport, and Rural England'.

6 – Jackson, 'Mid-Victorianism. W. M. Thackeray', p. 301, and see next note.

7 – For the first quotation, ibid., 'Creevey Papers – The Regency', p. 169; for the second, ibid., 'Mid-Victorianism. W. M. Thackeray', pp. 300–1: 'This feeling of shame for having practised some perfectly reputable calling [trade] has had I believe very serious results ... It has destroyed a commercial aristocracy and put a plutocracy in its place. It tended for a time to substitute prudery and respectability for real Christianity; and, before the war at least, even these poor substitutes were growing so out of fashion as to be regretted. It has also deepened the rift between the classes.'

8 – Ibid., 'George Crabbe [1754–1832]', p. 58: Jackson's maternal grandparents,

Mr and Mrs Burcham, had afforded Crabbe hospitality when, in 1780, he had gone to London to pursue a literary career.

9 – John Wesley (1703–91), see *ibid.*, 'Life in the Eighteenth Century Illustrated by the Career of John Wesley'. Margaret Catchpole (1773–1841) – an adventuress whose life was fictionalised by Rev. Richard Cobbold and published in 3 vols in 1845 – see *ibid.*, 'Margaret Catchpole'.

10 – Jackson, 'Sport, and Rural England', p. 302. For VW on English sporting life, see 'Jack Mytton', *V VW Essays* and *CR2*.

Mr Symons's Essays

Somewhere in the present volume Mr Symons quotes the saying of Charles Lamb, 'I love books about books', and adds that that is the test of the book-lover[2] – the test of him, we sometimes think, not because such books are boring or difficult, but rather because they are demoralising. Books about books are apt, one hardly knows why, to reduce Literature to a safe and comfortable pursuit for elderly valetudinarians by the fireside on winter evenings; and to love them seems to mean that such is our love of their subject that we can extract good even from these doubtful surroundings. But there is another sense in which we may take this remark – a sense in which it would certainly apply to the book before us – and that is that to be able to love and understand true criticism of writing is the final test of a love of books, and one of the sweetest rewards of it. Certainly, to be able to write such criticism is so rare a gift that one is inclined to doubt whether it is ever done save by the poets themselves. Our best criticism we owe to them. Coleridge and Lamb, Arnold and Sainte-Beuve[3] were all poets, either with the right hand or with the left. Indeed, it seems impossible for anyone who is not actually dealing with the problems of art to know the nature of them; or – and this is of greater importance – to have a lively enough passion for the artist's view to be in sympathy with the different forms of it.

Mr Symons is a very distinguished poet; as, indeed, we could have guessed from the character of his criticism. These papers are for the most part short: but they are aimed so directly at the heart of the subject that in each case they seem to show us something we had missed before. And it is always done as the poet knows how to do it: without display of knowledge or chain of argument, but directly, simply, and, in spite of the narrow bounds of the essay, fully. He has so fine an instinct for the aim and quality of each writer that the result seems effortless and brimming with truth. Naturally we do not accept all that Mr Symons says; but we must consistently pay homage to the spirit in which he approaches these different writers. It is the spirit of a man to whom art is as undoubtedly a part of life as bread, or air; but who, though his days are spent in the presence of it, never loses his sense of its divinity. In writing of Coventry Patmore he says:

... while he talked to me of the basis of poetry, and of metres and cadences, and of poetical methods, what meant more to me than anything he said, though not a word was without its value, was the profound religious gravity with which he treated the art of poetry, the sense he conveyed to me of his own reasoned conception of its immense importance, its divinity.[4]

'Profound religious gravity' expresses exactly the spirit of Mr Symons's essays; but there goes along with it a sense, most rare and refreshing, that to care for art is the most natural thing in the world. Very often it is the effect of criticism to make art appear so intricate and so remote from the interests of ordinary people that it is useless for them to try to care for it, let alone to attempt the practice of it. They persuade themselves that they are glad not to be artists, and make allowances for those who are. Mr Symons, on the other hand, treats literature with a kind of natural seriousness which should make even the least lettered aware that to write is the most normal occupation for man, or woman either; and we may study and love writing without being in the least queer ourselves. Those who care for literature already may repeat what Mr Symons has said of Coventry Patmore. If he had no other quality save this religious gravity, this reasoned conception of the immense importance, the divinity of poetry, we should be deeply grateful to him; as it is, we must also rejoice in the subtlety of his mind and in his brilliant intelligence. His work is more than a support to us; it serves to stimulate us to quicker feelings.

As to the brilliance, we do not suppose that Mr Symons cares to lay claim to much of that rather doubtful virtue. He has trained himself, as he says with perfect truth, to be 'infinitely careful in all matters of literature'.[5] But it is not seldom that his thought and language fuse themselves in a flash, perhaps a little to the surprise of the author and much to the delight of the reader. We may quote his saying about Meredith: 'In prose he would have every sentence shine; in verse he would have every line sparkle; like a lady who puts on all her jewelry at once, immediately after breakfast.'[6] This, too, is very true: 'To write poetry as if it had never been written before is to attempt what the greatest poets never attempted.'[7] And here is a comment upon Charles Lamb, so penetrating that we wonder, now that it is said, why it was never said before:

The quality which came to him from that germ of madness which lay hidden in his nature had no influence upon his central sanity. It gave him the tragic pathos and mortal beauty of his wit, . . . and, also, a hard, indifferent levity, which, to brother and sister alike, was a rampart against obsession, or a stealthy way of temporising with the enemy. That tinge is what gives its strange glitter to his fooling: madness playing safely and lambently around the stoutest common sense.[8]

As we read through Mr Symons's essays we come to recognise, as is the case with all true critics, a certain vein of thought which underlies many of his judgments and gives them personality. He has so great a passion for beauty that he is a little hard upon work which has other qualities, perhaps more valuable than beauty. On this account he seems to us less than just to Ibsen and more than generous to Swinburne.[9] He can write of Ibsen – 'Given the character and the situation, what Ibsen asks at the moment of crisis is, What would this man be most likely to say? not, What would be the finest, the most deeply revealing thing that he could say? In that difference lies all the difference between prose and poetry'.[10] That, to us, is a complete misunderstanding. In such crises, we should say, Ibsen's attempt has been to give what is deeply revealing together with what is likely, and from that source springs his tremendous power. No doubt he failed often, and when he failed he produced either 'the language of the newspaper recorded with the fidelity of the phonograph',[11] or a fantastic symbolism which serves merely to throw dust in our eyes. But when he succeeds his success is based upon the fact that he has not flinched from the prosaic look of things as they are and yet has made them yield as true a poetry as any to be found in the plays of Swinburne. The danger of asking oneself, What is the finest, the most deeply revealing thing that I can make my character say? is demonstrated over and over again by Swinburne, and by most of our poetic dramatists. When their inspiration flags they continue automatically to produce fine words with the semblance of beauty on them; and that is a disease of which it will take many Ibsens and not a few Walt Whitmans[12] to cure us.

Probably Mr Symons intends his distinction between prose and poetry to refer only to the particular prose under discussion – that of Ibsen. But all through his volume there is an evident glory in the beauty of poetry, an exaltation of poetry as the most inspired form which literature can take. Perhaps we may account for this by the curious fact that it was not until he read Pater's *Studies in the History of the Renaissance* that he 'realised that prose also could be a fine art'.[13] And, unconsciously no doubt, he is led to lay stress upon this predilection of his because the temper of the age is impatient with beauty and the particular skill in which he delights. Too fine a critic not to feel worth where it exists, he will not admit the poetic power of Ibsen, and calls *Leaves of Grass* the 'most monstrous and magnificent failure of the nineteenth century'.[14] But the interesting point is not whether one style is bad and another good, or whether we exalt poetry or prefer prose, but that prose has been the chosen medium of the greatest writers of our time – of Dostoevsky, of Carlyle, of Tolstoy.[15] And modern poetry seems more and more to glance at prose and make trial of the methods of prose. Nor can we attribute this to a shallow impatience with tradition or to a failure of artistic power. It springs rather from the belief that there is a form to be found in literature for the life of the present day – for a life lived in little houses separated only by a foot or two of brick wall; for the compli-cated, intense and petty emotions of the drawing room; for the acts and sights of the streets, and for the whole pageant of life without conceal-ment of its ugly surface. The language which shall express all this is neither the speech of the poets nor the speech of actual life, but it, too, is the result of that 'crystallisation in which direct emotion or sensation deviates exquisitely into art',[16] as Mr Symons puts it, writing of John Donne. The form of prose produces prolonged and cumulative effects; the form of poetry produces instant and intense effects; and for this, among other reasons, what we have to say now seems to shape itself more easily in the form of prose than in the form of poetry. But to place any limit upon either, or to predict that one will supersede the other, is to play with generalities and to force a living being between the walls of a rigid mould. The book of Mr Symons's essays should warn us against any excess of this kind; for whatever his own prejudices may be, he invariably brings all his imagination and all his skill to the understand-ing of the work before him.

1 – A review in the *TLS*, 21 December 1916, (Kp c62) of *Figures of Several Centuries* (Constable & Co., 1916) by Arthur Symons (1865–1945), poet, trans-lator, critic and editor, friend of W. B. Yeats and of Walter Pater, and a considerable

influence on the young writers and artists of the 1890s. He was the author of several books of verse, including his first collection *Days and Nights* (1889), and also, notably, of *The Symbolist Movement in Literature* (1899).

2 – Symons, 'Charles Lamb [1775–1834]', p. 21, source unidentified.

3 – S. T. Coleridge (1772–1834); Matthew Arnold (1822–88); Charles Augustine Sainte-Beuve (1804–69).

4 – Symons, 'Coventry Patmore', p. 365; Coventry Patmore (1823–96), author of *The Angel in the House* (1854–62), *The Unknown Eros* (1877) etc.

5 – *Ibid.*, 'Walter Pater [1839–94]', p. 323: '. . . it was through his [Pater's] influence and counsels that I trained myself to be infinitely careful . . .'

6 – *Ibid.*, 'George Meredith as a Poet', p. 142, which has: 'shine, in verse'; George Meredith (1828–1909).

7 – *Ibid.*, 'John Donne [c. 1571–1631]', p. 97.

8 – *Ibid.*, 'Charles Lamb', pp. 35–6.

9 – Henrik Ibsen (1828–1906); Algernon Charles Swinburne (1837–1909).

10 – Symons, 'Henrik Ibsen', pp. 266–7.

11 – *Ibid.*, p. 265.

12 – Walt Whitman (1819–92).

13 – Symons, 'Walter Pater', p. 322; *Studies in the History of the Renaissance* (1873).

14 – *Ibid.*, 'Coventry Patmore', p. 374; Walt Whitman, *Leaves of Grass* (1855).

15 – Fyodor Dostoevsky (1821–81); Thomas Carlyle (1795–1881); L. N. Tolstoy (1828–1910).

16 – Symons, 'John Donne', p. 104: 'It is always useful to remember Wordsworth's phrase of "emotion recollected in tranquillity", for nothing so well defines that moment of crystallisation in which direct emotion or sensation deviates exquisitely into art. Donne is intent on the passion itself, the thought, the reality; so intent that he is not at the same time, in that half-unconscious way which is the way of the really great poet, equally intent on the form, that both may come to ripeness together.'

1917

<hr>

'Romance'

This little book entitled *Romance* contains two lectures, the first upon the origin of Romance, the second upon imitation and forgery. Each, the lazy reader may say, might well have split itself into another pair at least; but Sir Walter Raleigh has never had the interests of the lazy reader at heart. We must be prepared, then, to hold a slim little book in our hands and to find that each sentence holds enough matter to fill a page. The pleasure and the risk of such reading rather resemble the pleasure of finding oneself suddenly out of one's depth at sea. In the first place many of our most trusty props are removed. 'The best way', we are told, 'to restore the habit of thinking is to do away with the names.'[2] Is Romance, then, or the revival of Romance, to which heading our literary primers have accustomed us, merely a name? We mean something when we use it; but Sir Walter Raleigh is not going to tell us what we mean. He intends that we should find out for ourselves. Like all scholars who know what there is to be known and mix their learning with love, he discards those convenient but indigestible little pellets which between them have made the history of English literature about as interesting as Bradshaw,[3] although of course not so accurate. He touches his subject with life, and invests it with all the uncertainty, the possibility, and the vagueness of a living thing.

You cannot define Romance; you cannot classify and explain the significance of men and books; 'to study the ascertained facts concerning men and books is to study . . . the only competent and modest part of the history of literature.'[4] The greater part of these lectures, therefore, is devoted to a sketch of the history of Romance, and there is only a tentative definition of Romance itself. But this sketch does much to define and clarify our ideas. For let us suppose that we have come into the lecture room believing rather vaguely that the romantic revival was a reaction against the school of Pope and Dryden; that it is chiefly marked by a return to nature; and that its most typical examples are to be found in 'Kubla Khan' and the 'Ode to a Nightingale'.[5] The lecturer knocks down our neat compartments one after another by observing that the great writers of all ages have always returned to nature, Pope no less than Wordsworth; that you may find the purest Romance in Virgil; that the Romance writers proper were distinguished by being actual, modern and realistic; that Romance became as bookish as decadent classicism. As for there being one period that is exclusively romantic, and another that is without romance, wherever we look in English literature we shall find Romance in the upper or in the under world. Further, even the age which we associate particularly with the revival of Romance contains Wordsworth, who 'drew straight from life' and 'shunned what is derived from other books',[6] and Scott, whose 'love for the knighthood and monkery was real but it was playful. His heart was with Fielding.'[7] Evidently it is a good thing to avoid, 'except for pastime, the discussion of tendencies and movements',[8] and stick as far as we can to the men and the books.

But there are some facts which may lead us to a clearer view. Many of our misconceptions about Romance may be attributed to a wrong understanding of another famous and ill-used name – the Renaissance. The study of Greek and Latin, for which that name stands, was consummated not in the fifteenth or sixteenth centuries, but in the eighteenth; thus the romantic revival was a reaction against the Renaissance. Fashion turned against the classics now that the classics were familiar and demanded a return to medieval Romance and chivalry. According to Sir Walter the strange thing about this movement was that it was not the supply which created the demand, but the demand which created the supply. Romance had to be made artificially in the forgeries of Ossian and at Strawberry Hill[9] before there arose a generation which could make the real thing.

So curious a state of things suggests speculations which will no doubt lead us to break our necks over another definition of Romance. For how does a country demand romantic poetry? And is it conceivable that sham castles and forged manuscripts, the products of a perfectly false feeling, had it in them to inspire certain little boys with the germs of some of the most genuine feelings that have ever existed? We cannot help thinking that the process was different, and infinitely complex, and that you make your poet as you make your demand for poetry, by a thousand influences which probably have very little to do with art. But the artistic influences are the easiest to trace. It is evident, as Sir Walter points out, that landscape painting, by inducing people to imagine themselves among mountains and sunsets and precipices, played an enormous part in the revival of Romance. We may also find matter for thought in those eighteenth-century gardens which were so strangely unlike the houses they surrounded. What did the gentleman in knee breeches and brocade think about when he stepped from his exquisitely civilised drawing room into a garden that was all green-covered ponds, ruins and blue distances? One may suppose that he thought a great deal about himself, and, removed from the constraint of furniture, rambled in a wilderness among the disorderly recesses of his own mind. To think about oneself is, of course, to think about a great many other things and people too; but perhaps there is truth in the distinction which Sir Walter draws between the 'modern romantic poet', who 'must keep himself aloof from life, that he may see it', and the epic poet 'who holds his reader fast by strong moral bonds of sympathy with the actors in the poem'.[10]

We mean a great many things when we say that a poem is romantic. We refer to an atmosphere of vagueness, mystery, distance; but perhaps we most constantly feel that the writer is thinking more of the effect of the thing upon his mind than of the thing itself. And up to a point there is nothing more real than the effect of things upon one's mind. The difficulty is to resist the temptation of conjuring up sensations for the pleasure of feeling them; and when he does that the writer is lost. For such a one,

> . . . lives alone,
> Housed in a dream, at distance from the Kind.[11]

The great poets, as Sir Walter Raleigh says, are those who 'face the discipline of facts and life'.[12] They may begin as Keats began, with a sense of the wonder of the visible world; of passion and love and beauty; but there comes a time when the passion turns to dream, and only the greatest wake themselves from that and make poetry with their eyes open. For, as Sir Walter says very finely, 'the poetry which can bear all naked truth and still keep its singing voice is the only immortal poetry'.[13]

1 – A review in the TLS, 18 January 1917, (Kp c63) of *Romance. Two Lectures* (Princeton, 1916) by Sir Walter Raleigh (1861–1922), Professor of English Literature, Oxford University, Fellow of Merton College. Raleigh, a relation by marriage of Lytton Strachey, whom he had taught at Liverpool University, delivered the Louis Clark Vanuxem Foundation Lectures ('The Origin of Romance' and 'Imitation and Forgery') at Princeton University on 4 and 5 May 1915. See also 'Trafficks and Discoveries', *I VW Essays*, and 'A Professor of Life', *IV VW Essays*.
2 – Raleigh, 'The Origin of Romance', p. 3.
3 – I.e., the *Railway Time-Tables, Monthly Railway Guide, Continental Railway Guide* etc, originally published by George Bradshaw (1801–53).
4 – Raleigh, 'The Origin of Romance', pp. 8–9; the ellipsis marks the omission of 'biography and bibliography, two sciences which between them supply'.
5 – S. T. Coleridge, 'Kubla Khan, a Vision in a Dream' (1816); John Keats, 'To a Nightingale' (1819). Alexander Pope (1688–1744); John Dryden (1631–1700).
6 – Raleigh, 'The Origin of Romance', p. 33; William Wordsworth (1770–1850).
7 – *Ibid.*; Sir Walter Scott (1771–1832); Henry Fielding (1707–54).
8 – *Ibid.*, p. 10.
9 – The poet Ossian and his Gaelic epics were the creation of James Macpherson (1736–96). Strawberry Hill: the gothic mansion near Twickenham created by Horace Walpole (1717–99), author of *The Castle of Otranto* (1764), whose name is also associated with that of Thomas Chatterton (1752–70), by whose gothic fabrications he was initially deceived.
10 – Raleigh, 'The Origin of Romance', p. 39; p. 40.
11 – William Wordsworth, 'Elegiac Stanzas – suggested by a picture of Peele Castle, in a storm, painted by Sir George Beaumont' (1807), ll. 53–4, not quoted by Raleigh.
12 – Raleigh, 'Imitation and Forgery', p. 84.
13 – *Ibid.*

Tolstoy's 'The Cossacks'

It is pleasant to welcome Tolstoy's *The Cossacks and other tales of the Caucasus*[2] to the World Classics. 'The greatest of Russia's writers,' say Mr and Mrs Maude in their introduction.[3] And when we read or re-read these stories, how can we deny Tolstoy's right to the title? Of late years both Dostoevsky and Tchehov[4] have become famous in England, so that there has certainly been less discussion, and perhaps less reading, of Tolstoy himself. Coming back to him after an interval the shock of his genius seems to us quite surprising; in his own line it is hard to imagine that he can ever be surpassed. For an English reader proud of the fiction of this country there is even something humiliating in the comparison between such a story as 'The Cossacks', published in 1863, and the novels which were being written at about the same time in England. As the lovable immature work of children compared with the work of grown men they appear to us; and it is still more strange to consider that, while much of Thackeray and Dickens⁵ seems to us far away and obsolete, this story of Tolstoy's reads as if it had been written a month or two ago.

It is as a matter of fact an early work, written for the most part some years before it was published, and preceding both the great novels. He gathered the materials when he was in the Caucasus for two years as a cadet, and the chief character is the same whom we meet so often in the later books, the unmistakable Tolstoy. As Olenin he is a young man who has run into debt and leaves Moscow with a view to saving a little money and seeing a fresh side of life. In Moscow he has had many experiences, but he has always said to himself both of love and of other things, 'That's not it, that's not it.'⁶ The story – and like most of Tolstoy's stories it has no intricacy of plot – is the story of the development of this young man's mind and character in a Cossack village. He lives alone in a hut; observes the beauty of the Cossack girl Maryanka, but scarcely speaks to her, and spends most of his time with Daddy Eroshka in shooting pheasants and talking about sport. At length he comes to know the girl and asks her to marry him, to which she seems inclined to consent; but at that very moment the soldier to whom she is engaged is wounded, and she refuses to have anything more to do with Olenin. He therefore gets himself put upon the staff and leaves the district. When he has said good-bye to them all, he turns to look back. 'Daddy Eroshka was talking to Maryanka, evidently about his own affairs, and neither the old man nor the girl looked at Olenin'.⁷ Nothing is finished; nothing is tidied up; life merely goes on.

But what a life! Perhaps it is the richness of Tolstoy's genius that strikes us most in this story, short though it is. Nothing seems to escape him. The wonderful eye observes everything; the blue or the red of a child's frock; the way a horse shifts its tail; the action of a man trying to put his hands into pockets that have been sewn up; every gesture seems to be received by him automatically, and at once referred by his brain to some cause which reveals the most carefully hidden secrets of human nature. We feel that we know his characters both by the way they choke and sneeze and by the way they feel about love and immortality and the most subtle questions of conduct. In the present selection of stories, all the work of youth and all laid in a wild country far from town civilisation, he gives freer play than in the novels to his extraordinary keenness of physical sensation. We seem actually able to see the mountains, the young soldiers, the grapes, the Cossack girls, to feel the firmness of their substance, and to see the bright colours with which the sun and the cold air have painted them. Nowhere perhaps has he written with greater zest of the excitement of sport and of the beauty of fine horses; nowhere has he made us feel more acutely how fiercely desirable the world appears to the senses of a strong young man. At the same time the thought which unites these scenes and gives them so keen an edge is the thought which goes on incessantly in the brain of Olenin. He throws himself down in the middle of the hunt to rest under the brambles in a lair where a stag has just lain:

And it was clear to him that he was not a Russian nobleman, a member of Moscow society, the friend and relation of so-and-so and so-and-so, but just such a mosquito or pheasant or deer as those that were now living all round him. 'Just as they, just as Daddy Eroshka. I shall live awhile and die, and as he says truly: grass will grow and nothing more.'[8]

'But what though the grass does grow?' he continued thinking. 'Still I must live, and be happy, because happiness is all I desire . . . How then must I live to be happy, and why was I not happy before?' . . . and suddenly a new light seemed to reveal itself to him. 'Happiness is this!' he said to himself. 'Happiness lies in living for others' . . .[9] He was so glad and excited when he had discovered this, as it seemed to him, new truth, that he jumped up and began impatiently seeking someone to sacrifice himself to, to do good to, and to love. 'Since one wants nothing for onself', he kept thinking, 'why not live for others?'[10]

But Lukashka, to whom he gives a horse, suspects his motives for making such a valuable gift; and Eroshka, whom he treats as a friend and to whom he gives a gun, forgets him as soon as his back is turned. Perhaps then he is on the wrong tack after all. Here, as everywhere, Tolstoy seems able to read the minds of different people as certainly as we count the buttons on their coats; but this feat never satisfies him; the knowledge is always passed through the brain of some Olenin or Pierre or Levin,[11] who attempts to guess a further and more difficult riddle – the riddle which Tolstoy was still asking himself, we may be sure, when he died. And the fact that Tolstoy is thus seeking, that there is always in the centre of his stories some rather lonely figure to whom the surrounding world is never quite satisfactory, makes even his short stories entirely unlike other short stories. They do not shut with a snap like the stories of Maupassant and Mérimee.[12] They go on indefinitely. It is by their continuous vein of thought that we remember them, rather than by any incident; by thoughts such as that which comes to him in the middle of battle.

The spectacle was truly magnificent. The one thing that spoilt the general impression for me, who took no part in the affair, and was unaccustomed to it, was that this movement, and the animation and the shouting, appeared unnecessary. Involuntarily the comparison suggested itself to me of a man swinging his arms from the shoulders to cut the air with an axe.[13]

And thus we end by thinking again of the unlikeness between ourselves and the Russians; and by envying them that extraordinary union of extreme simplicity combined with the utmost subtlety which seems to mark both the educated Russian and the peasant equally. They do not rival us in the comedy of manners, but after reading Tolstoy we always feel that we could sacrifice our skill in that direction for something of the profound psychology and superb sincerity of the Russian writers.

1 – A review in the *TLS*, 1 February 1917, (Kp c64) of *The Cossacks and Other Tales of the Caucasus . . . translated by Louise and Aylmer Maude* (O.U.P., 1916) by Leo Tolstoy (1828–1910). See also *Tolstoi's Love Letters* and *Talks With Tolstoi*, both translated by S. S. Koteliansky and Virginia Woolf and published by the Hogarth Press in 1923.
2 – The stories concerned are: 'The Raid' (1853), 'The Wood-Felling' (1855), 'Meeting a Moscow Acquaintance in the Detachment (from Prince Nekhlyudov's Caucasian Memoirs)' (1856), 'The Cossacks' (1863).
3 – Tolstoy, Pref., p. viii.
4 – Fyodor Dostoevsky (1821–81), see 'More Dostoevsky' and 'A Minor Dostoevsky' below; Anton Chekhov (1860–1904), see 'Tchehov's Questions' below.
5 – W. M. Thackeray (1811–63); Charles Dickens (1812–70).
6 – Tolstoy, 'The Cossacks', ch. II, p. 13.
7 – *Ibid.*, ch. XLII, p. 234, the story's final sentence.
8 – *Ibid.*, ch. XX, p. 120.
9 – *Ibid.*
10 – *Ibid.*, p. 121.
11 – Pierre Bezuhov in *War and Peace* (1865–72); Constantine Levin in *Anna Karenina* (1875–6).
12 – Guy de Maupassant (1850–93); Prosper Mérimée (1803–70).
13 – Tolstoy, 'The Raid', p. 263.

Melodious Meditations

The poets of the eighteenth century were fond of making their verse sound dignified by spelling certain qualities with a capital letter. It required a very good poet to make such personifications acceptable even then, and the habit has long been dropped. But we sometimes fancy that these antiquated ghosts merely took ship to America, lodged with the best families, and now walk abroad in those essays which the Americans write so frequently upon Old Age, Old Maids, On Being Ill, and Sorrow.[2] In those abstract contemplations we seem to recognise their nearly featureless faces, bloodless cheeks, and impeccable dignity of deportment. Life is difficult, but the good man triumphs; sorrow is not always evil; happiness depends upon what we are and not upon what we have; our truest friends are to be found among our books. If all these substantives began with capital letters, and if the lines were trimmed to the right length, we should at once have an eighteenth-century ode contributed by some country clergyman to the *Gentleman's Magazine*.[3]

And why this eternal commotion? Is all this turmoil the struggle of a baser element to attain self-realisation, to achieve psychic life? Is the whole universe seeking more life and fuller? Or is life our original sin, and death the great purifier? Is it beneficent death that is striving to cast out the vexing seeds of life and restore a universal calm? Is death the great ocean of peace to which all the rivers of existence flow? Is the blotting out of the universe, &c.[4]

This passage is taken at random from one of Mr Sedgwick's essays. Almost any novel, certainly any book of facts, seems to us better reading than these melodious meditations; and we say this emphatically in order to correct what we believe to be a misunderstanding on the part of Mr Wister. The American essayists, he says, unlike the novelists, 'save our face. We can point to them without blushing.' They show the stranger that 'some of us are writers and readers of civilised intelligence'.[5] Anyone who has read even a little of American literature hardly needs such assurance; there is nothing to blush at in the whole of it, except perhaps Walt Whitman;[6] and that is the worst we have to say of it. Their intelligence seems, oddly enough, more civilised, gentler, lower in tone than ours. And perhaps the studious refinement of their great writers is the result of this determination to show the stranger that they are people of civilised intelligence. Certainly Mr Sedgwick's essays carry out this theory, for they are not all as mild and melancholy as the above quotation would seem to show. When he writes upon Goethe, the Classics, Literature and Cosmopolitanism[7] he writes with a great deal of sense and energy, and enables us at least to understand the point of view of cultivated Americans towards their literature. He looks to literature to refine and restrain the boisterous spirit of democracy. He would give democracy supreme power over politics and economics; but then 'it must no longer seek to lay its hand on literature, art, higher education, pure science, philosophy, manners'.[8] The men of genius and learning are to constitute a priesthood, held in special reverence; and the intellectual traditions of generations of educated men should be taught by them as a special cult.

Was there ever a plan better calculated to freeze literature at the root than this one? We must imagine all our writers and artists properly pensioned and quartered in comfortable rooms in Oxford and Cambridge, where so long as they live the masses shall do them honour. In the Victorian age, which for all its faults was prolific of genius, this system was to some extent put into practice; the great men were secluded and worshipped, with the result that they wrote twice as much as they ought to have written, and, being geniuses all day long and every day, were for the most part extremely ill at ease and out of temper.[9] That seems to be the inevitable effect of a Priesthood upon the Priests who compose it; and though to reverence may be very good for the soul of the masses, still the best artistic work is done by people who mix easily with their fellows. Even with us art is far too much of a mystery and a luxury, but it is evidently still more beyond the reach of ordinary people in America. For the American critic attaches enormous importance to the appreciation of art, and seems to care very little for the making of it. It has been their misfortune perhaps to inherit our language with all those traditions which can hardly be taught, but must be felt naturally if they are to blossom into beauty. With a language of their own which would make its own traditions, they would have greater self-confidence, and would lose their excessive sensitiveness to the criticisms of those English professors who examine them from time to time and send them to the very bottom of the class. For no one can doubt that theirs is a splendid opportunity; or if any one is sceptical as to the future of American art let him read Walt Whitman's preface to the first edition of *Leaves of Grass*. As a piece of writing it rivals anything we have done for a hundred years, and as a statement of the American spirit no finer banner was ever unfurled for the young of a great country to march under:

There will soon be no more priests. Their work is done [. . .] A new order shall arise, and they shall be the priests of man, and every man shall be his own priest [. . .] They shall find their inspiration in real objects today, symptoms of the past and future. They shall not deign to defend immortality or God, or the perfection of things, or liberty, or the exquisite beauty and reality of the soul. They shall arise in America, and be responded to from the remainder of the earth.[10]

1 – A review in the *TLS*, 8 February 1917, (Kp c65) of *An Apology for Old Maids* . . . With a Preface by Owen Wister (Macmillan & Co., 1917) by Henry Dwight Sedgwick (1861–1957), American essayist and historian. 'We are going skating today,' VW wrote to Saxon Sydney-Turner on 3 February 1917 (*II VW Letters*, no. 821), 'on the Pen Ponds [Richmond Park] and tomorrow we have induced Lytton to come too . . . All the morning I have been reviewing with great labour an American essayist; and therefore I can't think of any good jokes.'

2 – Sedgwick's subjects include: 'An Apology for Old Maids', 'On Being Ill' (upon which VW was herself to write, see *IV VW Essays*), and 'The House of Sorrow', but not 'Old Age' as such.

3 – The monthly miscellany founded in 1731 by Edward Cave, to and upon which, during the period 1739–48, Dr Johnson was an important contributor and influence.

4 – Sedgwick, 'On Being Ill', p. 102, which continues: 'universe beyond the farm road, the reduction of it to a small sickroom, the diminution of the innumerable *dramatis personae* to one white-capped white-aproned nurse, a sample of the divine effort towards simplicity and peace?'

5 – *Ibid.*, Pref., p. xiii; Owen Wister (1860–1938), American lawyer and author, Overseer, Harvard University, 1912–18, 1919–25.

6 – Walt Whitman (1819–92), to whom no allusion is made in Sedgwick.

7 – Sedgwick writes on Goethe (1749–1832) – 'the great apostle of cosmopolitanism' (p. 211) – in 'A Forsaken God'. The other titles are: 'The Classics Again' and 'Literature and Cosmopolitanism'.

8 – *Ibid.*, 'A Forsaken God', pp. 162–3; the essay begins by addressing itself to 'certain frank opinions about America' expressed 'not long ago' (but otherwise unspecified) by Goldsworthy Lowes Dickinson (1862–1932), Fellow of King's College, Cambridge, Apostle, and friend of Bloomsbury.

9 – Cf. 'A Sketch of the Past', *MoB*, pp. 108–10, where VW expatiates upon Victorian 'genius', as the phenomenon affected her father Leslie Stephen; and note p. 109: 'Those who had genius in the Victorian sense were like the prophets . . . They were invariably "ill to live with".'

10 – *Leaves of Grass* (New York, 1855), p. xi, which has an ellipsis after 'past and future', and no comma after 'God', 'liberty', or 'America'.

More Dostoevsky

Each time that Mrs Garnett[2] adds another red volume to her admirable translations of the works of Dostoevsky we feel a little better able to measure what the existence of this great genius who is beginning to permeate our lives so curiously means to us. His books are now to be found on the shelves of the humblest English libraries; they have become an indestructible part of the furniture of our rooms, as they belong for good to the furniture of our minds. The latest addition to Mrs Garnett's translation, *The Eternal Husband*, including also 'The Double' and 'The Gentle Spirit', is not one of the greatest of his works, although it was produced in what may be held to be the greatest period of his genius, between *The Idiot* and *The Possessed*.[3] If one had never read anything else by Dostoevsky, one might lay the book down with a feeling that the man who wrote it was bound to write a very great novel some day; but with a feeling also that something strange and important had happened. This strangeness and this sense that something important has happened persist, however, although we are familiar with his books and have had time to arrange the impression that they make on us.

Of all great writers there is, so it seems to us, none quite so surprising, or so bewildering, as Dostoevsky. And although 'The Eternal Husband' is nothing more than a long short story which we need not compare with the great novels, it too has this extraordinary power; nor while we are reading it can we liberate ourselves sufficiently to feel certain that in this or that respect there is a failure of power, or insight, or craftsmanship; nor does it occur to us to compare it with other works either by the same writer or by other writers. It is very difficult to analyse the impression it has made even when we have finished it. It is the story of one Velchaninov, who, many years before the story opens, has seduced the wife of a certain Pavel Pavlovitch in the town of T———. Velchaninov has almost forgotten her and is living in Petersburg. But now as he walks about Petersburg he is constantly running into a man who wears a crepe hat-band and reminds him of someone he cannot put a name to. At last, after repeated meetings which bring him to a state bordering on delirium, Velchaninov is visited at two o'clock in the morning by the stranger, who explains that he is the husband of Velchaninov's old love, and that she is dead. When Velchaninov visits him the next day, he finds him maltreating a little girl, who is, he instantly perceives, his own child. He manages to take her away from Pavel, who is a drunkard and in every way disreputable, and give her lodging with friends, but almost immediately she dies. After her death Pavel announces that he is engaged to marry a girl of sixteen, but when, as he insists, Velchaninov visits her, she confides to him that she detests Pavel and is already engaged to a youth of nineteen. Between them they contrive to pack Pavel off to the country; and he turns up finally at the end of the story as the husband of a provincial beauty, and the lady, of course, has a lover.

These, at least, are the little bits of cork which mark a circle upon the top of the waves while the net drags the floor of the sea and encloses stranger monsters than have ever been brought to the light of day before. The substance of the book is made out of the relationship between Velchaninov and Pavel. Pavel is a type of what Velchaninov calls 'the eternal husband'.[4] 'Such a man is born and grows up only to be a husband, and, having married, is promptly transformed into a supplement of his wife, even when he happens to have an unmistakable character of his own ... ⟨Pavel⟩ could only as long as his wife was alive have remained all that he used to be, but, as it was, he was only a fraction of a whole, suddenly cut off and set free, that is something wonderful and unique.'[5] One of the peculiarities of the eternal husband is that he is always half in love with the lovers of his wife, and at the same time wishes to kill them. Impelled by this mixture of almost amorous affection and hatred, he cannot keep away from Velchaninov, in whom he breeds a kind of reflection of his own sensations of attraction and repulsion. He can never bring himself to make any direct charge against Velchaninov; and Velchaninov is never able to confess or to deny his misconduct. Sometimes, from the stealthy way in which he approaches, Velchaninov feels certain that he has an impulse to kill him; but then he insists upon kissing him, and cries out, 'So, you understand, you're the one friend left me now!'[6] One night when Velchaninov is ill and Pavel has shown the most enthusiastic devotion Velchaninov wakes from a nightmare to find Pavel standing over him and attempting to murder him with a razor. Pavel is easily mastered and slinks away shamefaced in the morning. But did he mean to murder him, Velchaninov muses, or did he want it without knowing that he wanted it?

But did he love me yesterday when he declared his feeling and said 'Let us settle our account'? Yes, it was from hatred that he loved me; that's the strongest of all loves ... It would be interesting to know by what I impressed him. Perhaps by my clean gloves and my knowing how to put them on . . . He comes here 'to embrace me and weep', as he expressed it in the most abject way – that is, he came here to murder me and thought he came 'to embrace me and to weep'. But, who knows? If I had wept with him, perhaps, really, he would have forgiven me, for he had a terrible longing to forgive me! . . . Ough! wasn't he pleased, too, when he made me kiss him! Only he didn't know then whether he would end by embracing me or murdering me . . .[7] The most monstrous monster is the monster with noble feelings . . . But it was not your fault, Pavel Pavlovitch, it was not your fault: you're a monster, so everything about you is bound to be monstrous, your dreams and your hopes.[8]

Perhaps this quotation may give some idea of the labyrinth of the soul through which we have to grope our way. But being only a quotation it makes the different thoughts appear too much isolated; for in the context Velchaninov, as he broods over the bloodstained razor, passes over his involved and crowded train of thought, without a single hitch, just, in fact, as we ourselves are conscious of thinking when some startling fact has dropped into the pool of our consciousness. From the crowd of objects pressing upon our attention we select now this one, now that one, weaving them inconsequently into our thought; the associations of a word perhaps make another loop in the line, from which we spring back again to a different section of our main thought, and the whole process seems both inevitable and perfectly lucid. But if we try to construct our mental processes later, we find that the links between one thought and another are submerged. The chain is sunk out of sight and only the leading points emerge to mark the course. Alone among writers Dostoevsky has the power of reconstructing those most swift and complicated states of mind, of rethinking the whole train of thought in all its speed, now as it flashes into light, now as it lapses into darkness; for he is able to follow not only the vivid streak of achieved thought, but to suggest the dim and populous underworld of the mind's consciousness where desires and impulses are moving blindly beneath the sod. Just as we awaken ourselves from a trance of this kind by striking a chair or a table to assure ourselves of an external reality, so Dostoevsky suddenly makes us behold, for an instant, the face of his hero, or some object in the room.

This is the exact opposite of the method adopted, perforce, by most of our novelists. They reproduce all the external appearances – tricks of manner, landscape, dress, and the effect of the hero upon his friends – but very rarely, and only for an instant, penetrate to the tumult of thought which rages within his own mind. But the whole fabric of a book by Dostoevsky is made out of such material. To him a child or a beggar is as full of violent and subtle emotions as a poet or a sophisticated woman of the world; and it is from the intricate maze of their emotions that Dostoevsky constructs his version of life. In reading him, therefore, we are often bewildered because we find ourselves observing men and women from a different point of view from that to which we are accustomed. We have to get rid of the old tune which runs so persistently in our ears, and to realise how little of our humanity is expressed in that old tune. Again and again we are thrown off the scent in following Dostoevsky's psychology; we constantly find ourselves wondering whether we recognise the feeling that he shows us, and we realise constantly and with a start of surprise that we have met it before in ourselves, or in some moment of intuition have suspected it in others. But we have never spoken of it, and that is why we are surprised. Intuition is the term which we should apply to Dostoevsky's genius at its best. When he is fully possessed by it he is able to read the most inscrutable writing at the depths of the darkest souls; but when it deserts him the whole of his amazing machinery seems to spin fruitlessly in the air. In the present volume, 'The Double', with all its brilliancy and astonishing ingenuity, is an example of this kind of elaborate failure; 'The Gentle Spirit', on the other hand, is written from start to finish with a power which for the time being turns everything we can put beside it into the palest commonplace.

1 – A review in the *TLS*, 22 February 1917, (Kp c66) of *The Eternal Husband, and Other Stories. From the Russian by Constance Garnett* (William Heinemann, 1917) by Fyodor Dostoevsky (1821–81). See also 'A Minor Dostoevsky' below; 'Dostoevsky in Cranford' and 'Dostoevsky the Father', *III VW Essays*; and see *Stavrogin's Confession* (Hogarth Press, 1922) by F. M. Dostoevsky, translated by S. S. Koteliansky and VW. Reprinted: *B&P*.

2 – Constance Garnett, *née* Black (1862–1946), took a first in classics at Newnham College, Cambridge, in 1883, and in the early 1890s began to learn Russian. Her classic translations from the Russian include the whole of Dostoevsky's oeuvre. The wife of the author and publisher's reader Edward Garnett, she was the mother of the novelist David Garnett (1892–1981), one of the younger generation in Bloomsbury.

3 – 'The Eternal Husband' (1870), 'The Double' (1846), 'The Gentle Spirit' (1876), *The Idiot* (1868–9), *The Possessed* (1872).

4 – Dostoevsky, ch. VII, p. 29: 'Velchaninov was convinced that there really was such a type of woman ['born to be unfaithful wives' p. 28]; but, on the other hand, he was also convinced that there was a type of husband corresponding to that woman, whose sole vocation was to correspond with that feminine type. To his mind, the

essence of such a husband lay in his being, so to say, "the eternal husband", or rather in being, all his life, a husband and nothing more.'

5 – *Ibid.*; the passage up to the ellipsis quotes Velchaninov's thoughts directly and is punctuated accordingly in the original, which also has: 'to have unmistakable character'.

6 – *Ibid.*, ch. VII, p. 57.

7 – *Ibid.*, ch. XVI, p. 125, which has: 'impressed him?'; and 'who knows? if I had wept'.

8 – *Ibid.*, p. 126.

'Before Midnight'

Before reviewing Mrs Elinor Mordaunt's new volume of short stories, *Before Midnight*, we ought to confess two, perhaps unreasonable, prejudices: we do not like the war in fiction, and we do not like the supernatural. We can only account for the first of these prejudices by the feeling that the vast events now shaping across the Channel are towering over us too closely and too tremendously to be worked into fiction without a painful jolt in the perspective; but, reasonable or unreasonable, this feeling is roused by one of Mrs Mordaunt's stories only. Better reasons for disliking the use of the supernatural might be given, especially in the case of a writer like Mrs Mordaunt, who has shown in her novels so great a gift for presenting the natural. Nobody can deny that our life is largely at the mercy of dreams and visions which we cannot account for logically; on the contrary, if Mrs Mordaunt had devoted every page of her book to the discovery of some of these uncharted territories of the mind we should have nothing but thanks for her. But we feel a little aggrieved when the writers who are capable of such delicate work resort instead to the methods of the conjurer and ask us to be satisfied with a trick.

As an example of what we mean let us take the second story, 'Pan'. Here a fashionable lady, who is recovering her health in the north meets a man out fishing who possesses himself of her heart in the most immediate and mysterious way, so that she follows him every day without knowing who he is, and is finally drowned at night in her endeavour to cross the river to reach him. All this is an allegory – but it is founded upon a theory which might form the basis of a deeply interesting study.

Yes, the country is a dangerous place if one once lets oneself become intimate with it, slipping one's soul free fom the stolid correctness of country folk, that correctness which has gained them the reputation of piety, and is, really, due to lack of imagination. For the fact is this: only the stolid, the unimaginative remain; the rest have gone back to the gods.[2]

That seems to promise extremely well. But to drag in the pointed ears, the shaggy hoofs, the strange music of the hemlock pipes in exchange for an analysis of the lady's state of mind seems to us equivalent to saying that the situation is too difficult to be pursued any further. Mrs Mordaunt has, as usual, so many shrewd and original things to say about the men and women of flesh and blood before she has recourse to magic that we resent the powers of darkness more than ever.

But it is not fair to say that she always avails herself of these short cuts. The first story in the book is rather a study in heredity than in magic, and so is the last;[3] and there are traces in both of them of that individuality which, whether it is the result of saying what one thinks or whether it is a special grace of nature, is certainly among the most refreshing of gifts. At the same time we must own that we like Mrs Mordaunt best when she is most resolutely matter-of-fact. Indeed, it is when she is keeping strictly to what she has observed that we catch sight of those curious hidden things in human life which vanish instinctively directly there is talk of ghosts or of gods.

1 – A review in the TLS, 1 March 1917, (Kp c67) of Before Midnight (Cassell & Co. Ltd., 1917) by Elinor Mordaunt (pseudonym for Evelyn May Mordaunt, née Clowes, 1877–1942), prolific author of fiction and travel books. In the original article in the TLS, but not in the earlier review of her novel The Park Wall (see above), she is referred to throughout as Miss rather than Mrs Mordaunt; the text here has been altered to accord with her married status and the earlier usage. Reprinted: CW.

2 – Mordaunt, 'Pan', p. 58.

3 – For the first story, 'The Weakening Point', ibid., pp. 3–54; and the second, 'Parentage', pp. 269–326.

Parodies

A good parody is rather a complex thing, for it should be amusing in itself, and should also do the work of the critic with greater daring than the critic can usually display. Mr Squire's parodies are very good examples of what he terms 'a not wholly admirable art';[2] first they make us laugh, and then they make us think. Instead of analysing his author's gifts and fitting them as closely as he can with the right epithets, he makes a little model of the work in question and expresses his sense of the defects of that work by a few deft pinches and twists which bring out the absurdity without destroying the likeness. Although we may laugh we cannot deny that he tells us more about Mr Belloc, or Mr Wells, or Sir H. Newbolt[3] than many serious and industrious articles where the gifts and failings of these writers are scrupulously weighed to an ounce. Thus when we read,

> And as I watch bees in a hive,
>   Or gentle cows that rub 'gainst trees,
> I do not envy men who live,
>   No fields, no books upon their knees.
> I'd rather lie beneath small stars
> Than with rough men who drink in bars[4]

we recognise Mr Davies wearing an air of artless innocence only a little in excess of his natural expression. And if we read, very quickly,

> It was eight bells in the forenoon and hammocks running sleek
>   (It's a fair sea flowing from the West),
> When the little Commodore came a-sailing up the Creek
>   (Heave Ho! I think you'll know the rest)[5]

we get the same hearty feeling as of an old sea-dog rolling across the harbour in a salt sou'-wester which the genuine works of Sir Henry Newbolt are wont to produce. And it needs a second glance to assure us that it is all nonsense. Mr Wells is very good, too:

v

And then it was that Mary Browne came into my life ⟨...⟩ But now there was about her a certain quality of graciousness, very difficult to define, but very unescapable when it is present, that gave to her mouse-grey hair and rather weak blue eyes a beauty very rare and very subtle. She had spent, she told me, two years in the East End at some social work or other ...

VI

And then I met Cecilia Scroop . . .[6]

Of the parodies of modern writers, that of Mr Shaw[7] seems to us the least successful. His style is much too workmanlike to present any obviously weak points to the caricaturist; and to parody his matter you would have to be quicker and more agile of intellect than he is himself. Moreover, Mr Shaw parodies himself far better than anyone else could do it.

As a rule, we imagine, it is much easier to hit off one's own contemporaries, whose little foibles are as well known to us as those of our friends, than it is to dress up in the clothing of some old and famous poet so as to look precisely like him. This is really playing the sedulous ape as Stevenson prescribed it to those in search of a style,[8] and means that at one time or another you have done homage very humbly to the poet in question. If we had to teach children how to write English, no doubt this would be one of our instruments of torture. And Mr Squire complicates the exercise still further. He imagines how Gray would have written the *Spoon River Anthology*, or Lord Byron the 'Passing of Arthur' or Pope 'Break, break, break'.[9] We get the same sort of pleasure from noting his skilful translations from one style to another that scholars find in savouring Greek versions of English poetry. What could be more charming than,

> Nor the bright smiles of ocean's nymphs command
> The pleasing contact of a vanished hand[10]

as an Augustan version of mid-Victorian Tennyson? We can almost see the imperturbable good breeding and courtesy with which Pope, as Mr Squire presents him, receives the lyrical cry of his successor, contemplates it with a little distress, and smooths it out, into impeccable rhyming couplets. It is, indeed, a vivid little summary of a whole chapter of the history of literature.

1 – A review in the *TLS*, 8 March 1917, (Kp c68) of *Tricks of the Trade* (Martin Secker, 1917) by J. C. (John Collings) Squire (1884–1958), man of letters, literary editor of the *New Statesman*, 1913–19, and contributor to *Georgian Poetry 1916–1917* (1917) – 'that ridiculous Squire', VW was soon to call him (*I VW Diary*, 3 January 1918), a verdict she never felt inclined to revise.

See also 'Imitative Essays' and 'Bad Writers' below.

2 – From Squire's dedication to Robert Lynd.

3 – Hilaire Belloc (1870–1953); H. G. Wells (1866–1946); Sir Henry Newbolt (1862–1938).

4 – Squire, p. 10; from the first of two parodies of the work of W. H. Davies (1871–1940).

5 – *Ibid.*, p. 12; in which the last line is italicised.

6 – *Ibid.*, p. 35.

7 – For Squire's parody of George Bernard Shaw (1856–1950), 'Fragment from an Unwritten Play Mahomet the Prophet', *ibid.*, p. 39.

8 – Robert Louis Stevenson, *Memories & Portraits* (Chatto & Windus, 1887), 'A College Magazine', p. 59; 'Whenever I read a book or a passage that particularly pleased me, in which a thing was said or an effect rendered with propriety, in which there was either some conspicuous force or some happy distinction in the style, I must sit down at once and set myself to ape that quality . . . I have thus played the sedulous ape to Hazlitt, to Lamb, to Wordsworth, to Sir Thomas Browne, to Defoe, to Hawthorne, to Montaigne, to Baudelaire and to Oberman.'

9 – For Thomas Gray as the author of Edgar Lee Masters's *Spoon River Anthology* (1915), *ibid.*, p. 61; Byron as the author of Tennyson's 'The Passing of Arthur' (1869), *ibid.*, p. 71; and for Alexander Pope as the author of Tennyson's 'Break, Break, Break' (1842), *ibid.*, p. 59.

10 – *Ibid.*, p. 59.

'Sir Walter Raleigh'

To most of us, says Miss Hadow in her introduction to a book of selections from the prose of Sir Walter Raleigh, 'the Elizabethan Age stands for one of two things: it is the age of jewelled magnificence, of pomp and profusion and colour, of stately ceremonial and Court pageant, of poetry and drama; or it is the age of enterprise and exploration'.[2] But though we have every reason for being grateful to Miss Hadow for her part in the production of this astonishing little book, we cannot go with her in this initial distinction. If Shakespeare, as literature is the only thing that survives in its completeness, may be held to represent the Elizabethan age, are not enterprise and exploration a part of Shakespeare? If there are some who read him without any thought save for the poetry, to most of us, we believe, the world of Shakespeare is the world of Hakluyt[3] and of Raleigh; on that map Guiana and the River of the Plate are not very far distant or easily distinguishable from the Forest of Arden and Elsinore. The navigator and the explorer made their voyage by ship instead of by the mind, but over Hakluyt's pages broods the very same lustre of the imagination. Those vast rivers and fertile valleys, those forests of odorous trees and mines of gold and ruby, fill up the background of the plays as, in our fancy, the blue of the distant plains of America seems to lie behind the golden cross of St Paul's and the bristling chimneys of Elizabethan London.

No man was a truer representative of this Elizabethan world than Sir Walter Raleigh. From the intrigues and splendours of the Court he sailed to an unknown land inhabited by savages; from discourse with Marlowe and Spenser[4] he went to sea-battle with the Spaniard. Merely to read over the list of his pursuits gives one a sense of the space and opportunity of the Elizabethan age; courtier and admiral, soldier and explorer, member of Parliament and poet, musician and historian – he was all these things, and still kept such a curiosity alive in him that he must practise chemistry in his cabin when he had leisure at sea, or beg an old hen-house from the Governor of the Tower in which to pursue his search for 'the Great Elixir'.[5] It is little wonder that Rumour should still be telling her stories about his cloak, his pipe with the silver bowl, his potatoes, his mahogany, his orange trees, after all these years; for though Rumour may lie, there is always good judgment in her falsehood.

When we come to read what remains of his writing – and in this little book the indispensable part of it is preserved – we get what Rumour cannot give us: the likeness of an extremely vigorous and individual mind, scarcely dimmed by the 'vast and devouring space'[6] of the centuries. It is well, perhaps, to begin by reading the last fight of the *Revenge*,[7] the letters about Cadiz and Guiana, and that to his wife written in expectation of death, before reading the extracts from the *Historie of the World*, and to end with the preface to that work, as one leaves a church with the sound of the organ in one's ears. His adventures by sea and land, his quest of Eldorado and the great gold mine of his dreams, his sentence of death and long imprisonment – glimpses of that 'day of a tempestuous life'[8] are to be found in these pages. They give us some idea of its storm and its sunshine. Naturally the style of them is very different from that of the preface. They are full of hurry and turmoil, or impetuosity and self-assertiveness. He is always eager to justify his own daring, and to proclaim the supremacy of the English among other peoples. Even 'our common English soldier, leavied in haste, from following the Cart, or sitting on the shop-stall',[9] surpasses in valour the best of Roman soldiers. Of the landing in Fayal in the year

1597 he writes, 'For I thought it to belong unto the honor of our Prince & Nation, that a few Ilanders should not think any advantage great enough, against a fleet set forth by Q. Elizabeth'; although he had to admit that 'I had more regard of reputation, in that businesse, than of safetie.'[10]

But if we had to justify our love of these old voyagers we should not lay stress upon the boastful and magnificent strain in them; we should point, rather, to the strain of poetry – the meditative mood fostered by long days at sea, sleep and dreams under strange stars, and lonely effort in the face of death. We would recall the words of Sir Humfrey Gilbert, when the storm broke upon his ship, 'sitting abaft with a book in his hand . . . and crying (so oft as we did approach within hearing) "We are as near to Heaven by sea as by land."'[11] And so Sir Walter Raleigh, whose character was subject to much criticism during his lifetime, who had been alternately exalted and debased by fortune, who had lived with the passion of a great lover, turns finally to thoughts of the littleness of all human things and to a magnanimous contemplation of the lot of mankind. His thoughts seem inspired by a knowledge of life both at its best and its worst; in the solitude of the Tower his memory is haunted by the sound of the sea. From the sea he takes his most frequent and splendid imagery. It comes naturally to him to speak of the 'Navigation of this life', of 'the Port of death, to which all winds drive us'.[12] Our false friends, he says, 'forsake us in the first tempest of misfortune and steere away before the Sea and Winde'.[13] So in old age we find that our joy and our woe have 'sayled out of sight'.[14] Often he must have looked into the sky from the deck of his ship and thought how 'The Heavens are high, farr off, and unsearcheable';[15] and his experience as a ruler of uncivilised races must have made him consider what fame 'the boundless ambition in mortal men'[16] is wont to leave behind it:

They themselves would then rather have wished, to have stolen out of the world without noise, than to be put in minde, that they have purchased the report of their actions in the world, by rapine, oppression, and crueltie, by giving in spoile the innocent and labouring soul to the idle and insolent, and by having emptied the cities of the world of their ancient Inhabitants, and filled them againe with so many and so variable sorts of sorrowes.[17]

But although the sounds of life and the waves of the sea are constantly in his ears, so that at any moment he is ready to throw away his pen and take command of an expedition, he seems in his deepest moods to reject the show and splendour of the world, to see the vanity of gold mines and of all expeditions save those of the soul.

For the rest, as all fables were commonly grounded upon some true stories of other things done; so might these tales of the Griffins receive this moral. That if those men which fight against so many dangerous passages for gold, or other riches of this world, had their perfect senses ... they would content themselves with a quiet and moderate estate.[18]

The thought of the passing of time and the uncertainty of human lot was a favourite one with the Elizabethans, whose lives were more at the mercy of fortune than ours are. In Raleigh's prose the same theme is constantly treated, but with an absence of the characteristic Elizabethan conceits, which brings it nearer to the taste of our own time; a divine unconsciousness seems to pervade it. Take this passage upon the passing of youth:

So as who-so-ever hee bee, to whome Fortune hath beene a servant, and the Time a friend: let him but take the accompt of his memory (for wee have no other keeper of our pleasures past) and truelie examine what it hath reserved, either of beauty and youth, or foregone delights; what it hath saved, that it might last, of his dearest affections, or of whatever else the amorous Springtime gave his thoughts of contentment, then unvaluable; and hee shall finde that all the art which his elder yeares have, can draw no other vapour out of these dissolutions, than heavie, secret, and sad sighs . . .[19] Onely those few blacke Swans I must except; who having had the grace to value worldly vanities at no more than their owne price; doe, by retayning the comfortable memorie of a well acted life, behold death without dread, and the grave without feare; and embrace both, as necessary guides to endlesse glorie.[20]

This is no sudden effort of eloquence; it is prefaced and continued by words of almost equal beauty. In its melody and strength, its natural symmetry of form, it is a perfect speech, fit for letters of gold and the echoes of cathedral aisles, or for the tenderness of noble human intercourse. It reaches us almost with the very accent of Raleigh's voice. There is a magnificence with which such a being relinquishes his hopes in life and dismisses the cares of 'this ridiculous world'[21] which is the counterpart of his great zest in living. We hear it in the deeply burdened sigh with which he takes his farewell of his wife. 'For the rest, when you have travailled and wearied all your thoughts, over all sorts of worldly cogitations, you shall but sitt downe by sorrowe in the end.'[22] But it is most evident in his thought upon death. The thought of death tolls all through Elizabethan literature lugubriously enough in our ears, for whom, perhaps, existence has been made less palpable by dint of much thinking and death more of a shade than a substance. But to the Elizabethans a great part of the proper conduct of life consisted in meeting the idea of death, which to them was not an idea but a person, with fortitude. And to Raleigh in particular, death was a very definite enemy – death, 'which doth pursue us and hold us in chace from our infancy'.[23] A true man, he says, despises death. And yet even as he says this there come to life before his eyes the 'mishapen and ouglye shapes'[24] with which death tortures the imagination. And at last, when he has taken the idea of death to him and triumphed over it, there rises from his lips that magnificent strain of reconciliation and acknowledgement which sounds for ever in the ears of those who have heard it once: 'O eloquent, just and mightie Death! whom none could advise, thou hast perswaded: what none hath dared, thou hast done.'[25]

1 – A review in the TLS, 15 March 1917, (Kp c69) of Sir Walter Raleigh [1552?–1618]. Selections from his Historie of the World, his Letters etc. ed. with an introduction and notes by G. E. Hadow (O.U.P., 1917). See also 'Trafficks and Discoveries' below and the article of the same title in I VW Essays, and 'The Elizabethan Lumber Room', IV VW Essays and CR1. Reprinted: G&R, CE.
2 – Raleigh, intro., p. 7.
3 – William Shakespeare (1564–1616), Richard Hakluyt (1552?–1616), author of Principal Navigations, Voyages, and Discoveries of the English Nation (1589, 1598–1600).
4 – Christopher Marlowe (1564–93), Edmund Spenser (1552?–99).
5 – Raleigh, intro., p. 7: '[Raleigh] spent his leisure time at sea in the study of chemistry to such effect that he discovered "the Great Elixir" and was called upon to prescribe for the heir to the throne when the court physicians had given up all hope'; and p. 20: 'he had access to the governor's garden [at the Bloody Tower] and was allowed . . . to turn the hen-house into a chemical laboratory'.
6 – The origin of this phrase, which VW also quotes in 'Papers on Pepys' below, has resisted all attempts at discovery.
7 – Raleigh, 'The Last Fight of the Revenge', pp. 144–66, originally published as A Report of the Truth of the fight about the Iles of Açores, this last Sommer. Betwixt the Revenge, one of her Majesties Shippes, And an Armada of the King of Spaine (London, 1591).
8 – Ibid., 'The Historie of the World', Pref., p. 36.
9 – Ibid., 'A Comparison Between Roman and English Soldiers', p. 91.
10 – For these two quotations, ibid., 'Concerning Naval Transport', p. 112; pp. 111–12.
11 – This description of the dying moments off the coast of Newfoundland of Sir Humphrey Gilbert (1539–83) – Sir Walter's half-brother – was also quoted by VW, though not as fully as here, in 'Trafficks and Discoveries', I VW Essays, from

Professor Walter Raleigh, *The English Voyages of the Sixteenth Century* (James MacLehose & Sons, 1906), p. 59.

12 – For both quotations, Raleigh, 'The Historie of the World', Pref., p. 51.

13 – *Ibid.*, p. 47.

14 – *Ibid.*, p. 54.

15 – *Ibid.*, p. 45, which continues: ': wee have sense and feeling of corporal things; and of eternall grace, but by revelation'.

16 – *Ibid.*, 'Of the Fall of Empires', p. 116.

17 – *Ibid.*, p. 115, which begins: 'Which were it otherwise, and the extreame ill bargaine of buying this lasting discourse, understood by them which are dissolved; they themselves . . .'; and has 'without noise;'; and 'Cities'.

18 – *Ibid.*, 'Of Griffins', p. 80, which has: 'things done:'; and 'Morall'. The ellipsis marks the omission of ', and were not deprived of halfe their eye-sight (at least of the eye of right reason and understanding)'.

19 – *Ibid.*, Pref., p. 54, which has: 'what ever'; and 'Spring-time'.

20 – *Ibid.*, p. 55, which has: 'Swannes I must except:'.

21 – *Ibid.*, p. 56: 'For seeing God, who is the Author of all our tragedies, hath written out for us, and appointed us all the parts we are to play . . . Certainly there is no other account to be made of this ridiculous world, than to resolve, That the change of fortune on the great Theater, is but as the change of garments on the lesse. For when on the one and the other, every man weares but his own skin; the Players are all alike.'

22 – *Ibid.*, 'Letters', 'The Copy of a Letter, written by Sir Walter Raleigh, to his wife, the Night before hee expected to be putt to death att winchester. 1603', p. 183.

23 – *Ibid.*, 'The Historie of the World', Pref., p. 54, which has: 'in chace, from our infancie'.

24 – *Ibid.*, 'Letters', p. 184.

25 – *Ibid.*, 'The Historie of the World', 'Of the Falls of Empires', p. 117, which has: 'perswaded;'; and continues '; and whom all the world hath flattered, thou only hast cast out of the world and despised: thou hast drawne together all the farre stretched greatnesse, all the pride, crueltie, and ambition of man, and covered it all over with these two narrow words, *Hîc iacet*'.

'The House of Lyme'

After reading Lady Newton's[2] history of the house of Lyme and looking at the pictures which adorn it we are inclined to think that the production of such works by the people who inherit such houses should be made compulsory by Act of Parliament. To have in one's possession this private door into the past, through which one can see back to the pale beginnings of English life four or five centuries ago, and to keep it locked against the public, is no less heinous an offence than to burn a portrait by Velasquez[3] once a year. It is true that we are still under the spell of Lady Newton's narrative, and her gifts, unfortunately, are by no means common ones. We are still looking through the door which she has thrown open at many generations of the family of Legh, at much of the history of England. Owing to her skilful arrangement and to a freshness of feeling which imparts a most delightful naturalness to her story, we are able for the moment to forget the substantial veil of the present and to gaze upon the lives which have receded from us but have not disappeared. To Lady Newton, we fancy, the veil is a very thin one, and to her the Leghs of the past are people of distinct character, tastes, clothing, appearances. She writes of them as if she had known them, and when she quotes their letters they take up the story with the most natural intonation. For although nothing, we imagine, would be more out of keeping with the family tradition than to rattle behind wainscots at dawn or indulge in other ghostly antics, we can scarcely believe that the dead Leghs have gone very far from their beloved possessions. No house can have a greater share of those happier ghosts who are with us in the daytime. It was surely at the prompting of one of these spirits that Lady Newton was led to open that 'fireproof cupboard the existence of which was unknown or had been forgotten', and take from it 'a large quantity of papers', tied up in bundles, labelled "Old Letters"'.[4] Certainly, if the ghosts felt the need of an interpreter, they could not have made a better choice.

On a high spot in the park of Lyme there stand two pillars of rough stone whose origin has never been accounted for, although it is agreed that they are of great antiquity. Beneath them spreads the plain of Cheshire and around them lie the hills of Derbyshire − 'an almost boundless view'[5] − and, in the days when those stones were set there, a view without sign of building or population. It is as if those old pagans had placed a mark here, and decreed that here a limit should be set to the wilderness of nature and man build himself a dwelling-place. The name of Lyme, indeed, stands for *limes*, a border, for the three counties of Cheshire, Lancashire, and Derbyshire come together at this point. And here, some time in the beginning of the fifteenth century, a house was built for the family of Legh; another house succeeded it in the middle of the sixteenth century, and the building and rebuilding of the house continued until the middle of the nineteenth century, when the designs of Leoni[6] were at last accomplished. If we consider these facts we shall see that Lady Newton has chosen her title well. Here in the same spot the same family has been building at the same house for something like five centuries. A son has succeeded a father, one tomb has been placed beside another, a new wing has been added to the house, or the windows have been altered. So slow is the growth of the house, so orderly the progress of life, that watching the gradual development we lose count of time and wake with a start to find that, while we have watched the house being built and one Sir Piers[7] succeed another, we have traversed the greater part of our English history. We have passed from the Middle Ages to the world as we know it now.

The Leghs were not a race to disturb the continuity of their history by any startling adventures. One, perhaps, fought at Flodden; another at Agincourt; a third sailed with Essex against the Spaniard and was knighted by Queen Elizabeth.[8] But for the most part they have been content to stay at home and do their duty; or, if compelled to serve in Parliament, have shown no anxiety to dictate the laws of the country, but hastened back to Lyme to shoot their stags or race their horses. The country might change its king or its religion without greatly disturbing the peace of mind of the master of Lyme; and by luck and wise conformity they lived through many troubled ages without losing their lives or their fortunes. The only one of the race who suffered a short term of imprisonment in the cause of the Stuarts[9] very soon came to his senses and, when the rising of '45[10] once more tempted the rasher heads of the county to venture their lives, sensibly refused to have anything to do with it. A set of Jacobite drinking glasses with the Stuart roses engraved upon them bears witness to a little post-prandial enthusiasm for the King over the water, and in congenial company a clock would chime out twelve Jacobite airs, as indeed it does to the present day.

The indifference of contemporaries to events which to us seem of the greatest, perhaps of the only, importance is one of the surprises which family letters generally hold in store for us. The Legh letters are no exception to the rule. Lady Newton tells us of a tradition that one of the Leghs, writing from London on the day that King Charles[11] had his head cut off, makes no mention of that fact; but this, of course, may be attributed to caution rather than negligence. Later, however, when news of the Plague and the Fire of London would, one thinks, have filled up a letter to the country very pleasantly, there is only one mention of either of them, and that, characteristically, introduces a compliment to Lyme, 'where health and wealth conspire to make you happy'.[12] To us this seems very right and fitting. The great value and interest of such letters as these lies in the fact that they drown the drums and trumpets of history with a deeper and subtler music of their own. We do not need the evidence of state papers or the eloquence of the College of Heralds to prove that Peter and Thomas and Richard Legh[13] were all gentlemen of the highest integrity and of the greatest importance to their corner of the world. By them the law was made and administered, they were the fountains of charity, the arbiters of right and wrong, the source of such influence as no one family in England wields today. We need not wonder that to go up to London and play a minute part in the passing of some Act of Parliament or even to take arms for a Cromwell[14] or a Stuart seemed to them of less importance than other work lying closer at hand. Their house was not only a house in every room of which traditions of their race had accumulated, but a law court, a theatre, a public building, and an hotel all in one; a self-sufficient community highly organised in each of its departments, and the centre of civilisation in that district. They did their duty also by their library, and at one time possessed a band of musicians. When visitors of importance came a play was provided.

Much labour and contrivance was continually needed to keep such an institution in working order. In the year 1607, for instance, eighty or a hundred people were employed in the house every day; the staff had to include brewers, spit-turners, glaziers, 'tincklers', carpet-makers, tailors, marlers, plasterers, gutterers, besides mole catchers, rat catchers, carters, and bricklayers.[15] The house, we must remember, was always being altered, furnished, and rebuilt, gardens dug and terraces levelled. In addition to the usual brewing, baking, and dairying, they slaughtered their own cattle, and made their own candles and soap. Besides the people regularly employed in these pursuits there was a floating population consisting of visitors from the great families in the neighbourhood, a sprinkling of poor relations who assisted at all births and marriages, and were expert at needlework and pastry making, and the squires who came for the racing and the hunting and stayed late to drink such toasts as 'May Aristocracy Rise on the Ashes of Democracy', or, 'A Fresh Earth and a High Metaled Terrier', or 'A Cellar well filled and a House Full of Friends'.[16] The Leghs were not a family to take to the pen without cause, and this is generally provided by some cock-fight or horse-race, or business connected with the famous herd of red deer. There is an amusing account of a hunt in Lancashire which tells how the writer returned after the fox was killed 'to drink a bowle of Hott Punch with ye fox's foot stew'd in it. Sr Willm drank pretty plentifully, and just at last perceiv'd he should be fuddled, "but," quoth he, "I care not if I am, I have kill'd a fox today."'[17] And whenever they are away they long that Parliament may rise and let them get back to 'sweet Lyme'[18] again and their wives and children. 'Dearest,' writes the delightful Richard, 'I want nothing this night to compleat the joy I am in but thy deare company and the brats.'[19]

Moving against this background of servants and dependents, household cares and country sports in the house which gradually changes and is rebuilt over their heads we see old Sir Piers[20] and the Peters and Richard discharging their businesses, making matches, settling disputes, doing their duty, and presiding over the life of the house, much to the satisfaction of their neighbours. The changes in the house correspond to a change which slowly transforms the race which lives in it. Nothing is more curious than to watch the gradual thawing of the human race from the monolithic isolation of Elizabethan days to the humanity and garrulity of the eighteenth century. The bare and comfortless rooms of the sixteenth century become furnished; the beds have cushions; the chairs are easy chairs; there are forks to eat with, and some regard for intimacy and privacy. Even the speech ceases to be the dialect of the district, and educated people have to observe the same laws of spelling. No longer can old Sir Peter thunder forth his commands and extort obedience from his grown-up sons; and by the time the book is finished the inaccessible House of Lyme is in close touch with the gossip and the shops of London.

But the most profound impression left upon us by this delightful and absorbing book is not one of change; it is one of continuity. The red deer have roamed the park for upwards of five hundred years; the famous mastiffs of Lyme, though 'now alas, threatened with extinction',[21] still exist whose ancestors followed their master in the Battle of Agincourt; the oak still stands beneath which the Duke of York killed a stag; the clock which Richard bought in 1675 is still keeping time for his descendants;[22] and the red hair for which the Leghs were marked five hundred years ago grows once more upon the head of their latest descendant. In a world which seems bent on ruin and oblivion we cannot refuse a feeling of affectionate respect for the courage with which such old houses still confront life, cherish its traditions, and are a sanctuary for the lovely wreckage of the past.

1 – A review in the *TLS*, 29 March 1917, (Kp C70) of *The House of Lyme. From its Foundation to the End of the Eighteenth Century* (William Heinemann, 1917) by the Lady Newton. 'I didn't honestly think that Lady Newton had made the best of her Lyme papers,' VW wrote to Violet Dickinson, 10 April 1917 (*II VW Letters*, no. 827), 'the truth was that the Legh's were almost invariably stupid – which accounts, I suppose, for their centuries of life on the same spot. Do you know them in the flesh? I should like immensely to write a book of that sort, if someone would trust me to tell the truth about their relations. It's so queer the sentiment she had for them.'

2 – Evelyn Caroline Newton, *née* Bromley-Davenport (d. 1931), wife of Thomas Wodehouse Legh, 2nd Baron Newton, diplomat and politician.

3 – Diego Rodríguez de Silva y Velasquez (1599–1660) – and see Newton, ch. III, p. 42: 'In the great picture by Velasquez of the children of Philip IV, the *Las Meniñas* . . . a large mastiff is seen in the foreground, one of the children rubbing its back with his foot. The dog is precisely the same as the Lyme mastiffs of the present day, having all their characteristics, and was no doubt a descendant of the pair presented by James I to Philip III in 1604.'

4 – *Ibid.*, intro, p. xiii, adapted.

5 – *Ibid.*, ch. II, p. 23.

6 – *Ibid.* ch. XXVII, 'Leoni's Alterations', pp. 370–82. Giacomo Leoni (1686–1764), Venetian architect, who settled in England in the early eighteenth century.

7 – For Sir Piers Legh (1360?–99), grantee of Lyme, who had the misfortune to be beheaded at Chester by Henry IV – and was 'the first of a long succession of Sir Piers' – see *ibid.*, ch. I, p. 1, and see the Legh family tree appended to Newton.

8 – For the Sir Piers (1455–1527) who possibly fought against James IV at Flodden Field, in 1513, *ibid.*, ch. I, p. 19; p. 21. For Sir Piers (or Peter) (d. 1422), who fought at Agincourt, 1415, *ibid.*, ch. I, p. 7. For the 'third' Sir Piers (1563–1635/6), knighted at Greenwich in 1598, *ibid.*, ch. IV, pp. 49–50. Robert Devereux, 2nd Earl of Essex (1567–1601).

9 – *Ibid.*, ch. XXVI, 'Imprisonment of Peter Legh [1669–1743/4]', pp. 360–9. Legh had become involved, in July 1694, in the so-called Lancashire Plot, one of a series of Jacobite conspiracies, and was arrested but discharged by the courts in the absence of substantial evidence against him. In 1696 he was once more apprehended, for high treason, and again discharged.

10 – *Ibid.*, ch. XXIX, p. 388; Peter Legh (1707–92) was the member of the family concerned at the time of the Jacobite Rising in 1745.

11 – *Ibid.*, ch. X, p. 158; Charles I was executed at Whitehall on 30 January 1649.

12 – *Ibid.*, ch. XVI, p. 237, Lady Anne Saville to her stepdaughter Elizabeth Legh, 16 October 1665: 'The general sicklynes of the yeare exempts few places but Lyme where . . .' The Great Fire raged 2–6 September 1666 and destroyed some two-thirds of London.

13 – VW appears to be referring here to Thomas Legh (1594–1639), doctor of divinity, rector of Sefton and Walton, father of Richard Legh (1634–87), M.P. for Cheshire, 1656, and for Newton, 1659–1678/9, and the latter's son Peter Legh (1669–1743/4), M.P. for Newton 1685.

14 – Oliver Cromwell (1599–1658).

15 – Newton, ch. IV, p. 61; p. 64.

16 – *Ibid.*, ch. XXVII, p. 369.

17 – *Ibid.*, ch. XXV, p. 357.

18 – *Ibid.*, intro., p. XIV, ch. XVIII, p. 263.

19 – *Ibid.*, ch. XVI, Richard to Elizabeth Legh, 19 February 1669/70, p. 242.

20 – VW is presumably referring to Sir Piers Legh (1513–90), original builder of the House of Lyme.

21 – *Ibid.*, ch. III, p. 42.

22 – For the oak, *ibid.*, ch. XIX, p. 283; and for the clock, *ibid.*, p. 281.

'Poe's Helen'

The real interest of Miss Ticknor's volume lies in the figure of Mrs Whitman,[2] and not in the love letters from Poe, which have already been published. It is true that if it had not been for her connection with Poe we should never have heard of Helen Whitman; but it is also true that Poe's connection with Mrs Whitman was neither much to his credit nor a matter of moment to the world at large. If it were our object to enhance the charm of 'the only true romantic figure in our literature',[3] as Miss Ticknor calls him, we should have suppressed his love letters altogether. Mrs Whitman, on the other hand, comes very well out of the ordeal, and was evidently, apart from Poe, a curious and interesting person.

She wrote poetry from her childhood, and when in early youth she was left a widow she settled down to lead a literary life in earnest. In those days and in America this was not so simple a proceeding as it has since become. If you wrote an essay upon Shelley,[4] for example, the most influential family in Providence considered that you had fallen from grace. If, like Mr Ellery Channing, you went to Europe and left your wife behind, this was sufficient proof that you were not a 'great perfect man',[5] as the true poet is bound to be. Mrs Whitman took her stand against such crudities, and, indeed, rather went out of her way to invite attack. Whatever the fashion and whatever the season she wore her 'floating veils'[6] and her thin slippers, and carried a fan in her hand. By means of 'inverting her lamp shades'[7] and hanging up bits of drapery her sitting room was kept in a perpetual twilight. It was the age of the Transcendentalists, and the fans and the veils and the twilight were, no doubt, intended to mitigate the solidity of matter, and entice the soul out of the body with as little friction as possible. Nature too had been kind in endowing her with a pale, eager face, a spiritual expression, and deep-set eyes that gazed 'beyond but never at you'.[8]

Her house became a centre for the poets of the district, for she was witty and charming as well as enthusiastic. John Hay, G. W. Curtis, and the Hon. Wilkins Updike[9] used to send her their works to criticise, or in very long and abstruse letters tried to define what they meant by poetry. The mark of that particular set, which was more or less connected with Emerson and Margaret Fuller, was an enthusiastic championship of the rights of the soul. They ventured into a sphere where words naturally were unable to support them. 'Poetry', as Mr Curtis said, 'is the adaption of music to an intellectual sphere. But it must therefore be revealed through souls too fine to be measured justly by the intellect . . . Music . . . is a womanly accomplishment, because it is sentiment, and the instinct declares its nature,' etc.[10] This exalted mood never quite deserted them when they were writing about matters of fact. When Mrs Whitman forgot to answer a letter Mr Curtis inquired whether she was ill 'or has the autumn which lies round the horizon like a beautifully hued serpent crushing the flower of summer fascinated you to silence with its soft, calm eyes?'[11] Mrs Whitman, it is clear, was the person who kept them all up to this very high standard. Thus things went on until Mrs Whitman had reached the age of forty-two. One July night, in 1845, she happened to be wandering in her garden in the moonlight when Edgar Allan Poe passed by and saw her. 'From that hour I loved you,' he wrote later. '. . . your unknown heart seemed to pass into my bosom – there to dwell for ever.'[12] The immediate result was that he wrote the verses 'To Helen' which he sent her. Three years later, when he was the famous poet of 'The Raven', Mrs Whitman replied with a valentine, of which the last stanza runs –

> Then, oh grim and ghastly Raven
> Wilt thou to my heart an ear
> Be a Raven true as ever
> Flapped his wings and croaked 'Despair'?
> Not a bird that roams the forest
> Shall our lofty eyrie share.[13]

For some time their meeting was postponed, and no word of prose passed between them. It might have been postponed for ever had it not been for another copy of verses which Mrs Whitman ended with the line

> I dwell with 'Beauty which is Hope'.[14]

Upon receipt of these verses Poe immediately procured a letter of introduction and set off to Providence. His declaration of love took place in the course of the next fortnight during a walk in the cemetery. Mrs Whitman would not consent to an engagement, but she agreed to write to him, and thus the famous correspondence began.

Professor Harrison can only compare Poe's letters to the letters of Abelard and Eloise or to the *Sonnets from the Portuguese*;[15] Miss Ticknor says that they have won themselves a niche among the world's classic love letters. Professor Woodberry,[16] on the other hand, thinks that they should never have been published. We agree with Professor Woodberry, not because they do damage to Poe's reputation, but because we find them very tedious compositions. Whether you are writing a review or a love letter the great thing is to be confronted with a very vivid idea of your subject. When Poe wrote to Mrs Whitman he might have been addressing a fashion plate in a ladies' newspaper – a fashion plate which walks the cemetery by moonlight, for the atmosphere is one of withered roses and moonshine. The fact that he had buried Virginia a short time before, that he denied his love for her, that he was writing to Annie[17] at the same time and in the same style, that he was about to propose to a widow for the sake of her money – all his perfidies and meannesses do not by themselves make it impossible that he loved Mrs Whitman genuinely. Were it not for the letters we might accept the charitable view that this was his last effort at redemption. But when we read the letters we feel that the man who wrote them had no emotion left about anything; his world was a world of phantoms and fashion plates; his phrases are the cast-off phrases that were not quite good enough for a story. He could see neither himself nor others save through a mist of opium and alcohol. The engagement, which had been made conditional upon his reform, was broken off; Mrs Whitman sank on to a sofa holding a handkerchief 'drenched in ether'[18] to her face, and her old mother rather pointedly observed to Poe that the train was about to leave for New York.

Cynical though it sounds, we doubt whether Mrs Whitman lost as much as she gained by the unfortunate end of her love affair. Her feeling for Poe was probably more that of a benefactress than of a lover; for she was one of those people who 'devoutly believe that serpents may be reclaimed. This is only effected by patience and prayer – but the results are wonderful.'[19] This particular serpent was irreclaimable; he was picked up unconscious in the street and died a year later. But he left behind him a crop of reptiles who taxed Mrs Whitman's patience and needed her prayers for the rest of her life. She became the recognised authority upon Poe, and whenever a biographer was in need of facts or old Mrs Clemm[20] was in need of money they applied to her. She had to decide the disputes of the different ladies as to which had been loved the most, and to keep the peace between the rival historians, for whether a woman is more vain of her love or an author of his work has yet to be decided. But the opportunities which such a position gave her of endless charity and literary discussion evidently suited her, and the good sense and wit of the bird-like little woman, who was extremely poor and had an eccentric sister to provide for, seem to justify her statement that 'the results are wonderful'.

1 – A review in the *TLS*, 5 April 1917, (Kp C71) of *Poe's Helen* (John Lane, 1917) by Caroline Ticknor. See also 'Thoreau' below, 'Emerson's Journals', *I VW Essays*; and see (for Caroline Ticknor) 'Glimpses of Authors', *III VW Essays*. Reprinted: *G&R, CE*.

2 – Sarah Helen Whitman, *née* Power (1803–78), poet, born at Providence, Rhode Island, was the widow of an inconspicuous lawyer, John Winslow Whitman (d. 1833). Her first volume of poems *Hours of Life* appeared in 1853; her other publications include *Edgar Poe and His Critics* (1860) and *Poems* (1879).

3 – This precise form of words has not been discovered, but see Ticknor, Pref., p. vii: 'After the lapse of half a century, Poe still remains the one romantic figure in the field of American Letters . . .'

4 – *Ibid.*, ch. III, p. 24, the essay is not identified; Percy Bysshe Shelley (1792–1822).

5 – *Ibid.*, ch. III, p. 27, quoting George William Curtis (1824–92), essayist, editor and reformer, who had been a student at Brook Farm. William Ellery Channing (1818–1901), poet, nephew of the unitarian minister W. E. Channing who exerted a considerable influence upon the Transcendentalists – members of the literary movement that flourished in New England, 1836–60, chief among whom were Ralph Waldo Emerson (1803–82), Henry David Thoreau (1817–62) and Margaret Fuller (1810–50). The younger Channing was a friend of Hawthorne and of Thoreau – of whom he wrote a biography, *Thoreau, the Poet-Naturalist* (1873) – and married Margaret Fuller's sister.

6 – *Ibid.*, ch. II, p. 15: 'In the matter of clothes she was entirely unconventional, dressing in a style all her own; she loved silken draperies, lace scarfs, and floating veils, and was always shod in dainty slippers'.

7 – *Ibid.*, ch. XV, p. 281, quoting Professor William Whitman Bailey: 'She had a trick of inverting her lamp shades so that a flood of light would be thrown upon and suffuse some particular painting or print, leaving the rest of the room in darkness . . .'

8 – Ticknor, ch. I, p. 5, quoting Mrs Whitman's friend Sarah S. Jacobs, which has: 'the dreamy look of deep-set eyes that gazed over and beyond, but never at you'.

9 – John Hay (1838–1905), writer and diplomat, author of *Pike County Ballads* (1871) and also of the 10-vol. *Abraham Lincoln: a History* (1890). Hon. Wilkins Updike (1784–1867), author of *Memoirs of the Rhode Island Bar* (1842) and of the *History of the Episcopal Church in Narrangansett* (1847).

10 – *Ibid.*, ch. III, p. 24, quoting G. W. Curtis to Mrs Whitman, letter 9 April 1845, which has: 'Music, so imperfect here, foreshadows a state more refined and delicate. It is a womanly accomplishment, because it is sentiment, and the Instinct declares its nature, when it celebrates heaven and the state where glorified souls chant around the throne. Poetry is the adaptation of music to an Intellectual sphere . . .'

11 – *Ibid.*, ch. III, p. 28, letter undated, which has: 'Autumn', and 'Summer'.

12 – *Ibid.*, ch. V, p. 60, letter 1 October 1848, which has: 'I cannot better explain to you what I felt than by saying that your unknown heart seemed to pass into my bosom – there to dwell forever – while mine, I thought, was translated into your own. From that hour I loved you.' Edgar Allan Poe (1809–40), poet and critic, found fame with the publication of *The Raven and Other Poems* (1845); the second of the two poems by Poe entitled 'To Helen' (published in November 1848) is addressed to Mrs Whitman.

13 – *Ibid.*, ch. IV, 'To Edgar Allan Poe', dated Providence, R.I., 14 February 1848, p. 46.

14 – *Ibid.*, ch. IV, p. 52.

15 – *Ibid.*, ch. V, p. 56; Professor James Albert Harrison author of *Life and Letters of Edgar Allan Poe* (1903). Pierre Abélard (1079–1142) and Héloïse (d. 1163), whose celebrated correspondence has been published in numerous editions. Elizabeth Barrett Browning (1806–61), *Sonnets from the Portuguese* (1850).

16 – George E. Woodberry, author of a biography of Poe in the American Men of Letters series, 1885, and of *The Life of Edgar Allan Poe. Personal and Literary* (2 vols, 1909). The source of his opinion on the publication of Poe's letters has not been traced.

17 – Virginia Poe, *née* Clemm (d. 1847), Poe's cousin, whom he married in 1836. Mrs Annie Richmond, of Lowell, Mass., another of Poe's passions, to whom he addressed the poem 'For Annie' (published in April 1849).

18 – *Ibid.*, ch. VIII, p. 120: 'The scene which ensued has been often described. Mrs Whitman herself quite ill, and worn out by worry and argument, returned to Poe certain letters and papers, then dropping upon a couch and placing a handkerchief drenched in ether to her face she relapsed into a semiconscious state.

'Poe fell upon his knees beside her and continued his protestations, begging her to reconsider and to speak to him.'

19 – *Ibid.*, ch. XI, p. 174, Mrs Whitman to her friend Mrs Freeman, otherwise unidentified, letter dated March 1857.

20 – Maria Clemm, mother of Virginia.

A Talker

When one opens a book of poetry and discovers the lines:

> In 1863 Charles publishes
> How Orchid Flowers are Fertilized by Insects,

or

> In 1833 a man named Hallam,
> A friend of Alfred's, died at twenty-two,[2]

one may be either delighted or annoyed; one may feel that this method is the genuine, unhumbugging speech which poets would always use if they were sincere; or one may inquire with some asperity why, if Mr Masters wants to say this sort of thing, he does not run all his lines into one, and say it in prose. But this last seems to us a stupid criticism: the lines would be no better if they were all of the same length, and, moreover, they would not be prose. The lines we have quoted are not prose; the lines that follow are not prose.

> Up there in the city
> Think sometimes of the American village and
> What may be done for conservation of
> The souls of men and women in the village.[3]

The difficulty of describing Mr Masters lies precisely in the fact that if he is not a prose writer, still less is he a poet. And for this reason it is not necessary to consider him as a man who is making serious experiments in metre like the Imagists or the Vers Librists. He has none of the sensibility which, whether we think it irritable or perverted or inspired, is now urging them to break up the old rules and devise new ones, more arduous than the old. He seems to us to have little ear for the sound of words, and no poetic imagination. When he does an exercise in the classical style, such as 'Marsyas', or 'Apollo at Pherae', he is as smooth and dull and conscientious as a prize poet at one of our universities. His metaphors are then of this description:

> And looking up he saw a slender maid
> White as gardenias, jonquil-haired, with eyes
> As blue as Peneus when he meets the sea[4]

or,

> And once he strove with music's alchemy
> To turn to sound the sunlight of the morn
> Which fills the senses as illuminate dew
> Quickens the ovule of the tiger-flower.[5]

Whatever poetry may be, it is nothing at all like this; and although we very much prefer

> For when they opened him up
> They found his heart was a played out pump,
> And leaked like a rusty cup,[6]

we doubt whether that is any more in the right direction.

But if Mr Masters is neither a poet nor a prose writer, we must, after reading 280 pages of his work, find a name for him; and on the whole we think it nearest the mark to call him a talker. His jerky, creaking style, the inconsecutiveness of his thought, his slap-dash use of language, his openness and plain speaking (the best of his poems is too frank to be quoted)[7] all seem to mark him as a person who utters his ideas in talk, without stopping very long to think what he is saying. As the above quotations will have shown, when he stops to think he becomes the shadow of other respectable people; even the restraint of a rhyme seems to shackle him at once. But when he is most at his ease, and therefore at his best, we seem to see him in the corner of a New England public house, telling stories about Jerry Ott, Cato Braden, Malachy Degan, or Slip Shoe Lovey,[8] with considerable shrewdness, humour, and sentimentality. In this mood he resembles a very primitive and provincial Robert Browning.[9] And when there is a political crisis he gets upon his feet and delivers a harangue about life in general – for he is extremely didactic – more in the style of one of our village orators, save that his background is made of great advertisement hoardings, factory chimneys, and skyscrapers, instead of ancient churches and the oaks of ancestral parks.

> Suppose you do it, Republic.
> Get some class.
> Throw out your chest, lift up your head,
> Be a ruler in the world.
> And not a hermit in regimentals with a flint-lock.
> Colossus with one foot in Europe,
> And one in China,
> Quit looking between your legs for the reappearance
> Of the star of Bethlehem –
> Stand up and be a man![10]

To a stranger the familiarity of this colloquial style seems to show that Mr Masters is at any rate a true son of the house. The chief interest of his work, indeed, comes from the fact that it is self-consciously and self-assertively American; and it is for that reason we suppose that the American public hails it with delight, on the principle, with which we must agree, that one native frog is of more importance than a whole grove full of sham nightingales.

1 – A review in the *TLS*, 12 April 1917, (Kp C72) of *The Great Valley* (T. Werner Laurie, 1916) by Edgar Lee Masters (1869–1950), the poet of small-town America, whose *Spoon River Anthology*, published anonymously in 1915, found instant popularity.
2 – For the first quotation, Masters, 'The Great Valley, VII, Autochthon', p. 40; and for the second, *ibid.*, p. 36.
3 – Masters, 'Cato Braden', p. 119.
4 – *Ibid.*, 'Apollo at Pherae', p. 169.
5 – *Ibid.*, 'Marsyas', p. 157.
6 – *Ibid.*, 'Steam Shovel Cut', p. 177
7 – VW is possibly referring to the poem 'To a Spirochaeta', *ibid.*, pp. 104–5, in which acknowledgement is made of Robert Burns's 'To a Louse'.
8 – The character Jerry Ott appears in the poem 'Cato Braden'; for the other characters referred to see 'Malachy Degan' and 'Slip Shoe Lovey'.
9 – Robert Browning (1812–89).
10 – Masters, 'Come, Republic', pp. 74–5.

'In Good Company'

We have enjoyed Mr Kernahan's book so much that we find ourselves asking what the reason can be. For the most part snapshot reminiscences of celebrities, though we can no more help reading them than we can help turning the pages of a picture paper, leave us with a slight feeling of depression. The little pictures are so real, so authentic – and yet if Tennyson really said this or did that have we missed so very much by never having known Tennyson? And thus we determine to check our natural instinct of reverence, and come rather to disbelieve in great men. The impression that Mr Kernahan's book produces is the exact opposite of this. He is a good but by no means a blind hero-worshipper; he makes little use of stories or personalities; and some of his heroes are hardly to be counted among the great or even the celebrated. But he succeeds very singularly in making us feel that to all these men life was a rich and remarkable affair, and that, after all, is what we want to know about; that is what we cannot altogether get from their books. The average person is chiefly struck by the eccentricities of the great; Mr Kernahan, on the other hand, bears witness to the fullness, sincerity, and passion with which great men live compared with lesser men. It is our method, indeed, of passing time and spending money that should rightly be called eccentric — not theirs.

Consider, for instance, what the present of a bunch of flowers meant to Swinburne.[2]

In an ecstasy of delight, he took the flowers from my outstretched hand . . . He bent his head over them in a rapture that was almost like a prayer, his eyes when he looked up to thank me for the gift alight and brimming over with thoughts that were not far from tears . . . Then he turned to Miss Watts[3] with his courtly bow. 'As you have been as equally honoured as I, you will not think me robbing you if I carry my bunch away with me to put them in water and to place them in my own room. I want to find them there when I wake in the morning.'[4]

This was an important event to him; his next day would begin with a solitary ecstasy over a bunch of flowers. We must change our focus altogether if we want to understand how the day which begins with the contemplation of lilies is lived by the poet. Many incidents must be blurred; others brought out with a sudden and amazing intensity. And this impression of a change in the focus is still with us when Mr Kernahan writes of Watts-Dunton,[5] although, of course, it is a very different change. His day was spent not in ecstasies over bunches of flowers, but in a busy interminable traffic with ideas and literature. Never, as Mr Kernahan says, a professional literary man, he was steeped in every sort of literary knowledge and memory which somehow made it impossible for him ever to become an author himself. A book of some kind – on the first principles of literary criticism, a biography, a novel – was always impending over his head; every day his equipment became more stupendous; the fame of the unwritten masterpiece was such that publishers would come down in order to induce him at last to pluck the ripe fruit. '"Yes," he would say, "I cannot deny that I could write such a book. Such a book, I do not mind saying in confidence, has long been in my mind, and in the minds of friends who have repeatedly urged me to such work."'[6] He toyed complacently with the idea of fame and accomplishment. He would then telegraph to one or two of his friends for their advice, and in imagination the book was already completed.

But sitting down to write the first words of it, he was overcome by doubts; suddenly it seemed essential to use that particular hour for the composition of one of his innumerable letters, and so, although his intentions for books were enough to fill a large space in the British Museum, he left only two published volumes behind him.[7]

The study of Edward Whymper[8] gives us another view of the life which has got itself out of the rut, though in his case this was achieved by no bias of extraordinary genius, unless, as sometimes seems to be the case, to be a 'character' is to be an artist, although you produce no work of art. The account of this masterful, independent, and self-isolated man, who lived for choice at the top of a high house in Southend, with a house-keeper in the basement and the intervening storeys completely unfurnished, so that he might feel himself alone, interests us like one of those portraits of queer people painted to perfection by Borrow.[9] We would draw attention in particular to the delightful scene with the photograph of himself when he had already kept Mr Kernahan waiting from 8.30 to 12.30 for his supper.[10] Mr Kernahan was very hungry; he could see nothing remarkable in the photograph. At length Whymper tapped it with the stem of his pipe. 'What I wondered was whether you'd notice that the smoke coming from the bowl of the pipe has been painted-in upon the negative . . . When you get to know me better you'll find that I'm slow and methodical, but minutely accurate, even about little things.'[11] But, like all Mr Kernahan's studies, this is a portrait, and we have no right to spoil it by picking out a handful of eccentricities; for he makes us understand that the queer ways of the great are for the most part only an impatient short cut to a life beyond our reach.

1 – A review in the TLS, 12 April 1917, (Kp c73) of In Good Company. Some personal recollections of Swinburne, Lord Roberts, Watts-Dunton, Oscar Wilde, Edward Whymper, S. J. Stone, Stephen Phillips (John Lane, The Bodley Head, 1917) by Coulson Kernahan (1858–1943). See also 'Swinburne As I Knew Him', III VW Essays.

2 – Algernon Charles Swinburne (1837–1909), author of Atalanta in Calydon (1865) and Poems and Ballads (1st series, 1866; 2nd series, 1878), etc.

3 – Teresa Watts, sister of Theodore Watts-Dunton (see n. 5).

4 – Kernahan, pp. 26–7.

5 – Theodore Watts-Dunton (1832–1914), critic, novelist, poet, friend and protector of Swinburne, with whom he shared his home at The Pines, Putney, from 1879 until Swinburne's death.

6 – Kernahan, p. 92.

7 – His book of verse scenes, The Coming of Love and Other Poems (1897), and the

novel, *Aylwin* (1898), books with characters in common and dealing with gipsy life. Watts-Dunton's collection of literary portraits, *Old Familiar Faces*, and the novel *Vesprie Towers* were published posthumously, in 1916.

8 – Edward Whymper (1840–1911), wood-engraver and Alpinist, a friend of Leslie Stephen.

9 – George Borrow (1803–81), author of *Lavengro* (1851), *The Romany Rye* (1857), *Wild Wales* (1862), etc.

10 – Kernahan, p. 163.

11 – *Ibid.*

A Cambridge V.A.D.

The war, so people say, is breaking down barriers between the classes which seemed of adamant. Many individuals would have something of the kind to relate of havoc wrought within their own personalities by the same disaster. They have been made aware, to their delight, that they possess powers and desires which are entirely at variance with each other and with their accepted beliefs about themselves. Here we have the case of Miss Spearing, a late Fellow of Newnham, engaged when war broke out upon 'research work on certain Elizabethan dramas'.[2] Not even this war, one might have thought, would have disturbed an occupation so utterly alien to itself; and yet the proofs of her book sent to the Louvain University Press were among the first things to perish in the flames. She found compensation 'and much more'[3] for its loss by becoming a V.A.D. at Cambridge, and this little book consists of notes and diaries she wrote there and later when she was nursing at hospitals in various parts of France. She does not attempt to analyse her feelings very closely, as no doubt she had little time to indulge in them; but something of the excitement of a student plunged from books into practical work and finding herself quite capable of it is perceptible in her account and exhilarating to the reader.

Her first taste of camp life was not a mild one. The hospital camp was among chalk hills swept by the wind; the tents were blown down in the middle of the night; the camp was a sea of mud; the month November. When the snow came 'it was difficult to creep out of the tent without allowing a heavy mass of snow to fall in and overwhelm everything.' 'Yet most of us,' Miss Spearing adds, 'find camp life decidedly congenial.'[5] It is very healthy, for one thing; and then 'one makes friends quickly',[5] such conditions, one may suppose, providing a fine test of friendship. As for the soldiers, her patients, Miss Spearing has the usual story to tell – so usual that we have almost forgotten how remarkable it is. They are very gentle, very grateful, very much like children, and yet in some respects the conventional picture does not do them justice. Beneath a surface which is so much alike that it resembles a uniform assumed for convenience, 'the modern Tommy is often a highly strung individual, very sensitive to pain',[6] a man living in abnormal conditions, and showing naturally some qualities that one would not expect. Among them there is his taste, which Miss Spearing found a little puzzling, for highly sentimental songs, about 'home and mother and sweetheart', which he will get up and sing with 'the utmost seriousness'.[7] But this surely is of a piece with the desire for noise and merriment which breaks out unreasonably as a reaction from the strain of the trenches. 'We all,' she says, 'live very much for the day,'[8] and try to get as much into the day as possible, for it is a short one, and those who meet now may be moved elsewhere tomorrow.

This concentration of life is, perhaps, the secret of the fascination which so many people find in a hard and dangerous existence. The best qualities, and the most real, which might be hidden in the slow intercourse of normal life, come quickly to the surface. They find the readiest expression, so far as the English are concerned, in humour. But in the nurses, and in the soldiers, such experiences are forming deeper thoughts, of 'an underlying reality',[9] of a 'community of suffering';[10] and it is this which is in Miss Spearing's mind when she writes, 'I have had horrors enough to last me my whole life, but still I don't think I would have missed it if I had been given my choice.'[11] And yet she by no means shares the sentimental illusions about wounded soldiers and the effects of war on the character which she found rife in England on her return. A time in the trenches does not make bad men good; soldiers 'are very ordinary people, with an unfortunate weakness for getting drunk, and an inability to say "No" to a pretty girl.'[12] But among all these conflicting impressions there are two which in her case grow ever stronger – the love of poetry and the love of England. The poetry is the poetry of today, and England is the English country, the Cambridge country – 'the slow, quiet river … the old Roman highway … the yellow cornfields, the pleasant green meadows'.[13]

1 – A review in the TLS, 10 May 1917, (Kp C74) of From Cambridge to Camiers

Under the Red Cross (W. Heffer & Sons Ltd., 1917) by E. M. Spearing (Mrs Evelyn Mary Simpson, 1885–1963), associate and late Fellow of Newnham College, Cambridge. V.A.D. – Voluntary Aid Detachment, a nursing service auxiliary to the armed forces. (See *I VW Diary*, Saturday, 23 January 1915: 'Jean [Thomas] asked us to go & hear some V.A.D.'s sing; but the fire after tea was too tempting'.)

2 – Spearing, Pref., p. vii.

3 – *Ibid.*

4 – *Ibid.*, 'Winter in a Camp Hospital in France', p. 26.

5 – *Ibid.*, p. 27.

6 – *Ibid.*, 'The Aftermath of the Big Push (July, 1916)', p. 62.

7 – *Ibid.*, 'Songs in the Night', p. 79, slightly adapted.

8 – *Ibid.*, p. 75, which has: 'Moreover, we all live very much for the day and let the morrow take care of itself'.

9 – *Ibid.*, p. 75: 'Not that war may not, in many cases, have given men a new sense of underlying reality, and a deep steadiness of purpose. But on the surface, at any rate, the reaction from the strain of the trenches shows itself often in bursts of high spirits and a desire to make plenty of noise.'

10 – *Ibid.*, 'The Aftermath of the Big Push (July, 1916)', p. 59.

11 – *Ibid.*

12 – *Ibid.*, 'Cambridge Again', p. 80: '"Our demigods in the trenches," as I see one journalist calls them, know perfectly well that in ordinary circumstance they are very ordinary people . . .'

13 – *Ibid.*, pp. 83–4.

The Perfect Language

To those who count themselves lovers of Greek in the sense that some ragged beggar might count himself the lover of an Empress in her robes, the Loeb Library,[2] with its Greek or Latin on one side of the page and its English on the other, came as a gift of freedom to a very obscure but not altogether undeserving class. The existence of the amateur was recognised by the publication of this Library, and to a great extent made respectable. He was given the means of being an open and unabashed amateur, and made to feel that no one pointed the finger of scorn at him on that account; and in consequence, instead of exercising his moribund faculties almost furtively upon some chance quotation met in an English book, he could read a whole play at a time, with his feet on the fender. With such treatment, too, his little stock of Greek became improved, and occasionally he would be rewarded with one of those moments of instant understanding which are the flower of reading. In them we seem not to read so much as to recollect what we have heard in some other life.

Of course, no translation, as Mr Paton[3] would probably be the first to agree, is going to reproduce the bloom and scent, the natural poise and sequence, all that we feel before we understand the meaning, of the original words. No one is going to translate —

> O Proserpina,
> For the flowers now, that frighted thou let'st fall
> From Dis's waggon![4]

It is necessary perhaps to be English to understand that. But there are other qualities which can be rendered. A spirited version will give the movement and the form of a play so that a thousand suggestions can be received by a mind unable to grasp a fraction of them when weighed down with the labour of translation. It is important to read quickly, if only because the friction of speed creates in the reader the arrogant and, in this case, scarcely warrantable belief that he knows precisely what Aeschylus meant, that the misunderstood Aeschylus reserved a peculiar meaning for him, that he is for the first time building up a perfectly original figure of the poet. Without this conviction the reading of the classics is apt to become insipid, and the burden of other people's views a weight too heavy to be borne. But, once fired with the spirit of the partisan, it is wonderful what hardships no longer repel us, and how little respect is paid to the authority of the great. It is true that humiliation has generally to be faced at the end of these outbursts of zeal, for the reason that Greek is an immensely difficult language. A great deal of knowledge is essential for the moderate understanding of it, and not easy to come by. How many people in England can read Homer as accurately as a child of eight can read the morning paper? for example; and the few who read Sophocles perfectly are about as singular as acrobats flying through space from bar to bar.

To our thinking the difficulty of Greek is not sufficiently dwelt upon, chiefly perhaps because the sirens who lure us to these perilous waters are generally scholars of European reputation. They have forgotten, or never knew, or for reasons of their own choose to belittle, what those difficulties are. But for the ordinary amateur they are very real and very great; and we shall do well to recognise the fact and to make up our minds that we shall never be independent of our Loeb. And the more we own the difficulty, and confess the sense of unrewarded effort, the consciousness of pygmy understanding, the more we must testify to the miracle of the language. It will not let us go. It will not agree to be a respectable branch of learning which we are well content to admire in the possession of others. A branch of learning suggests a withered stick with a few dead leaves attached to it. But Greek is the golden bough; it crowns its lovers with garlands of fresh and sparkling leaves. We have only to open this volume of the anthology at haphazard to fall once more beneath the spell:

I Brotachos, a Gortynian of Crete, lie here, where I came not for this end, but to trade.[5]

The serene, restrained, and penetrating sound of that detaches itself at once from all others, even in the English version. What is added to it by the Greek words it is impossible to define. To appreciate them fully one would have, no doubt, to be born a Greek. But we are not aware of any affectation when we say that once having read them we know, even with our imperfect understanding, that there is a beauty in the Greek language which is unlike and beyond any that we have met elsewhere. Let us turn the page and read:

I am the tomb of a shipwrecked man; but set sail, stranger; for when we were lost other ships voyaged on.[6]

or,

If to die will be the chief part of virtue, Fortune granted this to us above all others; for striving to endue Hellas with freedom, we lie here possessed of praise that groweth not old.[7]

or,

Tears, the last gift of my love, even down through the earth I send to thee in Hades, Heliodora . . .[8]

Here we have the peculiar magic, the lure that will lead us from youth to age, groping through our island fogs and barbarities towards that unattainable perfection. But perfection has a chill sound. It scarcely seems the right word for that extremely individual and definite spirit which is the flame of the Greek character. No one can read the few lines quoted above without feeling not only their extreme beauty, but also their extreme unlikeness to anything in any other language. It is an unlikeness that perpetually rouses our curiosity about them. These lines, in the first place, seem to be written neither in the infancy nor in the old age of the world, but in its maturity. There is no prettiness as there is no mysticism in them. We hear the voice of men whose outlook on life was perfectly direct and unclouded. There is, of course, that virtue of restraint so often praised in the Greeks that we tend to forget that it is most of all a virtue when, as in the present case, there is much to restrain. And although the present volume of the anthology is devoted to epigrams upon the dead, it is evident that this people had everything to restrain, a love of man or woman, a love of earth, a love of life itself more passionate, it seems, than ours. Nevertheless they are able to dismiss life with stoical clearness of sight, and of all their grief allow only one cry to escape them.

The difference between them and ourselves is made very clear in these epigrams where feelings of such depth and scope are concentrated into so small a space. They have to do with individual men and women; and we see, as in a vignette, a little view of the house, of the daily work, of the country outside the door. We can see the sharp lines of the mountains, the changing colour of the sea, the little vines stooping with grapes, and hear the harsh song of the crickets. It is the South, but it is not Italy. It is life, but it is not our life. When we attempt to visualise the Greek world we see it standing in outline against the sky without crowd or detail. One is inclined to think of their literature, too, as a succession of complete and perfect utterances; for (to the amateur at least) there are no schools in Greek literature, or imitations, no bad shots at great things which tend to blur the outline of the masterpiece when it is achieved. For us at least no chance saying in Greek, or association of words, opens up a view of irrelevant vulgarity such as it is well nigh impossible to exclude from the pages of those who write in a living tongue. On the contrary, we feel that if by chance the veil lifts in their writing it is to reveal something beautiful, something strong and sincere.

But we doubt whether it is right to use our English word beauty so perpetually when we speak of the Greeks, for they do not seem to have our conception of beauty, or of its rarity or of its value. Another power seems to be theirs – the power of gazing with absolute candour upon the truth of things, and beauty seems to come of its own accord, not as an ornament to be applied separately but as an essential part of the world as it appears to them. Theirs is a beauty of the whole rather than of parts; and although it would be possible, no doubt, to make a book of the beauties of their poets, we should miss much more by this treatment of them than we should if it were applied to our own Elizabethans. Among the epigrams of the anthology there are many examples of this flawless quality; save among the latest it would be hard to find one without a trace of it. It is a quality which has the likeness of impersonality were it not for that inflection of the voice with which they charge their words with all the sorrow, the passion, or the joy that words can say, or, more marvellously still, leave unsaid.

Now the white violet blooms, and blooms the moist narcissus, and bloom the wandering mountain lilies; and now, dear to her lovers, spring flower among the flowers, Zenophile, the sweet rose of Persuasion, has burst into bloom. Meadows, why·idly laugh in the brightness of your tresses? For my girl is better than garlands sweet to smell.[9]

The beauty of that seems to us incomparable and yet it is only a reflection of the beauty of the Greek.

But we could go on multiplying quotations and seeking and persuading ourselves that we find new reasons for our love of them indefinitely. For the truth is that, even to an amateur, Greek literature is not so much literature as the type of literature, the supreme example of what can be done with words. Even to him the words have their strong and unmistakable accent. Other words of other languages may come nearer to us, but what in Latin or English has this stamp of finality, what in any other literature so convinces us that the perfect form of human utterance has been found once and for all? Found easily, as we feel, almost unconsciously, such was the genius of the race for expression. And, although it seems ungracious to add this when we have owned so much indebtedness to translators, some knowledge of the language is a possession not to be done without. With the best will in the world the translators are bound to stamp their individuality or that of their age upon the text. Our minds are so full of echoes that a single word such as 'aweary'[10] will flood a whole page for an English reader with the wrong associations. And such is the power of the Greek language that to know even a little of it is to know that there is nothing more beautiful in the world.

1 – A review in the *TLS*, 24 May 1917, (Kp C75) of *The Greek Anthology*. With an English translation by W. R. Paton, vol. ii. The Loeb Classical Library (Heinemann, 1917). VW set immense store by Greek, which she saw as not only 'the perfect language' but also the privileged preserve of the educated male. Several of her friends were classical scholars, as indeed was LW. She began her own study of the language attending classes at King's College, London, in 1897, and took private lessons from Dr Warre, in 1898, and from Janet Case in 1902. See also 'On Not Knowing Greek', *IV VW Essays*, and *CR1*; and see *Jacob's Room* (1922), *passim*.

2 – Founded and endowed by James Loeb (1867–1933), American banker and philanthropist.

3 – William Roger Paton (d. 1921), classical scholar and archaeologist, educated at Eton and University College, Oxford, where he graduated in 1879.

4 – Shakespeare, *The Winter's Tale*, iv, 4, ll. 117–19.

5 – Paton, bk vii, no. 254A, by Simonides, p. 143, complete.

6 – *Ibid.*, no. 282, by Theodoridas, p. 155, complete.

7 – *Ibid.*, no. 253, by Simonides, p. 141, complete.

8 – *Ibid.*, no. 476, by Meleager, p. 259, which continues: '– tears ill to shed, and on thy much-wept tomb I pour them in memory of longing, in memory of affection. Piteously, piteously doth Meleager lament for thee who art still dear to him in death, paying a vain tribute to Acheron. Alas! Alas! Where is my beautiful one, my heart's desire? Death has taken her, has taken her, and the flower in full bloom is defiled by the dust. But Earth my mother, nurturer of all, I beseech thee, clasp her gently to thy bosom, her whom all bewail.'

9 – J. W. Mackail, *Select Epigrams from the Greek Anthology* (Longman's, Green & Co., 1890), no. xix, by Meleager, which has: 'mountain-wandering lilies'. VW possessed a 1907 edition of Mackail, probably the gift of Saxon Sydney-Turner, to which she alluded in a letter to Sydney-Turner on 31 December 1916 (*II VW Letters*, no. 813), announcing: 'Now I am going to read the Greek Anthology (in a copy you gave me once) which I find very hard and quite absorbing', and at its close, in Greek, quoted Meleager's epigram.

10 – E.g. Mackail, no. lxvii by Asclepiades, p. 117: 'I am not two and twenty yet, and I am aweary of living; O Loves, why misuse me so? why set me on fire; for when I am gone, what will you do? Doubtless, O Loves, as before you will play with your dice, unheeding.'

Mr Sassoon's Poems

As it is the poet's gift to give expression to the moments of insight or experience that come to him now and then, so in following him we have to sketch for ourselves a map of those submerged lands which lie between one pinnacle and the next. If he is a true poet, at least we fill up in thought the space between one poem and another with speculations that are half guesses and half anticipations of what is to come next. He offers us a new vision of the world; how is the light about to fall? What ranges, what horizons will it reveal? At least if he is a sincere artist this is so, and to us Mr Sassoon seems undoubtedly sincere. He is a poet, we believe, meaning by that that we cannot fancy him putting down these thoughts in any form save the one he has chosen. His vision comes to him directly; he seems almost always, before he began to get his words into order, to have had one of those puzzling shocks of emotion which the world deals by such incongruous methods, to the poet often, to the rest of us too seldom for our souls' good. It follows that this one slim volume is full of incongruities; but the moments of vision are interesting enough to make us wish to follow them up very carefully.

There are the poems about the war, to begin with. If you chance to read one of them by itself you may be inclined to think that it is a very clever poem, chiefly designed with its realism and its surface cynicism to shock the prosperous and sentimental. Naturally the critical senses rise in alarm to protect their owner from such insinuations. But read them, continuously, read in particular 'The Hero' and 'The Tomb-Stone Maker', and you will drop the idea of being shocked in that sense altogether.

> 'Jack fell as he'd have wished,' the Mother said,
> And folded up the letter that she'd read.
> 'The Colonel writes so nicely.' Something broke
> In the tired voice that quavered to a choke.
> She half looked up. 'We mothers are so proud
> 'Of our dead soldiers.' Then her face was bowed.
>
> Quietly the Brother Officer went out . . .
>
> He thought how 'Jack', cold-footed, useless swine,
> Had panicked down the trench that night the mine
> Went up at Wicked Corner; how he'd tried
> To get sent home; and how at last he died,
> Blown to small bits. And no one seemed to care
> Except that lonely woman with white hair.[2]

What Mr Sassoon has felt to be the most sordid and horrible experiences in the world he makes us feel to be so in a measure which no other poet of the war has achieved. As these jaunty matter-of-fact statements succeed each other such loathing, such hatred accumulates behind them that we say to ourselves, 'Yes, this is going on; and we are sitting here watching it,' with a new shock of surprise, with an uneasy desire to leave our place in the audience, which is a tribute to Mr Sassoon's power as a realist. It is realism of the right, of the poetic kind. The real things are put in not merely because they are real, but because at a certain moment of emotion the poet happened to be struck by them and is not afraid of spoiling his effect by calling them by their right

names. The wounded soldier looking out of the train window sees the
English country again –

> There shines the blue serene, the prosperous land,
> Trees, cows, and hedges; skipping these, he scanned
> Large friendly names that change not with the year,
> Lung Tonic, Mustard, Liver Pills, and Beer.[3]

To call back any moment of emotion is to call back with it the strangest
odds and ends that have become somehow part of it, and it is the weeds
pulled up by mistake with the flowers that bring back the extraordinary
moment as a whole. With this straight, courageous method Mr Sassoon
can produce such a solid and in its way beautiful catalogue of facts as
that of the train leaving the station – 'The Morning Express'.

But we might hazard the guess that the war broke in and called out this
vein of realism before its season; for side by side with these pieces there
are others very different, not so effective perhaps, not particularly
accomplished, but full of a rarer kind of interest, full of promise for the
future. For the beauty in them, though fitful, is of the individual,
indefinable kind which comes, we know not how, to make lines such as
we read over each time with a renewed delight that after one comes the
other.

> Where have you been, South Wind, this May-day morning,
> With larks aloft, or skimming with the swallow,
> Or with blackbirds in a green, sun-glinted thicket?
>
> Oh, I heard you like a tyrant in the valley;
> Your ruffian haste shook the young, blossoming orchards;
> You clapped rude hands, hallooing round the chimney,
> And white your pennons streamed along the river.
>
> You have robbed the bee, South Wind, in your adventure,
> Blustering with gentle flowers; but I forgave you
> When you stole to me shyly with scent of hawthorn.[4]

Here we have evidence not of accomplishment, indeed, but of a gift
much more valuable than that, the gift of being a poet, we must call it;
and we shall look with interest to see what Mr Sassoon does with his gift.

1 – A review in the TLS, 31 May 1917, (Kp c76) of *The Old Huntsman and Other
Poems* (Heinemann, 1917) by Siegfried Sassoon (1886–1967), by this date a captain
in the Royal Welch Fusiliers. Sassoon had been injured in April 1917. He was
currently convalescing in England and, while doing so, protesting, through the press
and through parliament, at what he saw to be the deliberate prolongation of the war.

In August, declared by the under-secretary for war to be suffering from shell shock, he would be sent to Craiglockhart War Hospital, near Edinburgh, there to meet the young poet Wilfred Owen, who died in action on 4 November 1918.

A letter from Sassoon, which does not survive, expressing his appreciation of the review, was forwarded to VW by Lady Ottoline Morrell, to whom VW wrote on 5 June: 'I am so glad he liked the review. I've reviewed so little poetry that I was rather nervous, and I liked his poems very much.' (*II VW Letters*, no. 839; and see no. 860). See also 'Two Soldier Poets' below. Reprinted: *B&P*.

2 – Sassoon, 'The Hero', p. 48, the first stanza, the first line of the second stanza, and the whole of the final stanza.

3 – *Ibid.*, 'Stretcher Case' '[To Edward Marsh]', p. 50, which has: 'There shone the blue serene'; and 'Large, friendly'.

4 – *Ibid.*, 'South Wind', p. 87, the entire poem.

'Creative Criticism'

Mr Spingarn has some hard things to say of American criticism, of its dependence on the decayed and genteel tradition of Victorian England, of its 'hopeless chaos in the face of new realities of art',[2] which we admit that we have sometimes wished to say for ourselves, but they come with greater force and grace from the lips of an American. He demolishes more decayed and genteel traditions than the Victorians can justly be taxed with; and in the face of new realities his enthusiasm is so keen and clear-sighted that we wish that he would give us a few examples of the art besides this spirited defence of it. We wish indeed that he had written a longer book; for the subjects he deals with are very complex, and many of the interesting things that he says would be still more interesting if they were discussed more fully.

Mr Spingarn's chief object is to confute those people who still hold that the critic is an inferior being, and his art a base one. He sets out to show that his opinion is founded upon a misconception of the power that 'poets and critics share together';[3] for whatever the power is, he asserts that 'in their most significant moments the creative and the critical instinct are one and the same'.[4] This conception of the nature of criticism is of very modern date. It depends upon the assumption that the task of the critic is to ask himself – 'What has the poet tried to express and how has he expressed it?'[5] As Mr Spingarn shows, in a very interesting and suggestive summary of the history of criticism, this question was never asked with any unanimity until we come to the nineteenth century, and in particular to Coleridge, Carlyle, and Sainte-Beuve.[6] Horace asked whether there were more than three actors on the stage, or more than five acts in the drama; Dr Johnson whether the poet numbered 'the streaks of the tulip';[7] innumerable critics of less importance applied yet more arbitrary tests before they tied on the right label – epic, pastoral, tragedy, comedy as the case might be. It was little wonder that the critic and his art fell into disrepute, for the first act of any vigorous writer was to break all the laws and tear up all the labels. Nowadays, thanks to Sainte-Beuve and others, the conception of criticism has changed; we try to enter into the mind of the writer, to see each work of art by itself, and to judge how far each artist has succeeded in his aim. We do not think that our work is done when we have taken his measure by a standard roughly adapted to fit that particular class.

The important change of course, as we think that Mr Spingarn is right in saying, was the change which led critics to conceive of literature as an art of expression. A great deal might be said about this view of art, and about the statement that 'art has performed its function when it has expressed itself'.[8] But if you hold that view a great many questions that used to be taken into account have to be thrown overboard. Mr Spingarn makes a long and a bold list of them. In his phrase we have 'done with'[9] the old rules; we have done with the *genres*; we have done with technique as separate from art; we have done with the history and criticism of poetic themes; we have done with the race, the time, the environment of the poet; we have done with all moral judgment of literature; we have done with the 'evolution'[10] of literature. None of these questions, though each is interesting in itself, has anything to do with the value of a work of art. Possibly this may be so, although we cannot help thinking that of two poems the one with a higher morality is better aesthetically than the one with a lower morality. The critic then is confronted by the work of art in itself. He has to reproduce in his own mind the 'essence of unmixed reality',[11] if we like to call it so, and to say how completely it has been expressed. In order to do this, says Mr Springarn, 'aesthetic judgment becomes nothing more or less than creative art itself'.[12] That any writer capable of this feat is deserving of the highest praise is indisputable; but that his genius is of the same order as that of the poet we are not so certain. For criticism is not merely the re-creation of a work of art; the process of re-creation gone through by the critic is very different from the process which created the original work.

Criticism is largely the interpretation of art, and it is difficult to see how a work which contains the element of interpretation can be a work of art in the sense in which a poem is a work of art. There is a difference not of degree but of kind between Coleridge's *Lectures on Shakespeare* and the *Ancient Mariner*.[13] It does not seem possible to say of critical work, as it is possible to say of poetical work, that 'beauty is its own excuse for being'.[14] But to decide the exact amount of the difference, or the relative value of the two gifts, supposing them to be distinct, is not of great importance, even were it possible to do so. On the other hand, it is of very great importance to open the mind as widely as possible to see what each writer is trying to do, and in interpreting him only to frame rules which spring directly from our impression of the work itself.

For how in criticism are we to go altogether without 'rules'? Is not the decision to do so merely another rule? Although to feel is of the first importance, to know why one feels is of great importance too. There can be no doubt, however, that to be free to make one's own laws and to be alert to do it afresh for every newcomer is an essential part of any criticism worth having. And that criticism is worth having Mr Spingarn has proved conclusively; in another essay he might go on to tell us the reason why.

1 – A review in the *TLS*, 7 June 1917, (Kp C77) of *Creative Criticism: Essays on the Unity of Genius and Taste* (Henry Holt & Co., 1917) by J. E. [Joel Elias] Spingarn (1875–1939), professor of comparative literature at Columbia University, 1899–1911, author of *A History of Literary Criticism in the Renaissance* (1899) and *The New Criticism* (1911). From 1919 to 1932 Spingarn was a member of the publishing firm Harcourt, Brace and Company, VW's American publisher. A revised edition of *Creative Criticism* appeared in 1931.

2 – Spingarn, 'Prose and Verse', p. 99.

3 – *Ibid.*, 'The New Criticism', p. 4.

4 – *Ibid.*, pp. 42–3.

5 – *Ibid.*, p. 42.

6 – S. T. Coleridge (1772–1834); Thomas Carlyle (1795–1881); Charles Augustin Sainte-Beuve (1804–69).

7 – Spingarn, 'The New Criticism', p. 21, quoting Dr Johnson (1709–84), *The History of Rasselas, Prince of Abyssinia* (1759), ch. x (ed. D. J. Enright, Penguin, 1976, pp. 61–2): 'The business of a poet, said Imlac, is to examine, not the individual, but the species; to remark general properties and large appearances: he does not number the streaks of the tulip, or describe the different shades in the verdure of the forest.'

8 – *Ibid.*, p. 20: 'It was they [the Germans] who first realised that art has performed ...; it was they who first conceived of criticism as the study of expression.'

9 – *Ibid.*, p. 24.
10 – *Ibid.*, p. 40.
11 – *Ibid.*, p. 19.
12 – *Ibid.*, p. 42.
13 – S. T. Coleridge, *Notes and Lectures upon Shakespeare* ... (1849), most of which were first published in *Literary Remains* (1836–8); the lectures were originally given in 1810–11. *The Ancient Mariner* (1798).
14 – Spingarn, 'The New Criticism', p. 32.

'South Wind'

We have no quarrel with the shape or size or colour of this novel; but we believe that if, instead of being a brown, plump, freshly printed volume, it were slim, a little yellow, the date about 1818, the cover of a faded green, marked, perhaps, with the rim of an ancient tea cup – if, in short, it resembled the first edition of *Nightmare Abbey* or *Crotchet Castle*[2] – there would be people willing to sift the old bookstalls in search of it, to pay a sovereign for it: people fond of taking it from the shelf and reading their favourite passages aloud, and apt to remark, when they put it back again, 'What a pity it is that novelists don't write like this nowadays!' They very seldom do write like this. But when the reader, a few pages deep and beginning to feel settled in the new atmosphere, collects himself, his first comment is likely to be that it is a very strange thing that no one has thought of writing this book before Mr Douglas. The comment is a compliment, although there is a trace of annoyance in it. It signifies that the idea is one of those fresh and fruitful ideas that have been sailing just out of range on the horizon of our minds and now have been brought to shore and all their merchandise unladen by another.

Take all the interesting and eccentric people you can think of, put them on an island in the Mediterranean beyond the realms of humdrum but not in those of fantasy: bid them say shamelessly whatever comes into their heads: let them range over every topic and bring forth whatever fancy, fact, or prejudice happens to occur to them: add, whenever the wish moves you, dissertations upon medieval dukes, Christianity, cookery, education, fountains, Greek art, millionaires, morality, the sexes: enclose the whole in an exquisite atmosphere of pumice rocks and deep blue waves, air with the warm and stimulating breath of the South Wind – the prescription begins something in this way. But we have left out the most important element of all. We are at a loss to define the quality of the author's mind, his way of presenting these men and women, of turning his ideas. We glance at Peacock, and then, for a second, at Oscar Wilde.[3] Peacock is superbly eccentric and opinionated; Wilde is persuasive and lucid. Mr Douglas possesses these qualities, but they are his own. His book has a distinguished ancestry, but it was born only the day before yesterday. So individual is the character of his mind that as we read we frequently congratulate him upon having found the right form for a gift that must have been hard to suit. As frequently we congratulate ourselves on the fact that the whole affair is turning out so surprisingly and delightfully successful.

Upon the Island of Nepenthe, then, 'an islet of volcanic stone rising out of the blue Mediterranean',[4] are congregated for various reasons a great many people of marked idiosyncrasy – Mr Keith, Mr Eames, Miss Wilberforce, Mr and Mrs Parker, Count Caloveglia, Mme Steynlin, Mr Denis, and the Duchess of San Martino, to name only the most prominent. The Bishop of Bampopo, Mr Heard, alights here for a short stay on his way home from episcopal duties in the Equatorial Regions. He is introduced to them all one after another. We scarcely venture to attempt any summary of their characters or of their conversation. We may say, however, that Mr Eames was engaged in annotating Perrelli's *Antiquities*. But 'it is not true to say that he fled from England to Nepenthe because he forged his mother's will, because he was arrested while picking the pockets of a lady at Tottenham Court Road station, because he refused to pay for the upkeep of his seven illegitimate children'.[5] None of this is true at all. He once had a love affair, which left him chronically sensitive on the subject of balloons. But Mr Eames was the reverse of Mr Keith. Mr Keith collected information for its own sake. 'He could tell you how many public baths existed in Geneva in pre-Reformation days, what was the colour of Mehemet Ali's whiskers, why the manuscript of Virgil's friend Gallius had not been handed down to posterity, and in what year and what month the decimal system was introduced into Finland.'[6] His was a complex character; he held marked and peculiar views upon the origin of our English spleen; he was an epicure; and, 'chaster than snow as a conversationalist, he prostituted his mother tongue in letter-writing to the vilest of uses'. We are not surprised on the whole that 'friends of long standing called him an obscene old man'.[7] Of Mrs Parker we need only say that she treasured and displayed in her drawing room a piece of fine blue material fished from the floating *débris* of a millionaire's yacht, from which she deduced and expressed certain opinions as to the habits of travelling millionaires. Of the millionaire himself, what can be said? The Malthusian philosophy had no more distinguished supporter, and the part he played when in the opinion of the island it became necessary to protect Miss Wilberforce from herself was much to his credit. This poor lady, of unblemished descent and connections, having lost her lover at sea had taken to the bottle and given way to noctambulous habits, when she was liable to divest herself of her raiment. The Duchess, it is true, was not a duchess at all, but as she talked and behaved like one the right was conceded her. Mme Steynlin, on the other hand, 'cared little what frocks she wore so long as somebody loved her'.[8] The reader must imagine how they talked, and how one of them was induced incidentally to slip over the edge of a precipice.

But as we have left out all mention of the Alpha and Omega Club, of Buddha and the Little White Cows, together with innumerable other interesting and delightful facts, we must cease to summarise. Indeed, a summary of their conduct and conversation is too likely to give the impression that the characters are merely a gallery of whimsical grotesques, mouthpieces for the brilliant and well-informed mind of their author. That is far from the truth. There are an astonishing number of things that never get into novels at all and yet are of the salt of life; and the achievement of *South Wind* is that is has arrested a great number of these things and proved once more what a narrow convention the novelist is wont to impose on us. Meanwhile, although the hot season has dispersed the original party, Mr Keith is still in residence; Mr Roger Rumbold, the advocate of Infanticide for the Masses, and Mr Bernard, author of *The Courtship of Cockroaches,* have lately arrived. How often in the coming months will our thoughts seek relief if not repose in the Island of Nepenthe, and with what eagerness shall we await a further and even fuller report of its history!

1 – A review in the *TLS*, 14 June 1917, (Kp C78) of *South Wind* (Martin Secker, 1917) by Norman Douglas (1868–1952). Reprinted: *CW*.
2 – *Nightmare Abbey* (1818) and *Crotchet Castle* (1831) by Thomas Love Peacock (1785–1866).
3 – Oscar Wilde (1854–1900).
4 – Douglas, ch. 16, p. 193.
5 – *Ibid.*, ch. 3, p. 33, part of a longer sentence, which begins: 'It was not true to say'.
6 – *Ibid.*, ch. 9, pp. 120–1.

7 – For this and the preceding quotation, *ibid.*, p. 121; each is a complete sentence in the original.
8 – *Ibid.*, ch. 6, p. 72.

'Books and Persons'

There are two kinds of criticism – the written and the spoken. The first, when it gets into print, is said to be the cause of much suffering to those whom it concerns; but the second, we are inclined to think, is the only form of criticism that should make an author wince. This is the criticism which is expressed when, upon finishing a book, you toss it into the next armchair with an exclamation of horror or delight, adding a few phrases by way of comment, which lack polish and ignore grammar but contain the criticism which an author should strain all his forces to overhear. If criticism can ever help, he will be helped; if it can ever please, he will be enraptured; the pain, even, is salutary, for it will be severe enough either to kill or to reform. One or two writers there are who can put this criticism into prose; but for the most part the adjectives, the grammar, the logic, the inkpot – to say nothing of humanity and good manners – all conspire to take the dash and sincerity out of it, and by the time speech becomes a review there is nothing left but grammatical English.

Mr Arnold Bennett is one of the few who can catch their sayings before they are cold and enclose them all alive in very readable prose. That is why these aged reviews (some are nearly ten years old) are as vivacious and as much to the point as they were on the day of their birth. They have another claim upon our interest. They deal for the most part with writers who are still living, whose position is still an open question, about whom we feel more and probably know more than we can with honesty profess to do about those dead and acknowledged masters who are commonly the theme of our serious critics. At the time when Mr Bennett was Jacob Tonson of the *New Age*,[2] Mr Galsworthy, Mr Montague, Mrs Elinor Glyn, Mr W. H. Hudson, Mr John Masefield, Mr Conrad, Mr E. M. Forster, Mr Wells and Mrs Humphry Ward[3] were not exactly in the positions which they occupy today. The voice of Jacob Tonson had something to do with the mysterious process of settling them where, as we think, they will ultimately dwell. It is true that we are not going to rank any book of Mr Galsworthy's with *Crime and*

Punishment,[4] and we dissent a little from the generosity of the praise bestowed upon the novels of Mr Wells. But these are details compared with the far more important question of Mr Bennett's point of view. We have said that his is spoken criticism; but we hasten to add that it is not at all what we are accustomed to hear spoken at dinner tables and in drawing rooms. It is the talk of a writer in his workroom, in his shirt sleeves. It is the talk, as Mr Bennett is proud to insist, of a creative artist. 'I am not myself a good theoriser about art,'[5] he says. 'I . . . speak as a creative artist, and not as a critic.'[6] The creative artist, he remarks, on another occasion, produces 'the finest, and the only first-rate criticism'.[7]

We do not think that this is a book of first-rate criticism; but it is the book of an artist. Nobody could read one of these short little papers without feeling himself in the presence of the father of fifty volumes.[8] The man who speaks knows all that there is to be known about the making of books. He remembers that a tremendous amount of work has gone to the making of them; he is versed in every side of the profession – agents and publishers, good seasons and bad seasons, the size of editions and the size of royalties, he knows it all – he loves it all. He never affects to despise the business side of the profession of writing. He will talk of high-class stuff,[9] thinks that authors are quite right in getting every cent they can for it, and will remark that it is the business of a competent artist to please, if not *the*, certainly *a*, public. But it is not in this sense only that he is far more professional than the English writer is apt to be or to appear; he is professional in his demand that a novel shall be made absolutely seaworthy and well constructed. If he hates one sin more than another it is the sin of 'intellectual sluggishness'.[10] This is not the attitude nor are these the words of 'mandarins' or 'dilettanti'[11] – the professors and the cultivated people whom Mr Bennett hates much as the carpenter hates the amateur who does a little fretwork.

London swarms with the dilettanti of letters. They do not belong to the criminal classes, but their good intentions, their culture, their judiciousness, and their infernal cheek amount perhaps to worse than arson or assault . . . They shine at tea, at dinner, and after dinner. They talk more easily than ⟨the artist⟩ does, and write more easily too. They can express themselves more readily. And they know such a deuce of a lot.[12]

Whether we agree or disagree we are reminded by this healthy outburst of rage that the critic has not merely to deal out skilfully measured doses of praise and blame to individuals, but to keep the atmosphere in a right state for the production of works of art. The atmosphere, even seven years ago, was in a state so strange that it appears almost fantastic now. Canon Lambert was then saying, 'I would just as soon send a daughter of mine to a house infected with diphtheria or typhoid fever as'[13] let her read *Ann Veronica*. About the same time Dr Barry remarked, 'I never leave my house . . . but I am forced to see, and solicited to buy, works flamingly advertised of which the gospel is adultery and the apocalypse the right of suicide.'[14] We must be very grateful to Mr Bennett for the pertinacity with which he went on saying in such circumstances 'that the first business of a work of art is to be beautiful, and its second not to be sentimental'.[15]

But if we were asked to give a proof that Mr Bennett is something more than the extremely competent, successful, businesslike producer of literature, we would point to the paper on 'Neo-Impressionism and Literature'.[16] These new pictures, he says, have wearied him of other pictures; is it not possible that some writer will come along and do in words what these men have done in paint? And suppose that happens, and Mr Bennett has to admit that he has been concerning himself unduly with inessentials, that he has been worrying himself to achieve infantile realisms? He will admit it, we are sure; and that he can ask himself such a question seems to us certain proof that he is what he claims to be – a 'creative artist'.[17]

1 – A review in the *TLS*, 5 July 1917, (Kp C79) of *Books and Persons. Being comments on a past epoch 1908–1911* (Chatto & Windus, 1917) by Arnold Bennett (1867–1931) whose 'comments' were originally published in the *New Age*, under the pseudonym Jacob Tonson.

In dealing as it does with Bennett's article 'Neo-Impressionism and Literature', VW's review anticipates amicably the more heated controversy she was to pursue in 'Character in Fiction' ('Mr Bennett and Mrs Brown'), *III VW Essays*, in which volume see also the first of the two articles VW entitled 'Mr Bennett and Mrs Brown'.

The present review appeared in the same month as that in which VW published her experimental story 'The Mark on the Wall' and, probably, shortly before she began to write *Kew Gardens* (1919). Reprinted: *CW*.

2 – Edited by A. L. Orage, 1907–22.

3 – By the end of Bennett's period of activity as Jacob Tonson, in 1911, John Galsworthy (1867–1933) was chiefly known as the author of *The Man of Property* (1906) – discussed by Bennett in the *New Age*, 14 July 1910 (Bennett, pp. 214–16) – *The Country House* (1907), *Fraternity* (1909), *The Patrician* (1911), and the plays, *The Silver Box* and *Strife*, both produced in 1909. VW was shortly to review Galsworthy's *Beyond* (1917): see 'Mr Galsworthy's Novel' below.

C. E. Montague (1867–1928), author, dramatic critic, and journalist with the

Manchester Guardian, 1890–1914, 1919–25. Bennett reviewed Montague's first novel *A Hind Let Loose* (1910) in the *New Age*, 10 March 1910 (Bennett, pp. 201–3). Montague published a volume of criticism, *Dramatic Values* in 1911, and a second novel *The Morning's War* in 1913. After the 1914–18 War he made himself quite a different reputation as the author of anti-militaristic essays and fiction.

Elinor Glyn (1864–1943) wrote popular 'society' novels, one of which, *His Hour* (1910), Bennett reviewed in the *New Age*, 10 November 1910 (Bennett, pp. 271–7).

By 1911, W. H. Hudson (1841–1922) had published most of the works for which he is now known, including *The Purple Land* (1885), *Green Mansions* (1904) and *A Shepherd's Life* (1910), which was discussed by Bennett in the *New Age*, 24 November 1910 (Bennett, pp. 278–9). Hudson's autobiographical masterpiece *Far Away and Long Ago* appeared in 1918; for VW's review of it, see 'Mr Hudson's Childhood' below.

John Masefield (1878–1967) had published *Salt-Water Ballads* (1909), *Ballads and Poems* (1910), several collections of short stories, essays, plays, and a number of novels, including *The Street of To-day* (1911), on which Bennett wrote in the *New Age*, 20 April 1911 (Bennett, pp. 311–14).

Joseph Conrad (1857–1924) had published most of his major works by 1911. Bennett made several references to him in his *New Age* articles and wrote about him specifically, and his treatment at the hands of the *Athenaeum*, in the *New Age*, 19 September 1908 (Bennett, pp. 36–40).

E. M. Forster (1879–1970) had published *Howards End* in 1910 and this was discussed by Bennett in the *New Age*, 12 January 1911 (Bennett, pp. 292–3).

H. G. Wells (1866–1946) had also published most of his major works by 1911. Bennett frequently referred to Wells in his *New Age* column; he discussed his work in general in the issue for 4 March 1909 (Bennett, pp. 109–16), and his *The New Machiavelli* (1911), in that for 2 February 1911 (Bennett, pp. 294–9).

Mrs Humphry Ward (1851–1920) was the author of a great many popular novels, including *Robert Elsmere* (1888), *Eleanor* (1900), *Lady Rose's Daughter* (1903) and *The Testing of Diana Mallory* (1908). Bennett wrote about her heroines in the *New Age*, 3 October 1908 (Bennett, pp. 47–52).

4 – Bennett, 'John Galsworthy', p. 216; Fyodor Dostoevsky, *Crime and Punishment* (1866).

5 – *Ibid.*, 'Neo-Impressionism and Literature', p. 283 (*New Age*, 8 December 1910).

6 – *Ibid.*, 'W. W. Jacobs and Aristophanes', p. 56 (*New Age*, 24 October 1908); William Wymark Jacobs (1863–1943) was the author of several collections of stories.

7 – *Ibid.*, 'Artists and Critics', p. 158 (*New Age*, 21 October 1909).

8 – *Books and Persons* was Bennett's fifty-third published book.

9 – E.g., Bennett, 'The Literary Periodical', p. 243: 'High-class stuff is like radium.' (*New Age*, 8 September 1910).

10 – *Ibid.*, 'W. W. Jacobs and Aristophanes', p. 55.

11 – There are several references in *Books and Persons* to these phenomena.

12 – Bennett, 'The British Academy of Letters', pp. 229–30 (*New Age*, 18 August 1910).

13 – *Ibid.*, 'Censorship by the Libraries', p. 186 (*New Age*, 24 February 1910);

Canon Lambert was a member of the Hull Libraries Committee which banned H. G. Wells's *Ann Veronica* (1909).

14 – *Ibid.*, 'Unclean Books', p. 143 (*New Age*, 8 July 1910).

15 – *Ibid.*, 'The Length of Novels', p. 249 (*New Age*, 22 September 1910).

16 – 'Neo-Impressionism and Literature' (Bennett, pp. 280–5; *New Age*, 8 December 1910) was inspired by the First Post-Impressionist Exhibition (Manet and the Post-Impressionists), organised by Roger Fry at the Grafton Galleries, London, 8 November 1910–15 January 1911. It discussed the great British public's notoriously hostile reactions to the show and the possible implications of Post-Impressionism for the future of the novel.

17 – Bennett's concluding words (as revised in *ibid.*, pp. 284–5) were: 'The average critic always calls me, both in praise and dispraise, "photographic"; and I always rebut the epithet with disdain, because in the sense meant by the average critic I am not photographic. But supposing that in a deeper sense I were? Supposing a young writer turned up and forced me, and some of my contemporaries – us who fancy ourselves a bit – to admit that we had been concerning ourselves unduly with inessentials, that we had been worrying ourselves to achieve infantile realisms? Well, that day would be a great and disturbing day – for us.'

Thoreau

A hundred years ago, on 12 July, 1817, was born Henry David Thoreau, the son of a pencil-maker in Concord, Massachusetts.[2] He has been lucky in his biographers, who have been attracted to him not by his fame so much as by their sympathy with his views, but they have not been able to tell us a great deal about him that we shall not find in the books themselves. His life was not eventful; he had, as he says, 'a real genius for staying at home'.[3] His mother was quick and voluble, and so fond of solitary rambling that one of her children narrowly escaped coming into the world in an open field. The father, on the other hand, was a 'small, quiet, plodding man',[4] with a faculty for making the best lead pencils in America, thanks to a secret of his own for mixing levigated plumbago with fuller's earth and water, rolling it into sheets, cutting it into strips, and burning it. He could at any rate afford with much economy and a little help to send his son to Harvard, although Thoreau himself did not attach much importance to this expensive opportunity.[5] It is at Harvard, however, that he first becomes visible to us. A class-mate saw much in him as a boy that we recognise later in the grown man, so that instead of a portrait we will quote what was visible about the year 1837 to the penetrating eye of the Rev. John Weiss:

He was cold and unimpressible. The touch of his hand was moist and indifferent, as if he had taken up something when he saw your hand coming, and caught your grasp on it. How the prominent grey-blue eyes seemed to rove down the path, just in advance of his feet, as his grave Indian stride carried him down to University Hall. He did not care for people; his class-mates seemed very remote. This reverie hung always about him, and not so loosely as the odd garments which the pious household care furnished. Thought had not yet awakened his countenance; it was serene, but rather dull, rather plodding. The lips were not yet firm; there was almost a look of smug satisfaction lurking round their corners. It is plain now that he was preparing to hold his future' views with great setness and personal appreciation of their importance. The nose was prominent, but its curve fell forward without firmness over the upper lip, and we remember him as looking very much like some Egyptian sculpture of faces, large-featured, but brooding, immobile, fixed in a mystic egoism. Yet his eyes were sometimes searching, as if he had dropped, or expected to find, something. In fact his eyes seldom left the ground, even in his most earnest conversations with you ...[6]

He goes on to speak of the 'reserve and inaptness'[7] of Thoreau's life at college.

Clearly the young man thus depicted, whose physical pleasures took the form of walking and camping out, who smoked nothing but 'dried lily stems',[8] who venerated Indian relics as much as Greek classics, who in early youth had formed the habit of 'settling accounts'[9] with his own mind in a diary, where his thoughts, feelings, studies, and experiences had daily to be passed under review by that Egyptian face and searching eye – clearly this young man was destined to disappoint both parents and teachers and all who wished him to cut a figure in the world and become a person of importance. His first attempt to earn his living in the ordinary way by becoming a schoolmaster was brought to an end by the necessity of flogging his pupils. He proposed to talk morals to them instead. When the committee pointed out that the school would suffer from this 'undue leniency' Thoreau solemnly beat six pupils and then resigned, saying that school-keeping 'interfered with his arrangements'.[10] The arrangements that the penniless young man wished to carry out were probably assignations with certain pine trees, pools, wild animals, and Indian arrowheads in the neighbourhood, which had already laid their commands upon him.

But for a time he was to live in the world of men, at least in that very remarkable section of the world of which Emerson was the centre and which professed the Transcendentalist doctrines.[11] Thoreau took up his lodgings in Emerson's house and very soon became, so his friends said, almost indistinguishable from the prophet himself. If you listened to them both talking with your eyes shut you could not be certain where Emerson left off and Thoreau began. '. . . in his manners, in the tones of his voice, in his modes of expression, even in the hesitations and pauses of his speech, he had become the counterpart of Mr Emerson.'[12] This may well have been so. The strongest natures, when they are influenced, submit the most unreservedly; it is perhaps a sign of their strength. But that Thoreau lost any of his own force in the process, or took on permanently any colours not natural to himself the readers of his books will certainly deny.

The Transcendentalist movement, like most movements of vigour, represented the effort of one or two remarkable people to shake off the old clothes which had become uncomfortable to them and fit themselves more closely to what now appeared to them to be the realities. The desire for readjustment had, as Lowell has recorded and the memoirs of Margaret Fuller[13] bear witness, its ridiculous symptoms and its grotesque disciples. But of all the men and women who lived in an age when thought was remoulded in common, we feel that Thoreau was the one who had least to adapt himself, who was by nature most in harmony with the new spirit. He was by birth among those people, as Emerson expresses it, who have 'silently given in their several adherence to a new hope, and in all companies do signify a greater trust in the nature and resources of man than the laws of the popular opinion will well allow'.[14] There were two ways of life which seemed to the leaders of the movement to give scope for the attainment of these new hopes; one in some cooperative community, such as Brook Farm;[15] the other in solitude with nature. When the time came to make his choice Thoreau decided emphatically in favour of the second. 'As for the communities,' he wrote in his journal, 'I think I had rather keep bachelor's quarters in hell than go to board in heaven.'[16] Whatever the theory might be, there was deep in his nature 'a singular yearning to all wildness'[17] which would have led him to some such experiment as that recorded in *Walden*,[18] whether it seemed good to others or not. In truth he was to put in practice the doctrines of the Transcendentalists more thoroughly than any one of them, and to prove what the resources of man are by putting his entire trust in them. Thus, having reached the age of twenty-seven, he chose a piece of land in a wood on the brink of the clear deep green waters of Walden Pond, built a hut with his own hands, reluctantly borrowing an axe for some part of the work, and settled down, as he puts it, 'to front only the essential facts of life, and see if I could not learn what it had to teach, and not, when I came to die, discover that I had not lived'.[19]

And now we have a chance of getting to know Thoreau as few people are known, even by their friends. Few people, it is safe to say, take such an interest in themselves as Thoreau took in himself; for if we are gifted with an intense egoism we do our best to suffocate it in order to live on decent terms with our neighbours. We are not sufficiently sure of ourselves to break completely with the established order. This was Thoreau's adventure; his books are the record of that experiment and its results. He did everything he could to intensify his own understanding of himself, to foster whatever was peculiar, to isolate himself from contact with any force that might interfere with his immensely valuable gift of personality. It was his sacred duty, not to himself alone but to the world; and a man is scarcely an egoist who is an egoist on so grand a scale. When we read *Walden*, the record of his two years in the woods, we have a sense of beholding life through a very powerful magnifying glass. To walk, to eat, to cut up logs, to read a little, to watch the bird on the bough, to cook one's dinner – all these occupations when scraped clean and felt afresh prove wonderfully large and bright. The common things are so strange, the usual sensations so astonishing that to confuse or waste them by living with the herd and adopting habits that suit the greater number is a sin – an act of sacrilege. What has civilisation to give, how can luxury improve upon these simple facts? 'Simplicity, simplicity, simplicity!' is his cry. 'Instead of three meals a day, if it be necessary eat but one; instead of a hundred dishes, five; and reduce other things in proportion.'[20]

But the reader may ask, what is the value of simplicity? Is Thoreau's simplicity simplicity for its own sake, and not rather a method of intensification, a way of setting free the delicate and complicated machinery of the soul, so that its results are the reverse of simple? The most remarkable men tend to discard luxury because they find that it hampers the play of what is much more valuable to them. Thoreau himself was an extremely complex human being, and he certainly did not achieve simplicity by living for two years in a hut and cooking his own dinner. His achievement was rather to lay bare what was within him – to let life take its own way unfettered by artificial constraints. 'I did not wish to live what was not life, living is so dear; nor did I wish to practise resignation, unless it was quite necessary. I wanted to live deep and suck out all the marrow of life . . .'[21] *Walden* – all his books, indeed – are packed with subtle, conflicting, and very fruitful discoveries. They are not written to prove something in the end. They are written as the Indians turn down twigs to mark their path through the forest. He cuts his way through life as if no one had ever taken that road before, leaving these signs for those who come after, should they care to see which way he went. But he did not wish to leave ruts behind him, and to follow is not an easy process. We can never lull our attention asleep in reading Thoreau by the certainty that we have now grasped his theme and can trust our guide to be consistent. We must always be ready to try something fresh; we must always be prepared for the shock of facing one of those thoughts in the original which we have known all our lives in reproductions. 'All health and success does me good, however far off and withdrawn it may appear; all disease and failure helps to make me sad and do me evil, however much sympathy it may have with me or I with it.' 'Distrust all enterprises that require new clothes.' 'You must have a genius for charity as well as for anything else.'[22] That is a handful, plucked almost at random, and of course there are plenty of wholesome platitudes.

As he walked his woods, or sat for hours almost motionless like the sphinx of college days upon a rock watching the birds, Thoreau defined his own position to the world not only with unflinching honesty, but with a glow of rapture at his heart. He seems to hug his own happiness. Those years were full of revelations – so independent of other men did he find himself, so perfectly equipped by nature not only to keep himself housed, fed, and clothed, but also superbly entertained without any help from society. Society suffered a good many blows from his hand. He sets down his complaints so squarely that we cannot help suspecting that society might one of these days have come to terms with so noble a rebel. He did not want churches or armies, post offices or newspapers, and very consistently he refused to pay his tithes and went into prison rather than pay his poll tax. All getting together in crowds for doing good or procuring pleasure was an intolerable infliction to him. Philanthropy was one of the sacrifices, he said, that he had made to a sense of duty. Politics seemed to him 'unreal, incredible, insignificant',[23] and most revolutions not so important as the drying up of a river or the death of a pine. He wanted only to be left alone tramping the woods in his suit of Vermont grey, unhampered even by those two pieces of limestone which lay upon his desk until they proved guilty of collecting the dust, and were at once thrown out of the window.

And yet this egoist was the man who sheltered runaway slaves in his hut; this hermit was the first man to speak out in public in defence of John Brown;[24] this self-centred solitary could neither sleep nor think when Brown lay in prison. The truth is that anyone who reflects as much and as deeply as Thoreau reflected about life and conduct is possessed of an abnormal sense of responsibility to his kind, whether he chooses to live in a wood or to become president of the Republic. Thirty volumes of diaries which he would condense from time to time with infinite care into little books prove, moreover, that the independent man who professed to care so little for his fellows was possessed with an intense desire to communicate with them. 'I would fain,' he writes, 'communicate the wealth of my life to men, would really give them what is most precious in my gift . . . I have no private good unless it be my peculiar ability to serve the public . . . I wish to communicate those parts of my life which I would gladly live again.'[25] No one can read him and remain unaware of this wish. And yet it is a question whether he ever succeeded in imparting his wealth, in sharing his life. When we have read his strong and noble books, in which every word is sincere, every sentence wrought as well as the writer knows how, we are left with a strange feeling of distance; here is a man who is trying to communicate but who cannot do it. His eyes are on the ground or perhaps on the horizon. He is never speaking directly to us; he is speaking partly to himself and partly to something mystic beyond our sight. 'Says I to myself,' he writes, 'should be the motto to my journal,'[26] and all his books are journals. Other men and women were wonderful and very beautiful, but they were distant; they were different; he found it very hard to understand their ways. They were as 'curious to him as if they had been prairie dogs'.[27] All human intercourse was infinitely difficult; the distance between one friend and another was unfathomable; human relationships were very precarious and terribly apt to end in disappointment. But, although concerned and willing to do what he could short of lowering his ideals, Thoreau was aware that the difficulty was one that could not be overcome by taking pains. He was made differently from other people. 'If a man does not keep pace with his companions, perhaps it is because he hears a different drummer. Let him step to the music which he hears, however measured or far away.'[28] He was a wild man, and he would never submit to be a tame one. And for us here lies his peculiar charm. He hears a different drummer. He is a man into whom nature has breathed other instincts than ours, to whom she has whispered, one may guess, some of her secrets.

'It appears to be a law,' he says, 'that you cannot have a deep sympathy with both man and nature. Those qualities which bring you near to the one estrange you from the other.'[29] Perhaps that is true. The greatest passion of his life was his passion for nature. It was more than a passion, indeed; it was an affinity; and in this he differs from men like White and Jefferies.[30] He was gifted, we are told, with an extraordinary keenness of the senses; he could see and hear what other men could not; his touch was so delicate that he could pick up a dozen pencils accurately from a box holding a bushel; he could find his way alone through thick woods at night. He could lift a fish out of the stream with his hands; he could charm a wild squirrel to nestle in his coat; he could sit so still that the animals went on with their play round him. He knew the look of the country so intimately that if he had waked in a meadow he could have told the time of year within a day or two from the flowers at his feet. Nature had made it easy for him to pick up a living without effort. He was so skilled with his hands that by labouring forty days he could live at leisure for the rest of the year. We scarcely know whether to call him the last of an older race of men, or the first of one that is to come. He had the toughness, the stoicism, the unspoilt senses of an Indian, combined with the self-consciousness, the exacting discontent, the susceptibility of the most modern. At times he seems to reach beyond our human powers in what he perceives upon the horizon of humanity. No philanthropist ever hoped more of mankind, or set higher and nobler tasks before him, and those whose ideal of passion and of service is the loftiest are those who have the greatest capacities for giving, although life may not ask of them all that they can give, and forces them to hold in reserve rather than to lavish. However much Thoreau had been able to do, he would still have seen possibilities beyond; he would always have remained, in one sense, unsatisfied. That is one of the reasons why he is able to be the companion of a younger generation.

He died when he was in the full tide of life, and had to endure long illness within doors. But from nature he had learnt both silence and stoicism. He had never spoken of the things that had moved him most in his private fortunes. But from nature, too, he had learnt to be content, not thoughtlessly or selfishly content, and certainly not with resignation, but with a healthy trust in the wisdom of nature, and in nature, as he says, there is no sadness. 'I am enjoying existence as much as ever,' he wrote from his deathbed, 'and regret nothing.'[31] He was talking to himself of moose and Indian when, without a struggle, he died.

1 – A commemorative essay in the *TLS*, 12 July 1917, (Kp c80) based on Thoreau's works and on material in *The Life of Henry David Thoreau* (Richard Bentley & Son, 1890) by H. S. Salt. See also 'Poe's Helen', above, and 'Ralph Waldo Emerson', *I VW Essays*. Reprinted: *B&P*.

2 – Henry David Thoreau (1817–62), was the third child of John Thoreau and Cynthia Dunbar.

3 – Salt, ch. I, p. 24, quoting Thoreau writing to Daniel Ricketson, 1 February 1855.

4 – *Ibid.*, ch. I, p. 4.

5 – Thoreau was a student at Harvard, 1833–7: 'He is said to have refused to take his degree on the ground that five dollars was too high a price to pay for that honour' (Salt, p. 17).

6 – Salt, ch. I, p. 18, quoting Rev. John Weiss, *Christian Examiner*, Boston, July 1865, which has: 'grasp upon it', and 'sculptures'.

7 – *Ibid.*: 'He would smile to hear the word "collegiate career" applied to the reserve and inaptness of his college life.'

8 – *Ibid.*, p. 20.

9 – *Ibid.*, p. 23, quoting Thoreau's student theme 'Of Keeping a Private Journal', 1835.

10 – For Thoreau's leniency, Salt, ch. II, p. 26; and for his resignation, *ibid.*, p. 27, quoting William Ellery Channing, *Thoreau: The Poet-Naturalist* (Boston, Roberts Brothers, 1873).

11 – Ralph Waldo Emerson (1803–82), poet and essayist, leading light in the Transcendentalist movement, settled at Concord in 1834.

12 – Salt, ch. III, p. 57, quoting David Greene Haskins, *Ralph Waldo Emerson* (Boston, George H. Ellis, 1887).

13 – James Russell Lowell (1819–91), poet, essayist and diplomat, friend of Leslie Stephen and, effectively, VW's godfather; for his account of Thoreau see *My Study Windows* (Boston, James, R. Osgood and Company, 1871).

Margaret Fuller (1810–50), sometime editor of *Dial*, the Transcendentalist organ, author of *Summer on the Lakes in 1843* (1844), and *Woman in the Nineteenth Century* (1845); her memoirs, edited by R. W. Emerson, W. H. Channing and J. F. Clarke, were published in 1852.

14 – Emerson's observation does not occur in his biographical sketch of Thoreau (*The Writings of Henry David Thoreau*, xi vols, Houghton Mifflin Co., 1893, vol. x, *Miscellanies*, pp. 1–33), perhaps the most likely source, and its origin has not been traced.

15 – The so-called Institute of Agriculture and Education, 1841–7, established at West Roxbury in Massachusetts by the Transcendentalists George and Sarah Ripley.

16 – Thoreau's Journal, 3 March 1841, which has: 'these communities', and 'bachelor's hall', also quoted in Salt, ch. III, p. 79.

17 – Salt, ch. V, p. 128; original source untraced.

18 – *Walden* (1854).

19 – *Ibid.*, 'Where I Lived' (*Writings*, vol. II, p. 143); (also quoted in Salt, ch. III, p. 82).

20 – For the first quotation, *ibid.*, p. 144 (Salt, ch. IX, p. 236); and for the second, *ibid.*, pp. 144–5 (Salt, ch. IV, p. 93).

21 – *Ibid.*, p. 143 (Salt, ch. III, p. 82).

22 – For the three preceding quotations, *ibid.*, 'Economy', p. 125; *ibid.*, p. 39, which has: 'I say, beware of all enterprises that require new clothes, and not rather a new wearer of clothes'; *ibid.*, p. 116.

23 – Salt, ch. IX, p. 234.

24 – John Brown (1800–59), the abolitionist, whom Thoreau first met in 1857 and for whom he spoke in his 'Plea for Captain John Brown' at Concord Town Hall, 30 October 1859, following Brown's arrest at Harper's Ferry earlier in the month. (Brown was hanged at Charles Town, 2 December 1859.) See also, *Writings,* vol. X, 'The Last Days of John Brown' and 'After the Death of John Brown'.

25 – Journal, 26 March 1842 (the first two sentences only are quoted in Salt, ch. II, p. 33).

26 – *Ibid.*, 11 November 1851.

27 – *Walden,* 'The Village', p. 262.

28 – *Ibid.*, 'Conclusion', p. 502.

29 – Journal, 11 April 1852 (Salt, ch. V, p. 115).

30 – Gilbert White (1720–93) and Richard Jefferies (1848–87), to both of whom Salt alludes.

31 – Salt, ch. VIII, p. 213, quoting Thoreau writing to Myron B. Benton, 21 March 1862.

'Lord Jim'

This new edition of *Lord Jim* will be succeeded, we suppose, by the rest of Mr Conrad's works – those that are already published, and the many, as we hope, that are still to come. But will they all appear in the binding which disfigured *The Shadow Line*[2] and now afflicts us once more in *Lord Jim*? Will they all be of a sad green colour, and sprinkled with chocolate-brown nautical emblems such as might be stamped upon club note-paper, or upon some florid philanthropic pamphlet drawing attention to the claims of sea-captains' widows? As a general rule we submit to the will of publishers in silence, but it is time to cry out when they ask us to disfigure our shelves upon so large a scale as this. It is not a question of luxury, but of necessity: we have to buy Mr Conrad; all our friends have to buy Mr Conrad; and that Mr Conrad of all people should be robbed even of a shred of that dignity and beauty which he more than any living writer is able to create seems quite distressingly inappropriate.

Let us give thanks, however, for the portrait, and especially for the few words of introduction which Mr Conrad prefixes to the book. He tells us two facts of great interest: there is, or was, in existence a lady who does not like *Lord Jim*. That, though discreditable to her, is possible. But what are we to say of her reason? '"You know," she said, "it is all so morbid."' . . . 'The pronouncement,' writes Mr Conrad, 'gave me food for an hour's anxious thought.'[3] That is sufficiently surprising, too. If Mr Conrad had taken this extravagantly bad shot into account for the space of a minute, we should have thought it an excessive compliment to the unknown lady; for is there any word in the language less applicable to *Lord Jim* than 'morbid'? In the second place, Mr Conrad has a few words to say about the origin of the story. He tells us that his first thought was of a short story concerned only with the pilgrim-ship episode; but after writing a few pages he became discontented, and laid them aside. But Mr Blackwood happened to ask him for a story, and 'it was only then that I perceived that the pilgrim-ship episode was a good starting point for a free and wandering tale'.[4] A great many of his readers we think, will say that this statement explains a great deal: it explains that difficult break in the narrative; it explains the one criticism which we have ever formulated against this superb romance – that the second part of the book does not develop satisfactorily out of the first. The adventures at Patusan are not quite on a level with the rest.

Nevertheless, after reading *Lord Jim* again we are inclined to agree with what appears to be Mr Conrad's own opinion and to put *Lord Jim* at the head of all his works. There is *The Heart of Darkness*; there is 'Youth'; there is *Typhoon*;[5] there is *The Shadow-Line*; for ourselves, we should claim a very high place for that beautiful fragment of *Reminiscences*[6] still unfinished; but in *Lord Jim* Mr Conrad seems to have found once for all the subject that brings out his rare and wonderful qualities at their best. By a chance that does not come to every novelist, he has found his opportunity and made use of it to the very utmost. But it is not for us while he is still, happily, midway in his career to attempt to place Mr Conrad's books in order of merit or to weigh this famous work once more in our scales. Indeed, those critical susceptibilities which are set on edge by nine books out of ten and insist upon recording their complaints lie down happily and sleep in this case, and leave us with leisure to ruminate one or two ideas about Mr Conrad's work.

It is in *Lord Jim* that one of those passages occurs which interest us almost more for what they reveal of the writer than for any light they throw on the story. Marlow is drinking with that French naval officer who appears very distinctly for a few pages and then drops out altogether, and he remarks:

As if the appointed time had arrived for his moderate and husky voice to come out of his immobility, he pronounced 'Mon Dieu, how the time passes!' Nothing could have been more commonplace than this remark; but its utterance coincided for me with a moment of vision. It's extraordinary how we go through life with eyes half shut, with dull ears, with dormant thoughts... Nevertheless, there can be but few of us who had never known one of these rare moments of awakening, when we see, hear, understand ever so much – everything – in a flash, before we fall back again into our agreeable somnolence. I raised my eyes when he spoke, and I saw him as though I had never seen him before.[7]

That, so it strikes us, is the way in which Mr Conrad's mind works; he has a 'moment of vision' in which he sees people as if he had never seen them before; he expounds his vision, and we see it, too. These visions are the best things in his books. In *Lord Jim* particularly, how they crowd about us, these wonderful figures – Brierly, Chester, Stein – with their strange experiences all laid bare for an instant before, just as they come from darkness, they fade into darkness again! The gift of seeing in flashes is, of course, a limitation as well as a gift; it explains what we may call the static quality of Mr Conrad's characters. They change and develop very slightly; they are for the most part people whose characters are made up of one or two very large and simple qualities, which are revealed to us in flashes. But Mr Conrad's genius is a very complex one; although his characters remain almost stationary they are enveloped in the subtle, fine, perpetually shifting atmosphere of Marlow's mind; they are commented upon by that voice which is so full of compassion, which has so many deep and fine cadences in its scale. Mr Conrad has told us that it is his conviction that the world rests on a few very simple ideas, 'so simple that they must be as old as the hills'.[8] His books are founded upon these large and simple ideas; but the texture through which they are seen is extremely fine; the words which drape themselves upon these still and stately shapes are of great richness and beauty. Sometimes, indeed, we feel rather as if we were lying motionless between sea and sky in that atmosphere of profound and monotonous calm which Mr Conrad knows so strangely how to convey. There is none of the harassing tumult and interlocking of emotion which whirls through a Dostoevsky[9] novel, and to a lesser extent provides the nervous system of most novels. The sea and the tropical forests dominate us and almost overpower us; and something of their largeness, their latent inarticulate passion seems to have got into these simple men and these old sea-captains with their silent surfaces and their immense reserves of strength.

1 – A review in the *TLS*, 26 July 1917, (Kp c81) of *Lord Jim. A Tale* (J. M. Dent & Sons Ltd., 1917) by Joseph Conrad (1857–1924). See also *Youth* and 'Mr Conrad's Crisis', below; 'A Disillusioned Romantic', 'A Prince of Prose', 'Mr Conrad: A Conversation', *III VW Essays*; 'Joseph Conrad', *IV VW Essays* and *CR1*.
2 – *The Shadow-Line* (1917).
3 – Conrad, Author's Note, p. ix.
4 – *Ibid.*, p. viii, the first part of a sentence, which concludes '; that it was an event, too, which could conceivably colour the whole "sentiment of existence" in a simple and sensitive character'. William Blackwood, editor of *Blackwood's Magazine*.
5 – 'The Heart of Darkness', published in *Youth – A Narrative; and Two Other Stories* (1902); *Typhoon* (1903).
6 – *Some Reminiscences* (1912).
7 – Conrad, ch. XIII, p. 142, which begins: 'I kept him company; and suddenly, but not abruptly, as if . . .' VW's ellipsis marks the omission of 'Perhaps it's just as well; and it may be that it is this very dulness that makes life to the incalculable majority so supportable and so welcome'.
8 – *Some Reminiscences* (Eveleigh Nash, 1912), 'A Familiar Preface', p. 20.
9 – Fyodor Dostoevsky (1821–81).

'John Davidson'

If you write a thesis 'in partial fulfilment of the requirements for the degree of Doctor of Philosophy' upon a poet, it is inevitable perhaps that you should approach that poet solemnly and heavily, and, if he is not among the great, should attribute to him an importance which makes his familiar features appear strained and unnatural. Mr Fineman has not been able to avoid this common error. His essay opens with a cannonade of sonorous general statements about Victorian life and literature which it is difficult to bring into relation with actual books and facts. No doubt there is a connection between the discovery of electricity and the growth of realism in art, but it is a statement which puts a great strain upon the imagination; nor is it easy to make flesh and blood of an analysis of our modern view of romance, such as the following:

It either became symbolism; and this appealed to an age of increased intensity of commercial production because of the nerve-irritation that symbolic methods of double interpretation and aroused expectancy involved and implied; or else it became the romance of cruelty and tragic endings with occasional by-products of Wellsian science-romances and Davidsonian cosmological testaments.[2]

But when Mr Fineman gets on to Davidson[3] himself he is not so heavy-handed and he has plenty of interesting things to say. He takes Davidson from the point of view of the philosopher, and there is, of course, much in Davidson that the reader who is primarily interested in thought will find it worth his while to unravel. It is possible, and Mr Fineman's study lends support to this view, that to future generations Davidson will be interesting chiefly as the man who expressed most forcibly a material-istic view of the world in poetry. But Mr Fineman sends us back to Davidson's books and, leaving the views of future generations out of account, we try to take stock of our own.

It is less than ten years since Davidson died, leaving behind him the tragic preface in which, among other reasons for making an end, he stated that he had to 'turn aside and attempt things for which people will pay'.[4] His books came out in the last years of the nineteenth century and in the first years of this. The tragedy and whatever of achievement there is in the work are quite close to us; and yet already his voice has become a strange one. That is always so with a poet who is not great enough to be in the air as well as in print; when you do not read him he ceases to exist. But the neglect, at least in the case of Davidson, brings its compensation, for surprise is uppermost in re-reading him that anyone so good should be so little famous. And when we call him good, we mean, first and foremost, energetic, passionate, sincere, and master of his own method of expression. Take for example the first half of the *Testament of John Davidson*.[5] He wishes to do no less than re-fashion our conception of the universe. We are to admit no vision of another existence than ours; we are to realise that gods, centaurs, goblins, the lands of faery and romance, the whole 'wonderful Cosmogony of Other World',[6] are merely the reflections of man's unenlightened mind.

> Upon the mirror of eternity.[7]
> ... God and gods
> Are man's mistake; no brain exists
> Behind the galaxies, above them or beneath;

No thought inhabiteth eternity,
No reason, no intelligence at all
Till conscious life begins.[8]

The first half of the poem, in which man states his claim for supremacy to Hecate, has not only beauty in the poetic sense, but also a degree of interest which experience has scarcely led us to expect in such circumstances. It seems as if the fire of the new faith were to shrivel up finally those pallid and abstract gods and goddesses whose help is so often invoked by the academic poets for the sake of the poetic atmosphere which they create. Davidson is wholly in earnest; he sees and feels with remarkable force the vast conceptions which he is trying to express; and, above all, he is absolutely convinced of the paramount importance of his theme. And that, so we think, is his undoing. When man unrolls the whole origin, construction, and pageant of the universe, he is so burdened by all the facts which prove him right in his materialism that the poem breaks down beneath their weight; it becomes a lecture upon biology and geology delivered by an irate and fanatical professor. The facts which cumber his lines may be correct, but we do not want them stated as the following lines state them:

Secreted by the primal atom, all
The other atoms, the planets cooled,
Became; and all the elements, how much
So ever differing in appearance, weight,
Amount, condition, function, volume (gold
From iodine, argon from iron) wrought
Of the purest ether, in electrons sprang
As lightning from the tension filling space.[9]

Our quarrel is not at all with the words, which might very well take their place in poetry, or with the subject, which is magnificent, but with the proselytising spirit, which makes the truth of the facts of more importance than the poetry, and with the growing arrogance and acerbity of manner, as of one dinning the Gospel into the heads of an indifferent public. It is an open question how far Milton and Dante[10] believed the truth of the doctrines which they sang, and it is possible to enjoy them to the utmost without agreeing with them. But Davidson raises a spirit of controversy which makes it plain that if you do not agree with him you are damned.

Yet there are very few modern poets who need to be reduced to their proper stature by the august shades of Milton and Dante. The sturdy persistence with which Davidson thinks out his theme stands him in good stead now that the years have gone over him. He is always an interesting poet, and a far better spokesman for his time than others more mellifluous, although nature denied him the faculty of making even one of those little poems which everybody knows by heart. His shorter work, like the *Fleet Street Eclogues* and the *Ballads*,[11] has more chance of this form of popularity, but the chief interest of it, too, comes from the attitude of his thought; as Mr Fineman says, '. . . it is not the passing vision of ordinary joys and sorrows that haunts his imagination but rather the queries that lie back of it.'[12] His philosophy was no mood but a deep-seated conception which modified his views on language, on metre, on everything that had to do with his art. He thought that modern poetry has lost its strength because the poets still feign a belief in what they know to be false. '. . . the material forces of mind and imagination,' he wrote, 'can now re-establish the world as if nothing had ever been thought or imagined before.'[13] He meant to see the world anew, and to create an unliterary literature as if nothing had been written in the past, and the new poets were to be greater than Shakespeare. Literature, he said, is the greatest foe to literature.

> Lo! thirty centuries of literature
> Have curved your spines and overborne your brains![14]

And in order to lay the foundations of the new age he began by bringing into literature not only scientific words that were hitherto unknown there, but he took for his poems subjects that are superficially prosaic – Fleet Street, the Crystal Palace, Liverpool Street and London Bridge railway stations.[15] To our mind these are the best of his poems. They are original without being prophetic, they show his curious power of describing the quality of matter, and they are full of observation and of sympathy with the sufferings of man. The Bank Holiday scene at the Crystal Palace is a first-rate piece of description:

> Courageous folk beneath
> The brows of Michael Angelo's Moses dance
> A cakewalk in the dim Renascence Court.
> Three people in the silent Reading-room
> Regard us darkly as we enter: three
> Come in with us, stare vacantly about,
> Look from the window and withdraw at once.
> A drama; a balloon; a Beauty Show; –
> People have seen them doubtless, but none of those

> Deluded myriads walking up and down
> The north nave and the south nave anxiously –
> And aimlessly, so silent and so sad.[16]

The mood reminds us of that of Gissing[17] in his novels of middle-class life in London. Both men knew and felt the horror of the sordid and the squalid with peculiar intensity; Gissing because he was at heart a scholar, Davidson because he was by conviction, at least, an aristocrat. Indeed, here we come to that strange combination of different strands of thought which gives the poems of Davidson their very individual flavour. On the one hand we have:

> I see the strong coerce the weak,
> And labour overwrought rebel;
> I hear the useless treadmill creak,
> The prisoner cursing in his cell;
> I see the loafer-burnished wall;[18]

and on the other:

> Soul, disregard
> The bad, the good:
> Be haughty, hard,
> Misunderstood.[19]

Be an Overman,[20] be an Englishman, be a man of imperious imagination who stamps his will upon the world, be one of those dukes, marqueses, earls, or viscounts to whom the *Testament of John Davidson* is dedicated, and if that is impossible, submit to be ruled by your superiors. Having disposed of the gods of the old mythology, he sets up a new god, man himself, to rule over man. It may seem a harsh and insolent creed, but Davidson nevertheless lavishes beauty on it, and sings it not only with conviction, but with the sensibility of a poet:

> Stand up; behold
> The earth, life, death, and day and night!
> Think not the things that have been said of these;
> But watch them and be excellent, for men
> Are what they contemplate.[21]

---

1 – A review in the *TLS*, 16 August 1917, (Kp c82) of *John Davidson: A Study of the Relation of his Ideas to his Poetry*, 'A Thesis presented to the Faculty of the Graduate School in Partial Fulfilment of the Requirements for the Degree of Doctor of Philosophy' (University of Pennsylvania, 1916) by Hayim Fineman.
2 – Fineman, p. 3.

3 – John Davidson (1857–1909), Scottish poet, gave up schoolmastering and in 1889 settled in London where he associated with members of the Rhymers' Club, earned a scant living by journalism, and enjoyed friendships with such diverse literary personalities as Max Beerbohm and George Gissing. Davidson, who committed suicide, became a disciple of Nietzsche and a radical materialist.

4 – Fineman, p. 43, quoting Davidson, *Fleet Street and Other Poems* (1909), 'Prefatory Note'.

5 – *The Testament of John Davidson* (Grant Richards, 1908).

6 – *Ibid.*, p. 104:

> Till conscious life begins. The ouphs and elves,
> The satyrs, centaurs, goblins, gnomes and trolls,
> The ancient lands of faery and romance,
> Infernal and supernal domiciles,
> The dreadful dwellers there, and wonderful
> Cosmogony of Other World (perverse
> Reflexions of his unenlightened mind
> Upon the mirror of eternity,
> And on the mirrors of the sun and moon,
> The stars, the flowers, the sea, the woods, the wilds)
> With immaterial nothings deceived mankind,
> Even as his shadow on a darksome way
> Looms like a ghost and daunts the pilgrim still.

7 – *Ibid.*, see previous note.

8 – *Ibid.*, pp. 103–4, which has: 'Gods and God'; and 'mistake:'.

9 – *Ibid.*, pp. 98–9.

10 – John Milton (1608–74); Dante Alighieri (1265–1321).

11 – *Fleet Street Eclogues* (1893), second series (1896); *New Ballads* (1897); *The Last Ballad* (1899).

12 – Fineman, p. 17.

13 – *The Testament of John Davidson*, 'Dedication', p. 31.

14 – *The Testament of a Man Forbid* (Grant Richards, 1901), p. 9.

15 – 'Fleet Street', 'Railway Stations', 'The Crystal Palace' in *Fleet Street and Other Poems* (Grant Richards, 1909).

16 – *Ibid.*, 'The Crystal Palace', p. 37.

17 – George Gissing (1857–1903).

18 – *St George's Day. A Fleet Street Eclogue* (John Lane, 1895), p. 6, spoken by Menzies.

19 – *The Last Ballad and Other Poems* (John Lane, 1899), 'The Outcast', p. 153.

20 – For Davidson's version of Nietszche's *Übermensch* see *The Testament of John Davidson*, 'Dedication', 'To the Peers Temporal of the United Kingdoms of Great Britain and Ireland', pp. 17–18.

21 – *The Testament of a Man Forbid*, p. 10.

A Victorian Echo

This reprint is, much to our pleasure, illustrated by the original woodcuts of Arthur Hughes.[2] A reader who knows nothing of painting could
scarcely fail to date these pictures within a year or two accurately
enough; and, although literature is not so easy to classify as painting, we
think we could give reasons for placing Dr Hake in the middle of the
nineteenth century in spite of the claim that Rossetti made for him:

> ...Dr Gordon Hake is, in relation to his own time, as original a poet as one can well
> conceive possible. He is uninfluenced by any styles or mannerisms of the day to so
> absolute a degree as to tempt one to believe that the latest English singer he may have
> even heard of is Wordsworth.[3]

It is quite true, as Rossetti goes on to point out, that one thinks of a good
many writers (Quarles, Bunyan, Pope and Gray[4] are the ones he selects)
while reading Dr Hake, although his substance is remarkably his own.
But there are two qualities which seem to us to stamp his date upon him
very visibly — his simple way of accepting the current morality, and his
Victorian method of describing Nature.

Turning to his pages after reading our Georgians we feel ourselves, as
far as morality is concerned, back in the nursery. His imagination liked
to work upon rather obvious themes rich in sentiment and rounded with
a moral. We have the orphan child wandering in the woods to seek food
for her starving grandparent and coming home to find him dead:

> No sound, no breath she heard above,
>   Where grandsire in the garret lay.
> But one was there whose looks of love,
>   'Poor little orphan,' seemed to say.
> She knew the chaplain's kindly face;
> The bearer of the lady's grace.[5]

Dr Hake believed in the chaplain, he believed in the noble lady and her
stately pile, and when he had a heroine he called her quite seriously the
Lady May of Alton Moor.[6] All this side of him is very charmingly
represented by the minute story-telling woodcuts of Mr Hughes, where
the more you peer into the shadows the more horn spectacles and family
Bibles you discover. But the strange thing is that we only call either
poems or pictures sentimental by an afterthought; and upon seeking a

reason it seems to be that if you are going to tell stories about orphan girls, blind boys, and deserted children the way to do it is with the perfect sincerity and good faith of Dr Hake. It is an art known to the Victorians. They heard a sad story; they were genuinely moved by it; they wrote it down straightforwardly, asking no questions and without a trace of self-consciousness; and this is what we cannot do, and this is what we find most strange in them.

But the youngest of our critics could not dismiss Dr Hake as nothing more than a simple-minded and sentimental story-teller. He may have high-born ladies and maidens who, when asked their names, reply with 'looks that gave a sweetness out, "Lily of the Vale"',[7] but he is quite capable of sending the cripple child to the workhouse; his most indignant lines are about the evils of the public house; and the most remarkable poem in the book, 'Old Souls',[8] satirises one vice or humbug after another very deftly and with a neatness which recalls the satirists of the eighteenth century. Above all – and this is the quality which gave him his high repute with such critics as Rossetti and Mrs Meynell[9] – he was an artist; a writer with an exquisite sense of language, a strange and individual sense of humour, and a power, urged on we are told by a rigorous self-criticism, of working at his verse until nothing is left but terse original speech giving his meaning exactly and carrying the narrative on firmly and lightly. It is excellent story-telling. The ground is covered from one point to another without going round or going back or losing the way. And each one of his poems contains some beautifully accurate description of Nature. For example:

> Of loving natures, proudly shy,
>   The stock-doves sojourn in the tree,
> With breasts of feathered cloud and sky,
>   And notes of soft though tuneless glee;
> Hid in the leaves they take a spring,
> And crush the stillness with their wing.[10]

or,

> Before the sun, like golden shields,
>   The clouds a lustre shed around;
> Wild shadows gambolling o'er the fields
>   Tame shadows stretching o'er the ground.
> Towards noon the great rock-shadow moves,
> And takes slow leave of all it loves.[11]

Each of the quotations seems to us typically Victorian. Each is an example of the Victorian passion for getting Nature perfectly accurately, for her own sake, into poetry. And when, with much observation, much matching of words and of similes, the right description is found, down it goes, and the emotions of the poem pass round it as if it were an island in mid-stream and leave it unmoved.

1 – A review in the *TLS*, 23 August 1917, (Kp c83) of *Parables and Tales* by Thomas Gordon Hake. With a Preface by his son, Thomas Hake. Illustrated by Arthur Hughes (Elkin Mathews, 1917).

2 – Arthur Hughes (1832–1915), pre-Raphaelite painter, and illustrator, notably of works by William Allingham, Tennyson, Christina Rossetti, George MacDonald, and of the original edition of *Parables and Tales* (1872) by Thomas Gordon Hake (1809–95), physician and poet, friend of D. G. Rossetti (1828–82) and of George Borrow. Hake published several volumes of verse, including *Madeline and Other Poems* (1871) and *The New Day* (1890), and a volume of autobiography *Memoirs of Eighty Years* (1892).

3 – Hake, Pref., p. 13, quoting D. G. Rossetti on Hake's *Madeline* (1871), which continues: 'while in some respects his ideas and points of view are newer than the newest in vogue; and the external affinity frequently traceable to elder poets only throws this essential independence into startling and at times almost whimsical relief.'

4 – *Ibid.*; Francis Quarles (1592–1644), author of the book of devotional poems *Emblems* (1635); John Bunyan (1628–88); Alexander Pope (1688–1744); Thomas Gray (1716–71).

5 – *Ibid.*, 'The Lily of the Valley', stanza 40, p. 73.

6 – *Ibid.*, 'Mother and Child', stanza 23, p. 9.

7 – *Ibid.*, 'The Lily of the Valley', stanza 11, p. 64, which has:

> When folk who gossipped thereabout
>   Asked the child's name, – the child so pale, –
> With looks that gave a sweetness out,
>   She answered, 'Lily of the Vale'.
> Not then her eyes had dew-drops shed
> In early tribute to the dead.

8 – *Ibid.*, 'Old Souls', pp. 46–59.

9 – *Ibid.*, Pref., p. 15, quoting Alice Meynell in her preface to a selection of Hake's poems published in 1894.

10 – *Ibid.*, 'The Lily of the Valley', stanza 3, p. 61.

11 – *Ibid.*, 'The Blind Boy', p. 23.

Mr Galsworthy's Novel

Everyone, especially in August, especially in England, can bring to mind the peculiar mood which follows a long day of exercise in the open air. The body is tired out; the mind washed smooth by countless gallons of fresh air, and for some reason everything seems dangerously simple, and the most complex and difficult decisions obvious and inevitable. There is something truly or falsely spiritual about this state, and it is one which if prolonged may easily lead to disaster. In Mr Galsworthy's new novel the people fill us with alarm, because they appear all more or less under the influence of the great narcotic and therefore not quite responsible for their actions. They have been out hunting all day for so many generations that they are now perpetually in this evening condition of physical well-being and spiritual simplicity. With minds one blur of field and lane, hounds and foxes, they make sudden and tremendous decisions marked by the peculiar lightness and boldness of those who are drugged out of self-consciousness by the open air. Just before they drop off to sleep they decide that they must get married tomorrow, or elope with a housemaid, or challenge someone to fight a duel. This, of course, is an exaggeration, but some theory of the kind must be fabricated to explain this rather queer book, *Beyond*.

Charles Clare Winton, a major in the Lancers, was evidently in the condition described when he fell in love and had a child by a lady who was already the wife of a country squire, his friend. Nothing was more against all his ideas and, what is more important in the case of Major Winton, his tradition of good breeding than such behaviour. The child, a girl called Gyp, was left to his guardianship by the unsuspecting squire; and he salved his conscience to some extent by looking after her affairs and improving her investments. She lived with him and took his name. Being his daughter she was naturally extremely well-bred, loved dogs, and rode like a bird; but being a woman, very attractive, in an ambiguous position, and endowed with a passion for music, her lot was evidently to be complicated by queer sudden impulses on the part of others besides those which she felt for herself. At her first dance she was kissed on the elbow; by the time she was twenty-two she was involved in an affair with a long-haired Swedish violinist, called Fiorsen, whom she met when her father went to take the waters at Wiesbaden. In a second, as it seems to our apprehensive eyes, she is embraced by him; next minute she is actually married to a man whose past has been disreputable, and whom her father dislikes. 'That long, loping, wolfish, fiddling fellow with the broad cheek bones and little side whiskers (good God!) and greenish eyes, whose looks at Gyp he secretly marked down, roused his complete distrust.'[2] But he was a man of few words, and his own experience of love had convinced him that it was useless to interfere. The alarming thing was that Gyp herself had never given the matter any serious thought; her talks with Fiorsen, in spite of the embraces, had been of the most elementary and formal description. For example, coming home 'bone-tired'[3] from a long day's hunting, she hears that Fiorsen is in the house; she has a hot bath and does for a moment consider what will happen if she refuses him. 'The thought staggered her. Had she, without knowing it, got so far as this? Yes, and further. It was all no good. Fiorsen would never accept refusal even if she gave it. But, did she want to refuse? She loved hot baths, but had never stayed in one so long. Life was so easy there, and so difficult outside.'[4] She was not in love with Fiorsen; the only serious element in her decision was that, according to a certain Baroness, Fiorsen wanted saving from himself; and the task appealed to her. No wonder, then, that when she finds herself alone with her husband for the first time after the wedding, 'she thought of her frock, a mushroom-coloured velvet cord'.[5]

From these quotations it is not possible, perhaps, to gather that Mr Galsworthy is giving Gyp his closest and most serious attention. He represents her not only as a very finely organised being, fastidious, sensitive, and proud, but she lives her life and meets the harsh and inevitable blows of fate by a code of morality which has Mr Galsworthy's respect. It is by this time a matter of course that whatever Mr Galsworthy respects we must take seriously; whatever story he writes is likely to be not merely a story but also a point of view. But this time we must admit that we have not been able to get ourselves into that sympathetic state in which we read if not with agreement still with conviction. At every crisis in Gyp's fate, instead of feeling that the laws of society have forced her into positions where her passion and her courage vindicate her behaviour completely, we feel that she acts without enough thought to realise what she is doing – and therefore callously and conventionally; without enough passion to carry her triumphantly 'beyond'. She never forgets what the servants will think; and at a terrible moment she can remember that she is walking down

Baker Street without any gloves on and can forget her emotion in buying a pair. Behind her behaviour there is no code of morality; there is only a standard of manners which she was taught, no doubt, by the charming maiden aunt who lives in Curzon Street. This, of course, would be all very well if there were any trace of satire or of protest in Mr Galsworthy's portrait of her and her surroundings; but there is none. If you try to read the book as a satire upon honourable officers in the Lancers who hunt all day and sleep all night, to see in Gyp an amiable and innocent girl who has been flung disastrously from her dogs and ponies to sink or swim in the whirlpool of the world without any weapon save good manners, you are painfully at cross-purposes with your author. Gyp, he is careful to point out, is neither a 'new woman', nor is she a 'society woman';[6] she is a woman of temperament, or refinement, and of courage. And we are asked to believe that in the great things of life she was carried 'beyond' other people, and that these weapons of hers were good enough to fight her battles very finely, and to leave her in the end mistress of her soul and able to say, although her heart is broken and she can only find comfort in a Home for Poor Children, 'I wouldn't have been without it.'[7]

There are many other characters in the book, but they have, unfortunately, as we think, to comply with the standard which Gyp accepts. Fiorsen and Rosek are men of rather unpleasant character; Summerhay is a man of rather pleasant character. Gyp sums him up very well by her remark: 'I like men who think first of their dogs.'[8] Unfortunately she is led to exclaim more than once in the book also, 'What animals men are!'[9] Did she give them a chance, we wonder, of being anything much better? But the whole society seems to us to have had its sting, whether for good or for evil, for happiness or unhappiness, drawn long ago, and to be living rather a colourless than a vicious or beautiful life. There is nothing coarse or boisterous about this world; nobody seems to want anything very much, and when we think it all over at the end we remember, and this we mean sincerely and not satirically, a great many most delightful dogs.

1 – A review in the *TLS*, 30 August 1917, (Kp c84) of *Beyond* (William Heinemann, 1917) by John Galsworthy (1867–1933), among whose best-known works at this date were the novel *The Man of Property* (1906) and the play *Strife* (1909). See also 'Books and Persons' above and 'Character in Fiction', *III VW Essays*. Reprinted: CW.

2 – Galsworthy, pt I, ch. IV, pp. 43–4.

3 – *Ibid.*, ch. V, p. 55, which has: 'Ah, she was tired; and it was drizzling now. She would be nicely stiff to-morrow.'

4 – *Ibid.*, pp. 55–6, which has: 'It was all no good; Fiorsen would never accept refusal, even if she gave it!'

5 – *Ibid.*, pt. II, ch I, p. 65, which has 'Gyp thought of her frock'.

6 – For the first quotation, *ibid.*, ch. VII, p. 120; the second appears to be a paraphrase drawn fom *ibid.*, ch. V, p. 99, where Gyp is said to have felt she did not 'belong' either to 'high bohemia' or to 'that old orthodox, well-bred world' of her Aunt Rosamund.

7 – *Ibid.*, pt IV, ch. XII, p. 438.

8 – *Ibid.*, pt III, ch. I, p. 246.

9 – *Ibid.*, pt II, ch. XX, p. 227.

To Read Or Not To Read

There was once an old gentleman who could, if you gave him time, trace every evil of public and private life, and he thought them both in a bad way, to one and the same cause – the prevalence of the rat. He died, unfortunately, from the bite of one of the black or Hanoverian species before he was able to collect his arguments in a book, and the principles of his faith are lost to us for ever. Let us, therefore, make the most of Viscount Harberton while we have him; he has not rediscovered the lost theory of the rat, alas! but he has invented one that will do almost as well. Whenever our old friend would have wagged his head, looked very solemn, and ejaculated, 'Rats!' Lord Harberton goes through the same process and cries, 'Books!' What sin do you most abhor? Is it drunkenness or lying, cruelty or superstition? Well, they all come from reading books. What virtues do you most admire? Pluck them in handfuls, wherever you like, the answer is still the same; that is the result of not reading books. The trouble is that somehow or other the vicious race of readers has got the virtuous race of non-readers into its power. Wherever you look you find the readers in authority. 'Every administrative post throughout the Empire is being confined more and more to minds that can display a distorted faculty for reading and remembering what they are told, instead of judging for themselves what they care to read and remember.'[2] Worse than this, 'our scholastics' have 'managed

to acquire complete control in moulding the minds of the next generations'.[3] The vice is spreading daily, and things have come to such a pass
that if we do not look out the aristocracy will have forfeited their special
merit of 'disliking study and being more interested in their own opinions
than in those of their author'.[4]

But at this point the prophet's message seems capable of two interpre-
tations, each capable of founding a different sect. We are told with great
emphasis that all the power is in the hands of the readers, but upon
another page we – the well-to-do gentry, that is – are warned that it is
owing to our vicious habit of reading that the Labour leaders have us at
their mercy. Let the Socialists and trade unionists have every opportunity for reading, Lord Harberton advises; but let us stop at once, for it is
only by so doing that we shall regain our lost ascendancy. It is really very
difficult to know what to do. And there is another source of confusion. It
is laid down on page 55 that the gift of writing is no more 'guarantee of
sense than the gift of song or the gift of the gab'. We are to remember that
'few men of letters are absolutely sane, and their silly side is the main
factor of their popularity'.[5] No sooner have we grasped this principle
and jeered where we used to do honour than we are presented with a list
of untaught, unread people, and bidden to own at once that 'in actual
writing, in drama, poetry, and fiction', in the art, that is to say, which
needs no gift and is best practised by insane people, 'they have more than
held their own'.[6]

In spite of these obscure passages it would be mere affectation to
pretend that there is any doubt about Lord Harberton's meaning. The
unread man is a kind of natural genius, nosing his way through the
world with an instinctive eye for the good and the right which is utterly
beyond the reach of thought, and can only be compared with the flick of
the wrist of a first-rate racquets player. Once common enough, these
creatures, owing to the spread of books, have become so rare that it will
be necessary in time for every household to keep one in its employ, so as
to preserve a contact with reality; Lord Harberton himself has one
already. The well-read man, on the other hand, is the 'champion bigot',[7]
the spirit of evil in our midst, who has endowed each one of the
professions with its long ears of pedantic absurdity. Look (merely to
look is enough) at Darwin; look at Lord Lister; look at Huxley, 'that old
bone-man';[8] look in the frontispiece at the faces of Swinburne,
Goldsmith, Wordsworth, and Gibbon, and compare them with the face
of William Whiteley, the Universal Provider. You will see that he is

'more alert, quite as intelligent, and with twice the vitality and character'.[9]

But though we have tried to show by these quotations that Lord Harberton makes good his claim for himself – 'education resisted, faith small; degrees none'[10] – there is a great deal in his book that might have been written by anyone. Take this, for example: 'There are plenty of minds who might read all the best authors at their own convenience and yet never be led to think at all; but when they are doing something practical the mind is alive and on the watch, and afterwards they think about it and how to do better, and they discover small improvements and inventions'.[11] That is almost the remark of a professor. And to say that the examination test has been a failure, and that letters after one's name are no proof of ideas within one's head – all this has been said by the schoolmasters over and over again. Nevertheless, such is the bustle and sprightliness of Lord Harberton's mind, such the audacity with which he flies from Tariff Reform to inoculation, from Party Government to Home Rule, to settle finally upon the flanks of the incorrigible reader, that we were just laying a faggot to our bookcase in the hope of catching his style, when we came upon the names of Schopenhauer and Herbert Spencer.[12] No praise is too high for them; in their books, we are told, we shall find the secret of the universe. After all, then, Lord Harberton is merely one of those cultivated people who play the innocent for a holiday. Still, one reader will give him the benefit of the doubt and take his advice to the extent of refraining for ever from the pages of Schopenhauer.

1 – A review in the *TLS*, 6 September 1917, (Kp c85) of *How To Lengthen Our Ears. An enquiry whether learning from books does not lengthen the ears rather than the understanding* (C. W. Daniel Ltd, 1917) by Viscount Harberton – Ernest Arthur George Pomeroy, 7th Viscount Harberton (1867–1944), soldier, educated at Charterhouse and Trinity College, Cambridge, formerly a captain in the Royal Dublin Fusiliers, author of *Salvation by Legislation; or Are We All Socialists?* (1908) and of works of classical scholarship.

2 – Harberton, ch. III, p. 26.

3 – *Ibid*.

4 – *Ibid*., ch. VI, p. 82.

5 – *Ibid*., ch. V, p. 55.

6 – For both quotations, *ibid*., p. 68.

7 – *Ibid*., p. 67.

8 – *Ibid*., ch. VI, p. 72; Charles Darwin (1809–82); Joseph Lister, 1st Baron Lister (1827–1912); Thomas Huxley (1825–95).

9 – *Ibid.*, ch. xv, p. 197; Algernon Charles Swinburne (1837–1909); Oliver Goldsmith (1730–74); William Wordsworth (1770–1850); Edward Gibbon (1737–94). William Whiteley (1831–1907), founder of a chain of shops in London and of a mail order business which undertook to supply every kind of goods and by which Whiteley, the son of a Yorkshire corn factor, became a millionaire.

10 – *Ibid.*, p. 206.

11 – *Ibid.*, ch. IV, p. 37.

12 – Harberton frequently alludes to Arthur Schopenhauer (1788–1860) and to Herbert Spencer (1820–1903), and prefaces his book, and several of his chapters, with epigraphs from their works.

Mr Conrad's 'Youth'

Mr Arnold Bennett recently protested against those people who, when Mr Conrad is mentioned, exclaim 'Ah, Conrad!'[2] as if that were a different thing altogether, as if you were now talking about something that mattered. It is a form of exclusiveness that is very irritating, no doubt, particularly if you happen to be a novelist yourself; but when a new novel, or a reprint of an old novel, by Mr Conrad comes into our hands how can we suppress that exclamation? How can we help feeling that it is a different thing altogether – so different, indeed, that even our minute duties with regard to it attain a momentary dignity? There are two novelists in England today, so we feel spontaneously if wrongly, whom it seems no waste of time to criticise, whose work, we feel certain, is of such lasting importance that we are even serving a useful purpose when we try to value it, to make its shape a little more definite, its beauty a little more evident. Some naturalists, we are told, put their specimens into ant heaps to be eaten clean of unnecessary flesh – a humble office much like ours where these great men are concerned. Innumerable critics each armed with his pick and shovel do in the end, perhaps, clear away a few encumbrances. But Mr Hardy[3] and Mr Conrad are the only two of our novelists who are indisputably large enough to engage the services of a whole anthill. They are not men of one success, or one impression; they are men whose art has been large enough to develop now on this side, now on that, so that it is only by laying one book beside another that you can make out what the proportions and circumference of the giant really are.

'Youth' was first published in 1902; it is now republished by Mr Dent, with a note by the author. He tells us something of his relations with Marlow which we are glad to know:

He haunts my hours of solitude, when, in silence, we lay our heads together in great comfort and harmony; but as we part at the end of a tale I am never sure that it may not be for the last time. Yet I don't think that either of us would care much to survive the other . . . Of all my people he's the one that has never been a vexation to my spirit. A most discreet, understanding man. . .[4]

He has not very much to say about the three stories – 'Heart of Darkness' and 'The End of the Tether' are, of course, the other two – and that is what one might have expected; there is not much to be said. But he says that each one is the product of experience, pushed in the case of 'Heart of Darkness' 'a little (and only very little) beyond the actual facts of the case for the perfectly legitimate, I believe, purpose of bringing it home to the minds and bosoms of readers'.[5] He also says that the three stories lay no claim to unity of artistic purpose. And yet, though the mood is distinct and different in each, it is surely not difficult to see that these three stories are the work of one and the same period, just as *Chance* and *Victory*[6] are the work of another period. After reading them again one is inclined to say that here Mr Conrad is at his best; but it would be more just to say not that he is better, but that he is different. We probably mean that in these stories he gives us the most complete and perfect expression of one side of his genius – the side that developed first and was most directly connected with his own experience. It has an extraordinary freshness and romance. It is not so subtle or so psychological as the later mood. His characters are exposed far more to the forces of sea and forest, storm and shipwreck, than to the influence of other human beings. And these great powers, working in their large and inscrutable fashion, bring into action those qualities in mankind which always seem most dear to Mr Conrad's heart – courage, fidelity, magnanimity in the face of suffering. They are the qualities which mark those men who seem to have most of nature in them; they have been overlaid by civilisation and need the particular tests of nature to call them out, but they exist, so Mr Conrad seems to tell us, in the poorest and most apparently worthless of men. Those 'profane scallywags without a redeeming point'[7] plucked from the heart of a Liverpool slum, when tested by the supreme test of sea and fire, will be found to conceal these great possessions in the depths of their hearts. The ship is burning and 'we went aloft to furl the sails[8] . . . What made them do it?'[9] Was it praise, or sense of duty, or their most inadequate pay? 'No; it was something in them, something inborn and subtle and everlasting . . .'[10] There was a completeness in it, something solid like a principle, and masterful like an instinct – a disclosure of something secret – of that hidden something, that gift of good or evil, that makes racial difference, that shapes the fate of nations.'[11]

'There was a completeness in it.' Perhaps it is that quality which satisfies us so enormously in these stories. When the burning ship sinks, when Marlow adventures into the Heart of Darkness, and, most of all, when old Captain Whalley,[12] betrayed by nature and by man, fills his pockets with iron and drops into the sea we feel a rare sense of adequacy, of satisfaction, as if conqueror and conquered had been well matched and there is here 'nothing to wail'.[13] Mr Conrad, it is needless to say, has done other things supremely well; but in these first visions of life there is often a simplicity, a sense of perfect harmony, which is broken up as life goes on; and in the case of Mr Conrad we feel that this simplicity reveals the largest outlines, the deepest instincts.

1 – A review in the TLS, 20 September 1917, (Kp c86) of *Youth: A Narrative and two other stories* (J. M. Dent & Sons, 1917) by Joseph Conrad (1857–1924). See also '*Lord Jim*' above, 'Mr Conrad's Crisis' below; 'A Disillusioned Romantic', 'A Prince of Prose', 'Mr Conrad: A Conversation', *III VW Essays*; and 'Joseph Conrad', *IV VW Essays* and CR1.
2 – Arnold Bennett, *Books and Persons* (Chatto & Windus, 1917), 'The British Academy of Letters', p. 231. See also VW's review 'Books and Persons' above.
3 – Thomas Hardy (1840–1928).
4 – Conrad, 'Author's Note', p. viii.
5 – *Ibid.*, p. ix, which has: 'of the readers'.
6 – *Chance* (1914), *Victory* (1915).
7 – Conrad, 'Youth', p. 29.
8 – *Ibid.*, pp. 28–9, a complete sentence.
9 – *Ibid.*, p. 29, which has: 'What made them do it – what made them obey me when I, thinking consciously how fine it was, made them drop the bunt of the foresail twice to try and do it better. What?'
10 – *Ibid.*
11 – *Ibid.*, p. 30, which has: 'good or evil that makes'.
12 – For Captain Whalley see 'The End of the Tether'; for his death, *ibid.*, p. 363.
13 – John Milton, *Samson Agonistes* (1671), Manoa speaking, l. 1721:

> 'Nothing is here for tears, nothing to wail
> Or knock the breast, no weakness, no contempt,
> Dispraise, or blame; nothing but well and fair,
> And what may quiet us in a death so noble.'

Flumina Amem Silvasque

It is a proof of the snobbishness which, no doubt, veins us through that the mere thought of a literary pilgrim makes us imagine a man in an ulster looking up earnestly at a house front decorated with a tablet, and bidding his anaemic and docile brain conjure up the figure of Dr Johnson. But we must confess that we have done the same thing dozens of times, rather stealthily perhaps, and choosing a darkish day lest the ghosts of the dead should discover us, yet getting some true pleasure and profit nevertheless. We cannot get past a great writer's house without pausing to give an extra look into it and furnishing it as far as we are able with his cat and his dog, his books and his writing table. We may justify the instinct by the fact that the dominion which writers have over us is immensely personal; it is their actual voice that we hear in the rise and fall of the sentence; their shape and colour that we see in the page, so that even their old shoes have a way of being worn on this side rather than on that, which seems not gossip but revelation. We speak of writers; the military or medical or legal pilgrim may exist, but we fancy that the present of his heroes' old boots would show him nothing but leather.

Edward Thomas[2] was as far removed from our imaginary pilgrim as well may be. He had a passion for English country and a passion for English literature; and he had stored enough knowledge of the lives of his heroes to make it natural for him to think of them when walking through their country and to speculate whether the influence of it could be traced in their writing. The objection that most writers have no particular country he met in a variety of ways, which are all excellent, and many of them illuminating, because they spring from the prejudices and preferences of a well-stocked mind. There is no need to take alarm, as we confess to have done, at finding that the counties are distributed among the poets; there is no trace whatever of the 'one can imagine' and 'no doubt' style of writing.

On the contrary the poets and the counties are connected on the most elastic and human principle; and if in the end it turns out that the poet was not born there, did not live there, or quite probably had no place at all in his mind when he wrote, his neglect is shown to be quite as characteristic as his sensibility. Blake, for instance, comes under London and the Home Counties; and it is true that, as it is necessary to live somewhere, he lived both in London and at Felpham, near Bognor. But there is no reason to think that the tree that was filled with angels was peculiar to Peckham Rye, or that the bulls that 'each morning drag the sulphur Sun out of the Deep'[3] were to be seen in the fields of Sussex. 'Natural objects *always did and do* weaken, deaden, and obliterate imagination in me!'[4] he wrote; and the statement, which might have annoyed a specialist determined to pin a poet down, starts Mr Thomas off upon a most interesting discussion of the state of mind thus revealed. After all, considering that we must live either in the country or in the town, the person who does not notice one or the other is more eccentric than the person who does. It is a fine opening into the mind of Blake.

But the poets, as Mr Thomas shows, are an extremely capricious race, and do for the most part show a bird's or butterfly's attachment to some particular locality. You will always find Shelley near the water; Wordsworth among the hills; and Meredith within sixty miles of London. Matthew Arnold,[5] although associated with the Thames, is, as Mr Thomas points out in one of those critical passages which make his book like the talk of a very good talker, most particularly the poet of the garden and of the highly cultivated land.

> I know these slopes; who knows them, if not I?

'has the effect of reducing the landscape to garden scale'. There is, he points out, 'a kind of allegorical thinness' about Arnold's country, 'as if it were chiefly a symbol of escape from the world of "men and towns"'.[6] Indeed, if one takes a bird's-eye view of Arnold's poetry, the background seems to consist of a moonlit lawn, with a sad but not passionate nightingale singing in a cedar tree of the sorrows of mankind.[7] It is much less easy to reduce our vision of the landscape of Keats to something marked upon a map. We should be inclined to call him more the poet of a season than the poet of a place. Mr Thomas puts him down under London and the Home Counties because he lived there. But although he began as most writers do by describing what he saw, that was exercise work, and very soon he came to 'hate descriptions'.[8] And thus he wrote some of the most beautiful descriptions in the language, for in spite of many famous and exact passages the best descriptions are the least accurate, and represent what the poet saw with his eyes shut when the landscape had melted indistinguishably into the mood. This brings us, of course, into conflict with Tennyson.[9] The Tennysonian method of sifting words until the exact shade and shape of the flower or the cloud had its equivalent phrase has produced many wonderful examples of minute skill, much like the birds' nests and blades of grass of the pre-Raphaelite painters. Watching the dead leaves fall in autumn, we may remember that Tennyson has given precisely the phrase we want, 'flying gold of the ruin'd woodlands'; but for the whole spirit of autumn we go to Keats.[10] He has the mood and not the detail.

The most exact of poets, however, is quite capable of giving us the slip if the occasion seems to him to demand it; and as his theme is most often a moment of life or of vision, so his frozen stream, or west wind, or ruined castle is chosen for the sake of that mood and not for themselves. When that 'sense of England',[11] as Mr Thomas calls it, comes over us driving us to seek a book that expresses it, we turn to the prose writers most probably – to Borrow, Hardy, the Brontës, Gilbert White.[12] The sense of country which both Mr Hardy and Emile Brontë possess is so remarkable that a volume might be spent in discussion of it. We should scarcely exaggerate our own belief if we said that both seem to forecast a time when character will take on a different aspect under the novelist's hand, when he will be less fearful of the charge of unreality, less careful of the twitterings and chatterings which now make our puppets so animated and for the most part so ephemeral. Through the half-shut eyes with which we visualise books as a whole, we can see great tracts of Wessex and of the Yorkshire Moors inhabited by a race of people who seem to have the rough large outline of the land itself. It is not with either of these writers a case of the word-painter's gift; for though they may have their detachable descriptions, the element we mean is rubbed deep into the texture and moulds every part. Ruskin,[13] we observe, who did the description pure and simple to perfection, is not quoted by Mr Thomas; and the omission, which seems to us right, is a pleasant sign of the individual quality of the pilgrimage. We have seldom read a book indeed which gives a better feeling of England than this one. Never perfunctory or conventional, but always saying what strikes him as the true or interesting or characteristic thing, Mr Thomas brings the very look of the fields and roads before us; he brings the poets, too; and no one will finish the book without a sense that he knows and respects the author.

1 – A review in the TLS, 11 October 1917, (Kp c87) of A Literary Pilgrim in England ... with eight illustrations in colour and twelve in monotone (Methuen & Co. Ltd., 1917) by Edward Thomas. The title of the article may be translated: 'Let

me adore the rivers and the woods.' See also, on the subject of literary pilgrimage, 'Haworth, November, 1904', 'Literary Geography', *I VW Essays,* and 'Great Men's Houses', *V VW Essays* and *The London Scene* (1982). Reprinted: *B&P.*

2 – (Philip) Edward Thomas (1878–1917), poet, essayist and critic, had been killed at Arras on 9 April 1917, serving with the Royal Garrison Artillery, having originally enlisted in the Artists' Rifles in July 1915. He was not at this date generally known to the public as a poet but as the author of prose studies of country life, including *Rest and Unrest* (1910), *Light and Twilight* (1911) and *The South Country* (1909). Thomas also published numerous critical pot-boilers and, notably, an account of *Richard Jefferies, His Life and Work* (1909).

3 – Thomas, 'William Blake [1757–1827]', p. 13, quoting Blake's poem 'Milton', bk 1, pt 21, l. 20.

4 – *Ibid.,* p. 12, quoting Blake's 'note to Wordsworth' [1770–1850], an annotation Blake made in his copy of Wordsworth's *Poems* (2 vols, 1815).

5 – Thomas discusses Percy Bysshe Shelley (1792–1822) and Matthew Arnold (1822–88) in the section on 'The Thames'; William Wordsworth (1770–1850) in 'The North'; and George Meredith (1828–1909) in 'London and the Home Counties'.

6 – Thomas, 'Matthew Arnold', p. 77, quoting and commenting on Arnold's poem 'Thyrsis', stanza 12, l. 1.

7 – This observation provoked some correspondence. See *TLS,* 18 October 1917, 'Arnold as a Poet of Nature', a letter from 'C.L.D.' who, having paraphrased VW's remark, commented: 'It is difficult to think of any other poet whose "backgrounds" and local "settings" have such variety as well as beauty . . . To speak of his muse as confined within garden walls, or clinging to cultivated land, is surely quite a mistake. His poetry is full of the fascination of mountain and forest and sea'. In which view 'C.L.D.' was supported two weeks later (*TLS,* 1 November 1917) by W. G. Waters of 7 Mansfield Street, W.

8 – *Ibid.,* 'Keats [1795–1821]', p. 36: 'Thus [by means of 'Hyperion'] Keats became "an old stager in the picturesque", as he said himself. Thus he learned to "hate descriptions", so that his poems thereafter contained no mere details verified from a notebook, but only broad noble features as suitable for heaven or hell as for the earth.'

9 – Thomas discusses Alfred, Lord Tennyson (1809–92) in the section on 'The East Coast and Midlands'.

10 – For the reference to Keats, *ibid.,* p. 38, where Thomas quotes from 'To Autumn'; the line by Tennyson, which Thomas does not quote, is from *Maud; A Melodrama,* pt I, iii, l. 12: 'And out he walk'd when the wind like a broken worldling wail'd, / And the flying gold of the ruin'd woodlands drove thro' the air'.

11 – *Ibid.,* 'Hilaire Belloc [1870–1953]', p. 155.

12 – Thomas discusses George Borrow (1803–81), in the section on 'The East Coast and Midlands'; Thomas Hardy (1840–1928) and Gilbert White (1720–93) in 'The South Downs and the South Coast'; and of 'the Brontës', only Emily (1818–48), in 'The North'.

13 – Thomas makes two passing references to John Ruskin (1819–1900). He also, incidentally, refers to Leslie Stephen (1832–1904) and the Sunday Tramps. Thomas

quotes (pp. 44–5) George Meredith on Stephen's 'unlimited paternal despotism' and his 'solicitous look of a schoolmaster'.

A Minor Dostoevsky

The second-rate works of a great writer are generally worth reading, if only because they are apt to offer us the very best criticism of his masterpieces. They show him baffled, casting about, hesitating at the branching of the paths, breaking into his true vein, and, misled by temptation, lashing himself in despair into a caricature of his own virtues and defects until the plan of his mind is very clearly marked out. The latest of Mrs Garnett's[2] translations, *The Gambler* (it includes also 'Poor People' and 'The Landlady'), will throw a good deal of light upon the processes of the mind whose powers seem almost beyond analysis in such works as *The Idiot* and *The Brothers Karamazov*.[3] If we call it second-rate compared with these, we mean chiefly that it impresses us as a sketch flung off at tremendous and almost inarticulate speed by a writer of such abundant power that even into this trifle, this scribbled and dashed-off fragment, the fire of genius has been breathed and blazes up, though the flame is blown out and the whole thing thrown to the ground in the same sudden and chaotic manner as that in which it comes into existence.

To begin with, all the characters – that is, a whole room full of Russian generals, their tutors, their stepdaughters, and the friends of their stepdaughters, together with miscellaneous people whose connection is scarcely defined – are talking with the greatest passion at the tops of their voices about their most private affairs. That, at least, is our confused and despairing impression. We are not certain whether we are in an hotel, what has brought all these people together, or what has set them off at this rate. And then, in the usual miraculous manner in the midst of ever-thickening storm and spray, a rope is thrown to us; we catch hold of a soliloquy; we begin to understand more than we have ever understood before, to follow feverishly, wildly, leaping the most perilous abysses, and seeming, as in a crisis of real life, to gain in flashes moments of vision such as we are wont to get only from the press of life at its fullest. Then the facts begin to emerge. The hero of the story is tutor in the General's family; he is in love with the General's stepdaughter Polina; she is involved with the French Marquis de Grieux; and her stepfather is in debt to the Marquis and in love also with a French adventuress. The stepfather's aunt, an old lady of seventy-five who should save them by dying, turns up in perfect health and proceeds to gamble away her fortune at the tables. They are all staying at Roulettenburg, and it is always possible to put everything to rights by a lucky spell at the tables. In order to save Polina the tutor begins to gamble, is sucked into the whirlpool, and never comes out again. All this is going at full speed at the moment of our first introduction to them; and to crowd the atmosphere still further, everyone is made to appear as if he or she had come upon the scene with all the preoccupations and tendencies which other circumstances have bred in them, so that we are speculating about all kinds of things that may happen in the spacious margin that lies on either side of Dostoevsky's page.

No one but Dostoevsky is able even to attempt this method successfully, and in 'The Gambler' where he is not completely successful one can see what fearful risks it entails – how often in guessing the psychology of souls flying at full speed even his intuition is at fault, and how in increasing the swiftness of his thought, as he always tends to do, his passion rushes into violence, his scenes verge upon melodrama, and his characters are seized with the inevitable madness or epilepsy. Every scene either ends or threatens to end with an attack of unconsciousness, or one of those inconsequent outbursts into which he falls, we cannot help feeling, when the effort to think is too exhausting. For example:

She cried and laughed all at once. Well, what was I to do? I was in a fever myself. I remember she began saying something to me – but I could scarcely understand anything. It was a sort of delirium – a sort of babble – as though she wanted to tell me something as rapidly as possible – a delirium which was interrupted from time to time with the merriest laughter, which at last frightened me.[4]

To control this tendency there is not in Dostoevsky, as there always is in Tolstoy, a central purpose which brings the whole field into focus. Sometimes in these stories it seems as if from exhaustion he could not concentrate his mind sufficiently to exclude those waifs and strays of the imagination – people met in the streets, porters, cabmen – who wander in and begin to talk and reveal their souls, not that they are wanted, but because Dostoevsky knows all about them and is too tired to keep them to himself.

Nevertheless, one finishes any book by Dostoevsky with the feelin that, though his faults may lie in this direction or in that, the range is s vast that some new conception of the novelist's art remains with us in th end. In this case we are left asking questions about his humour. There is scene in 'The Gambler' where the General and the Marquis try to drav the old aunt from the gaming tables with visions of a little expeditio into the country.

'There are trees there . . . we will have tea . . .' the General went on, utterly desperate 'Nous boirons du lait, sur l'herbe fraîche,' added De Grieux, with ferocious fury.

There is very little more, so little that when we come to re-read it we ar astonished at the effect of humour that has been produced. Given th same circumstances, an English writer would have developed an insisted upon a humorous scene; the Russian merely states the facts an passes on, leaving us to reflect that, although humour is bound up with life, there are no humorous scenes.

1 – A review in the *TLS*, 11 October 1917, (Kp c88) of *The Gambler and Othe Stories* (William Heinemann, 1917) by Fyodor Dostoevsky [1821–81]. From th Russian by Constance Garnett. See also 'More Dostoevsky' above; 'Dostoevsky i Cranford', 'Dostoevsky the Father', *III VW Essays*; and *Stavrogin's Confessio* (Hogarth Press, 1922) by F. M. Dostoevsky, translated by S. S. Koteliansky and VW. 2 – Constance Garnett, *née* Black (1862–1946), for biographical details see 'Mor Dostoevsky', n. 2.
3 – *The Idiot* (1868–9), *The Brothers Karamazov* (1879–80).
4 – *The Gambler*, title story, ch. xv, p. 107.
5 – *Ibid.*, ch. xII, p. 80.

The Old Order

With this small volume, which brings us down to about the year 1870, the memories of Henry James break off. It is more fitting to say that they break off than that they come to an end, for although we are aware that we shall hear his voice no more, there is no hint of exhaustion or of leave-taking; the tone is as rich and deliberate as if time were unending and matter infinite; what we have seems to be but the prelude to what we are to have, but a crumb, as he says, of a banquet now forever withheld. Someone speaking once incautiously in his presence of his 'completed' works drew from him the emphatic assertion that never, never so long as he lived could there be any talk of completion; his work would end only with his life;[2] and it seems in accord with this spirit that we should feel ourselves pausing, at the end of a paragraph, while in imagination the next great wave of the wonderful voice curves into fullness.

All great writers have, of course, an atmosphere in which they seem most at their ease and at their best; a mood of the great general mind which they interpret and indeed almost discover, so that we come to read them rather for that than for any story or character or scene of separate excellence. For ourselves Henry James seems most entirely in his element, doing that is to say what everything favours his doing, when it is a question of recollection. The mellow light which swims over the past, the beauty which suffuses even the commonest little figures of that time, the shadow in which the detail of so many things can be discerned which the glare of day flattens out, the depth, the richness, the calm, the humour of the whole pageant – all this seems to have been his natural atmosphere and his most abiding mood. It is the atmosphere of all those stories in which aged Europe is the background for young America. It is the half light in which he sees most, and sees farthest. To Americans, indeed, to Henry James and to Hawthorne,[3] we owe the best relish of the past in our literature – not the past of romance and chivalry, but the immediate past of vanished dignity and faded fashions. The novels teem with it; but wonderful as they are, we are tempted to say that the memories are yet more wonderful, in that they are more exactly Henry James, and give more precisely his tone and his gesture. In them his benignity is warmer, his humour richer, his solicitude more exquisite, his recognition of beauty, fineness, humanity more instant and direct. He comes to his task with an indescribable air of one so charged and laden with precious stuff that he hardly knows how to divest himself of it all – where to find space to set down this and that, how to resist altogether the claims of some other gleaming object in the background; appearing so busy, so unwieldy with ponderous treasure that his dexterity in disposing of it, his consummate knowledge of how best to place each fragment, afford us the greatest delight that literature has had to offer for many a year. The mere sight is enough to make anyone who has ever held a pen in his hand consider his art afresh in the light of this extraordinary example of it. And our pleasure at the mere sight soon merges in the thrill with which we recognise, if not directly then by hearsay, the old world of London life which he brings out of the shades and sets tenderly and solidly before us as if his last gift were the most perfect and precious of the treasures hoarded in 'the scented chest of our savings'.[4]

After the absence from Europe of about nine years which is recorded in *Notes of a Son and Brother*, he arrived in Liverpool on 1 March, 1869, and found himself 'in the face of an opportunity that affected me then and there as the happiest, the most interesting, the most alluring and beguiling that could ever have opened before a somewhat disabled young man who was about to complete his twenty-sixth year'.[5] He proceeded to London, and took up his lodging with a 'kind slim celibate',[6] a Mr Lazarus Fox – every detail is dear to him – who let out slices of his house in Half Moon Street to gentlemen lodgers. The London of that day, as Henry James at once proceeded to ascertain with those amazingly delicate and tenacious tentacles of his, was an extremely characteristic and uncompromising organism. 'The big broom of change' had swept it hardly at all since the days of Byron at least.[7] She was still the 'unaccommodating and unaccommodated city ... the city too indifferent, too proud, too unaware, too stupid even if one will, to enter any lists that involved her moving from her base and that thereby ... enjoyed the enormous "pull", for making her impression, of ignoring everything but her own perversities and then of driving these home with an emphasis not to be gainsaid'.[8] The young American ('brooding monster that I was, born to discriminate *à tout propos*')[9] was soon breakfasting with the gentleman upstairs (Mr Albert Rutson), eating his fried sole and marmalade with other gentlemen from the Home Office, the Foreign Office, the House of Commons, whose freedom to lounge over that meal impressed him greatly, and whose close questioning as to the composition of Grant's first Cabinet embarrassed him not a little.[10] The whole scene, which it would be an impiety to dismember further, has the very breath of the age in it. The whiskers, the leisure, the intentness of those gentlemen upon politics, their conviction that the composition of cabinets was the natural topic for the breakfast table, and that a stranger unable, as Henry James found himself, to throw light upon it was 'only not perfectly ridiculous because perfectly insignificant'[11] – all this provides a picture that many of us will be able to see again as we saw it once perhaps from the perch of an obliging pair of shoulders.

The main facts about that London, as all witnesses agree in testifying, were its smallness compared with our city, the limited number of distractions and amusements available, and the consequent tendency of all people worth knowing to know each other and to form a very accessible and, at the same time, highly enviable society. Whatever the quality that gained you admittance, whether it was that you had done something or showed yourself capable of doing something worthy of respect, the compliment was not an empty one. A young man coming up to London might in a few months claim to have met Tennyson, Browning, Matthew Arnold, Carlyle, Froude, George Eliot, Herbert Spencer, Huxley, and Mill.[12] He had met them; he had not merely brushed against them in a crowd. He had heard them talk; he had even offered something of his own. The conditions of those days allowed a kind of conversation which, so the survivors always maintain, is an art unknown in what they are pleased to call our chaos. What with recurring dinner parties and Sunday calls, and country visits lasting far beyond the week-ends of our generation, the fabric of friendship was solidly built up and carefully preserved. The tendency perhaps was rather to a good fellowship in which the talk was wide-sweeping, extremely well informed, and impersonal than to the less formal, perhaps more intense and indiscriminate, intimacies of today. We read of little societies of the sixties, the Cosmopolitan and the Century,[13] meeting on Wednesday and on Sunday evenings to discuss the serious questions of the times, and we have the feeling that they could claim a more representative character than anything of the sort we can show now. We are left with the impression that whatever went forward in those days, either among the statesmen or among the men of letters – and there was a closer connection than there is now – was promoted or inspired by the members of this group. Undoubtedly the resources of the day – and how magnificent they were! – were better organised; and it must occur to every reader of their memoirs that a reason is to be found in the simplicity which accepted the greatness of certain names and imposed something like order on their immediate neighbourhood. Having crowned their king they worshipped him with the most whole-hearted loyalty. Groups of people would come together at Freshwater, in that old garden where the houses of Melbury Road now stand,[14] or in various London centres, and live as it seems to us for months at a time, some of them indeed for the duration of their lives, in the mood of the presiding genius. Watts and Burne-Jones in one quarter of the town, Carlyle in another, George Eliot in a third,[15] almost as much as Tennyson in his island, imposed their laws upon a circle which had spirit and beauty to recommend it as well as an uncritical devotion.

Henry James, of course, was not a person to accept laws or to make one of any circle in a sense which implies the blunting of the critical powers. Happily for us, he came over not only with the hoarded curiosity of years, but also with the detachment of the stranger and the critical sense of the artist. He was immensely appreciative, but he was also immensely observant. Thus it comes about that his fragment revives, indeed stamps afresh, the great figures of the epoch, and, what is no less important, illumines the lesser figures by whom they were surrounded. Nothing could be happier than his portrait of Mrs Greville, 'with her exquisite good nature and her innocent fatuity',[16] who was, of course, very much an individual, but also a type of the enthusiastic sisterhood which, with all its extravagances and generosities and what we might unkindly, but not without the authority of Henry James, call absurdity, now seems extinct. We shall not spoil the reader's impression of the superb passage describing a visit arranged by Mrs Greville to George Eliot by revealing what happened on that almost tragic occasion.[17] It is more excusable to dwell for a moment upon the drawing room at Milford Cottage,

the most embowered retreat for social innocence that it was possible to conceive . . . The red candles in the red shades have remained with me, inexplicably, as a vivid note of this pitch, shedding their rosy light, with the autumn gale, the averted reality, all shut out, upon such felicities of feminine helplessness as I couldn't have prefigured in advance, and as exemplified, for further gathering in, the possibilities of the old tone.[18]

The drawn curtains, the 'copious service', the second volume of the new novel 'half-uncut' laid ready to hand, 'the exquisite head and incomparable brush of the domesticated collie'[19] – that is the familiar setting. He recalls the high-handed manner in which these ladies took their way through life, baffling the very stroke of age and disaster with their unquenchable optimism, ladling out with both hands every sort of gift upon their passage, and bringing to port in their tow the most incongruous and battered of derelicts. No doubt 'a number of the sharp truths that one might privately apprehend beat themselves beautifully in vain'[20] against such defences. Truth, so it seems to us, was not so much disregarded as flattered out of countenance by the energy with which they pursued the beautiful, the noble, the poetic, and ignored the possibility of another side of things. The extravagant steps which they would take to snare whatever grace or atmosphere they desired at the moment lend their lives in retrospect a glamour of adventure, aspiration, and triumph such as seems for good or for evil banished from our conscious and much more critical day. Was a friend ill? A wall would be knocked down to admit the morning sun. Did the doctor prescribe fresh milk? The only perfectly healthy cow in England was at your service. All this personal exuberance Henry James brings back in the figure of Mrs Greville, 'friend of the super-eminent'[21] and priestess at the different altars. Cannot we almost hear the 'pleasant growling note of Tennyson' answering her 'mild extravagance of homage' with 'Oh, yes, you may do what you like – so long as you don't kiss me before the cabman!'[22]

And then with the entrance of Lady Waterford,[23] Henry James ponders lovingly the quality which seems to hang about those days and people as the very scent of the flower – 'the quality of personal beauty, to say nothing of personal accomplishment as our fathers were appointed to enjoy it ... Scarce to be sated that form of wonder, to my own imagination I confess.'[24] Were they as beautiful as we like to remember them, or was it that the whole atmosphere made a beautiful presence, any sort of distinction or eminence indeed, felt in a way no longer so carefully arranged for, or so unquestionably accepted? Was it not all a part of the empty London streets, of the four-wheelers even, lined with straw, of the stuffy little boxes of the public dining rooms, of the protectedness, of the leisure? But if they had merely to stand and be looked at, how splendidly they did it! A certain width of space seems to be a necessary condition for the blooming of such splendid plants as Lady Waterford, who, when she had dazzled sufficiently with her beauty and presence, had only to take up her brush to be acclaimed the equal of Titian or of Watts.

Personality, whatever one may mean by it, seems to have been accorded a licence for the expression of itself for which we can find no parallel in the present day. The gift if you had it was encouraged and sheltered beyond the bounds of what now seems possible. Tennyson, of course, is the supreme example of what we mean, and happily for us Henry James was duly taken to that shrine and gives with extraordinary skill a new version of the mystery which in our case will supersede the old. 'The fond prefigurements of youthful piety are predestined, more often than not, I think, experience interfering, to strange and violent shocks . . .'[25] Fine, fine, fine, could he only be . . .'[26] So he begins, and so continuing for some time leads us up to the pronouncement that 'Tennyson was not Tennysonian'.[27] The air one breathed at Aldworth[28] was one in which nothing but the 'blest obvious, or at least the blest outright, could so much as attempt to live . . . It was a large and simple and almost empty occasion . . .[29] He struck me in truth as neither knowing nor communicating knowledge.'[30] He recited *Locksley Hall* and 'Oh dear, oh dear . . . I heard him in cool surprise take even more out of his verse than he had put in.'[31] And so by a series of qualifications which are all beautifully adapted to sharpen the image without in the least destroying it, we are led to the satisfactory and convincing conclusion, 'My critical reaction hadn't in the least invalidated our great man's being a Bard – it had in fact made him and left him more a Bard than ever.'[32] We see, really for the first time, how obvious and simple and almost empty it was, how 'the glory was without history', the poetic character 'more worn than paid for, or at least more saved than spent',[33] and yet somehow the great man revives and flourishes in the new conditions and dawns upon us more of a Bard than we had got into the habit of thinking him. The same service of defining, limiting, and restoring to life he performs as beautifully for the ghost of George Eliot, and proclaims himself, as the faithful will be glad to hear, 'even a very Derondist of Derondists.'[34]

And thus looking back into the past which is all changed and gone (he could mark, he said, the very hour of the change) Henry James performs a last act of piety which is supremely characteristic of him. The English world of that day was very dear to him; it had a fineness and a distinction which he professed half-humourously not to find in our 'vast monotonous mob'.[35] It had given him friendship and opportunity and much else, no doubt, that it had no consciousness of giving. Such a gift he of all people could never forget; and this book of memories sounds to us like a superb act of thanksgiving. What could he do to make up for it all, he seems to have asked himself. And then with all the creative power at his command he summons back the past and makes us a present of that. If we could have had the choice, that is what we should have chosen, not entirely for what it gives us of the dead, but also for what it gives us of him. Many will hear his voice again in these pages; they will perceive once more that solicitude for others, that immense desire to help which had its origin, one might guess, in the aloofness and loneliness of the artist's life. It seemed as if he were grateful for the chance of taking part in the ordinary affairs of the world, of assuring himself that, in spite of his absorption with the fine and remote things of the imagination, he had not lost touch with human interests. To acknowledge any claim that was in the least connected with the friends or memories of the past gave him, for this reason, a peculiar joy; and we can believe that if he could have chosen, his last words would have been like these, words of recollection and of love.

1 – A review in the TLS, 18 October 1917, (Kp c89) of The Middle Years (W. Collins Sons & Co. Ltd. 1917) by Henry James (1843–1916). 'I have promised to write a long article upon Henry James,' VW wrote to Vanessa Bell at Charleston on 21 September 1917 (II VW Letters, no. 872), 'and the book may arrive in a day or two, in which case I should have to spend next week doing it, and it means such a lot of reading as well as writing that there wouldn't be much point in coming to you . . .'; and on Wednesday, 10 October, she confided in her diary: 'No air raid; no further disturbance by our country's need . . . Late last night, I was told to have my Henry James done if possible on Friday, so that I had to make way with it this morning, & as I rather grudge time spent on articles, & yet cant help spending it if I have it, I am rather glad that this is now out of my power.'
  See also 'The Method of Henry James', below; 'Mr Henry James's Latest Novel', I VW Essays; 'Within the Rim', 'The Letters of Henry James', and 'Henry James's Ghost Stories', III VW Essays. Reprinted: DOM, CE.
2 – The person and occasion remain unidentified.
3 – Nathaniel Hawthorne (1804–64).
4 – Henry James, Notes of a Son and Brother (Macmillan & Co. Ltd, 1914), ch. v, p. 113.
5 – Middle Years, p. 3.
6 – Ibid., p. 17.
7 – For 'the big broom', Henry James, A Small Boy and Others (Macmillan & Co. Ltd, 1913), ch. xii, p. 323: 'I liked for my own part a lot of history, but felt in face of certain queer old obsequiosities and appeals, whinings and sidlings and hand-rubbings and curtsey-droppings, the general play of apology and humility, behind which the great dim social complexity seemed to mass itself, that one didn't quite want so inordinate a quantity. Of that particular light and shade, however, the big broom of change has swept the scene bare; more history still has been after all what it wanted.' James does not refer here to Lord Byron (1788–1824).
8 – Middle Years, p. 23.
9 – Ibid., pp. 104–5.
10 – Ibid., p. 29; Gen. Ulysses S. Grant (1822–85), a Republican, became in 1868 the 18th president of the United States; he served, with scandalous ineptitude and disregard for the laws of the land, for two terms.
11 – Ibid., p. 30.
12 – Alfred, Lord Tennyson (1809–92); Robert Browning (1812–89); Matthew Arnold (1822–88); Thomas Carlyle (1795–1881); J. A. Froude (1818–94); George Eliot (1819–80); Herbert Spencer (1820–1903); T. H. Huxley (1825–95); J. S. Mill (1806–73). (Another name VW might have added to this catalogue of eminent Victorians was that of her father, Leslie Stephen.)
13 – London clubs whose habitués tended to be of a radical and anti-clerical persuasion. (Leslie Stephen belonged for a period to both.)

14 – Farringford and, from *c.* 1874, The Briary, abutting properties at Freshwater in the Isle of Wight, were owned respectively by Tennyson and the painter G. F. Watts (1817–1904) – a milieu famously laughed at by VW in *Freshwater, A Comedy,* first performed in January 1935.

Melbury Road was the site in Kensington of the original Little Holland House, where Watts lived for about twenty-five years, from about 1850, with Henry Thoby Prinsep (1793–1878), of the Indian Civil Service, and his wife Sara, *née* Pattle (1816–67), a great-aunt of VW; and, less than 200 yards distant, of the new Little Holland House which Watts had built in the 1870s.

15 – Sir Edward Burne-Jones (1833–98), the painter, having first migrated from Bloomsbury to Kensington in 1864, finally settled in the following year at The Grange, North End Road, West Kensington; he was a frequent visitor at nearby Little Holland House. Carlyle lived in Chelsea, at no. 5 (now 24), Cheyne Row. George Eliot lived at The Priory, North Bank, Regent's Park, 1863–80.

16 – *Middle Years,* p. 74; Sabina Matilda (Mrs Richard) Greville, *née* Thellusson, of Milford Cottage, Surrey.

17 – *Ibid.,* pp. 79–82; the 'almost tragic occasion' refers to a visit James made, in the company of Mrs Greville, to Witley Villa, the Surrey retreat of George Eliot and G. H. Lewes (1817–78). The encounter ended with Lewes returning to James's hands 'a pair of blue-bound volumes' lent him by Mrs Greville. '". . . take them away, please, away, away!" I hear him unreservedly plead while he thrusts them at me,' James records (p. 82), 'and I scurry back into our conveyance, where . . . I venture to assure myself of the horrid truth that had squinted at me as I relieved our good friend of his superfluity. What indeed was this superfluity but the two volumes of my own precious "last" [*The Europeans* (1878).] – . . .'

18 – *Ibid.,* p. 76.

19 – For all three quotations, *ibid.,* p. 76.

20 – *Ibid.,* p. 75.

21 – *Ibid.,* p. 86.

22 – *Ibid.,* p. 102, which has: 'the pleasant growling note heard behind me, as the Bard followed with Mrs Greville'.

23 – Louisa, Marchioness of Waterford, *née* Stuart (d.1891), celebrated beauty and an accomplished painter, widow of the 3rd Marquess of Waterford (d.1859).

24 – *Middle Years,* p. 109, which has '"accomplishment"'.

25 – *Ibid.,* p. 88.

26 – *Ibid.,* p. 89.

27 – *Ibid.,* p. 90.

28 – Tennyson's second residence, near Haslemere in Surrey.

29 – *Middle Years,* p. 98, which has: 'it was a large'.

30 – *Ibid.,* p. 100.

31 – *Ibid.,* p. 104, from a more extensive sentence. *Locksley Hall* (1832).

32 – *Ibid.,* p. 105, from a more extensive sentence.

33 – For both quotations *ibid.,* p. 101, which has: 'If I should speak of this impression as that of glory without history, that of the poetic character more worn than paid for, or at least more saved than spent, I should doubtless much over-

emphasise; but such, or something like it, was none the less the explanation that met one's own fond fancy of the scene after one had cast about for it.'
34 – *Ibid.*, p. 85; George Eliot's *Daniel Deronda* was published in 1876.
35 – *Ibid.*, p. 114.

'Hearts of Controversy'

Although Mrs Meynell[2] is a true critic, courageous, authoritative, and individual, she will only consent to use her gift, publicly, in the cause of controversy. 'Exposition, interpretation,' she says, 'by themselves are not necessary. But for controversy there is cause.'[3] She sets no high value upon criticism – 'Poor little art of examination and formula!'[4] as she calls it. But we should suppose that no one today is more scrupulously careful than Mrs Meynell to determine what is to be said for and against any book that she thinks worth reading. We are conscious that she has made up her mind with unusual firmness, and that there is no writer of worth whom she has not by this time placed within a fraction of an inch of what she judges to be his right position. She, much more than most of us, knows what her standards are, and applies them as she reads. Her criticism, therefore, has a character and a definiteness which make it worth considering, worth testing, and worth disagreeing with.

The present volume of essays is an attempt to set right certain great reputations which, owing to our general habit of reading quickly and lazily accepting the current view of the case, are in danger of losing their proper proportions. The public version is a strange thing. It sways us much more than we are aware. We are swept along by an anonymous voice which alternatively debases Tennyson, exalts Swinburne, pits Thackeray against Dickens,[5] and bestows the laurel wreath and withdraws it on the impulse of the moment. Mrs Meynell's call to order is timely, and in many instances we come to heel with a good deal of contrition for our misdemeanours. The evident courage of her outspoken essay on Swinburne need not distract our attention from the profound though unwelcome truth of much of her criticism of him. But we have one complaint to lodge without entire confidence in its justness, so that we prefer to put it in the form of a question. Is it right that a critic should make his audience so conscious of their stupidity? May we not charge it partly to over-ingenuity on his part, although the main blame must rest with us? We were content in the belief that no one was going to say anything that we had not dimly foretold about Tennyson. And Mrs Meynell, with her precision and power of phrase, puts our dim foreboding perfectly. He is 'the poet with the great welcome style and the little unwelcome manner', she says. That is in the first place. But in the second he is, not so obviously, 'the poet who withstood France'.[6] Throwing out by the way the provocative remark that Matthew Arnold spoke of France as he spoke French, with 'an incurably English accent', she finally proclaims Tennyson 'our wild poet, . . . and wilder poet than the rough, than the sensual, than the defiant, than the accuser, than the denouncer'.[7] Wild is not the word we foresaw; but it is, of course, the exact word that Mrs Meynell means. Mrs Meynell never says a loose thing; and therefore we have to see, though we feel blind and blundering as we set about it, what we can do with this new ingredient in our conception. Then there is Dickens. Her distinction between exaggeration and caricature is admirably fine, and her reproof of our age in the person of Mr Lascelles Abercrombie is exquisite: 'My dear, you exaggerate.'[8] But then comes the queer shock that Mrs Meynell admires chiefly in Dickens, together with the humour and his dramatic tragedy, 'his watchfulness over inanimate things and landscape'.[9] The quotations she makes prove us partly in the wrong there too. If we give ourselves a bad mark for that oversight, must we have another because we are unable to trace the influence of Bolingbroke upon his style,[10] and a third because we cannot point directly to the two words that Dickens 'habitually misuses' although we are given the clue that Charles Lamb 'misuses one of them precisely in Dickens's manner'?[11] On the whole, we are inclined to make a distinction. Sometimes – the greater number of times by far – Mrs Meynell writes like a critic, and sometimes she writes like a specialist; sometimes she says the large sound thing, and sometimes she picks up the curious detail, puts it in the foreground, and lavishes upon it an attention which it does not deserve.

And where should we place the question of the English language – in the background or in the foreground? Our own prejudice would lead us to put it as far in the shadow of the background as possible. We prefer never to know, certainly never to mention, the pedigree of a word. We can see no reason for believing that a long pedigree makes a good word, or that there is any test of a word save the test of taste, which varies widely and should have every liberty to vary. The critic who brands certain words or phrases with the mark of his displeasure interferes with the liberty of the writer, and fetters his hand in the instinctive reach for what he wants. Let us then say nothing of words, let us leave grammar to right itself, and let us use them both as little consciously as possible. But here we are at variance with Mrs Meynell, whose sense of right and wrong in these matters is so clearly defined that she can make the question of Charlotte Brontë's use of English in the earlier books a cause of controversy. She wrote 'to evince, to reside, to intimate, to peruse'; she spoke of 'communicating instruction', 'a small competency', and so on.[12] It is quite true, and, to us, quite immaterial. A particle of dust, however, is not going to blind our eyes to the force and skill with which Mrs Meynell sends her arrow again and again to the heart of her target.

1 – A review in the TLS, 25 October 1917, (Kp C90) of Hearts of Controversy (Burns & Oates, 1917) by Alice Meynell. 'L[eonard]. out until 5 at his conference,' VW noted in her diary on Thursday, 18 October, '& the telephone rang constantly (so I thought, as I tried to pin Mrs Meynell down in a review)'.

2 – Alice Christiana Gertrude Meynell (1847–1922), poet and journalist, edited with her husband, Wilfrid Meynell, the Weekly Register, 1881–98, and the monthly Merry England, 1883–95, and contributed to the Pall Mall Gazette. Her work, both as essayist and poet, was admired and championed by Coventry Patmore, George Meredith and Francis Thompson, who addressed poems to her.

3 – Meynell, Intro., preliminary unnumbered page.

4 – Ibid., 'Swinburne's Lyrical Poetry', p. 56.

5 – Alfred, Lord Tennyson (1809–92); Algernon Charles Swinburne (1837–1909); W. M. Thackeray (1811–63); Charles Dickens (1812–70).

6 – For Tennyson in the first and in the second place, Meynell, 'Some Thoughts of a Reader of Tennyson', p. 8.

7 – For Matthew Arnold (1822–88) and his French accent, ibid., p. 9; and for Tennyson the wild poet, ibid., pp. 21–2, slightly adapted, and which concludes: 'Wild flowers are his – great poet – wild winds, wild lights, wild heart, wild eyes!'

8 – Ibid., 'Dickens as a Man of Letters', p. 28. The criticism of Lascelles Abercrombie (1881–1938) is directed at his poem 'Judith', published in Emblems of Love (1912).

9 – Ibid., p. 29.

10 – Ibid., p. 50; Henry St John, 1st Viscount Bolingbroke (1678–1751), statesman, friend of Pope and of Swift, and the author of brilliant political journalism, notably in the Craftsman, a periodical in which appeared his 'Remarks on the History of England by Humphry Oldcastle' (1730–1) and 'A Dissertation on Parties' (1733). His prose style is, according to Meynell, especially reflected in Esther Summerson's words in Bleak House (1852–3): 'There was nothing to be undone; no chain for him to drag or for me to break'.

11 – For the unspecified misuses of Dickens and of Charles Lamb (1775–1834), ibid., p. 44.

12 – For Charlotte Brontë (1816–55) and her use of English, ibid., 'Charlotte and Emily Brontë', p. 77; and see also 'Dickens as a Man of Letters', p. 45.

'A Russian Schoolboy'

The previous volumes of this chronicle, *Years of Childhood* and *A Russian Gentleman*,[2] left us with a feeling of personal friendship for Serge Aksakoff; we had come to know him and his family as we know people with whom we have stayed easily for weeks at a time in the country. The figure of Aksakoff himself has taken a place in our minds which is more like that of a real person than a person whom we have merely known in a book. Since reading the first volume of Mr Duff's translation we have read many new books; many clear, sharp characters have passed before our eyes, but in most cases they have left nothing behind them but a sense of more or less brilliant activity. But Aksakoff has remained – a man of extraordinary freshness and substance, a man with a rich nature, moving in the sun and shadow of real life so that it is possible, as we have found during the past year or two, to settle down placidly and involuntarily to think about him. Such words as these would not apply truthfully perhaps to some very great works of art; but nothing that produces this impression of fullness and intimacy can be without some of the rarest qualities and, in our opinion, some of the most delightful. We have spoken of Aksakoff as a man, but unfortunately we have no right to do that, for we have known him only as a boy, and the last volume of the three leaves him when he has but reached the age of fifteen. With this volume, Mr Duff tells us, the chronicle is finished; and our regret and desire to read another three, at least, is the best thanks we can offer him for his labour of translation. When we consider the rare merit of these books we can scarcely thank the translator sufficiently. We can only hope that he will look round and find another treasure of the same importance.

Ignorant as we are of the works of Aksakoff, it would be rash to say that this autobiography is the most characteristic of them; and yet one feels certain that there was something especially congenial to him in the recollection of childhood. When he was still a small boy he could plunge into 'the inexhaustible treasury of recollection'.[3] He is not, we think, quite so happy in the present volume because he passes a little beyond the scope of childhood. It deals less with the country; and the magic, which consists so much in being very small among people of immeasurable size so that one's parents are far more romantic than one's brothers and sisters, was departing. When he was at school the boys were on an equality with him; the figures were contracting and becoming more like the people whom we see when we are grown up. Aksakoff's peculiar gift lay in his power of living back into the childish soul. He can give to perfection the sense of the nearness, the largeness, the absolute dominance of the detail before the prospect has arranged itself so that details are only part of a well-known order. He makes us remember, and this is perhaps more difficult, how curiously the child's mind is taken up with what we call childish things together with premonitions of another kind of life, and with moments of extreme insight into its surroundings. He is thus able to give us a very clear notion of his father and mother, although we see them always as they appeared to a child. The effect of truth and vividness which is so remarkable in each of his volumes is the result of writing not from the man's point of view, but by becoming a child again; for it is impossible that the most tenacious memory should have been able to store the millions of details from which these books are fashioned. We have to suppose that Aksakoff kept to the end of his life a power of changing back into a different stage of growth at the touch of recollection, so that the process is more one of living over again than of remembering. From a psychological point of view this is a curious condition – to view the pond or the tree as it is now without emotion, but to receive intense emotion from the same sight by remembering the emotion which it roused fifty years ago. It is clear that Aksakoff, with his abundant and impressionable nature, was precisely the man to feel his childhood to the full, and to keep the joy of reviving it fresh to the end.

The happiness of childhood ⟨he writes⟩ is the Golden Age, the recollection of it has power to move the old man's heart with pleasure and with pain. Happy is the man who once possessed it and is able to recall the memory of it in later years! With many the time passes by unnoticed or unenjoyed; and all that remains in the ripeness of age is the recollection of the coldness or even cruelty of men.[4]

He was no doubt peculiar in the strength of his feelings, and singular compared with English boys in the absence of discipline at school and at college. As Mr Duff says, 'His university studies are remarkable; he learnt no Greek, no Latin, no mathematics, and very little science – hardly anything but Russian and French.'[5] For this reason, perhaps, he remained conscious of all those little impressions which in most cases fade and are forgotten before the power of expressing them is full grown. Who is there, for example, who will not feel his early memories of coming back to a home in the country wonderfully renewed by the description of the return to Aksakovo:

As before I took to bed with me my cat, which was so attached that she followed me everywhere like a dog; and I snared small birds or trapped them and kept them in a small room which was practically converted into a spacious coop. I admired my pigeons with double tufts and feathered legs . . . which had been kept warm in my absence under the stoves or in the houses of the outdoor servants . . . To the island I ran several times a day, hardly knowing myself why I went; and there I stood motionless as if under a spell, while my heart beat hard, and my breath came unevenly.[6]

Nor is it possible to read his account of butterfly collecting without recalling some such period of fanatical excitement. Indeed, we have read no description to compare with this one for its exact, prosaic, and yet most stirring reproduction of the succeeding stages of a child's passion. It begins almost by accident; it becomes in a moment the only thing in the world; of a sudden it dies down and is over for no perceptible reason. One can verify, as if from an old diary, every step that he takes with his butterfly net in his hand down that grassy valley in the burning heat until he sees within two yards of him 'fluttering from flower to flower a splendid *swallow-tail!*'[7] And then follows the journey home, where the small sister has begun collecting on her brother's account, and has turned all the jugs and tumblers in her room upside down, and even opened the lid of the piano and put butterflies alive inside of it. Nevertheless, in a few months the passion is over, and 'we devoted all our leisure to literature, producing [. . .] a manuscript magazine . . . I became deeply interested in acting also.'[8]

All childhood is passionate, but if we compare the childhood of Aksakoff with our memories and observations of English childhood we shall be struck with the number and the violence of his enthusiasms. When his mother left him at school he sat on his bed with his eyes staring wildly, unable to think or to cry, and had to be put to bed, rubbed with flannels, and restored to consciousness by a violent fit of shivering. His sensitiveness to any recollection of childhood was such, even as a child, that the sound of a voice, a patch of sunlight on the wall, a fly buzzing on the pane, which reminded him of his past, threw him into a fit. His health became so bad that he had to be taken home. These fits and ecstasies, in which his mother often joined him, will hardly fail to remind the reader of many similar scenes which are charged against Dostoevsky as a fault. The fault, if it is a fault, appears to be more in the Russian nature than in the novelist's version of it. From the evidence supplied by Aksakoff we realise how little discipline enters into their education; and we also realise, what we do not gather from Dostoevsky, how sane, natural and happy such a life can be. Partly because of his love of nature, that unconscious perception of beauty which lay at the back of his shooting and fishing and butterfly catching, partly because of the largeness and generosity of his character, the impression produced by these volumes is an impression of abundance and of happiness. As Aksakoff says in a beautiful description of an uncle and aunt of his, 'The atmosphere seemed to have something calming and life-giving in it, something suited to beast and plant.'[9] At the same time we have only to compare him, as he has been compared, with Gilbert White to realise the Russian element in him, the element of self-consciousness and introspection.[10] No one is very simple who realises so fully what is happening to him, or who can trace, as he traces it, the moment when 'the radiance' fades and the 'peculiar feeling of sadness'[11] begins. His power of registering these changes shows that he was qualified to write also an incomparable account of maturity.

He gives in this book a description of the process of letting water out of a pond. A crowd of peasants collected upon the banks. 'All Russians love to watch moving water . . . The people saluted with shouts of joy the element they loved, as it tore its way to freedom from its winter prison.'[12] The shouts of joy and the love of watching both seem the peculiar property of the Russian people. From such a combination one would expect to find one of these days that they have produced the greatest of autobiographies, as they have produced perhaps the greatest of novels. But Aksakoff is more than a prelude; his work in its individuality and its beauty stands by itself.

1 – A review in the *TLS*, 8 November 1917, (Kp c91) of *A Russian Schoolboy. Translated from the Russian by J. D. Duff* (Edward Arnold, 1917) by Serge Aksakoff (1791–1850). Both VW and LW were to read Aksakoff in the original when, in 1921, they took lessons in Russian from S. S. Koteliansky – see *II VW Letters*, no. 1172, and *I LW*, p. 23. See also 'Mr Hudson's Childhood', below. Reprinted: *B&P*.

2 – Published in J. D. Duff's translation by Edward Arnold, in 1916 and 1917 respectively, and originally in 1856. J. D. Duff (d. 1940) was a fellow of Trinity College, Cambridge, and, incidentally, a member of the Conversazione Society (the Apostles).

3 – Aksakoff, ch. I, p. 28.

4 – *Ibid.*, p. 7, which has 'that time'.
5 – *Ibid.*, 'Translator's Pref.', p. vii.
6 – *Ibid.*, ch. I, p. 6, which has: 'attached to me'; a comma where VW has an ellipsis between 'legs' and 'which'; and no comma between 'beat hard' and 'and my breath'.
7 – *Ibid.*, 'Butterfly-Collecting', p. 190.
8 – *Ibid.*, p. 214, which has: 'producing with much enthusiasm a manuscript magazine'.
9 – *Ibid.*, ch. III, p. 109, from a longer sentence.
10 – For the comparison with Gilbert White (1720–93), see Prince Kropotkin, *Russian Literature* (Duckworth & Co., 1905), p. 177.
11 – *Ibid.*, ch. II, p. 68: 'The radiance of some objects began to fade for me, and a peculiar feeling of sadness, such as I had never experienced before, began to cast a shadow over all the amusements and occupations I had loved so well.'
12 – *Ibid.*, p. 69, each extract is from a longer sentence.

Stopford Brooke

'As to Lord Selborne's Life, why do you read a book of that kind and done by a relation, too? One knows beforehand all that it will be, and that more than half will only be of interest to the relative and none to the world.'² Such was Stopford Brooke's opinion of the ordinary biography, and the reader who sits down to a couple of stout volumes dedicated to Brooke's own life, 'done by a relation, too',³ may nurse a question of the same sort at the back of his mind. Judged by some of the standards which justify lavish and minute biography, Stopford Brooke may be found wanting. He left behind him no literary work of the first class. Time seems already to have withered a little the profusion and vitality of much that he wrote, and it is scarcely fair to read as literature much that he spoke.⁴ But books are not the only test of greatness, even among those whose lives are spent in making them. The little circle of the great must be enlarged to include some of those who have spent themselves upon many things rather than concentrated upon a single one. But the question of greatness, always of little account in biography, need not trouble us at present. No reader of this book is likely to ask whether it was worth doing; and he will be wise, we think, not to attempt to sum up Stopford Brooke as this, that, or the other until he has read to the end, when the desire for such definitions may have left him.

For this biography has one quality at least which makes it very unlike the usual biography. It has the quality of growth. It is the record of the things that change rather than of the things that happen. Instead of knowing beforehand all that it will be, we constantly, as in life itself, find ourselves baffled and trying to understand. Much is due to the beautifully loving and alert skill with which Mr Jacks has done his work. Apart from the closeness of his relationship, he has by nature a singular insight into the qualities which made Stopford Brooke so memorable. He is peculiarly fitted to interpret the mass of documents which Brooke, with his passion for self-expression and his hatred of concealment, had written at all times of his life and left behind him. To our thinking, the result is a book not of revelations or confessions in the usual sense, but of spiritual development which carries the art of biography a step further in the most interesting direction now open to it — that of psychology.

The facts of Brooke's life are probably well known. Born in 1832, the son of a poor but well-born Irish clergyman, he was ordained in 1857, was curate at Kensington from 1859 to 1863, took the lease of St James's Chapel in 1865, and left the Church of England in 1880. From such a record we should expect to find conflicting strains at work in him. In his case they are so marked as to lie upon the surface, so profound as between them to rule his whole being.

One side of his nature ⟨says Mr Jacks⟩ belonged to religion; the other to art . . . He possessed a deep natural piety . . . but his feet were firmly planted on the earth; no pagan ever loved it better or received from contact with the things of sense a fuller current of the joy of life . . . and there is little doubt that had he lived in some age or society to which Christian culture was unknown he would have found satisfaction and won eminence . . . Between these two tendencies, the Christian and the Greek . . . the mediating power in Brooke was the impassioned love of beauty in all its forms, both natural and spiritual . . . His finest work, which ripened slowly and late, was the fruit of their union.[5]

In our age such a dual spirit is perhaps no uncommon inheritance; in the majority of cases one instinct triumphs and the other dies, or they both survive, imperfectly, in a state of chronic warfare. But it is extremely rare to find a mind open enough to widen year by year so that there is room for each different plant to come to flower. In the process the formal limitations devised by the hand of man might be swept aside, as indeed they were. Brooke, naturally enough, was marked down 'unsafe'[6] as a curate, and kept out of the danger of preferment by his superiors. He vacillated in the strangest way between Lisson Grove and Piccadilly, where he astonished the dowagers of that day by exclaiming, 'We must have more joy in life – I say, more joy!'[7] He found out in time that he was not meant to remain a curate. Nor would he go on acting as chaplain to the embassy at Berlin,[8] in spite of the opportunities which that position at one time seemed to promise of teaching future emperors of Germany the meaning of liberty. 'She ⟨the Crown Princess of Prussia⟩ wants an English tutor for her boys, to teach them, she said, "liberal principles, the English Constitution, and the growth of the nation into free government. Princes nowadays have no chance, Mr Brooke, unless they are liberal."'[9] He preferred to take his own chapel and preach his own message.

Then, after preaching for twenty-five years, he finds that the Church of England has become a fetter upon him, and he unloosens himself and passes on with no more effort, it seems, than a flower displays when it opens another bud. The faculty is puzzling and deserves our attention. 'No man,' says Mr Jacks, 'ever lived who was less in trouble about his soul than Brooke.'[10] 'His power of dismissing things,' said Mr Chesterton, 'is beyond praise'.[11] Mr Jacks's comment upon this is that when the issue was to be decided by argument Brooke's faculty of dismissing things 'would sometimes lead him to discharge the argument altogether and replace it with a bold statement of his own intuition'.[12] It is possible to suppose that if Brooke had been a deeper thinker this could not have been so; and, if, as Mr Jacks says, his position in the Church morally admitted of a very simple definition, 'that of a man who week by week publicly declares that he believes what he does not believe', it is strange that it should have taken him till he was nearly fifty to find that 'such a position is positively hateful'.[13]

But one must remember that Brooke attached very little importance to thinking – 'there is always the knowledge at the back of the mind that the secret of life is not in thinking, but in loving'.[14] And he spoke with impatience always of 'self-vivisecting souls ... twisting and turning incessantly in the labyrinth of their own spiritual entrails'.[15] But it is vain to attempt to summarise in a few words the many different intuitions and susceptibilities which resulted in Brooke's peculiar faith. It was the growth of his love of art, in which one may include the love of liberty and the love of humanity, his friendship with such men as Ruskin, Burne-Jones, Morris, and Holman Hunt, that chiefly made it impossible for him to wear 'an official uniform'[16] any longer. The story of a walk through the streets of London with his daughter illustrates in an amusing way his power of living in the world of imagination. They determined to act the 'Seven Ages of Man' as they went along in order that 'the Londoners might at last have the benefit of some really good Shakespearean acting'. Having astonished the Londoners who recognised their preacher, they burst at last into the room of J. R. Green, shouting 'Here we are, Green, *sans* eyes, *sans* teeth, *sans* taste, *sans* everything.'[17] Meanwhile, he was making a very beautiful house in Manchester Square.[18] There were books in precious bindings, and pictures everywhere, beautiful things which he loved to buy, loved to explain, and loved to give away. A stranger to that house and to that talk of literature and art would, says Mr Jacks, have guessed him to be an artist, but on hearing that he was a clergyman 'there would have been no ultimate surprise'.[19] And this we fancy is the point for the reader to hold fast in his mind. We have spoken of growth and change, but the goal is always towards some synthesis in which views generally found antagonistic are harmonised. The goal is pursued, moreover, down crowded streets and in the thick of men and women. His week contained many dinner parties and interviews and long delightful talks in the 'eagle's nest'[20] at the top of the house; but for all that this is not a life in which individual men and women are seen vividly or described intimately. Famous though many of the names are, the 'good stories'[21] are few or none. The aim was at some large community founded upon brotherhood rather than towards the salvation of the individual soul.

Significantly enough Mr Jacks has recourse to the words of an Indian writer and quotes from the *Sādhanā* of Tagore when he wishes to give 'the essential message' of Stopford Brooke. The passage, describing the unity between man and nature, is too long to quote in full; and it is difficult, we think, to understand it.[22] But even for those who are aware of an impediment in their understanding of such philosophies the last years of Brooke's life suggest many more ideas than can be dealt with at all adequately in a review. The bare facts are that he withdrew from London with powers unabated, ceased to work, and was completely happy. So rare is happiness that it sometimes seems as if the desire for it must be among the weakest of our desires. One has come to take it for granted that the possession of great intellectual gifts is equivalent, in the West at least, to unhappiness in manhood and an old age of resignation or battered peace at the best. One saying of Brooke's throws, we think, much light upon his reversal of the common experience. 'Green said, "I die learning." I say I shall die un-learning, and, 'pon my word, it's the wiser of the two sayings.'[23] We cannot help connecting the faculty of 'un-learning', which implies so much else, with that other power which is so marked and has such curious results in the memorable story of Brooke's old age. It happened that he found himself in 1898 at Homburg surrounded by people who reminded him of the characters in Ibsen – that is to say, people one would not touch 'even with a fishing rod ten yards long'.[24] As a way of escape he invented a myth in which the three springs of the place became people. Begun in play the story became something which he accepted as having actually taken place. We have not space to go into the details of this strange dream world, or of Mr Jacks's most interesting analysis of it. We call it strange because the expression of that state with anything like Brooke's degree of fullness is so rare; but we cannot help thinking that the experience in one shape or another is common enough, especially among those who are in the habit of putting their mental experiences into words. For the most part a moral objection of some sort tends to deny this side of the mind expression, and thus starves it of life. With Brooke the tendency is of the opposite kind. The whole story of his life is the story of a mind kept open in part by a powerful instinct of self-expression, and in part also by the tendency which became stronger and stronger in him against morality 'save as the expression of love'.[25] The record of the development of such a mind is one of the greatest interest, and one rarely attempted.

1 – A review in the *TLS*, 29 November 1917, (Kp C91.1) of *Life and Letters of Stopford Brooke* (John Murray, 1917) by Lawrence Pearsall Jacks. 'I don't like Sunday,' VW noted in her diary on 26 November 1917, 'the best thing is to make it a work day, & to unravel Brooke's mind to the sound of church bells was suitable enough.'

See also 'Philosophy in Fiction', below; and 'Fantasy', *III VW Essays*.

2 – Jacks, vol. ii, ch. xxvi, p. 524. The work referred to is *Memorials* (4 vols., Macmillan & Co. Ltd., 1896–8) by Roundell Palmer, 1st Earl of Selborne (1812–95), Lord Chancellor, 1872–4, 1880–5, under Gladstone.

3 – *Ibid.*; Lawrence Pearsall Jacks (1860–1955), unitarian divine, principal of Manchester College, Oxford, 1915–31, was Brooke's assistant at Bedford Chapel and in 1889 married his daughter Olive Cecilia.

4 – Stopford Augustus Brooke (1832–1916) had won prizes for English verse while at Trinity College, Dublin, but his literary legacy, such as it is, consists chiefly in criticism. His *Primer of English Literature* (1876) was received enthusiastically by Matthew Arnold and sold widely; VW quotes from it, without identifying her source, in her essay 'I Am Christina Rossetti', *V VW Essays* and *CR2*.

5 – Jacks, vol. i, ch. IV, pp. 55–7, which has: 'But his feet'; and 'an impassioned love'.

6 – *Ibid.*, vol. i, ch. VII, p. 114: 'Indeed, from the point of view of bishops and vicars in 1860 he was distinctly "unsafe", and his Broad Church views, extremely

moderate as they now seem, were a barrier which not even the influence of powerful friends could always overcome.'

7 – *Ibid.*, vol. i, ch. VI, p. 94; Brooke held his first curacy at St Matthew's, Lisson Grove, Marylebone, 1857–9, but enjoyed (*ibid.*, p. 92), at Piccadilly, Grosvenor Place, Portman Square, 'almost daily ... meetings with Ministers of State, Ambassadors, artists, men of letters – and ... other meetings too, "on a balcony, overlooking the Green Park", when Maud is quoted under the moon'.

8 – Brooke was chaplain at Berlin, 1863–4, ministering to the English court established around Victoria (1840–1901), the Princess Royal, who in 1858 had married Crown Prince Frederick of Prussia (1831–88), the future emperor of Germany.

9 – Jacks, vol. i, ch. XII, p. 219.

10 – *Ibid.*, ch. XI, p. 197, which has: 'But a man'.

11 – *Ibid.*, ch. XVI, p. 311, quoting G. K. Chesterton (1874–1936) on Brooke's *Browning* (1902), in the *Daily News*, 25 September 1902.

12 – *Ibid.*

13 – *Ibid.*, ch. XVI, p. 319, which has: 'believe; and it is not exaggeration to say that he found the position at this point positively hateful'.

14 – *Ibid.*, vol. ii, ch. XXX, p. 602.

15 – *Ibid.*, ch. XXIII, p. 481, adapted.

16 – *Ibid.*, vol. i, ch. XVI, p. 317; in addition to the personages cited by VW, Jacks also lists Tennyson, Arnold, the Earl and Countess of Carlisle, Giovanni Costa, the Italian painter, and Alphonse Legros, the French etcher, painter and sculptor.

17 – For both references to this Shakespearean episode, *ibid.*, vol. ii, ch. XX, p. 423. John Richard Green (1837–83), historian, author of a *Short History of the English People* (1874).

18 – No. 1 Manchester Square, Marylebone.

19 – Jacks, vol. ii, ch. XX, p. 413, which has: 'no ultimate incredulity'.

20 – *Ibid.*, p. 414.

21 – This phrase does not occur in Jacks.

22 – Jacks, vol. ii, ch. XXIX, p. 586; Brooke first became acquainted with the Indian poet and mystic Rabindranath Tagore (1861–1941) in 1911; Tagore's *Sādhanā*, addresses on life and its realisation, was published in 1913.

23 – *Ibid.*, p. 584.

24 – *Ibid.*, ch. XXVII, p. 554.

25 – *Ibid.*, ch. XXII, p. 454.

Mr Gladstone's Daughter

Those who say that the art of letter-writing is dead are not presumably the daughters of prime ministers.[2] We may make so bold as to suppose that these favoured people still sometimes sigh when their share of the postbag is meted out to them. The envelopes are not only numerous, but in some cases they are swollen beyond the scope of easy breakfast-table reading. In writing to Mrs Drew, Sir Mountstuart Grant Duff, for instance, would enclose a record of a twenty-six days' tour in India and proceed to make his statement about the condition of Hyderabad.[3] Lord Stanmore, then Sir Arthur Gordon, would give expression to the difficulties which beset a colonial governor conscious of a 'power of work and attention to detail with an ungrudging trust in my subordinates'.[4] Other correspondents remark that it is very important that the new Bishop (of London) shall be a Liberal;[5] and again someone pleads that a poet shall be given a pension, and does that pension last his lifetime or 'does it end if the country wants to be Tory'?[6]

That is the official side of Mrs Drew's correspondence, the inevitable privilege, or penalty, of being her father's daughter. But the men and women who came to Hawarden to see Mr Gladstone generally became almost independently of that the friends of Mrs Drew. The character of her correspondents makes it inadmissible to suppose that she was ever made use of – save with the completely open injunction, 'Please tell Mr Gladstone' – to take a message from the writer to her father. And yet some of the most amusing passages in these letters are amusing precisely because of the accident of her birth. People who, as we must feel, had no business in that sphere at all came fluttering through it in a delightfully audacious way. Ruskin had written an article which interested Mr Gladstone, and was invited to stay at Hawarden. He came, with a telegram of recall in his pocket, 'as suspiciously as a wild animal entering a trap'.[7] When he left he was on such cordial terms with them all that he wrote at once to his publisher to cancel certain strictures in *Fors*, being, as he put it, 'greatly dismayed'[8] to find how much more admirable Mr Gladstone was than he had expected to find him. All went well for two years. He was then moved to declare that he cared no more for Mr Gladstone or Mr Disraeli[9] than he did for two old bagpipes. This he could not retract, so he explained to Mrs Drew, because he meant it; nor would he mind if Mr Gladstone called him a 'broken bottle stuck on the top of a wall', upon which Mr Gladstone exclaimed with delight, 'He stands apart from and above all other men.'[10] Whether his further vociferations against Home Rule and in favour of land possession for all the world 'eternal as the mountains and the sea'[11] ever reached Mr Gladstone's ears we are not told; but when he and Burne-Jones talk about politics they do so with a freshness and a passion which might have made even Mrs Gladstone less bored by that subject than she was quite unashamed to be.[12]

Politics have their share in these letters, but no more than their share. The interest lies rather in the attitude of that particular group of highly privileged people towards the books and the pictures and the men and women of their time. The group ('chiefly drawn from the Gladstone, Balfour, and Lyttelton families')[13] was intimate, communicative, and honestly persuaded that nature as well as fortune had been generous at any rate to the others. They were alive to whatever went forward in a good many different worlds, and took their sides enthusiastically. The *Life of Carlyle* forms them into an anti-Froude society; *Progress and Poverty* goes the round from one earnest correspondent to another; *The Vulture Maiden* is 'devoured'; first impressions of *Robert Elsmere* are debated with extreme seriousness and not a little apprehension as to what the result of the book may be; the 'Maiden Tribute' crusade of Mr Stead is discussed passionately by Professor Stuart and gravely by Alfred Lyttelton.[14] And *Diana of the Crossways* and *The Minister's Wooing*, and 'Mme de Mauves' and the *Redemption of Edward Strachan*[15] are all coming out and getting inextricably mixed in importance and commendation.

Such was the nucleus of the larger group of the eighties 'styled, by those who did not belong to it, "The Souls"'.[16] Is there still, as the severity of these words implies, a public which impudently pretends to know more than it possibly can know about that gifted constellation, and in default of facts invents rumours? Here at any rate it is not going to be satisfied; here are only glimpses, not secrets. But these glimpses are certainly very pleasant. Mr Balfour stands at the top of a great double staircase and reflects, 'The worst of this staircase is that there is absolutely no reason why one should go down one side rather than the other. What am I to do?'[17] Joachim asks Miss Gladstone whether Wednesday would suit her 'to play with my accompaniment'.[18] In short, we can see quite enough to know that we should like to see more. The pity is that so little, not even the newspaper which was to advocate higher truths and at the same time let off the scum, survives for our edification. For although Mrs Drew's letters throw lights upon a past society significant even to the public and illuminating doubtless to friends, they are on the whole, and with the exception of Burne-Jones's letter, oddly inexpressive, oddly unformed and undistinguished, if you consider the names and the gifts of the writers. When it is a question of

Wyndhams and Lytteltons one can scarcely help considering their names and thinking of the eighteenth century, and remembering how Horace Walpole too was the son of a Prime Minister.[19]

1 – A review in the *TLS*, 6 December 1917, (Kp C92) of *Some Hawarden Letters. 1878–1913. Written to Mrs Drew (Miss Mary Gladstone). Before and after her marriage.* Chosen and arranged by Leslie March-Phillipps and Bertram Christian (Nisbet & Co. Ltd., 1917).

2 – William Ewart Gladstone (1809–98) was Prime Minister 1868–74, 1880–5, 1886, and 1892–4.

3 – *Letters*, ch. V, p. 153, 16 August 1884. Sir Mountstuart Elphinstone Grant Duff (1829–1906), statesman and author, Liberal M.P., 1857–81; he served under Gladstone as Under-Secretary of State for India, 1868–74, and for the Colonies, 1880–1, and was Lieutenant Governor of Madras, 1881–6.

4 – *Ibid.*, ch. IV, p. 98, 27 January 1882. Sir Arthur Charles Hamilton Gordon (1829–1912), created Baron Stanmore in 1893, had at one time been Gladstone's private secretary; he held several colonial governorships, including those of New Zealand, 1880–3, and Ceylon, 1883–90.

5 – *Ibid.*, ch. VI, p. 199, from Professor James Stuart of Trinity College, Cambridge, 10 January 1885. The new bishop of London, Frederick Temple (1821–1902), a future archbishop of Canterbury, was enthroned at St Paul's in April 1885; he was, indeed, a Liberal.

6 – *Ibid.*, ch. III, p. 85, from Edward Burne-Jones (1833–1898), concerning the pitman poet Joseph Shipsey, undated.

7 – *Ibid.*, ch. I, p. 6, editorial commentary. John Ruskin (1819–1900).

8 – *Ibid.*, ch. II, p. 21, John Ruskin, writing to his publisher, 18 January 1878: 'I have been greatly dismayed by the discovery to me of Mr Gladstone's real character, as I saw it at Hawarden: its intense simplicity and earnestness laying themselves open to every sort of misinterpretation – being unbelievable unless one saw him. I must cancel all my attack on him in *Fors*.' *Fors Clavigera* (1871–84), a series of letters addressed to the workmen and labourers of Britain.

9 – Benjamin Disraeli (1804–81), Tory Prime Minister, 1867–8, 1874–80.

10 – For the first quotation, *ibid.*, ch. III, p. 65, 23 October 1880; and for the second, *ibid.*, p. 63, editorial commentary, which continues: 'He is an exception and must never be judged by ordinary standards'.

11 – *Ibid.*, ch. IV, p. 102, 29 March 1882.

12 – *Ibid.*, Pref., pp. xii–xiii: ' "She contrived," Lady Lovelace says of her, "to combine the keenest interest and quick apprehension of all that concerned her husband's career with the most unashamed boredom with politics in general." '

13 – *Ibid.*, ch. IV, p. 135. Gladstone was an intimate friend of George William, 4th Baron Lyttelton (1817–76), who had married Mary Glynne, Mrs Gladstone's sister. Arthur James Balfour, 1st Earl of Balfour (1848–1930), philosopher and statesman, was intimate with Baron Lyttelton's extensive family and in 1875 had become engaged to his daughter May Lyttelton, who died a month or so after Balfour's proposal.

14 – J. A. Froude, *Thomas Carlyle: A History of his Life in London. 1834–1881* (1884); for its responsibility for the anti-Froude society, *ibid.*, ch. III, p. 91, editorial commentary. Henry George, *Progress and Poverty* (1879). For the devouring of *The Vulture Maiden* (1876), by Wilhelmine von Hillern, *ibid.*, ch. IV, letter from H. S. Holland, 1883, p. 133. For the agitation of W. T. Stead (1849–1912), editor of the *Pall Mall Gazette*, 1883–90, *ibid.*, ch. VI, pp. 200–1, 206–7. In July 1885 Stead published an attack on immorality in England entitled 'The Maiden Tribute of Modern Babylon', in which he indirectly implicated several public figures. As a result, parliament was galvanised into passing a Criminal Law Amendment Act, over which it had dragged its feet for some time, raising the age of consent to sixteen; and Stead, who had failed to substantiate some crucial evidence, spent three months in prison for libel.

15 – George Meredith, *Diana of the Crossways* (1885); Harriet Beecher Stowe, *The Minister's Wooing* (1859); Henry James, 'Mme de Mauves' (1873), collected in *A Passionate Pilgrim and Other Tales* (1875); W. H. Dawson, *The Redemption of Edward Strachan* (?1892).

16 – *Letters*, ch. IV, p. 135, editorial commentary.

17 – *Ibid.*

18 – *Ibid.*, ch. IV, p. 136, undated but of the period 1882–3. Joseph Joachim (1831–1907), Hungarian violinist and composer.

19 – The references, not previously noted, are to the family of George Wyndham (1863–1913), statesman and man of letters, sometime private secretary to Arthur Balfour, and chief secretary for Ireland, 1900–05; and to Horace Walpole (1717–97), fourth son of Sir Robert Walpole, prime minister, 1715–17, 1721–42.

'Charlotte Brontë'

Thirteen well-known writers,[2] twenty-eight illustrations and three maps here unite in testifying that Charlotte Brontë[3] is still a shining object to which the eyes of the living turn with love and question after a hundred years. Indubitably, she shines on, but it is also evident that no two people see the same star. Indeed, this book would be well worth reading were it only as a lesson in the meaning and nature of criticism. If we are ever inclined to think that the last word has been said and that our minds are made up for the rest of our lives, we may now change that opinion. Here are thirteen writers, all particularly fitted to define the character of this one woman and to pass judgment upon her three books, and each one of them is struck by a different quality, or values the same quality at a different rate. Nevertheless, although we must resign the comfort of depending upon an infallible support, by this means we get a much richer, more various, and finally, we believe, truer estimate than is usual. It is an example that might well be followed, were it not that few subjects lend themselves so happily to this particular treatment.

There are not many writers capable, after a century, of kindling such vivid sparks in such different minds. The essay by Mrs Humphry Ward[4] is on the whole the most comprehensive, not only because we read it before we have been disturbed, but because she is herself a novelist and has a wide knowledge of literature to lend authority to her view. She insists, quoting Renan, upon the Celtic nature of the Brontë genius;[5] the nature which grasps at passion and at poetry for their own sakes, which breaks all the rules and which neglects 'that shaping and fastidious instinct which is, in truth, the ultimate thing'. Charlotte Brontë, she says, lives because she is both dreamer and observer, 'bringing the poetic faculty to bear on the truth nearest to her'.[6] To this we should assent were it not that by doing so we must, according to Mrs Ward, sacrifice at least partially the curates in *Shirley*. Her art has not transmuted them from reality to literature, Mrs Ward explains; and yet if you cancel the first chapter of *Shirley* you lose, we think, the most convincing proof that Charlotte Brontë had a sense of humour.

But here already criticism has done part of its duty. It has revived our impression and given us the sense of possessing a live and combative conception of our author. Good criticism also is subtly suggestive; Mrs Ward whispers 'poetry, truth, feeling',[7] and sets us thinking how we too have felt the breath of the moors, and seen the purple sunset, and loved that angular honesty and rated it above wisdom. Still, Mr Gosse[8] interrupts, checking a mood which easily runs riot, have you ever thought how it would be to talk to Charlotte Brontë? 'It would probably have been disconcerting to the highest degree.'[9] She was without experience of the 'social amenities'. The atmosphere of Haworth was hard and dry; she lived in the 'blast of a perpetual moral east wind'.[10] 'She has the impatience, the unreasonable angers and revolts, of an unappreciated adolescent.'[11] All this, too, was latent in our conception, an important element, and one that has stamped itself irrevocably upon her work. If she had gone to Paris, not Brussels, if, as Mr Gosse suggests, she had studied Balzac,[12] if even she had enjoyed a few years of happiness, in what directions might she not have developed? It is tempting to speculate how humour and charity and genius itself would have ripened in the sun of a happy marriage. But such reflections are presently cut short by Bishop Welldon. 'If,' he says, 'Charlotte Brontë owed much to her own life, most of all did she owe to its sadness.'[13] For the moment this gives us pause; we grudge deeply any tribute to the value of sadness. The moral east wind and the anger bred of sadness are still too fresh in our minds. But then, after all, that intensity of passion which we honour most perhaps in Charlotte Brontë was only ground out by conflict; make her happy, make her amiable, make her fluent in society, and the writer we know has ceased to exist.

In spite of their diversities, however, these three critics have helped us to shape our conception and have not said anything which is so incompatible that we cannot make use of it. But there are more general questions to be considered, and upon these, too, the critics are at variance. Dr Garnett tells us that her principal shortcoming was that she could not create a character 'by sheer force of imagination',[14] and therefore, having to draw upon experience, had already exhausted her material. Completely though this verdict is reversed a few pages later by Professor Vaughan,[15] the question for us lies not in reconciling the critics, but in deciding what is meant by 'sheer force of imagination'. Tolstoy,[16] for example, drew far more accurately from life than Charlotte Brontë, but one can hardly charge him with a lack of creative power, or with poverty of material. Indeed, the opposite seems to be the truth; those who fix their eyes upon life itself depend more upon 'sheer force of imagination' than the purely subjective artists, if such there be, who create from their own resources. But the danger of using such ugly words as the old subjective and objective is illustrated by Dr Garnett, who, in spite of her dependence upon experience, puzzles us by placing Charlotte Brontë chief among those writers who are subjective.

But, although there are dangers, assumptions and questions of ill-defined scope leading us as far as we choose to go, the tenor of this book is unmistakable. She is the novelist of passion, of intensity, of revolt. Upon the general outlines all are agreed, but only one critic, Mr Chesterton,[17] makes, to our thinking, an unexpected contribution. An Irish friend of his, living in Yorkshire, 'once made to me the suggestive remark that the towering and over-masculine barbarians and lunatics who dominate the Brontë novels simply represent the impression produced by the rather boastful Yorkshire manners upon the more civilised and sensitive Irish temperament'.[18] That is all the more suggestive if you remember that the Brontës, being Irish and Cornish by birth, were as fanatical in their love of Yorkshire as adopted children are apt to be. There is, then, still much to ponder and much to guess; and yet, after all, the important thing after a hundred years is to feel what each of these writers feels, that whatever our differences we are all looking at a star. We have quoted Mr Gosse when he criticises Charlotte Brontë; let us end with his praise of her. 'She was, in her own words, "furnace-tried by pain, stamped by constancy", and out of her fires she rose, a Phoenix of poetic fancy, crude yet without a rival, and now, in spite of all imperfections, to live for ever in the forefront of creative English genius.'[19]

1 – A review in the TLS, 13 December 1917, (Kp c93) of *Charlotte Brontë 1816–1916. A Centenary Memorial*. Prepared by the Brontë Society. Edited by Butler Wood F.R.S.L. With a foreword by Mrs Humphry Ward and 3 maps and 28 illustrations (Fisher Unwin Ltd., 1918). See also 'Charlotte Brontë' above, 'Howarth, November, 1904', *I VW Essays*, *'Jane Eyre* and *Wuthering Heights'*, *IV VW Essays* and *CR1*.

2 – Of whom the following are not mentioned by VW: Arthur C. Benson ('Charlotte Brontë: A Personal Sketch'); M. H. Spielmann ('Charlotte Brontë: in Brussels'); H. E. Wroot ('Story of the Brontë Society'); Sir Sidney Lee ('Charlotte Brontë in London'); Halliwell Sutcliffe ('The Spirit of the Moors'); J. K. Snowden ('The Brontës as Artists and Prophets'); Butler Wood ('A Brontë Itinerary').

3 – Charlotte Brontë (1816–55), author of *Jane Eyre* (1847), *Shirley* (1849), *Villette* (1853); her first novel, *The Professor*, was published posthumously, in 1857.

4 – Mrs Humphry (Mary Augusta) Ward (1851–1920), 'Some Thoughts on Charlotte Brontë'.

5 – Wood, p. 22: '"Never laugh at us Celts!... We shall not build the Parthenon... But we know how to seize upon the heart and soul..."'; and p. 23: '"In the heart of our race there rises... a spring of madness."' Ernest Renan (1823–92), Breton-born philologist and historian, best known as the author of *Origines du Christianisme* (1863–83).

6 – For the two preceding quotations, *ibid.*, p. 23, p. 29.

7 – *Ibid.*, p. 29.

8 – Edmund Gosse (1849–1928), 'A Word on Charlotte Brontë'.

9 – Wood, p. 43.

10 – For the two preceding quotations, *ibid.*, p. 42.

11 – *Ibid.*, p. 43.

12 – *Ibid.*, p. 44; Honoré de Balzac (1799–1850).

13 – *Ibid.*, J. E. C. Welldon (1854–1937), 'Centenary Address at Haworth', p. 74.

14 – *Ibid.*, Dr Richard Garnett (1835–1906), 'The Place of Charlotte Brontë in Nineteenth Century Fiction', pp. 166–7.

15 – Professor C. E. Vaughan (1854–1922), 'Charlotte and Emily Brontë: A Comparison and a Contrast'.

16 – L. N. Tolstoy (1828–1910).

17 – G. K. Chesterton (1874–1936), 'Charlotte Brontë as a Romantic'.

18 – Wood, p. 52.   19 – *Ibid.*, p. 45.

'Rebels and Reformers'

Mr and Mrs Ponsonby's[2] book is intended for children or for those who are too busy to read books in many volumes. But the interest of it lies not in the necessarily short and simple narratives giving the story rather than the ideas, although these are done clearly and with spirit, but in the reflections which lie about those stories and lodge here and there in the reader's mind. Like all books worth reading, this one is the outcome of a mass of judgments and beliefs which may be very briefly expressed in the work itself but lend it the gift which in the case of human beings we call personality.

When the writers remark how few lives there are of rebels and reformers compared with those of men of action, when they say that 'life is conflict',[3] that most famous men are of humble origin, that it is even more difficult to struggle against luxury than against poverty, that indifference and indolence are the worst of failings, that history has hitherto been the history of wars, then, to use a homely phrase, we prick up our ears and attend. If we sat among the children to whom this book will be read aloud in the winter evenings we should have guessed by this time what answer would please our teachers. As this book is meant primarily for children, it may be worth while to consider what the effect upon them of such stimulus is likely to be. Will it stir them from an early age to redress the wrongs of the world, or is there not in the human mind a curious tendency to go against the ideas suggested in childhood, so that the effect may be precisely the opposite of what Mr and Mrs Ponsonby intend? Tolstoy,[4] we remember, refused to force his views upon his children. The truth may be that if you want to breed rebels and reformers you must impress upon them from the beginning the virtues of Tories and aristocrats.

Mr Ponsonby enforces a point which the lives of these twelve heroes illustrate over and over again. It is 'the very struggle and continuous effort that is the making of them'.[5] What sort of future must we expect if the light of reason and humanity is lit in the earliest dawn of understanding in the nursery? Multiply the enlightened nurseries of the world and the race of rebels and reformers is extinct, until, indeed, the next wave of reaction sets in. The argument may throw a little light upon the very puzzling tendency of the human race to resist its reformers and to burn its rebels. The fact that rebels and reformers are a race of people who live by struggle and conflict may be some slight justification for the peculiar shrinking with which the normal mind regards them. For ourselves we are in agreement with many doctrines explicit and implicit in Mr and Mrs Ponsonby's book; and yet even from their straightforward pages the shadow of the spectre looks out and chills us against our will and against our reason. A strange melancholy pervades us. It may be that the element of denial and destruction enters more largely than that of creation or belief into the reformer's attitude. It may be that circumstances force him to dwell disproportionately upon the bad and the wrong and to draw a circle round the right which excludes many of the things we care for most. It may be that the average human mind, so far as it desires anything, desires to create and to like. At any rate by easy stages of 'indolence and indifference'[6] back we slip into a mood demanding poetry, music, fiction – Shakespeare, perhaps, most of all.

Now Mr and Mrs Ponsonby provide us with four men of letters, Cervantes, Voltaire, Hans Andersen[7] and Tolstoy; but they are careful to explain that although they wrote some famous books they are here for reasons not connected with their art. The reasons are good ones; yet what more living and prolific source of reform is to be found than the plays of Shakespeare? His claim to the title of reformer is no doubt obscured by the fact that he burnt no one and died presumably in his own bed; but, as every scribbler knows, each sentence wins its way to existence through a crowd of temptations or dies at their hands, and the most effective victory over evil seems to lie not so much in Acts of Parliament as in a song or two.

But these reflections, which certainly have not escaped Mr and Mrs Ponsonby, only go to prove the truth of their main contention that those who have won the title of rebels and reformers are never given their due of admiration. Either we feel ourselves in opposition to them for one of the above reasons, or the evils which they overcame seem too gross to call for heroic qualities in those who vanquish them. William Lloyd Garrison did more than anyone to abolish slavery, yet we find ourselves, as Mrs Ponsonby points out, less inclined to admire him than to be shocked that such views should be rare enough to demand admiration. Perhaps at the root of all our grudging hesitation lies the deep-seated human vanity which is wounded, after all these years, as the record of human cruelty and superstition is unrolled before us. But the struggle still continues; we find the rebel flame burning at its purest in the cry of little Ivan Tolstoy, who, when his mother told him that Yasnaya was his property, stamped his foot and cried, 'Don't say that Yasnaya Polyana is mine! Everything is everyone else's'.[8] No less true and persistent is the other cry which comes to us from the mouth of Countess Tolstoy. Her husband, she knows, goes ahead of the crowd, pointing the way. 'But I am the crowd [. . .] I live in its current, and see the light of the lamp which every leader, and Leo of course, carries, and I acknowledge it to be the light. But I cannot go faster; I am held by the crowd and by my surroundings and habits.'[9]

1 – A review in the TLS, 20 December 1917, (Kp C94) of *Rebels and Reformers. Biographies for Young People* (George Allen & Unwin Ltd., 1917) by Arthur and Dorothea Ponsonby.
2 – Arthur Augustus William Harry Ponsonby (1871–1946), Liberal M.P., since 1908, outspoken pacifist, and his wife Dorothea, *née* Parry. He later joined the Independent Labour Party and in 1930 was created 1st Baron Ponsonby of Shulbrede.
3 – Ponsonby, 'Savonarola' [1452–98, Italian religious reformer], p. 16.
4 – L. N. Tolstoy (1828–1910).
5 – Ponsonby, 'Tycho Brahe' [1546–1601, Danish astronomer], p. 86, which has: 'this very struggle'.
6 – *Ibid.*, 'William Lloyd Garrison' [1805–79, American opponent of slavery], p. 233, which has: 'sloth and indifference'.
7 – Miguel de Cervantes Saavedra (1547–1616); François Marie Arouet de Voltaire (1694–1778); Hans Christian Andersen (1805–75).
8 – Ponsonby, 'Tolstoy', p. 293
9 – *Ibid.*, p. 294.

Sunset Reflections

Mr Martin's little book will be welcomed, we believe, particularly by Americans. It comes from Stratford-upon-Avon in the first place; and that appeal is enforced by a gentle resignation of tone, a placid smoothness of utterance, a tendency to indulge in moralities and mysticisms, to harp wistfully upon the past, which are characteristic more of the essayists of that country than of ours. As a vision of England before the war, too, it will have greater interest for them than for us. The face of Europe, Mr Martin points out in his dedication, is being changed out of all knowledge by the war, and therefore 'it has seemed well to gather together these few peace pictures of a vanishing landscape and of those who once made it their home'. 'There is a mystery and a loveliness' he proceeds, 'in the sun's setting, distinct and apart from the wonder of his rising.'[2]

Whether it is that the light of sunset is on his face, or whether our memories are short ones, we certainly have difficulty in recognising Mr Martin's greengrocer's boy. It was a wet morning in October when he came in and told Mr Martin that, although wet here, it was shining 'in the happy fields'. When asked where these might be, 'he was puzzled and even a little distressed'. [. . .] 'The happy fields where men sing as they work.'[3] And he shouldered his basket and went off, leaving Mr Martin to a whole morning of what we may call in his own phrase 'the compelled silence of easeful meditation'.[4] He provided a title for the book, however, and therefore may be excused. But the old woman in the Welsh village with whom Mr Martin lodged has no such claim upon our charity. When, after trying for six weeks to get into a field which he saw from his window, Mr Martin asked her why the field for ever eluded him, and why he might not pass through that unguarded entrance, she replied, 'Fields and hedges can keep their secrets as well as we, but maybe things look different seen near to.'[5] If the war has put an end to such greengrocers' boys and taught such old ladies to give a plain answer to a plain question, we shall have something to thank it for.

The lower classes, as we know, may always be used more or less for purposes of allegory, but even upon the upper, the cultivated classes, the sunset, according to Mr Martin, has had the same transforming effect. Two grown people, for instance, would sit down seriously to discuss whether on the whole they preferred the sky or the earth. The lady explained, at greater length than we can grant her, how she liked the sky better 'because the sky stays unchanging in the beauty of its thousand shifting scenes . . .[6] The gentleman replied that he preferred the earth, and as he has just exclaimed that the earth is his mistress, he has some right to be heard. 'We of the earth,' he wound up, 'would not change our wild wind-blown reeds for the faultless strings of Apollo.'[7] Again, before the war (and this we can verify from personal observation) poets were in the habit of saying that, given a crystal or allowed to make certain passes with the hands, they could make you see whatever vision they chose. In Mr Martin's version the lady holds an antique jewel in her delicate, thin-fingered hand, 'such a hand as Memling would have loved to paint', and her answer was always the same, 'I see a bright light,' until at last she said, 'I see flames everywhere, red flames burning like a great flower.'[8] The poet had meant her to see a lonely reed-covered lake. Now about the same time a poet was willing a lady of our acquaintance to see a burning rose; and to all his exhortations she would reply with the single word 'Frog.' We tell this story for the double purpose of showing that the visions presumably got mixed, and of assuring ourselves and any American readers that even in the time of the sunset we were occasionally monosyllabic.

But we are not altogether just to Mr Martin. Although devoted to every form of sunset himself, he recognises the fact that even in this land of decaying ruins, secular oaks, Shakespeare and the rest of it, some remain untouched. A case occurred in February 1912. There was then a sunset the like of which has never been seen and never will be seen by Mr Martin again. It affected even the spirits of his dog. But when he went about asking eagerly whether anyone else had seen the sunset, the replies were invariably disappointing. The dog then looked at him with 'grave silent reproach. What does it matter (so she seemed to say) what others have seen or think, when we two know; is it not enough that for us the heavens have been opened, and we have seen the glory of a new earth?'[9] She may have meant all that, but why not give the poor animal the benefit of the doubt?

1 – A review in the TLS, 20 December 1917, (Kp C95) of The Happy Fields. A Country Record (Shakespeare Head Press, 1917) by E. M. Martin, author also of Wayside Wisdom, a book for quiet people (1909) and Dreams in Wartime, a faithful record (1915).
2 – Martin, 'To Those Who Love the Country', preliminary unnumbered page, which has 'New beauty may come with this new harvesting of the nations; but there is . . .'
3 – Ibid., 'The Happy Fields', p. 4.
4 – Ibid., 'A Harrier of the Hedgeways', p. 49.
5 – Ibid., 'The Happy Fields', p. 10.
6 – Ibid., 'Weather Books', p. 28.
7 – Ibid., which has: 'It is the legend of Marsyas; but though stripped and flayed we of the earth . . .'
8 – Ibid., p. 22, which has: 'Memmling' [Hans Memling, c. 1430–94, Flemish religious painter].
9 – Ibid., p. 38.

The New Crusade

The process of making anything, whether it be a horseshoe, an ironclad, or a cigarette, has a fascination absent from the finished object, and of all creative processes that of the poet is the one we would give most to have the chance of watching were it possible. But of all makers poets are apt to be the least communicative about their processes, and, perhaps, owing in part to the ordinary nature of their material, have little or nothing that they choose to discuss with outsiders. The best way of surprising their secrets is very often to read their criticism. Thus, although Mr Drinkwater has many acute things to say about different poets in these papers, his most illuminating remarks are those which give us for a second a glimpse into his workshop. There we can see the unfinished stanzas, the litter of words, the chaos of conceptions from which at last the little poem of four lines is struck out by work 'colossal in its severity compared with that involved in any other kind of labour'.[2] Our fancy picture of Mr Drinkwater's workshop must represent a place without ornament or ease, but everywhere the signs of strife and austerity. His criticism bears the same stamp. He speaks of poets more as a soldier in a hard fought battle might speak of another soldier fighting with him or against him than as a critic looking from a distance and without share in the strife.

It is natural to consider further whether this point of view does not lie behind much of the best poetic work of our time, and in what directions that influence is making itself felt. When a poet speaks of poetry as the hardest labour in the world we may infer that he is up in arms against some popular fallacy which has at length goaded him to anger; nor does Mr Drinkwater leave us long in doubt as to the source of his irritation. 'We artists,' he writes in his dedication, 'have the world to fight. Prejudice, indifference, positive hostility, misrepresentation, a total failure to understand the purposes and the power of art, beset us on every side.'[3] The first few essays develop this position and are therefore extremely and almost wholly combative. Mr Drinkwater expresses with a certain stiffness, but with much honest eloquence, the view and the claims of the disinherited. Very possibly you will find the same sense of isolation in the artists of any period of the world's history; but it is no doubt more marked in such an age as ours where callings are sharply specialised and the artist cannot be a bank manager into the bargain. There is by nature, or there has come to be by custom, a deep gulf between the little body of visionaries and the great mass of practical people. But when we find Mr Drinkwater, who speaks for many of his generation, claiming his rights and asserting his capacities, we see that we are reaching a new phase in the old tacit hostility. The days of the truce which most of the poets of the past were quite content to observe are over, and there has gone with them perhaps a certain conception of the art of poetry. At least the conception of the artist himself has changed. It is we artists, says Mr Drinkwater, who are the strictly practical people, we 'who have our eyes set straight, not squinting; and so can see beyond our noses'.[4] Further, he threatens that if in the future, as in the past, no heed is paid to art, and it is treated as a luxury and not as a necessity, the work of civilisation is doomed. 'Here is the new crusade.'[5] The first step in the new crusade is to teach children to read poetry, and from that simple foundation all the civic virtues will grow of themselves. People who have learnt to love Shakespeare will, 'in less than a generation',[6] Mr Drinkwater insists, desire decent conditions to live in. Perhaps that does not overrate what, for brevity's sake, one calls poetry, but the possibility of teaching a love of poetry save by the indirect means of health and leisure seems to us problematical, to say the least of it.

But if Mr Drinkwater does not here discuss the practical part of the problem, we do not on that account accuse him of easy idealism or of irresponsible prophecy. This little book is solid testimony to the effect which such ideas have had upon his art. Tokens of the spirit which is inspiring the new crusade are scattered throughout Mr Drinkwater's pages. Poetry, he says, makes clarity and order out of vagueness and difficult confusion; it translates common simple life into the most exact and stirring beauty. As for the old taunt that a poet leads a life of luxury and indolence, Mr Drinkwater is almost too ready to enlarge upon the severity of discipline which he must be ready to undergo; but we must remark that the labour is of a special nature. It is not the labour of building up elaborate stanza structures, for 'the whole range of verse technique [...] may be covered in a perfectly regular five-foot quatrain'.[7] It is the labour rather of making what is vague clear, what is abstract concrete, what is common beautiful. Rightly or wrongly, we cannot help connecting these views of poetry with the belief that a capacity for the love of art is commoner than people allow. Mr

Drinkwater's anger is not the anger of the aristocrat who despises, but of the democrat who wishes to share. Whether such views are favourable to what used to be called inspiration we do not know; but we may prophesy that our age will be known not for one or two great poets, but because a large number of smaller men held such views as these and gave them the best shape they could.

Of the critical papers that on Rupert Brooke[8] will be read perhaps with most interest; and it is one of the few that do not inevitably suggest the question what Rupert Brooke himself would have said if he could come back to find himself thus idolised. To the loss of him his friends have had to add the peculiar irony of his canonisation; and any one who helps us to remember that volatile, irreverent, and extremely vivacious spirit before the romantic public took possession of his fame has a right to our gratitude. If the legend of Rupert Brooke is not to pass altogether beyond recognition, we must hope that some of those who knew him when scholarship or public life seemed even more his bent than poetry will put their view on record and relieve his ghost of an unmerited and undesired burden of adulation.

1 – A review in the *TLS*, 27 December 1917, (Kp C95.1) of *Prose Papers* (Elkin Mathews, 1917) by John Drinkwater (1882–1937), poet, dramatist and actor. See also 'Abraham Lincoln' below.

2 – Drinkwater, 'Frederick Tennyson', p. 131.

3 – From Drinkwater's dedicatory letter to William Rothenstein (1872–1945), painter and author.

4 – Drinkwater, 'The Value of Poetry in Education', p. 44.

5 – *Ibid.*, p. 45.

6 – *Ibid.*, p. 44: 'Let them use some of the money available for the purpose to send companies into the villages to play Shakespeare, and the work of other great or fine dramatists, and in less than a generation the people will desire decent conditions, and as soon as they desire them they will have them.'

7 – *Ibid.*, 'Frederick Tennyson', p. 136; the ellipsis marks the omission of ', from the veriest album incompetency to the most superb lyric mastery.'

8 – Rupert Brooke (1887–1915) on whom Drinkwater includes two papers: 'Rupert Brooke' and 'Rupert Brooke on John Webster'. See also VW on 'Rupert Brooke', below.

1918

'Visits to Walt Whitman'

The great fires of intellectual life which burn at Oxford and at Cambridge are so well tended and long established that it is difficult to feel the wonder of this concentration upon immaterial things as one should. When, however, one stumbles by chance upon an isolated fire burning brightly without associations or encouragement to guard it, the flame of the spirit becomes a visible hearth where one may warm one's hands and utter one's thanksgiving. It is only by chance that one comes upon them; they burn in unlikely places. If asked to sketch the condition of Bolton about the year 1885 one's thoughts would certainly revolve round the cotton market, as if the true heart of Bolton's prosperity must lie there. No mention would be made of the group of young men – clergymen, manufacturers, artisans, and bank clerks by profession – who met on Monday evenings, made a point of talking about something serious, could broach the most intimate and controversial matters frankly and without fear of giving offence, and held in particular the view that Walt Whitman was 'the greatest epochal figure in all literature'.[2] Yet who shall set a limit to the effect of such talking? In this instance, besides the invaluable spiritual service, it also had some surprisingly tangible results. As a consequence of those meetings two of the talkers crossed the Atlantic; a steady flow of presents and messages set in between Bolton and Camden; and Whitman as he lay dying had the thought of 'those good Lancashire chaps'[3] in his mind. The book recounting these events has been published before,[4] but it is well worth reprinting for the light it sheds upon a new type of hero and the kind of worship which was acceptable to him.

To Whitman there was nothing unbefitting the dignity of a human being in the acceptance either of money or of underwear, but he said that there is no need to speak of these things as gifts. On the other hand, he had no relish for a worship founded upon the illusion that he was somehow better or other than the mass of human beings. 'Well,' he said, stretching out his hand to greet Mr Wallace, 'you've come to be disillusioned, have you?'[5] And Mr Wallace owned to himself that he *was* a little disillusioned. Nothing in Walt Whitman's appearance was out of keeping with the loftiest poetic tradition. He was a magnificent old man, massive, shapely, impressive by reason of his power, his delicacy, and his unfathomable depths of sympathy. The disillusionment lay in the fact that 'the greatest epochal figure in all literature' was 'simpler, homelier, and more intimately related to myself than I had imagined'.[6] Indeed, the poet seems to have been at pains to bring his common humanity to the forefront. And everything about him was as rough as it could be. The floor, which was only half carpeted, was covered with masses of papers; eating and washing things mixed themselves with proofs and newspaper cuttings in such ancient accumulations that a precious letter from Emerson[7] dropped out accidentally from the mass after years of inter-ment. In the midst of all this litter Walt Whitman sat spotlessly clean in his rough grey suit, with much more likeness to a retired farmer who spends his time in gossip with passers-by than to a poet with a message. Like a farmer whose working days are over, it pleased him to talk of this man and of that, to ask questions about their children and their land; and, whether it was the result of thinking back over places and human beings rather than over books and thoughts, his mood was uniformly benignant. His temperament, and no sense of duty, led him to this point of view, for in his opinion it behoved him to 'give out or express what I really was, and, if I felt like the Devil, to say so!'[8]

And then it appeared that this wise and free-thinking old farmer was getting letters from Symonds and sending messages to Tennyson,[9] and was indisputably, both in his opinion and in yours, of the same stature and importance as any of the heroic figures of the past or present. Their names dropped into his talk as the names of equals. Indeed, now and then something seemed 'to set him apart in spiritual isolation and to give him at times an air of wistful sadness',[10] while into his free and easy gossip drifted without effort the phrases and ideas of his poems.

Superiority and vitality lay not in a class but in the bulk; the average of the American people, he insisted, was immense, 'though no man can become truly heroic who is really poor'.[11] And 'Shakespeare and suchlike' come in of their own accord on the heels of other matters. 'Shakespeare is the poet of great personalities.' As for passion, 'I rather think Aeschylus greater'.[12] 'A ship in full sail is the grandest sight in the world, and it has never yet been put into a poem.'[13] Or he would throw off comments as from an equal height upon his great English contemporaries. Carlyle, he said, 'lacked amorousness'.[14] Carlyle was a growler. When the stars shone brightly – 'I guess an exception in that country' – and someone said 'It's a beautiful sight,' Carlyle said, 'It's a *sad* sight' . . . 'What a growler he was!'[15]

It is inevitable that one should compare the old age of two men who steered such different courses until one saw nothing but sadness in the shining of the stars and the other could sink into a reverie of bliss over the scent of an orange. In Whitman the capacity for pleasure seemed never to diminish, and the power to include grew greater and greater; so that although the authors of this book lament that they have only a trivial bunch of sayings to offer us, we are left with a sense of an 'immense background or vista'[16] and stars shining more brightly than in our climate.

1 – A review in the *TLS*, 3 January 1918, (Kp c96) of *Visits to Walt Whitman in 1890–1891*. By Two Lancashire Friends. J. Johnston, M.D., and J. W. Wallace. With twenty illustrations. (George Allen & Unwin, 1917). Reprinted: *G&R*, *CE*.
2 – *Visits*, p. 20; Walt Whitman (1819–92).
3 – *Ibid.*, p. 259, Whitman writing to Dr Ducke, 25 June 1891, which has: 'I doubt if ever a fellow had such a splendid emotional send-back response as I have had f'm those Lancashire chaps under the lead of Dr J. & J.W.W. – it cheers & nourishes my very heart.'
4 – *Notes of a Visit to Walt Whitman . . . in July, 1890* (1890); *Diary Notes of a Visit to Walt Whitman and Some of His Friends* (1898).
5 – *Visits*, p. 90.
6 – *Ibid.*, p. 91.
7 – Ralph Waldo Emerson (1803–82).
8 – *Visits*, p. 137.
9 – John Addington Symonds (1840–93); Alfred, Lord Tennyson (1809–92).
10 – *Visits*, p. 222.
11 – *Ibid.*, p. 44: 'He quoted the saying of the Northern Farmer of "Lord Tennyson" as he called him: "Taake my word for it, Sammy, the poor in loomp is bad"; which he took exception to, saying that the poor in a lump were not bad. "And not so poor either; for no man can become truly heroic who is really poor. He must have food,

clothing and shelter, and," he added significantly, "a little money in the bank too, I think."'

12 – For the first allusion to Shakespeare, *ibid.*, p. 62, which has: 'Many of his visitors he said seemed to expect him to keep talking about "Shakespeare and poetry" and such-like, all the time; and Mr Whitman told him that he liked a little of the talk of everyday life occasionally – in fact, as Mr Whitman once put it, he "liked to be a sensible man *sometimes*!"' For the second allusion to Shakespeare, and Aeschylus, *ibid.*, p. 213.

13 – *Ibid.*, p. 47.

14 – *Ibid.*, p. 127; Thomas Carlyle (1795–1881).

15 – *Ibid.*, pp. 178–9.

16 – *Ibid.*, p. 219, quoting Whitman's friend and disciple Edward Carpenter (1844–1929).

Philosophy in Fiction

After one has heard the first few bars of a tune upon a barrel organ the further course of the tune is instinctively foretold by the mind and any deviation from that pattern is received with reluctance and discomfort. A thousand tunes of the same sort have grooved a road in our minds and we insist that the next tune we hear shall flow smoothly down the same channels; nor are we often disobeyed. That is also the case with the usual run of stories. From the first few pages you can at least half-consciously foretell the drift of what is to follow, and certainly a part of the impulse which drives us to read to the end comes from the desire to match our foreboding with the fact. It is not strange then that the finished product is much what we expected it to be, and bears no likeness, should we compare it with reality, to what we feel for ourselves. For loudly though we talk of the advance of realism and boldly though we assert that life finds its mirror in fiction, the material of life is so difficult to handle and has to be limited and abstracted to such an extent before it can be dealt with by words that a small pinch of it only is made use of by the lesser novelist. He spends his time moulding and remoulding what has been supplied him by the efforts of original genius perhaps a generation or two ago. The moulds are by this time so firmly set, and require such effort to break them, that the public is seldom disturbed by explosions in that direction.

These reflections arose when we try to account for the discomfort which so often afflicts us in reading the works of Mr Jacks.[2] We do not insinuate that he is therefore a great writer; he has not increased the stock of our knowledge very largely, nor has he devised a shape which seems completely satisfactory for his contributions; but nevertheless he is disconcerting. In the first place he has one distinction which we wish that more novelists shared with him, the distinction of being something besides a novelist. His bias towards philosophy and religious speculation leads him off the high road and carries him to blank spaces where the path has not been cut nor the name chosen. He is an explorer, and in view of that fact we can forgive him some wanderings which seem to lead nowhere and others which end, as far as our eyesight serves us, in a fog. We fancy that he reverses some of the common methods of those who write fiction. More often than not the seed which the novelist picks up and brings to flower is dropped in some congregation of human beings, from sayings, gestures, or hints; but we should guess that Mr Jacks most commonly finds his seed between the pages of a book, and the book is quite often a book of philosophy. That at once gives him a different method of approach and a different direction. He is acquainted with Moral Science:[3] he looks up from the page and wonders what would happen should some of its doctrines be put into practice. He conceives an undergraduate and sets him the task of atoning for the sins of a dissolute father according to the teachings he has learnt in the schools. The crisis of the story therefore takes the form of a philosophical argument between two undergraduates as to the morality of giving a shilling to a tramp, and the one who proves his case shall marry the lady. It seems to us extremely unlikely that anyone could hum the rest of that tune from hearing the first few bars. It is plain that if you are ordering your imaginary universe from this angle your men and women will have to adapt themselves to dance to a new measure. The criticism which will rise to the lips of every reader who finds himself put out by the unwonted sight is that the characters have ceased to be 'real' or 'alive' or 'convincing'. But let him make sure that he is looking at life and not at the novelist's dummy. Or he might do worse than reflect whether likeness to life is the prime merit in a novel; and, if that is agreed upon, whether life is not a much more ubiquitous presence than one is led by the novelist to suppose. Whether or not Mr Jacks has discovered a new vein of the precious stuff, some rare merit must be allowed a writer who through five volumes of stories lures us on to the last word of the last page.

He causes us to remember the exhilaration of driving by dusk when one cannot foresee the ups or the downs of the road. With Mr Jacks starting his story anywhere, following it anywhere and leaving it anywhere, as he is in the habit of doing, the incentive of the unexpected is constantly supplied to us. 'Oh, I'm nobody in particular,' he remarks in 'A Grave Digger's Scene'. 'Just passing through and taking a look round';[4] and anything that his eye lights upon may start a story, which story may be a parable, or a satire upon religious sects, or a ghost story, or a straightforward study of a farmer's character, or a vision, or an argument, with figures merely put in as pegs to mark the places. But although he disregards all the rules and effects a most arbitrary tidying up when he remembers them, there is one invariable partner in all his enterprises – a keen and educated intelligence.

Intelligence, with its tendency to acquire views and its impatience with the passive attitude of impartial observation, may be a source of danger in fiction should it get the upper hand; but even in a state of subjection it is so rare that we must welcome it on its own terms. The only reservation which we feel disposed to make in the case of Mr Jacks's intelligence is that it fills his mind too full with ideas derived from other sources to give him a wide and unprejudiced view of his subject. Instead of going on with his tale, he has views upon socialism, or sex problems, or education, or psychology which must be brought in and investigated at the expense of the individual. But even this reservation must be qualified. The portraits of Farmer Perryman, Farmer Jeremy and Peter Rodright[5] have the stuff in them of three-volume novels, and give the essence of different types without deviation into the mystical or the abnormal. On account of their solid truth we prefer them to the study of Snarley Bob in *Mad Shepherds*, whose portrait seems to have been made up from some cunning prescription found in the books rather than from direct observation. Yet as we make this criticism we are aware that it may merely represent the shudder of a conservative mind forced to consider what it has always shunned, invited to land upon one of the 'Desolate Islands'[6] not marked upon the map. Expectancy mingles itself in equal proportions with our distrust, for the things that Mr Jacks tries to bring into the light are among the deepest and the most obscure. 'Things from the abyss of time that float upwards into dreams – sleeping things whose breath sometimes breaks the surface of our waking consciousness, like bubbles rising from the depths of Lethe.'[7]

Inevitably it is extremely difficult to combine these new trophies of psychology with the old; and the results are often queer composite beings, monsters of a double birth, fit for the museum rather than the breakfast table. When, among other curiosities, we read of a mare which has mysteriously acquired the personality of a professor's lost love we can hardly help remarking, 'Piecraft is trying to live in two worlds, the world of imagination and the world of pure science; he will come to grief in both of them.'[8] But if we are more often interested than moved by Mr Jacks's stories, the balance is so seldom on that side that it would be churlish to demand a combination which only the very few can give us. For some reason or other intelligence is particularly rare in fiction. At first sight it seems that there must be something amiss with a story which is aimed at the reason; when we find sentence after sentence brief, pointed, and expressive we shiver at a nakedness that seems momentarily indecent. But when we have rid ourselves of a desire for the dusky draperies of fiction there is no small pleasure in being treated neither as child nor as sultan, but as an equal and reasonable human being. Mr Jacks uniformly achieves this wholesome result by writing with an exactness which gives a sharp idea of his meaning. Nothing is modified out of deference to our laziness. And occasionally, as in the remarkable paper called 'The Castaway', he writes what we may read not only for the light which it casts upon his methods, but for its own rare beauty. We quote the last passage:

Desolate Islands, more than I could ever explore, more than I could count or name, I found in the men and women who press upon me every day. Nay, my own life was full of them; the flying moment was one; they rose out of the deep with the ticking of the clock. And once came the rushing of a mighty wind; and the waves fled backward till the sea was no more. Then I saw that the Islands were great mountains uplifted from everlasting foundations, their basis one beneath the ocean floor, their summits many above the sundering waters – most marvellous of all the works of God.[9]

1 – A review in the TLS, 10 January 1918, (Kp c97) of *Mad Shepherds and other human stories* (1910), *Among the Idolmakers* (1911), *From the Human End* (1916). *All Men Are Ghosts* (1913), *Philosophers in Trouble* (1916), collected, 6 vols, Williams & Norgate, 1916–17, as *Writings* by L. P. Jacks. VW noted in her diary on Monday, 7 January 1918: 'To London today, L[eonard] with my Jack's article to the Times, I to Spiller about my spectacles; & I must get a new pair at a cost of £2.2. After that we met at the London Library . . .'
    See also 'Stopford Brooke' above and 'Fantasy', *III VW Essays*. Reprinted: CW.
2 – Lawrence Pearsall Jacks (1860–1955), unitarian divine, principal of Manchester College, Oxford, 1915–31.
3 – *Philosophers in Trouble*, 'Bracketed First', p. 34: 'Those who are unfamiliar

with the ways of our University may learn with a gentle surprise that in the one subject which, from its nature, deals with Practice, the highest Degrees are obtainable without any Practical Examination whatsoever. That subject is Moral Science.'

4 – *Mad Shepherds*, 'A Grave Digger Scene' [sic], p. 213.

5 – For Farmer Perryman see *Mad Shepherds*; for Farmer Jeremy and Peter Rodright, *Among the Idolmakers*.

6 – *Among the Idolmakers*, 'The Castaway', p. 23; see also at n. 9 below.

7 – *Mad Shepherds*, 'Shepherd Toller O' Clun Downs', p. 140, which has 'Time', and forms part of a longer sentence.

8 – *All Men Are Ghosts*, the title story, p. 110.

9 – *Among the Idolmakers*, 'The Castaway', p. 23.

A Book of Essays

The order of the serious sixpenny weekly paper must originally have been evolved like the now almost extinct order of the meats and the sweets, in deference to some demand of the public appetite. It is a rule that after the politics we come to the lighter form of essay and so to the reviews; and as this order is never upset, it must have been devised either for our pleasure or for our good. We are confessing an abnormality, then, when we say that to us the essay is the superfluous part of the feast. To be honest, we can only bring ourselves to read it if the train has stopped for more than twenty minutes in a fog and it is no longer amusing to speculate upon the lost terrier for whom a reward is offered in the advertisements. We find our justification in the belief that there is nothing quite so rare as a good essay and nothing quite so dismal as a bad one. The very titles are enough to darken the landscape; the groan of the slave at his task is audible to our ears. Our gorge rises at the thought of all the turns and twists and devices which some fellow-creature is going through in order to persuade us to swallow a fragment of the truth without recognising it. For the essay is now chiefly employed to mitigate the severity of Acts, reforms, and social questions; it entices us to perform the operation of thinking under an anaesthetic. Worse still, there may be no question of thinking; the only question may be how best to amuse the public for the space of 1,500 or 2,000 words, in which case the essay is no more than a dance upon the tight rope, where if a single caper is cut clumsily the acrobat suffers death or humiliation before our eyes.

For these reasons there is one course in our weekly dinner which we invariably omit, and thus it comes about that we read Mr Robert Lynd for the first time. With reasons to back us we do not intend to climb down unreservedly, but we must admit that we might do better than read the advertisements next time the train stops in a fog. Mr Lynd is so competent a writer that we need have no fear that he is going to break his bones, and there are sure signs that he enjoys his work. Whether he writes upon the 'Horrors of War', or 'Grub', upon 'Taking a Walk in London', or 'Revenge' he seems to be following his own bent without too much anxiety either for our good or for our entertainment. The narrowness of his limits does not obviously constrict him, nor does he think it necessary because he has only fifteen hundred words at his disposal to make each one do the work of ten. The exigencies of the time may make it necessary to consider either 'Courage', or 'Treating', or 'Refugees', but that forbidding signpost is in his mind, the centre of all sorts of pleasant paths which lead either to the humours of the public house or, by way of a red omnibus and the Strand, to the top of a little eminence such as this:

We are exiles, if not fugitives, from the perfect city. We are sojourners and strangers under the sun; we build houses of a day in the valleys of death. There seems to be no patriotism of the earth for many of those, like St Paul, whose patriotism is in Heaven. Their psalms and hymns are like native songs remembered by those who will admit no citizenship here. The saint is still a foreigner in every land, a sorrowing refugee from skies not ours.[2]

In addition to the literary skill here displayed, which could be matched easily by other quotations, Mr Lynd has all the merits of an open and generous mind. He is always tolerant and for the most part sanguine, and would rather spoil his period than make a point at the expense of some charity or decency. The streets of London offer so many charming thoughts to one of his fertile fancy that it would be most excusable in him to find no room for his final reflection: 'We must never be allowed to enjoy walking in London till London has been made fit to walk in.'[3] Thus remembering the claims of humanity he no doubt willingly suppresses what we take to be the chief stock-in-trade of the essayist – himself. It is a most serious omission. Whether a first-rate essay has ever been written which is not the ripe fruit of egoism may be doubted. The essays of Elia[4] are so many confidences which impart to us the most private secrets of Lamb's heart. There is room in them for all sorts of facts about his whims and habits, but there is very little concern for the public good. The most delightful parts of Montaigne's essays[5] are those where he breaks from the consideration of some abstract quality to explore the peculiarities of his body or his soul. It is the same with Hazlitt, or with Thackeray in the *Roundabout Papers*.[6] None of these men has the least fear of giving himself away, and, perhaps, in a short piece that is the only thing of value that one can give away. In 2,000 words you cannot do much to reform society or inculcate morality, but you can tell us about your imperfect sympathies, your poor relations, or 'Mackery End in Hertfordshire'.[7] When we consider that this gift of intimacy is the most difficult of all to make, and that to convey anything so personal needs the impersonality of the highest art, we need not wonder that it is not often offered us between the politics and the reviews. We have reason indeed to be grateful when an essayist like Mr Lynd writes well enough to make us remember the possibilities of his form.

1 – A review in the *TLS*, 17 January 1918, (Kp c98), of *If The Germans Conquered England and Other Essays* (Maunsel & Co. Ltd., 1917) by Robert (Wilson) Lynd (1879–1949), literary journalist and essayist, editor of the *Daily News* (which in 1930 became the *News Chronicle*) and regular contributor, as Y.Y., to the *New Statesman*, 1913–39.
2 – Lynd, 'Refugees', p. 38.
3 – *Ibid.*, 'On Taking a Walk in London', p. 109.
4 – Charles Lamb (1775–1834), *Elia* (1st series, 1823; 2nd series, 1828) and *The Last Essays of Elia* (1833).
5 – Michel Eyquem de Montaigne (1533–92), *Essais* (1580, 1588); see also VW's 'Montaigne', *IV VW Essays* and *CR1*.
6 – William Hazlitt (1778–1830); see also VW's 'William Hazlitt', *V VW Essays* and *CR2*; W. M. Thackeray (1811–63), *The Roundabout Papers* (1863).
7 – As did Charles Lamb in *Elia*: 'Imperfect Sympathies', 'My Relations' and 'Mackery End, in Hertfordshire'.

'The Green Mirror'

In the drawing room, over the mantelpiece, there hung a green mirror. Many generations of the Trenchard family had seen themselves reflected in its depths. Save for themselves and for the reflection of themselves they had never seen anything else for perhaps three hundred years, and in the year 1902 they were still reflected with perfect lucidity. If there was any room behind the figures for chair or table, tree or field, chairs, tables, trees and fields were now and always had been the property of the Trenchard family. It is impossible to limit the pride of this family in itself.

Not to be a Trenchard was to be a nigger or a Chinaman[2] ... The Trenchards had never been conceited people – conceit implied too definite a recognition of other people's position and abilities. To be conceited you must think yourself abler, more interesting, richer, handsomer than someone else – and no Trenchard ever realised anyone else.[3]

The reader who is acquainted with modern fiction will at this point reflect that he has met these people or their relations already; they must belong to that composite group of English families created by Mr Galsworthy, Mr Arnold Bennett and Mr E. M. Forster.[4] Very different in detail, they all share a common belief that there is only one view of the world, and one family; and invariably at the end the mirrors break, and the new generation bursts in.

This is said more in order to describe Mr Walpole's novel than to criticise it, although it is by this door that criticism will enter. There is no fault to be found with the theme. If the family theme has taken the place of the love theme with our more thoughtful writers, that goes to prove that for this generation it is the more fertile of the two. It has so many sides to it, like all living themes, that there is no reason why one book should repeat another. You may destroy the family and salute the dawn by any means at your disposal, passion, satire, or humour, provided that you are in love with your cause. But the danger of a cause which has had great exponents lies in its power to attract recruits who are converts to other people's reforms but are not reformers themselves. In so far as Mr Walpole presents the Trenchard family as a type of the pig-headed British race with its roots in the past and its head turned backwards he seems to us to fail. The place for the Trenchard type is the didactic stage. All the exaggerations of their insularity would hit the mark delivered from the mouths of actors, but from the mouths of people in a book with the merits of this book they sound forced and unreal. 'It was one of the Trenchard axioms that anyone who crossed the English Channel conferred a favour';[5] no Trenchard can marry a man who thinks 'Russia such a fine country'.[6] And quite in keeping with the limelight is the Uncle's well-known lecture upon the approaching break-up of his class. 'Nearly the whole of our class in England has, ever since the beginning of last century, been happily asleep ... Oh, young Mark's just one of the advance guard. He's smashing up the Trenchards with his hammer the same way that all the families like us up and down England are being smashed up.'[7] The hammer is thrown and the mirror comes down with a crash. Upstairs a very old Mr Trenchard falls back dead; and out we pour into the street looking askance at the passers-by as though we ought to tell them too that another English family has been smashed to splinters and freedom is stealing over the roof-tops.

Mr Walpole's gift is neither for passion nor for satire, but he possesses an urbane observant humour. He has a true insight into the nature of domesticity. He can render perfectly the 'friendly confused smell of hams and medicine, which is the Stores note of welcome'.[8] The psychology of a lady charged with the exciting duty of buying three hot-water bottles is no secret to him. We have seldom met a better account of a long Sunday in the country and the cold supper with which it ends. On this occasion the servants were out, and there was no soup. These are the small things in which Mr Walpole is invariably happy, and in our view it is no disparagement to a writer to say that his gift is for the small things rather than for the large. Scott was master of the large method, but Jane Austen[9] was mistress of the small. If you are faithful with the details the large effects will grow inevitably out of those very details. In its way the portrait of the hobbledehoy brother Henry is a large achievement, based though it is upon a careful study of hot-water bottles and Sunday suppers. The aunts, too, when they are not drawn violently from their orbits by the young man who has spent some years in Moscow, prattle, squabble, and make it up again in the warm soft atmosphere of true imagination. There is no reason for Mr Walpole to apologise for what is slow, uneventful, and old-fashioned in the world which he portrays. We feel convinced that in these respects the war has done nothing to change it. The Trenchard family, far from having sprung apart when the mirror was unfortunately broken, had it mended at an expensive shop in Bond Street, and it was hanging as usual over the mantelpiece on 4 August 1914. Mrs Trenchard never did anything so hysterical as to turn her daughter from her house because she married a young man who talked rather superficially about Russia. Mother and daughter are at this moment knitting comforters together. The only person who turned out badly, as Mrs Trenchard said he would, was Mr Philip Mark – but it is no business of ours to write other people's novels. We confess that in this case we should like to, but that is only because Mr Walpole has done it in many respects so extremely well himself.

1 – A review in the *TLS*, 24 January 1918, (Kp C99) of *The Green Mirror. A Quiet Story* (Macmillan & Co. Ltd., 1918) by Hugh Walpole (1884–1941). See also 'A View of the Russian Revolution' below. Reprinted: *CW*.

2 – Walpole, bk. i, ch. III, p. 42.

3 – *Ibid.*, p. 43.

4 – John Galsworthy (1867–1933); Arnold Bennett (1867–1931); E. M. Forster (1879–1970).

5 – Walpole, bk i, ch. III, p. 59, part of a longer sentence.

6 – *Ibid.*, bk i, ch. VI, p. 129.

7 – *Ibid.*, bk ii, ch. VI, pp. 277–8.

8 – *Ibid.*, bk ii, ch. II, p. 167, which has: 'friendly, confused'; and 'medicines which'.

9 – Sir Walter Scott (1771–1832), of whose work, incidentally, Walpole was a devoted admirer; Jane Austen (1775–1817).

Across the Border

When Miss Scarborough describes the results of her inquiries into the supernatural in fiction as 'suggestive rather than exhaustive'[2] we have only to add that in any discussion of the supernatural suggestion is perhaps more useful than an attempt at science. To mass together all sorts of cases of the supernatural in literature without much more system or theory than the indication of dates supplies leaves the reader free where freedom has a special value. Perhaps some psychological law lies hidden beneath the hundreds of stories about ghosts and abnormal states of mind (for stories about abnormal states of mind are included with those that are strictly supernatural) which are referred to in her pages; but in our twilight state it is better to guess than to assert, to feel than to classify our feelings. So much evidence of the delight which human nature takes in stories of the supernatural will inevitably lead one to ask what this interest implies both in the writer and in the reader.

In the first place, how are we to account for the strange human craving for the pleasure of feeling afraid which is so much involved in our love of ghost stories? It is pleasant to be afraid when we are conscious that we are in no kind of danger, and it is even more pleasant to be assured of the mind's capacity to penetrate those barriers which for twenty-three hours out of the twenty-four remain impassable. Crude fear, with its anticipation of physical pain or of terrifying uproar, is an undignified and demoralising sensation, while the mastery of fear only produces a respectable mask of courage, which is of no great interest to ourselves, although it may impose upon others. But the fear which we get from reading ghost stories of the supernatural is a refined and spiritualised essence of fear. It is a fear which we can examine and play with. Far from despising ourselves for being frightened by a ghost story we are proud of this proof of sensibility, and perhaps unconsciously welcome the chance for the licit gratification of certain instincts which we are wont to treat as outlaws. It is worth noticing that the craving for the supernatural in literature coincided in the eighteenth century with a period of rationalism in thought, as if the effect of damming the human instincts at one point causes them to overflow at another. Such instincts were certainly at full flood when the writings of Mrs Radcliffe[3] were their chosen channel. Her ghosts and ruins have long suffered the fate which so swiftly waits upon any exaggeration of the supernatural and substitutes our ridicule for our awe. But although we are quick to throw away imaginative symbols which have served our turn, the desire persists. Mrs Radcliffe may vanish, but the craving for the supernatural survives. Some element of the supernatural is so constant in poetry that one has come to look upon it as part of the normal fabric of the art; but in poetry, being etherealised, it scarcely provokes any emotion so gross as fear. Nobody was ever afraid to walk down a dark passage after reading *The Ancient Mariner*,[4] but rather inclined to venture out to meet whatever ghosts might deign to visit him. Probably some degree of reality is necessary in order to produce fear; and reality is best conveyed by prose. Certainly one of the finest ghost stories, Wandering Willie's Tale in *Redgauntlet*,[5] gains immensely from the homely truth of the setting, to which the use of the Scotch dialect contributes. The hero is a real man, the country is as solid as can be; and suddenly in the midst of the green and gray landscape opens up the crimson transparency of Redgauntlet Castle with the dead sinners at their feasting.

The superb genius of Scott here achieves a triumph which should keep this story immortal however the fashion in the supernatural may change. Steenie Steenson[6] is himself so real and his belief in the phantoms is so vivid that we draw our fear through our perception of his fear, the story itself being of a kind that has ceased to frighten us. In fact, the vision of the dead carousing would now be treated in a humorous, romantic or perhaps patriotic spirit, but scarcely with any hope of making our flesh creep. To do that the author must change his direction; he must seek to terrify us not by the ghosts of the dead, but by those ghosts which are living within ourselves. The great increase of the psychical ghost story in late years, to which Miss Scarborough bears witness, testifies to the fact that our sense of our own ghostliness has much quickened. A rational age is succeeded by one which seeks the supernatural in the soul of man, and the development of psychical research offers a basis of disputed fact for this desire to feed upon. Henry James, indeed, was of opinion before writing *The Turn of the Screw* that 'the good, the really effective and heart-shaking ghost stories (roughly so to term them) appeared all to have been told ... The new type, indeed, the mere modern "psychical case", washed clean of all queerness as by exposure to a flowing laboratory tap ... the new type clearly promised little'.[7] Since *The Turn of the Screw,* however, and no doubt largely owing to that masterpiece, the new type has justified its existence by rousing, if not 'the dear old sacred terror',[8] still a very effective modern representative. If you wish to guess what our ancestors felt when they read *The Mysteries of Udolpho* you cannot do better than read *The Turn of the Screw.*

Experiment proves that the new fear resembles the old in producing physical sensations as of erect hair, dilated pupils, rigid muscles, and an intensified perception of sound and movement. But what is it that we are afraid of? We are not afraid of ruins, or moonlight, or ghosts. Indeed, we should be relieved to find that Quint and Miss Jessel[9] are ghosts, but they have neither the substance nor the independent existence of ghosts. The odious creatures are much closer to us than ghosts have ever been. The governess is not so much frightened of them as of the sudden extension of her own field of perception, which in this case widens to reveal to her the presence all about her of an unmentionable evil. The appearance of the figures is an illustration, not in itself specially alarming, of a state of mind which is profoundly mysterious and terrifying. It is a state of mind; even the external objects are made to testify to their subjection. The oncoming of the state is preceded not by the storms and howlings of the old romances, but by an absolute hush and lapse of nature which we feel to represent the ominous trance of her own mind. 'The rooks stopped cawing in the golden sky, and the friendly evening hour lost for the unspeakable minute all its voice.'[10] The horror of the story comes from the force with which it makes us realise the power that our minds possess for such excursions into the darkness; when certain lights sink or certain barriers are lowered, the ghosts of the mind, untracked desires, indistinct intimations, are seen to be a large company.

In the hands of such masters as Scott and Henry James the

supernatural is so wrought in with the natural that fear is kept from a dangerous exaggeration into simple disgust or disbelief verging upon ridicule. Mr Kipling's stories 'The Mark of the Beast' and 'The Return of Imray'[11] are powerful enough to repel one by their horror, but they are too violent to appeal to our sense of wonder. For it would be a mistake to suppose that supernatural fiction always seeks to produce fear, or that the best ghost stories are those which most accurately and medically describe abnormal states of mind. On the contrary, a vast amount of fiction both in prose and in verse now assures us that the world to which we shut our eyes is far more friendly and inviting, more beautiful by day and more holy by night, than the world which we persist in thinking the real world. The country is peopled with nymphs and dryads, and Pan, far from being dead, is at his pranks in all the villages of England. Much of this mythology is used not for its own sake, but for purposes of satire and allegory; but there exists a group of writers who have the sense of the unseen without such alloy. Such a sense may bring visions of fairies or phantoms, or it may lead to a quickened perception of the relations existing between men and plants, or houses and their inhabitants, or any one of those innumerable alliances which somehow or other we spin between ourselves and other objects in our passage.

1 – A review in the *TLS*, 31 January 1918, (Kp C100) of *The Supernatural in Modern English Fiction* (G. P. Putnam's Sons, 1917) by Dorothy Scarborough, Ph.D., Instructor in English Extension, Columbia University. See also 'Henry James's Ghost Stories', *III VW Essays*. Reprinted, as 'The Supernatural in Fiction', *G&R*, *CE*.

2 – Scarborough, ch. VIII, p. 310.

3 – Ann Radcliffe (1764–1823), author of *The Mysteries of Udolpho* (1794) etc.

4 – S. T. Coleridge (1772–1834), *The Rime of the Ancient Mariner* (1798).

5 – Sir Walter Scott (1771–1832), *Redgauntlet* (1824), and the tale of Willie Steenson, the blind fiddler.

6 – I.e. Willie Steenson's father.

7 – Henry James (1843–1916), *The Novels and Tales of Henry James* (New York Edition, Macmillan & Co. Ltd, 1908), vol. xii, 'The Aspern Papers', 'The Turn of the Screw' etc., pref., pp. x–xi.

8 – *Ibid.*

9 – Peter Quint and Miss Jessel in *The Turn of the Screw* (1898).

10 – *The Turn of the Screw*, ch. III ('*The Aspern Papers*' and '*The Turn of the Screw*', ed. Anthony Curtis, Penguin, 1984, p. 165).

11 – Rudyard Kipling (1865–1936), whose 'The Mark of the Beast' (referred to by Scarborough, pp. 100–1, 167) and 'The Return of Imray' were published in *Life's Handicap. Being Stories of Mine Own People* (1891).

Coleridge as Critic

In his preface to the *Anima Poetae* Mr E. H. Coleridge[2] remarks that the *Table Talk*, unlike other of Coleridge's prose writings, still remains well known and widely read. We do not know that the brief article by Coventry Patmore prefixed to this new edition tells us much more than that Mr Patmore was himself a Conservative, but if the preface had any share in the republication of the *Table Talk*,[3] we owe it our thanks. It is always well to re-read the classics. It is always wholesome to make sure that they still earn their pedestals and do not merely cast their shadows over heads bent superstitiously from custom. In particular it is worth while to re-read Coleridge because, owing to his peculiarities of character and to the effect which they had upon such portrait painters as Hazlitt, De Quincey, and above all, Carlyle,[4] we possess a very visible ghost – Coleridge, a wonderful, ridiculous, impossibly loquacious old gentleman who lived at Highgate and could never determine which side of the path to walk on. The loquacity can hardly have been exaggerated, but read the *Table Talk* and you will get what no portrait painter can possibly catch – the divine quality of the old gentleman's mind, the very flash of his miraculous eye. Whether or no it is a test of true greatness, his own words give us at once not indeed a sense of perceiving the distinction between the reason and the understanding, but of knowing him as no second person can reveal him: there is a being in the book who still speaks directly to the individual mind.

The comparison between Coleridge and Johnson is obvious in so far as each held sway chiefly by the power of his tongue. The difference between their methods is so marked that it is tempting, but also unnecessary, to judge one to be inferior to the other. Johnson was robust, combative, and concrete; Coleridge was the opposite. The contrast was perhaps in his mind when he said of Johnson:

> his *bow-wow* manner must have had a good deal to do with the effect produced ... Burke, like all men of genius who love to talk at all, was very discursive and continuous; hence he is not reported; he seldom said the sharp, short things that Johnson almost always did, which produce a more decided effect at the moment, and which are so much more easy to carry off.[5]

Modesty may have required him to say Burke instead of Coleridge, but either name will do. The same desire to justify and protect one's type led him no doubt to perceive the truth that 'a great mind must be androgynous ... I have known strong minds with imposing, undoubting, Cobbett-like manners, but I have never met a great mind of this sort.'[6]

But the chief distinction between the talk of Coleridge and that of Johnson, or indeed, between the talk of Coleridge and that of most of the famous talkers, lay in his indifference to, in his hatred of, 'mere personality'.[7] That omission rules out more than gossip; it rules out the kind of portrait painting in which Carlyle excelled, or the profound human insight so often expressed by Johnson. One cannot suppose that Coleridge would ever have lifted a poor woman to his shoulders, but he could be 'pained by observing in others, and was fully conscious in himself of a sympathy' with the upper classes which he had not for the lower, until, hearing a thatcher's wife cry her heart out for the death of her child, 'it was given him all at once to feel' that, while sympathising equally with poor and rich in the matter of the affections — 'the best part of humanity'[8] — still with regard to *mental* misery, struggles and conflicts his sympathies were with those who could best appreciate their force and value. From this it is plain that if we seek Coleridge's company we must leave certain human desires outside, or rather we must be ready to mount, if we can, into an atmosphere where the substance of these desires has been shredded by infinite refinements and discriminations of all its grossness.

The incompatibility which certainly existed between Coleridge and the rest of the world arose, so the *Table Talk* persuades us, from the fact that even more than Shelley he was 'a beautiful and ineffectual angel'[9] — a spirit imprisoned behind bars invisible and intangible to the tame hordes of humanity, a spirit always beckoned by something from without. Very naturally, to his fellow prisoners behind the bars his interpretation was confused, and from a philosophic point of view inconclusive. But there has been no finer messenger between gods and men, nor one whose being kept from youth to age so high a measure of transparency. His criticism is the most spiritual in the language. His notes upon Shakespeare are, to our thinking, the only criticisms which bear reading with the sound of the play still in one's ears. They possess one of the marks which we are apt to discover in the finest art, the power of seeming to bring to light what was already there beforehand, instead of imposing anything from the outside. The shock, the surprise, the paradox, which so often prevail and momentarily illumine, are entirely absent from the art of Coleridge; and the purity of his criticism is further increased by his neglect here also of 'mere personality'. The possibility that one may throw light upon a book by considering the circumstances in which it was written did not commend itself to Coleridge; to him the light was concentrated and confined in one ray – in the art itself. We have, of course, to take into account the fact that he never produced any complete work of criticism. We have only imperfect reports of lectures, memories of talk, notes scribbled in the margins of pages. His views are therefore scattered and fragmentary, and it is usual to lament the ruin wrought by opium upon the vast and enduring fabric which should have been built from these broken stones. But this mania for size savours rather of megalomania. There is a great deal to be said for small books. It is arguable that the desire to be exhaustive, comprehensive, and monumental has destroyed more virtue than it has brought to birth. In literary criticism at least the wish to attain completeness is more often than not a will o' the wisp which lures one past the occasional ideas which may perhaps have truth in them towards an unreal symmetry which has none.

Coleridge's mind was so fertile in such ideas that it is difficult to conceive that, given the health of a coal-heaver and the industry of a bank clerk, he could ever have succeeded in tracking each to its end, or in embracing the whole of them with their innumerable progeny in one vast synthesis. A great number spring directly from literature, but almost any topic had power at once to form an idea capable of splitting into an indefinite number of fresh ideas. Here are some chosen for their brevity. 'You abuse snuff! Perhaps it is the final cause of the human nose!'[10] 'Poetry is certainly something more than good sense, but it must be good sense at all events.'[11] 'There is no subjectivity whatever in the Homeric poetry.'[12] 'Swift was *anima Rabelaisii habitans in sicco* – the soul of Rabelais dwelling in a dry place.'[13] 'How inimitably graceful children are before they learn to dance!'[14] 'There is in every human countenance either a history or a prophecy.'[15] 'You see many scenes which are simply Shakespeare's, disporting himself in joyous triumph and vigorous fun after a great achievement of his highest genius.'[16] A respectable library could be, and no doubt has been, made out of these ideas; and Coleridge, not content with carrying the stuff of many libraries in his head, had what in England is more remarkable, the germs of an equal susceptibility to painting and to music. The gifts should go together; all three are perhaps needed to complete each one. But if such gifts complete a Milton or a Keats[17] they may undo a Coleridge. The reader of the *Table Talk* will sometime reflect that although, compared with Coleridge, he must consider himself deaf and blind as well as dumb, these limitations, in the present state of the world, have protected him and most of his work has been done within their shelter. For how can a man with Coleridge's gifts produce anything? His demands are so much greater than can be satisfied by the spiritual resources of his age. He is perpetually checked and driven back; life is too short; ideas are too many; opposition is too great. If Coleridge heard music he wanted hours and hours of Mozart and Purcell;[18] if he liked a picture he fell into a trance in front of it; if he saw a sunset he almost lost consciousness in the rapture of gazing at it. Our society makes no provision for these apparitions. The only course for such a one to pursue is that which Coleridge finally adopted – to sink into the house of some hospitable Gillman[19] and there for the rest of his life to sit and talk. In better words, 'My dear fellow! never be ashamed of scheming! – you can't think of living less than 4,000 years, and that would nearly suffice for your present schemes. To be sure, if they go on in the same ratio to the performance, then a small difficulty arises; but never mind! look at the bright side always and die in a dream!'[20]

1 – A review in the TLS, 7 February 1918, (Kp C101) of *The Table Talk and Omniana of Samuel Taylor Coleridge* [1772–1834]. With a note on Coleridge by Coventry Patmore [1823–96] (O.U.P., 1917). See *I VW Diary*, Monday, 4 February 1918: 'Up to the Times with a Coleridge article; & once more I lost myself, owing to the multiplicity of Water Lanes . . .' See 'The Man at the Gate', 'Sara Coleridge', *VI VW Essays*; and (especially in the light of VW's remark in 'A Sketch of the Past') *MoB*, p. 115: 'I always read *Hours in a Library* by way of filling out my ideas, say of Coleridge, if I'm reading Coleridge', see also Leslie Stephen on Coleridge in both the *DNB* and *Hours in a Library* (vol. iv, 1904). Reprinted: *B&P*. Reading Notes (Berg xxx), reproduced in Appendix I.

2 – *Animae Poetae. From the unpublished Note-Books of Samuel Taylor Coleridge*, ed. Ernest Hartley Coleridge (William Heinemann, 1895), Pref., p. vii.

3 – Originally published as *Specimens of the Table Talk of Samuel Taylor Coleridge* (1835), with a preface by H. N. Coleridge.

4 – For William Hazlitt (1778–1830) on Coleridge: *The Spirit of the Age* (1825); for Thomas de Quincey (1785–1859): *Selections Grave and Gay* (vol. ii, 1854); and for Thomas Carlyle (1795–1881), *The Life of John Sterling* (1851).

5 – Coleridge, 'Table Talk', 4 July 1833, pp. 256–7; the ellipsis marks the omission of: ';'; – for no one, I suppose, will set Johnson before Burke – and Burke was a great and universal talker; – yet now we hear nothing of this except by some chance remarks in Boswell. The fact is, . . .' Dr Samuel Johnson (1709–84); Edmund Burke (1729–97).

6 – *Ibid.*, 1 September 1832, p. 201, which has: '. . . of this sort. And of the former,

they are at least as often wrong as right. The truth is, a great mind must be androgynous. Great minds – Swedenborg's, for instance – are never wrong but in consequence of being in the right, but imperfectly'; 'I have known *strong* minds'; and 'I have never met a *great* mind'.

7 – The origin of this phrase has not been traced, but for an example of Coleridge's strictures on 'this Age of Personality' see his 'Friend', no. 10.

8 – *Ibid.*, 'Allsop's Recollections', pp. 444–5: 'I have often been pained by observing in others, and was fully conscious in myself of a sympathy with those of rank and condition in preference to their inferiors, and never discovered the source of this sympathy until one day at Keswick I heard a thatcher's wife crying her heart out for the death of her little child. It was given me all at once to feel, that I sympathised equally with the poor and the rich in all that related to the best part of humanity – the affections; but that, in what relates to fortune, to mental misery, struggle, and conflicts, we reserve consolation and sympathy for those who can appreciate its force and value.'

9 – Matthew Arnold, *Essays in Criticism. Second Series* (Macmillan & Co., 1888), 'Byron', p. 203: 'But these two, Wordsworth and Byron, stand, it seems to me, first and preeminent in actual performance, a glorious pair, among the English poets of this century . . . I for my part can never even think of equalling with them any of their contemporaries; – either Coleridge, poet and philosopher wrecked in a mist of opium; or Shelley, beautiful and ineffectual angel, beating in the void his luminous wings in vain.'

10 – Coleridge, 'Table Talk', 4 January 1823, p. 41.

11 – *Ibid.*, 9 May 1830, p. 91, which continues: '; just as a palace is more than a house, but it must be a house at least.'

12 – *Ibid.*, 12 May 1830, p. 93.

13 – *Ibid.*, 15 June 1830, p. 116.

14 – *Ibid.*, 1 January 1832, p. 166.

15 – *Ibid.*, 'Omniana', p. 377, which continues: 'which must sadden, or at least soften, every reflecting observer'.

16 – *Ibid.*, 'Table Talk', 7 April 1833, p. 224, which has: 'You see many scenes and parts of scenes which are simply Shakespeare's, disporting . . .'

17 – John Milton (1608–74); John Keats (1795–1821).

18 – Coleridge, 'Table Talk', 6 July 1833, p. 258: 'Some music is above me; most music is beneath me. I like Beethoven and Mozart – or else some of the aerial compositions of the elder Italians, as Palestrina and Carissimi. – And I love Purcell.'

19 – The hospitable James Gillman lived with his wife at The Grove, Highgate, and there Coleridge resided and presided from 1816 until his death. Gillman was the dedicatee of the original edition of *Specimens of the Table Talk . . .* (1835) and the author of an unfinished *Life* of Coleridge (1838).

20 – The origin of this passage remains untraced.

Mr Conrad's Crisis

To possess a fuller account of the processes which have produced some notable books we should be willing to offer their distinguished authors liberal terms in the shape of our gratitude, or, if it suited them better, promise to forgo a chapter here, a volume there, in return for the gift of a few pages of spiritual autobiography. It is no impiety. We are not asking that the creator should dismember his own creatures. We ask only to be allowed to look more closely into the creative process and see those whom we know as Nostromo, Antonia, or Mrs Gould[2] as they were before they came into the world of Sulaco, while they existed merely in the rarer atmosphere of their maker's mind.

For whatever we learn of their pre-existence undoubtedly adds to our understanding of them when they come before us as men and women of established character and settled destiny. An artist like Mr Conrad, to whom his work is the life of his life, can only speak of his characters in the tone with which we speak of lives that have an existence independent of our own. There is a suggestive power in what he says about his intentions or his affections for these people which enables us to guess at more than is actually said. It is necessary to help out the words themselves with whatever power of intuition we may possess. In the Note, which is of course much too short for our satisfaction, Mr Conrad tells us that after writing *Typhoon* there occurred

a subtle change in the nature of the inspiration; a phenomenon for which I cannot in any way be held responsible. What, however, did cause me some concern was that after finishing the last story of the *Typhoon* volume it seemed somehow that there was nothing more in the world to write about.[3]

It is for us to guess what this check in the course of his development amounted to. We should like to fancy that we see how it happened that when one conception had worked itself out there was a season of seeming emptiness before the world again became full of things to write about; but they were not the same things, and we can guess that they had multiplied in the interval. The knowledge of this crisis, if such we can call it, lends vitality to an old dilemma into which it is common to find people plunging when *Nostromo* comes up for discussion. Is it 'astonishing', or is it a 'failure',[4] as critics according to Mr Conrad variously term it, or can one hold that it is both?

In either case it is illuminating to know that it is the work of a writer who has become aware that the world which he writes about has changed its aspect. He has not got used to the new prospect. As yet it is a world in which he does not see his way. It is a world of bewildering fullness, fineness, and intricacy. The relations of human beings towards each other and towards those impersonal ideals of duty and fidelity which play so large a part in Mr Conrad's scheme of life are seen to be more closely related and finely spun than had been visible to his youthful eye. From all this there results a crowding and suffocating superabundance which makes *Nostromo* one of those rare and magnificent wrecks over which the critics shake their heads, hesitating between 'failure' and 'astonishing', unable to determine why it is that so much skill and beauty are powerless to float the fabric into the main stream of active and enduring existence. The demon which attends Mr Conrad's genius is the demon of languor, of monotony, of an inertness such as we see in the quiescence of the caged tiger. In *Nostromo* the tiger broods superb, supine, but almost completely immobile.

It is a difficult book to read through. One might even say, had he not in later books triumphantly proved himself master of all his possessions, that the writer would have been better served by slighter gifts. Wealth of every sort pours its avalanche from different tributaries into his pages. It would be difficult to find half a dozen thin, colourless, or perfunctory sentences in the length of the book. Each is consciously shaped and contributes its stroke to the building up of a structure to which we are sometimes tempted to apply terms more applicable to the painter's art than to the writer's. ' . . . there was not a single brick, stone, or grain of sand of its soil that I had not placed in position with my own hands,'[5] he tells us in that passage of his *Reminiscences* where he records how for twenty months, 'neglecting the common joys of life,' he 'wrestled with the Lord'[6] for his creation. One may be aware, perhaps, of the extreme effort of this labour of construction, but one is also conscious of the astonishing solidity of the result. The sun is hot, the shadows profound, the earth weighted and veined with silver; the very plaster of Mrs Gould's drawing room appears rough to our touch, and the petals of her flowers are red and purple against it. But in a novel we demand something more than still life, and where the still life is thus superbly designed we want humanity as largely modelled and inspired by a vitality deep and passionate in proportion to the magnificence of the conception. As is apt to be the case with any work by Mr Conrad, his characters have the rare quality of erring upon the side of largeness. The gestures with which they move upon his wide stage are uniformly noble, and the phrases lavished upon them are beautiful enough to be carved for ever upon the pedestals of statues. But when critics speak of the 'failure' of *Nostromo* it is probable that they refer to something inanimate and stationary in the human figures which chills our warmer sympathies. We salute the tragedy with a bow as profound and deferential as we can make it; but we feel that nothing would be more out of keeping than an offering of tears.

1 – A review in the *TLS*, 14 March 1918, (Kp c102) of *Nostromo. A Tale of the Seaboard* (1904; J. M. Dent & Sons Ltd, 1918) by Joseph Conrad (1857–1924). 'A vile windy day,' VW noted in her diary on Sunday, 3 March 1918. 'Sent off my Conrad article, at last – & printed a few [honey pot] labels for Bunny [David Garnett], but we stayed in, & were very happy.'

See also 'Lord Jim' and 'Mr Conrad's *Youth*' above; 'A Disillusioned Romantic', 'A Prince of Prose', 'Mr Conrad: A Conversation', *III VW Essays*; and 'Joseph Conrad', *IV VW Essays* and *CR1*.

2 – For an account of these characters, see Conrad, 'Author's Note' (dated October 1917), pp. x–xiii.

3 – *Ibid.*, p. vii, which has: 'What however did'. *Typhoon* (1902).

4 – Conrad, *Some Reminiscences* (Eveleigh Nash, 1912), ch. v, p. 173: 'I was just then giving up some days of my allotted span to the last chapters of the novel *Nostromo*, a tale of an imaginary (but true) seaboard, which is still mentioned now and again, and indeed kindly, sometimes in connection with the word "failure" and sometimes in conjunction with the word "astonishing". I have no opinion on this discrepancy. It's the sort of difference that can never be settled.'

5 – *Ibid.*, p. 176, which has: 'of its soil I had not placed'.

6 – *Ibid.*, p. 173.

Swinburne Letters

It is possible that before opening this book of Swinburne's letters the reader may ask himself what pleasure, considering the poet's genius, he has a right to expect. The achievements of poets as letter writers in the past would warrant the highest hopes. There are people who would exchange all Byron's poems for half his letters, and upon many shelves *The Task* is spruce and virginal while Cowper's correspondence[2] has the dog's ears, the sloping shoulders, the easy, inevitable openings of a loved companion. Again, no one would wish to sacrifice a line that Keats ever wrote; but we cling as firmly to some of his letters as to some of his poems. So far as it is possible to judge at present, Swinburne is not with these men among the great letter-writers. Perhaps it may not be fantastic to seek some clue to his failure in this respect in the familiar portrait by Watts[3] which is reproduced as a frontispiece to the present volume. It is rather the portrait of a spirit than the portrait even of a poet's body. The eyes are set upon a distant vision. The mouth is slightly pursed in concentrated attention. The whole aspect is exquisitely poetical; but it is also strangely fixed and set. One can imagine how such a figure would take its way through crowded streets looking neither to right nor to left. One seems to perceive an underlying wholeness of nature in this man which would make it unusually hard to turn him from his purpose or to impress him with a different purpose of one's own. The authors[4] of the present book contradict these speculations in their suggestive recollections by dwelling upon the 'plastic and sensitive' nature of Swinburne's temperament. He 'speedily took on', they write, 'the colour (for good or ill) of his immediate environment', which statement they prove by the fact that he 'changed with almost miraculous alacrity' as soon as he came to live with Watts-Dunton.[5] This may be true and yet not exclude a rigidity of mental character which, while it increased the fervour of his admirations and the violence of his denunciations, did not lend itself happily to the give and take of familiar correspondence.

The letters in the present selection begin in 1869 and end some ten years before the poet's death. The early and more interesting letters are addressed chiefly to Rossetti,[6] but the greater number are written to Watts-Dunton in the years before they set up house together at Putney. It is safe to say that they will give a great deal of pleasure to lovers of Swinburne because, if they fail in the peculiar intimacies, abandonments and improvisations which mark certain famous letters, they by no means fail to conjure up the astonishing ghost of Swinburne. He appears in the beginning as the extremely careful and sagacious critic of poetry. In 1869 Rossetti asked him to criticise the proof sheets of his forthcoming volume.[7] He received the criticism which only a poet could give. In reading it we have a sense of watching a jeweller handling his diamonds and rubies. Here it is a question whether 'the break'[8] does not come too soon and suddenly; here it is a matter of sound – a choice between 'what's' and 'what is';[9] here 'I should unhesitatingly reject the five added lines in the Haymarket ... because they utterly deaden and erase the superb effect of the lines preceding . . .[10] The "yesterday's rose in the bosom" is better than beautiful, being so lifelike, but I would condense if I could the thought into a couplet.'[11] Many of the criticisms were accepted, suffused as they were with the glow of Swinburne's already rapturous commendation. 'I cannot tell you how ineffable in wealth of thought and word and every beauty possible to human work I see that set of sonnets to be . . . or how brutally inadequate I feel the best and most delicate comment possible on them to be.'[12] But at the age of thirty-two there was a mean between Swinburne's loves and his hates not so perceptible in later life, as a criticism upon *The Earthly Paradise* will prove. '⟨Morris's⟩ Muse is like Homer's Trojan women; she drags her robes as she walks. I really think any Muse (when she is neither resting nor flying) ought to tighten her girdle, tuck up her skirts, and step out . . . Top's is spontaneous and slow.'[13]

The impious wish must sometimes occur to us that some friend could have done for Swinburne's mind what Watts-Dunton did for his body. So much beauty and truth, such wit and insight seem to have been buried beneath the explosions of his amazing but in its later developments so sterile vocabulary. The talent, for instance, which is displayed in *Love's Cross Currents*[14] foretold the advent and indeed proclaimed the presence of a delightful and original novelist. But the prophecy was never fulfilled. The critic in his turn suffered the same extinction or dissipation; for Swinburne's praise or blame blots out the object of it as effectually as a dust storm conceals a daisy, and the verbal whirlwind of his later utterance becomes as monotonous as the smooth drone of a large humming top. In reading his letters, however, the criticism which we have impatiently uttered is disarmed. There is a gallantry about this enthusiastic figure which is irresistible. Moreover, it is impossible not to lay the blame for such catastrophe as there was upon a thousand circumstances which are hidden, as so much of Swinburne's life remains hidden, from our knowledge. The British public whom he delighted to flout and to tease did not surround their surprising fellow citizen with an atmosphere of sympathy. Perhaps, indeed, the man who could persuade the secretary of the Society for the Suppression of Vice to state in public that his Society did not, as the poet asserted, intend 'to burke' Rabelais, Shakespeare, and the Holy Bible,[15] deserved to do penance every Sunday of his life at Putney, shut up in his room because he dared not venture out in the midst of the holiday-making crowd. That day, according to the authors of this book, was the 'one prosaic time of Swinburne's life at the

Pines'.[16] The company of the Elizabethan dramatists was not sufficient; he was forced to extend his hours of sleep. On the other hand, Captain Webb had only to swim across the Channel and no voice was more vociferous in his praise. 'I consider it,' Swinburne wrote, 'the greatest glory that has befallen England since the publication of Shelley's greatest poem, whichever that may be.'[17]

But in truth the staple of these letters is composed neither of poetic meditation nor of invective against the public; matters of business provide the chief theme of the letters to Watts-Dunton, and would threaten them with dulness if that danger were not always averted by some delightful thrust or phrase or suggestion. When all the difficulties of his publishing affairs had been arranged, his landladies still had drunken husbands, his books were still left behind him in London, his letters still succeeded in getting lost, his tradesmen still insisted upon being paid.

'Such is the present excess of human baseness, and such the weltering abyss of social anarchy in which we live, that this demoralised Mammonite, whose all would be at my disposal – his life and his property alike – in a commonwealth duly based on any rational principle of order and good government, actually requires money for goods supplied to Me.'[18] In such crises of daily life Swinburne instinctively took up his pen and wrote a full and eloquent statement of the case to Watts-Dunton. In one such document, written, he declares, in great haste, it is possible to count seven separate commissions. Watts-Dunton is to draw up a form of subscription to the *Pall Mall*; to find an unfinished article in a drawer; to discover the lost letter of a Hungarian countess; to explain how to answer and direct it properly; to give an opinion upon both parties in a libel action; to forward a large number of books and manuscripts, and to order a variety of magazines. Finally, he need not trouble about the missing penholder; that has already been found.[19]

1 – A review in the *TLS*, 21 March 1918, (Kp c103) of *The Letters of Algernon Charles Swinburne*. With some personal recollections by Thomas Hake and Arthur Compton-Rickett (John Murray, 1918). Having pronounced herself 'rejected by the Times [Literary Supplement] (*I VW Diary*, Tuesday, 12 March 1918), VW declared on the 14th, 'My dismissal is revoked. A large book on Pepys arrived ['Papers on Pepys', below], which I spent the evening reading, & now another on Swinburne awaits me at the Railway station. I'm divided whether one likes to have books, or to write fiction without interruption. But I may make a few shillings to pay for my

Baskerville [edition of Congreve].' See also 'Watts-Dunton's Dilemma', *III VW Essays*.

2 – For VW on the poet William Cowper (1731–1800), see 'Cowper and Lady Austen', *V VW Essays* and *CR2*; the essay, based on Cowper's correspondence (4 vols, Hodder and Stoughton, 1904), contains, incidentally, a single buried quotation ('thistly sorrow') from *The Task* (1785).

3 – The quarter-length portrait in oils by G. F. Watts (1817–1904) is in the National Portrait Gallery (no. 1542).

4 – Thomas Hake (d. 1917) and Arthur Compton-Rickett (1869–1937), literary journalist, university lecturer, and author of several works including *A History of English Literature* (1912) and, with Hake, *The Life and Letters of Theodore Watts-Dunton* (1916).

5 – For all three quotations, *Letters*, p. 171, which has: 'This is shown by the almost miraculous alacrity with which he shed the "old Adam" as soon as he had come to live with Watts-Dunton.' Walter Theodore Watts-Dunton (1832–1914), critic, poet, and author of the novel *Aylwin* (1898), had first met Swinburne (1837–1907) in 1872. Seven years later, when Swinburne was in a state of nervous collapse, he invited him to stay at his home at The Pines, Putney Hill; and there Swinburne remained, 'quiet and sequestered' (*Letters*, p. 173), until his death.

6 – Dante Gabriel Rossetti (1828–82), following the tragic death of his wife in 1862, had shared a house with Swinburne, a fervent admirer of his work both as painter and poet, and with George Meredith, at 16 Cheyne Walk, Chelsea.

7 – *Poems* (1870).

8 – *Letters*, 10 December 1869, p. 23; the poem under discussion, not identified in the text, is 'Jenny' (ll. 9–13).

9 – *Ibid.*, 24 February 1870, p. 45: 'And I wish for my ear's sake, which liked the over-syllable, you had not (in "John of Tours") written "What's the crying," etc . . . these sprucifications of structure injure the ballad sound and style, which ought *not* to be level and accurate.'

10 – *Ibid.*, 10 December 1869, p. 22, which has: 'on the Haymarket'.

11 – *Ibid.*, p. 23, which concludes'; it reads a little draggingly.' The reference is to 'Jenny', probably paragraph nine.

12 – *Ibid.*, 24 February 1870, p. 44; the work under discussion is the cycle of love-sonnets 'Towards a work to be called The House of Life'.

13 – *Ibid.*, 10 December 1869, p. 25, which continues '; and, especially, my ear hungers for more force and variety of sound in the verse.' William Morris (1834–96), known to his friends as 'Topsy', published his poem *The Earthly Paradise* in 1868–70.

14 – Swinburne's *Love's Cross Currents* (1905) was originally published as *A Year's Letters* in the *Tatler*, (25 August–29 December 1877) as by 'Mrs Horace Manners'.

15 – *Letters*, to Edward Harrison, 7 July 1875, pp. 56–7, referring to an earlier correspondence in the *Athenaeum*; the secretary concerned is not identified. To 'burke': 'to kill secretly by suffocation or strangulation, or in order to sell the victim's body for dissection, as Burke did' (*OED*).

16 – *Ibid.*, p. 191.

17 – *Ibid.*, to Watts-Dunton, 27 August 1875, p. 58; Captain Webb swam the

English channel from Dover to Calais in just under twenty-four hours on 24 August 1875.
18 – *Ibid.*, to the same, 30 January 1873, which has '*Me*'.
19 – *Ibid.*, 22 June 1879. The discovery of the 'penholder' is in fact recorded earlier in the letter, before the reference to the (unidentified) Hungarian countess.

Papers on Pepys

The number of those who read themselves asleep at night with Pepys[2] and awake at day with Pepys must be great. By the nature of things, however, the number of those who read neither by night nor by day is infinitely greater; and it is, we believe, by those who have never read him that Pepys is, as Mr Wheatley complains, treated with contempt. The Pepys Club 'may be considered', Mr Wheatley writes, 'as a kind of missionary society to educate the public to understand that they are wrong in treating Pepys with affection, tempered with lack of respect'.[3] The papers published in the present volume would not have suggested to us so solemn a comparison. A missionary society, however, which dines well, sings beautifully old English songs, and delivers brief and entertaining papers upon such subjects as Pepys's portraits, Pepys's stone, Pepys's ballads, Pepys's health, Pepys's musical instruments,[4] although it differs, we imagine, in method from some sister institutions, is well calculated to convert the heathen. Lack of respect for Pepys, however, seems to us a heresy which is beyond argument, and deserving of punishment rather than of the persuasive voices of members of the Pepys Club singing 'Beauty Retire'.[5]

For one of the most obvious sources of our delight in the diary arises from the fact that Pepys, besides being himself, was a great civil servant. We are glad to remember that it has been stated on authority, however well we guessed it for ourselves, that Pepys was 'without exception the greatest and most useful Minister that ever filled the same situation in England, the acts and registers of the Admiralty proving this beyond contradiction'.[6] He was the founder of the modern Navy, and the fame of Mr Pepys as an administrator has had an independent existence of its own within the walls of the Admiralty from his day to ours. Indeed, it is possible to believe that we owe the diary largely to his eminence as an official. The reticence, the pomposity, the observance of appearances which their duties require, or at least exact, of great public servants must make it more congenial to them than to others to unbend and unbosom themselves in private. We can only regret that the higher education of women now enables the wives of public men to receive confidences which should have been committed to cipher. Happily for us, Mrs Pepys[7] was a very imperfect confidante. There were other matters besides those naturally unfit for a wife's ear that Pepys brought home from the office and liked to deliver himself upon in private. And thus it comes about that the diary runs naturally from affairs of State and the characters of ministers to affairs of the heart and the characters of servant girls; it includes the buying of clothes, the losing of tempers, and all the infinite curiosities, amusements, and pettinesses of average human life. It is a portrait where not only the main figure, but the surroundings, ornaments, and accessories are painted in. Had Mrs Pepys been as learned, discreet, and open-minded as the most advanced of her sex are now reputed to be, her husband would still have had enough over to fill the pages of his diary. Insatiable curiosity, and unflagging vitality were the essence of a gift to which, when the possessor is able to impart it, we can give no lesser name than genius.

It is worth reminding ourselves that because we are without his genius it does not follow that we are without his faults. The chief delight of his pages for most of us may lie not in the respectable direction of historical investigation, but in those very weaknesses and idiosyncrasies which in our own case we would die rather than reveal; but our quick understanding betrays the fact that we are fellow-sinners, though unconfessed. The state of mind that makes possible such admission of the undignified failings even in cipher may not be heroic, but it shows a lively, candid, unhypocritical nature which, if we remember that Pepys was an extremely able man, a very successful man and honourable beyond the standard of his age, fills out a figure which is perhaps a good deal higher in the scale of humanity than our own.

But those select few who survive the 'vast and devouring space'[8] of the centuries are judged not by their superiority to individuals in the flesh, but by their rank in the society of their peers, those solitary survivors of innumerable and nameless multitudes. Compared with most of these figures, Pepys is small enough. He is never passionate, exalted, poetic, or profound. His faults are not great ones, nor is his repentance sublime. Considering that he used cipher, and on occasion double cipher, to screen him in the confessional, he did not lay bare very deep or very intricate regions of the soul. He has little consciousness of dream or mystery, of conflict or perplexity. Yet it is impossible to write Pepys off as a man of the dumb and unanalytic past, or of the past which is ornate and fabulous; if ever we feel ourselves in the presence of a man so modern that we should not be surprised to meet him in the street and should know him and speak to him at once, it is when we read this diary, written more than two hundred and fifty years ago.

This is due in part to the unstudied ease of the language, which may be slipshod but never fails to be graphic, which catches unfailingly the butterflies and gnats and falling petals of the moment, which can deal with a day's outing or a merrymaking or a brother's funeral so that we latecomers are still in time to make one of the party. But Pepys is modern in a deeper sense than this. He is modern in his consciousness of the past, in his love of pretty civilised things, in his cultivation, in his quick and varied sensibility. He was a collector and a connoisseur; he delighted not only in books, but in old ballads and in good furniture. He was a man who had come upon the scene not so early but that there was already a fine display of curious and diverting objects accumulated by an older generation. Standing midway in our history, he looks consciously and intelligently both backwards and forwards. If we turn our eyes behind us we see him gazing in our direction, asking with eager curiosity of our progress in science, of our ships and sailors. Indeed, the very fact that he kept a diary seems to make him one of ourselves.

Yet in reckoning, however imperfectly, the sources of our pleasure we must not forget that his age is among them. Sprightly, inquisitive, full of stir and life as he is, nevertheless Mr Pepys is now two hundred and eighty-five years of age. He can remember London when it was very much smaller than it is now, with gardens and orchards, wild duck and deer. Men 'justled for the wall and did kill one another'.[9] Gentlemen were murdered riding out to their country houses at Kentish Town. Mr Pepys and Lady Paulina[10] were much afraid of being set upon when they drove back at night, though Mr Pepys concealed his fears. They very seldom took baths, but, on the other hand, they dressed in velvet and brocade. They acquired a great deal of silver plate too, especially if they were in the public service, and a present of gloves for your wife might well be stuffed with guineas. Ladies put on their vizards at the play – and with reason if their cheeks were capable of blushing. Sir Charles Sedley[11] was so witty once with his companion that you could not catch a word upon the stage. As for Lady Castlemaine,[12] we should never persuade Mr Pepys that the sun of beauty did not set once and for all with her decline. It is an atmosphere at once homely and splendid, coarse and beautiful, of a world far away and yet very modern that is preserved in his pages.

The Pepys Club, which draws its life from so fertile a source, may well flourish and multiply its members. The portraits reproduced here, in particular a page of Mr Pepys's 'individual features',[13] are of themselves sufficient to make this volume of memorable interest. And yet there is one contribution which we would rather have left unread. It consists only of a little Latin, a few signs, two or three letters of the alphabet, such as any oculist in Harley Street will write you out upon half a sheet of note-paper for a couple of guineas.[14] But to Samuel Pepys it would have meant a pair of spectacles, and what that pair of spectacles upon that pair of eyes might have seen and recorded it is tantalising to consider. Instead of giving up his diary upon 31 May 1669, he might with this prescription have continued it for another thirty years.[15] It is some relief to be told that the prescription is beyond the skill of contemporary oculists; but this is dashed by Mr Power's statement that had Pepys chanced to sit upon the 'tube spectacall'[16] of paper which his oculist provided so that he must read through a slit,

he would then have found his eye strain removed; his acute mind would have set itself to determine the cause; he would have pasted slips of black paper on each side of his glasses, and the diary might have been continued to the end of his life; whilst the paper he would certainly have read upon the subject before the Royal Society would have added still greater lustre to his name, and might have revolutionised the laws of dioptrics.[17]

But our regret is not purely selfish. How reluctant Pepys was to close his diary the melancholy last paragraph bears witness. He had written until the act of writing 'undid' his eyes, for the things he wished to write were not always fit to be written in long-hand, and to cease to write 'was almost as much as to see myself go into my grave'.[18] And yet this was a writing which no one, during his life at any rate, was to be allowed to read. Not only from the last sentence, but from every sentence, it is easy to see what lure it was that drew him to his diary. It was not a confessional, still less a mere record of things useful to remember, but the store house of his most private self, the echo of life's sweetest sounds, without which life itself would become thinner and more prosaic. When he went upstairs to his chamber it was to perform no mechanical exercise, but to hold intercourse with the secret companion who lives in everybody, whose presence is so real, whose comment is so valuable, whose faults and trespasses and vanities are so lovable that to lose him is 'almost to go into my grave'.[19] For this other Pepys, this spirit of the man whom men respected, he wrote his diary, and it is for this reason that for centuries to come men will delight in reading it.

1 – A review in the *TLS*, 4 April 1918, (Kp C104) of *Occasional Papers Read by Members at Meetings of the Samuel Pepys Club*. Ed. by the late H. B. Wheatley, First President of the Club, vol. i, 1903–14 (Pepys Club, printed at the Chiswick Press, 1918). See 'Swinburne's Letters', n.1 above. Reprinted: *B&P*.

2 – Samuel Pepys (1633–1703) whose diary was first edited in 1825 and not published in its entirety until 1893–6, in an edition prepared by H. B. Wheatley – also the author of *Samuel Pepys and the World He Lived In* (1880), a work cited by Leslie Stephen in his *DNB* entry on Pepys.

3 – *Occasional Papers*, H. B. Wheatley, 'The Growth of the Fame of Samuel Pepys', p. 173.

4 – *Ibid.*, Lionel Cust, 'Notes on the Portraits of Samuel Pepys', and Samuel Pepys Cockerell, 'Notes on Some Distinctive Features in Pepys's Portraits'; D'Arcy Power, 'Who Performed Lithotomy on Mr Samuel Pepys'; F. Sidgwick, 'The Pepys Ballads'; D'Arcy Power, 'The Medical History of Mr and Mrs Samuel Pepys'; Sir Frederick Bridge, 'Musical Instruments Mentioned by Pepys'.

5 – *Ibid.*, p. 1, 'Beauty Retire' (words from Davenant's 'Siege of Rhodes') was sung at all the club's dinners – immediately after the toast to Pepys's immortal memory.

6 – *Ibid.*, Wheatley, 'The Growth of the Fame of Samuel Pepys', p. 160, an unattributed quotation.

7 – Elizabeth St Michel (d. 1669) whom Pepys had married in 1655, when she was aged fifteen.

8 – The origin of this phrase, which VW also quotes in 'Sir Walter Raleigh', above, has resisted all attempts at discovery.

9 – The source of this quotation has not been found.

10 – Lady Paulina, daughter of Edward Montagu, 1st Earl of Sandwich (1625–72).

11 – Sir Charles Sedley (1639?–1701), wit and dramatist, author of *The Mulberry Garden* (1668) and of *Bellamira* (1687). For his witticisms at the theatre see Pepys's diary, 4 October 1664 and 18 February 1667.

12 – Barbara Villiers (afterwards Palmer), Countess of Castlemaine and Duchess of Cleveland (1641–1709), the notorious mistress of Charles II.

13 – *Occasional Papers*, Cockerell, 'Notes on Some Distinctive Features in Pepys's Portraits', illustrations between pp. 36–7, with portraits drawn or otherwise executed after the manner of Hayls, by Kneller, by Cavallier, and attributed to Le Marchand, and showing details extracted from these of Pepys's eyes, nose and mouth.

14 – *Ibid.*, D'Arcy Power, 'Why Samuel Pepys Discontinued his Diary', p. 75: 'For Samuel Pepys Esq. Spectacles – +2 D.c. + 0.50 D. cyl. axis 90°'.

15 – *Ibid.*, which has: 'with these glasses the Diary might have been continued at any rate for several subsequent years. Such a prescription would, however, have been impossible'.

16 – *Ibid.*, p. 71, quoting the diary, 11 August 1668.

17 – *Ibid.*, pp. 76–7, quoting the diary, 31 May 1669.

18 – *Ibid.*, p. 74, which has: 'And thus ends all that I doubt I shall ever be able to do with my own eyes in the keeping of my Journal, I being not able to do it any longer, having done it now so long as to undo my eyes almost every time that I take my pen in my hand . . .'

19 – *Ibid.*, which has: 'And so I betake myself to that course which is almost as much as to see myself go into my grave; for which and all the discomforts that will accompany my being blind, the good God prepare me!'

'Second Marriage'

Fiction is probably the most living form of literature in England at the present moment, and for that reason it is the most difficult to judge. Far from having reached its full height, it is in a state of growth and development; we scarcely know on opening a new novel what to expect; the most sagacious has difficulty in deciding where to draw the line, and nowhere perhaps do our personal prejudices so confuse what should be our aesthetic judgments. To sit with crossed hands impartially observant when everything that is said or done rouses some irrational antagonism or sympathy, is like or unlike what we are accustomed to call life, conflicts with or ignores rules tentatively framed beforehand, requires more than the usual degree of infallibility. Nothing is so hard to criticise as a new novel, but nothing is more interesting than to make the attempt.

Miss Viola Meynell[2] is not likely to upset anyone by the obvious novelty of her methods. She does not plunge you beneath the surface into a layer of consciousness largely represented by little black dots. She does not experiment with phrases that recur like the motive in a Wagner opera. She has no animosity against adjectives, nor does she exterminate verbs upon principle. Her characters are related to each other in the normal way, and they live in a house which is definitely stated to be situated in the Fen country.[3] All the same you will probably find yourself stopping before you have read very far in *Second Marriage* to ask yourself what Miss Meynell is after; for the picture is sufficiently unlike life to forbid anyone to rest in the belief that it is a straightforward story with one simple knot which the last chapter will successfully untie. The reader has always to answer some such question when the writer is anything of an artist; he has to adjust his sight to the focus of another. If in this case we have found the adjustment more difficult than usual it is not because there is any special complexity in the story. The story is too simple to require much analysis. It is made out of the different engagements and marriages of Rose, Ismay, and Esther, the three daughters of Mr and Mrs Glimour, of Skirth Farm, in the Fens. Concurrently with their story runs the story of the farm and in particular the story of the pumping engine, the invention of Arnold Glimour, a young man who has quarrelled with his cousins at the farm. Ismay Hunt, the incredibly beautiful daughter of the Glimours, returns home, a widow, after a year of marriage, endowed with three thousand pounds. Instead of using this sum to facilitate her sister's marriage, she invests it in the pumping engine, saves the land from the floods which threaten it, and finally marries the inventor.

And now the question is what impression Miss Meynell's arrangement of this story makes upon us. If it is for her to carry out her design faithfully, it is for us to attempt to see what she has meant us to see. In our case we must admit that the attempt has been attended with more of groping and straining than is consistent with complete pleasure, or indeed with the certainty that we have seen aright. The impression is a little inconclusive. In the first place the introduction of men and women with some degree of detail at once incites us to do what we can to imagine them alive and real. But the process has hardly begun when it is checked; for some reason, possibly connected with the flatness and scarcity of the dialogue, our instinct is snubbed; we begin to suspect that Miss Meynell does not care very much for life or reality.[4] If we are not to bother about life we must cast about until we find another track. It may be a novel of still life, a novel, such as Miss Meynell is well qualified to write, about substance and texture, with a design of men and women indicated like a fresco upon a wall. But from this conception of the right point of view we are roused by snatches of slang, by the apparatus of breakfast, dinner and tea, and by sudden attempts at brutality such as the scene when Arnold Glimour ties his young brother to a tree, stamps a shilling into the earth and laughs to see him grub it out with his teeth. The scene has a curiously medieval taste about it. The fight between Arnold and Maurice, for all its parade of violence, is best conveyed to us by one of Miss Meynell's precise observations: 'Up in the dark, raftered roof the cobwebs shook and waved in the wind of their fight.'[5]

In the end, then, we settle to listen to the reflections which life in general has suggested to a curious and very fastidious observer, to whom the Glimour family was known not very intimately but with discernment, and to whom the characters of trees and skies are as well worth watching as the character of human beings. The different aspects of water, the effect of summer mist upon the trees, the sound of a storm, are described not only with care but with a sudden unexpected intensity as if the writer, having allowed the mass of obvious ideas and commonplace words to stream past her, suddenly saw and selected the single one of interest to her.

For the wind never came with a clean smooth edge; what it was doing it was never doing right – like a diver who does not cut neatly into the water but falls flat upon it, to his own violence and destruction. The shuddering blow it gave the house was like all the violent things done wrong and awkwardly in the world; and one could imagine that the reason why the wind grew in fury was because every blow it gave with such awkward violence was as hurtful to itself as to what it struck.[6]

Applied to the lives of people – Ismay, Rose, Maurice, Arnold – this method has the effect of telling you some recondite detail about them while leaving entirely unnoticed the substance of which they are made. Moreover, by this method everything is told you; it never happens, nor is it ever said. Indeed the dialogue is curiously timid, put into the mouth, not issuing from it, and losing in its colloquial reality the beauty of quality which Miss Meynell so frequently attains in her carefully wrought passages of description and analysis. The fifteen minutes after a book is finished recreate the impression of the whole in the reader's mind as upon reaching home the course of a walk comes before you from start to finish. At the end of *Second Marriage* we see no particular person, we remember no particular scene, but we have a general impression of having examined in a pleasing and quiet way rather an intricate pattern, full of ornament and detail, hidden in a secluded place where the sun, falling through greenish panes of old glass, has no longer any heat.

1 – A review in the *TLS*, 25 April 1918, (Kp c105) of *Second Marriage* (Martin Secker, 1918) by Viola Meynell. 'Then I went to Guildford,' VW wrote in her diary on Thursday, 18 April. 'I don't see how to put 3 or 4 hours of Roger [Fry]'s conversation into the rest of this page; (& I must stop & read Viola Meynell) . . .'

2 – Viola Meynell (1886–1956), a daughter of the poet and essayist Alice Meynell (see 'Hearts of Controversy' above), was the author of several novels, a study of George Eliot (1913) and a memoir of the soldier-poet Julian Grenfell (1917).

3 – Meynell, bk 1, ch. 1, p. 7: 'From the edge of the fen into its farthest places one family had for ages past inhabited the drowned lands.'

4 – A point VW touched on earlier in writing, about an unspecified work, to Lady Robert Cecil, 18 February 1916 (*II VW Letters*, no. 743): 'I have also been reading . . . Miss Viola Meynell who depresses me with her lack of realism.'

5 – Meynell, bk 3, ch. III, p. 272.

6 – *Ibid.*, bk 1, ch, XI, pp. 132–3.

Two Irish Poets

That the song of a nightingale is sad and that a poet desires fame are two statements that have all the authority of legend behind them. Thus, Lord Dunsany will find room in a page or two of introduction to the *Last Songs* of Francis Ledwidge² to lament that the poet died before he saw his fame. The regret seems more fitting in the case of a poet than it would be in any other case, although at first sight the ungratified desire for fame seems merely pathetic and the attainment of the desire even a little ridiculous. Why should fame mean so much to anyone? The reason why it means so much to a poet will, perhaps, occur to the reader of these *Last Songs*. They seem to ask with a simplicity denied to poets of a richer or more powerful gift that we should be in sympathy with the singer. It is not praise that he wants, but that we should be on his side in liking what he likes.

Without some such assurance the task of writing the kind of poetry which this book contains must be difficult:

> I took a reed and blew a tune,
> And sweet it was and very clear
> To be about a little thing
> That only few hold dear.³

Most of Mr Ledwidge's poems are about those little things that only few hold dear not because they are rare or remote, but because they lie all about us, as common as grass and sky. There are poems about Spring, and Autumn, and Youth, and Love, and Home;⁴ and with no obvious ecstasy to thrill you it is difficult at first to see why Francis Ledwidge

ventured to make poetry where most of us are silent. But either you are
caught by a phrase like that about a tree at evening:

> And when the shadows muster and each tree
> A moment flutters, full of shutting wings,[5]

or by a sense of completeness such as the following lines, 'With Flowers',
convey:

> These have more language than my song,
> Take them and let them speak for me.
> I whispered them a secret thing
> Down the green lanes of Allary.
>
> You shall remember quiet ways
> Watching them fade, and quiet eyes,
> And two hearts given up to love,
> A foolish and an overwise.[6]

And you come to believe in the end that you, too, hold these things dear.
Mr Ledwidge has not made them great, or passionate, or different; but
he has believed in the worth of his own feelings; and he has believed that
there was enough sympathy with such feelings for him to confide in a
world rather ostentatiously interested in other things. His belief was
deep enough to give him delight in stating it whether the world listened
or not, whether the Irish fields were before his eyes or seen in imagination through the smoke of battle.

Irish blood produces a likeness which it would be easy to exaggerate,
and yet, reading first Mr Ledwidge and then Mr Stephens,[7] you cannot
deny that the likeness exists. It is to be found in a common rightness of
feeling, as if, with whatever difference of gift, it came by nature to them
to say neither too much nor too little, but to keep well in the middle of
the note. The lilt of the voice which we believe we can detect in their
literature no less than in their speech is also easy to feel though difficult
to analyse. Synge[8] was the most potent master of it, and in the hand of
his imitators we must confess to have grown a little tired of the Irish style
in prose. But in poetry the natural charm and natural turn of voice give
quality and style to slight verses which without that grace would be
almost negligible. The 'Reincarnations' of Mr Stephens are very graceful, but by no means negligible. Having printed his note at the end of the
book – a habit to be commended to all authors – we read through the
poems in the belief tl.at they were entirely his own work, and in that
belief admired his range and variety of mood. As a matter of fact

everything in the book 'can be referred to the Irish of some one hundred to three hundred years ago'.[9] In two cases only is the translation exact, and in the rest of the poems Mr Stephens himself could hardly tell at what point and in what measure his words have mixed themselves with the words of Raftery, O'Rahilly, and O'Bruadhair.[10] We get a generalised impression that Raftery was a master of easy melody, that O'Rahilly was a satirist, and that O'Bruadhair was the most complex of them all, well endowed with words and inclined to run them into an 'unending rebellious bawl':[11]

> As lily grows up easily,
> In modest gentle dignity
> To sweet perfection,
> So grew she,
> As easily.
>
> Or as the rose that takes no care
> Will open out on sunny air
> Bloom after bloom, fair after fair,
> Sweet after sweet;
> Just so did she,
> As carelessly.[12]

That is the voice of Raftery.

> The lanky hank of a she in the inn over there
> Nearly killed me for asking the loan of a glass of beer.
> May the devil grip the whey-faced slut by the hair,
> And beat bad manners out of her skin for a year.[13]

That is the style of the witty, eloquent and truculent O'Bruadhair. However closely or loosely these versions may fit the originals, each seems to come from the mouth of an Irishman, who writes from his tradition and not from ours. These poems, like the translations from the Chinese, make you aware of another attitude towards poetry, of another civilisation. The difference in this case may not be very profound; it may only be as the change from the Cockney accent to broad Devonshire; but, even so, the sound is welcome in our ears.

1 – A review in the *TLS*, 2 May 1918, (Kp c106) of *Last Songs* (Herbert Jenkins Ltd, 1918) by Francis Ledwidge and of *Reincarnations* (Macmillan & Co., 1918) by James Stephens.
2 – Francis Ledwidge (1891–1917), poet, labourer, and Irish nationalist, had joined the Royal Iniskillin Fusiliers in 1914 'to fight "neither for a principle, nor a people, nor a law, but for the fields along the Boyne, for the birds and the blue sky over

them"' (*DNB*); he was killed in Belgium on 31 July 1917. His two previous volumes of verse, *Songs of the Field* (1915) and *Songs of Peace* (1916), were also introduced by Lord Dunsany – Edward John Moreton Drax Plunkett, 18th Baron of Dunsany (1878–1957), author of plays and novels, who served as a captain in the R.I.F., 1914–18, and took part in the suppression of the Easter Rising, during which he was wounded and captured by the nationalists.

3 – Ledwidge, 'The Find', p. 63.

4 – *Ibid.*, 'Spring', pp. 58–9; 'Autumn', pp. 26–7; 'Youth', pp. 22–3; 'Spring Love', p. 40; 'Home', pp. 71–2.

5 – *Ibid.*, 'The One Who Comes Now and Then' (dated: Belgium, 22 July 1917), p. 68.

6 – *Ibid.*, 'With Flowers' (dated: France, April 1917), p. 62.

7 – James Stephens (1880?–1950), author of the classic Irish fantasy *The Crock of Gold* (1912).

8 – John Millington Synge (1871–1909), author of *The Playboy of the Western World* (1907), etc.

9 – Stephens, 'Note', p. 61.

10 – Anthony Raftery (1784–1834); Egan O'Rahilly (fl. 1690–1726); David O'Bruadhair (fl. 1650–94).

11 – Stephens, 'Note', p. 66.

12 – *Ibid.*, 'Peggy Mitchell', p. 6.

13 – *Ibid.*, 'Righteous Anger', p. 37.

Tchehov's Questions

An anonymous American critic, introducing *Nine Humorous Tales* by Tchehov to his contemporaries, defines the Russian writer thus: 'If Tchehov is more humanly self-revealing than de Maupassant, he is on the whole more deep than O. Henry. If O. Henry may be called the American Tchehov with a "punch", Tchehov may equally be termed the Russian O. Henry with a caress.'[2] You look at that rather as you look at an advertisement cow standing in a field among real cows. The critic has tried to cut out a pattern of Tchehov with a very large, but, alas! a very blunt pair of scissors. The shape is so grotesque that it does not fit even the shadow of Tchehov preserved from past readings; and this is the more disappointing because Tchehov is still one of the nebulous, undefined writers of whom one is glad to have even an outline.

Everyone has read him by this time; one can foretell a large and inquisitive public for the fifth and sixth volumes of his stories, but it seems doubtful whether there will result from all this reading a unanimous verdict such as was passed in so short a space of time upon Dostoevsky.³ That hesitation may be a sign that he is not on a level with the greatest of the Russian writers. He is at any rate not among the unmistakable and overwhelming geniuses who bend you, whether you are upstanding or flexible, in the way their spirit blows. He is more on a level with ourselves. He is not heroic. He is aware that modern life is full of a nondescript melancholy, of discomfort, of queer relationships which beget emotions that are half ludicrous and yet painful, and that an inconclusive ending for all these impulses and oddities is much more usual than anything extreme. He knows all this as we know it, and at first sight he seems no more ready than we are with a solution. The attentive reader who is on the alert for some unmistakable sign that now the story is going to pull itself together and make straight as an arrow for its destination is still looking rather more blankly when the end comes. Perhaps it comes in this way. 'With whom was he angry? Was it with people, with poverty, with the autumn nights?'⁴ That is the end of a story called 'The Post'. The postman has to drive a student to the station, and all the way the student tries to make the postman talk, but the postman remains silent, and at last the student falls silent too. Suddenly, just before they reach the station, the postman says unexpectedly, 'It's against the regulations to take anyone with the post . . . Yes. It makes no difference to me, it's true, only I don't like it, and I don't wish it.'⁵ And he walks up and down the platform with a look of anger on his face. But why was he angry?

The recurrence of this question, not only in the form of an actual note of interrogation but in the choice of incidents and of endings, produces at first a queer feeling that the solid ground upon which we expected to make a safe landing has been twitched from under us, and there we hang asking questions in mid air. It is giddy, uncomfortable, inconclusive. But imperceptibly things arrange themselves, and we come to feel that the horizon is much wider from this point of view; we have gained a sense of astonishing freedom. The method that at first seemed so casual and inconclusive, ordinary and upon the level of our own eyesight, now appears to be the result of an exquisitely fastidious taste, controlled by an honesty for which we can find no match save among the Russians themselves. There may be no answer to these questions, but at the same time let us never manipulate the evidence so as to produce something fitting, decorous, or agreeable to our vanity. Away fly half the conclusions of the world at once. Accept endlessly, scrutinise ceaselessly, and see what will happen.

But it is easy to make out a message that is momentarily satisfying, and to dwell too emphatically upon the philosophy of Tchehov. His philosophy is, of course, inseparable from all that he writes, but it has to blend itself with another element that springs with immense vigour and fecundity from a very deep source. He is a born story-teller. Wherever he looks, whatever he sees, wherever he goes, stories shape themselves quickly and with a sort of spontaneous directness which reminds one of an earlier age of the world's literature when story-telling was natural to man. The whole mass of Russia seems to be leavened with the spirit, instead of small patches or thin crusts. Frequently one of Tchehov's peasants will ask to be told a story, and his friend, who is also a peasant, will pour out a story which is not funny or an adventure, but the history of his life, told with coarseness perhaps, but with a subtlety and passion which we accept from him, though it would be impossible to imagine an English farmer speaking thus. "'It is interesting," said Savka ⟨the watchman and scarecrow⟩, "whatever one talks about is always interesting. Take a bird now, or a man ... or take this little stone; there's something to learn about all of them." "[6] Or it is an account of a dinner in a small country house, where the local doctor is one of the guests. He leads a very dull life, and when he has the chance over-eats himself enormously. Yet he begins almost at once upon the nature of life. 'Yes! if one thinks about it, you know, looks into it, and analyses all this hotch-potch, if you will allow me to call it so, it's not life, but more like a fire in a theatre!'[7] He goes on to describe his sensations in this blazing theatre. And this is not by any means the speech of Tchehov through a mask: the doctor speaks; he is there, alive, himself, an ordinary man, but he looks at things directly; there is in him too a fibre of individuality which gives out its own sharp vibration to the touch of life.

Innumerable as Tchehov's characters seem to be, they are all different, and their differences are indicated by fine clean strokes dealt with astonishing celerity and certainty, for the whole story often occupies only a page or two. And yet, we ask again, what aim is there behind this certainty? What was his purpose in defining so many scores of men and women, who are for the most part so disagreeable in themselves or in their circumstances so degraded? Did he find no connecting link, no final arrangement which is satisfying and harmonious in itself, although the parts which compose it are painful and mean? It is difficult not to ask that question, and the very fineness and delicacy of Tchehov's mind make it unusually difficult to be sure of an answer. He seems able with one tap to split asunder those emotions that we have been wont to think whole and entire, leaving them scattered about in small disconnected splinters. How much of your mental furniture remains entire when you have read 'A Dreary Story'?[8] Even when the tale is apparently straightforward, another view of it is reflected in some mirror in the background. But if he were merely cynical, brilliant, and destructive, we should have no question to ask; we should already know the answer. He is more profoundly disturbing than any cynic because his gifts are so rich and various. But among these gifts there are at least three which seem to contradict those who hold him the novelist of hopelessness and despair. There is no one who seems endowed, even through the necessarily coarse medium of a translation, with a keener sense of beauty. In some of the stories we may find that this beauty is by itself sufficient. Again, there is an originality in his choice of the elements that make up a story which sometimes produces an arrangement so unlike any we have met with before that it is necessary to consider whether he is not hinting at some order hitherto unguessed at, though perhaps never fully stated by him. 'Gusev'[9] is an example of this. And, finally, in his cruelty, in the harshness of his pictures, especially of the peasants and of their life is there not by implication a statement of the only sympathy which is creative?

1 – A review in the *TLS*, 16 May 1918, (Kp C107) of *The Wife and Other Stories, The Witch and Other Stories* ... translated by Constance Garnett (Chatto & Windus, 1918) and of *Nine Humorous Tales* (Boston: Stratford Publishing Co., ?1918) by Anton Tchehov. 'L[eonard Woolf] has gone to a [League of Nations] meeting at the House of Commons,' VW noted in her diary on Tuesday, 7 May 1918. 'I've had a rush of books as usual: three Tchekovs [sic], Logan, Squire and Merrick hanging over me.' See also 'The Russian Background', 'The Cherry Orchard', *III VW Essays*, and see 'The Russian Point of View', *IV VW Essays* and CR1.

2 – No copy of *Nine Humorous Tales* has been traced. Anton Chekhov (1860–1904). Guy de Maupassant (1850–93). O. Henry (William Sydney Porter, 1862–1910).

3 – Fyodor Dostoevsky (1821–81), see 'More Dostoevsky' and 'A Minor Dostoevsky', above.

4 – *The Witch*, 'The Post', p. 58; VW also quotes this passage in 'The Russian Point of View'.

5 – *Ibid.*, p. 57; the first sentence here is also quoted in 'The Russian Point of View'.

6 – *Ibid.*, 'Agafya', p. 123.
7 – *The Wife*, the title story, p. 60, spoken by Dr Sobol.
8 – *Ibid.*, 'From the Notebook of an Old Man', pp. 131–219.
9 – *The Witch*, pp. 147–67.

Imitative Essays

It is always a misfortune to feel oneself out of sympathy with another person's taste. You cannot reason about a question of taste; you can only feel for yourself; you are bound to feel strongly, and yet your feeling may be quite unintelligible to a third person. Mr Squire's book of essays provides us with a case in point. The first essay, 'The Gold Tree', describes a tree in a college garden, whose leaves turn gold in a wonderful autumn, hang miraculously beautiful for a season, and then vanish. The essay, after gently meandering through moralities which seem a little obvious, ends with this passage: 'But may it not be, perhaps, that when I am an old man, near my grave, I shall some day wander into the gardens below my window and find a second time the tree of gold, still and perfect, under a consoling autumnal sky?'[2] The sentiment of that is one that makes us uncomfortable. The murmur of voices, singing in church, a few chords struck gently in the dusk – these things also make us uncomfortable. We grow more and more solemn as we read with that uneasy solemnity which suddenly turns to untimely laughter. Let us quickly find something that it is permissible to laugh at. We hastily turn the page and light on this:

The cook, when middle-aged, had married a daughter of the keeper of the Great Seal; but she unhappily was one day killed by that ferocious animal (it was as large as a walrus) ... and left her husband a widower with an only son, a small boy, who spent much of his time wondering about vain and foolish things. He wondered, for example, why he often heard of aeroplanes turning turtle, but never of a turtle turning aeroplane; and also why it was that no one ever threw a third or a quarter of a brick at anyone else.'[3]

Our plight is worse than ever; we are as glum as an undertaker in the spring.

These are questions of taste, that must be decided by the individual judgment of each reader. But if you are so unhappy as to be neither charmed nor amused by such sentiment or such humour, you will find yourself asking how it comes about that a writer who has shown himself a vivacious satirist, and at least a serious writer of verse, can produce so insipid a volume of prose. The answer seems to be that he has failed because he has tried to write beautifully. The danger of trying to write beautifully in English lies in the ease with which it is possible to do something very like it. There are the old cadences humming in one's head, the old phrases covering nothing so decently that it seems to be something after all. Preoccupied with the effort to be smooth, rotund, demure, and irreproachable, sentimentality slips past unnoticed, and platitudes spread themselves abroad with an air of impeccable virtue. A quotation from one of the eighty-nine pages of this expensive and beautifully printed book will show what it is that we are objecting to:

As the long scroll of memory unfolded he felt that he had walked all his manhood among phantoms; and he derived no pain from the reflection that his friends were dead, and he himself already half-forgotten, save as a legend. For he knew, watching the stream, that it would have been better had he remained all his life in that garden with that river that did not change. The fountains of speech, now he would willingly converse with the river, were rusted and choked; why, when he was young had they been sealed? Why had he been compelled to go round the world to find himself?[4]

The fatal effect of such smoothing and mincing is that as you read on and on and on you gradually cease to feel or to think; edges are rounded, colours are faded, one trite simile follows another, and yet it is done so decorously that you can never put your finger upon a definite evil. A lover of literature will tolerate many varieties of failure and hold them fertilising in their season, but what good cause is served by a volume of plausible imitation? Is it worth making a protest, not only because Mr Squire is capable of doing much better work, but because, poured voluminously into a world too busy or too careless to discriminate, such writing does more harm, we fancy, than work which is marked all over with the stamp of the second-rate.

1 – A review in the *TLS*, 23 May 1918, (Kp C108) of *The Gold Tree* . . . with initials designed by Austin O. Spare and cut in wood by W. Quick (Martin Secker, 1917) by J. C. (John Collings) Squire (1884–1958), man of letters, literary editor of the *New Statesman*, 1913–19. See *I VW Diary*, 7 May 1918, and 28 May 1918: 'The rush of books [three Tchekovs, Logan, Squire & Merrick] was disposed of, & Squire was well drubbed too'.
2 – Squire, 'The Gold Tree', p. 7.
3 – *Ibid.*, 'The Walled Garden', p. 11, which has: 'a small boy who'.
4 – *Ibid.*, pp. 14–15, which has: 'river which did not change'.

Moments of Vision

To some readers the very sight of a book in which the plain paper so generously balances the printed paper will be a happy omen. It seems to foretell gaiety, ease, unconcern. Possibly the writer has written to please himself. He has begun and left off and begun again as the mood seized him. Possibly he has had a thought for our pleasure. At any rate, our attention is not going to be stretched on the rack of an extended argument. Here is a handful of chosen flowers, a dinner of exquisite little courses, a bunch of variously coloured air balloons. Anticipating pleasure of this rare kind from the fact that Mr Pearsall Smith's *Trivia* seldom do more than reach the bottom of the page and sometimes barely encroach upon its blankness, we deserve to be disappointed. We deserve to find moral reflections or hints for the economical management of the home. Perhaps our unblushing desire for pleasure of itself deserves to be disappointed. We can fancy that many of Mr Pearsall Smith's readers will placate their consciences for the sin of reading him by some excuse about going to bed or getting up. There are times, they will say, when it is impossible to read anything serious.

It is true that there is little to be got from this book except pleasure. It has no mission, it contains no information, unless you can dignify with that name the thoughts that come into the head, buzz through it, and go out again without improving the thinker or adding to the wealth of the world. The head of the author of *Trivia* contains, as he confesses, a vast store of book learning; but his thoughts have little serious concern with that; they may light upon some obscure folio as a robin might perch for a moment upon a book before flitting to the marble bust of Julius Caesar and so on to the shining brass head of the poker and tongs. This lightness, more justly to be compared to the step of a crane among wild flowers, is perhaps the first thing you notice. The second is that although Mr Pearsall Smith has preserved the freshness and idiosyncrasy of his idea he has done so by the unostentatious use of great literary skill. Nor can we long overlook the fact that his purpose is as serious as the purpose that fulfils itself in other books of more ambitious appearance. If we are not mistaken, it is his purpose to catch and enclose certain moments which break off from the mass, in which without bidding things come together in a combination of inexplicable significance, to arrest those thoughts which suddenly, to the thinker at least, are almost menacing with meaning. Such moments of vision are of an unaccountable nature; leave them alone and they persist for years; try to explain them and they disappear; write them down and they die beneath the pen.

One of the reasons which has led to Mr Pearsall Smith's success is that he has taken neither himself nor his thoughts too seriously. Most people would have been tempted to fill the blank pages. They would have strained to be more profound, more brilliant, or more emphatic. Mr Pearsall Smith keeps well on this side of comfort; he knows exactly how far his gift will carry him. He is on easy terms with what he calls 'that Masterpiece of Nature, a reason-endowed and heaven-facing Man' [. . .] 'What stellar collisions and conflagrations, what floods and slaughters and enormous efforts has it not cost the Universe to make me – of what astral periods and cosmic processes am I not the crown and wonder?'² Nevertheless, he is conscious of belonging to that sub-order of the animal kingdom which includes the orang-outang, the gorilla, the baboon, and the chimpanzee.³ His usual mood towards himself and towards the rest of us is one of ironic but affectionate detachment, befitting an elderly Pierrot conscious of grey hairs. The poplar tree delights him and the 'lemon-coloured moon'.⁴ 'After all these millions of years, she ought to be ashamed of herself!' he cries out, beholding the 'great amorous unabashed face of the full moon'.⁵ As he listens to the talk of the thoughtful baronet:

I saw the vast landscape of the world, dim, as in an eclipse; its population eating their bread with tears, its rich men sitting listless in their palaces, and aged Kings crying, 'Vanity, Vanity, all is Vanity!' laboriously from their thrones . . .⁶ When I seek out the sources of my thoughts, I find that they had their beginning in fragile chance; were born of little moments that shine for me curiously in the past . . . So I never lose a chance of the whimsical and perilous charm of daily life, with its meetings and words and accidents. Why, today, perhaps, or next week, I may hear a voice, and, packing up my Gladstone bag, follow it to the ends of the world.⁷

The voice may be the voice of Beauty, but all the same he does not forget to pack his Gladstone bag. Compared with the 'whimsical and perilous charm of daily life',⁸ compared with the possibility that one of these days one may discover the right epithet for the moon, are not all the ends of serious middle-aged ambition 'only things to sit on'?⁹

We have marked a number of passages for quotation, but as it would be necessary to quote them only in part we refrain. But the mark was not in the margin of the book; a finger seemed to raise itself here and there as if to exclaim, 'At last! It has been said.' And, without making extravagant claims for a gift which would certainly refuse to bear a weight of honour, to cut these passages into two or otherwise mutilate them would be to damage a shape so fitting and so characteristic that we can fancy these small craft afloat for quite a long time, if not in mid stream, still in some very pleasant backwater of the river of immortality.

1 – A review in the *TLS*, 23 May 1918, (Kp C109) of *Trivia* (Constable & Co., 1918) by Logan Pearsall Smith (1865–1946), American-born man of letters, educated at Harvard and Oxford, and from 1913 a British citizen. The Hogarth Press published his *Stories from the Old Testament* in 1920; *More Trivia* appeared in 1922.

'I write expecting Philip Morrell to dinner – not that one need dwell upon that – Wind East & violent rain & grey sky again . . .' VW noted in her diary on Tuesday, 7 May 1918, 'I must read Logan's Trivia now.'

See also 'English Prose', *III VW Essays*. Reprinted: CW.
2 – Smith, 'My Portrait', p. 14.
3 – *Ibid.*, 'The Author', p. ix.
4 – *Ibid.*, 'The Poplar', p. 138, which has: 'Moon'.
5 – *Ibid.*, 'The Full Moon', p. 53, which has: 'great, amorous, unabashed'.
6 – *Ibid.*, 'The Sound of the Voice', p. 25, which has: 'populations', and 'lugubriously', not 'laboriously'.
7 – *Ibid.*, 'The Coming of Fate', p. 9, which has: 'sense', not 'chance'.
8 – *Ibid.*
9 – *Ibid.*, 'Human Ends', p. 46.

Dreams and Realities

Several years ago, turning the pages of a miscellany of some kind in which bad verses abounded, the present reviewer chanced upon a scrap of poetry signed with the name of Walter de la Mare.[2] The name was then unfamiliar, and the little poem, since we have never seen it republished, did not perhaps seem to Mr de la Mare worthy of preservation. Yet to us the shock of surprise with which we encountered this sharply and, considering its surroundings, almost improperly individual voice is still memorable. Reading the verses once more in the expectation of reducing them to harmony with the mediocrity of their companions, we were forced by their persistent assertion of merit to conclude that someone by a fluke or a freak had brought off a success which he would never repeat again. In the light of Mr de la Mare's subsequent achievements this judgment, if we think it discriminating, was certainly pessimistic. The voice which sounded so fine and distinct in that obscure gathering of the commonplace now speaks not only to a large audience, but to a great number of listeners it is a voice which has no fellow. The surprise, the sense of finding an unseized emotion reduced to its unmistakable form of words, possesses us when we read his latest volume, as it possessed us then.

Of the many proofs of the value of poetry, the conviction that the poet has said what was hitherto unsaid is among the most conclusive. In future for that emotion or mood, which he seems half to create and half to reveal, there is no other poet who serves instead of him.

> Far are those tranquil hills,
> Dyed with fair evening's rose;
> On urgent, secret errand bent,
> A traveller goes.[3]

Many readers could recognise the authorship of that simple statement of a characteristic theme without a name to it. The shapes of the day have lost their form; the low limits of the world stretch far on the horizon; the voice comes to us from just beyond the verge of light. He is the poet of hush and silence, of the deserted house, of flowers bowed in the moonlight.

> Speak not – whisper not;
> Here bloweth thyme and bergamot;
> Softly on the evening hour
> Secret herbs their spices shower,
> Dark-spiked rosemary and myrrh,
> Lean-stalked, purple lavender;
> Hides within her bosom, too,
> All her sorrows, bitter rue.[4]

He is the poet who wakes when the world sleeps, the poet of dreams, the poet who, when slumber is heavy upon the earth, hears faint stirrings and far murmurs and footfalls, for above all, perhaps, he is the poet who rouses us to an expectation of something that we can neither hear nor see.

> 'Secrets,' sighs the night-wind,
> 'Vacancy is all I find;
> Every keyhole I have made
> Wail a summons, faint and sad,
> No voice ever answers me,
>   Only vacancy.'

> 'Once, once . . .' the cricket shrills,
> And far and near the quiet fills
> With its tiny voice, and then
> Hush falls again.[5]

The poem ends in silence and hush, but, strangely, the sound goes on. The quiet has become full of tremors and vibrations; we are still listening long after the words are done. Possessed of this secret, Mr de la Mare is able in a few verses to make full contact between the reader and some intangible feeling of mystery, wonder or fear.

Those who delight in marking out as definitely as may be the circumference of a poet's mind will not fail to point out that Mr de la Mare has not proved himself capable of writing anything so sustained as, shall we say, the *Prelude*.[6] A poet who is above all things personal is closely limited by the bounds of that personality. We may defer to this criticism to the extent of admitting that when Mr de la Mare takes upon himself to discharge a patriotic duty, as in 'Happy England' he writes what many others might have written. His verses to 'E.T.'[7] have also an air of being written in a broad daylight to which the writer is ill accustomed. But it is a mistake to suppose that because the whimsical and fantastic are specially akin to him he is therefore to be banished until the moon is up and the flowers of a June night are whispering with phantoms. He proves once more that the essence of reality is only to be reached through the substance.

> Where blooms the flower when her petals fade,
> Where sleepeth echo by earth's music made,
> Where all things transient to the changeless win,
> There waits the peace thy spirit dwelleth in.[8]

In poems like 'Vain Questionings', 'Eyes' and 'Life'[9] Mr de la Mare gives clear enough evidence of mortality. Far from being rapt on some moonlit island remote from human passion, he is conscious of 'an endless war twixt contrarieties' of a 'livelong tangle of perplexities'[10] of a necessity binding us to turn back from ecstasy to 'earth's empty track of leaden day by day'.[11] Without that understanding of the gross body which divides the seer from the seen his vision of the spirit in plant and man could not be so distinct, nor his command to seek beauty and love it above everything so imperious.

Look thy last on all things lovely,
Every hour. Let no night
Seal thy sense in deathly slumber
    Till to delight
Thou have paid thy utmost blessing;
Since that all things thou wouldst praise
Beauty took from those who loved them
    In other days.[12]

1 – A review in the *TLS*, 30 May 1918, (Kp c110) of *Motley and Other Poems* (Constable & Co. Ltd, 1918) by Walter de la Mare. See also 'The Intellectual Imagination', *III VW Essays*.

2 – Walter de la Mare (1873–1956), poet, novelist and anthologist; his publications to date included *Songs of Childhood* (1902), under the pseudonym Walter Ramal; *The Listeners* (1912) and *Peacock Pie* (1913).

3 – de la Mare, 'The Three Strangers', p. 60.

4 – *Ibid.*, 'The Sunken Garden', p. 3.

5 – *Ibid.*, 'The Empty House', p. 15.

6 – Wordsworth's *The Prelude* (1805–6, 1850).

7 – For 'Happy England', see de la Mare, pp. 47–8; and for 'To E.T.: 1917', *ibid.*, p. 55.

8 – *Ibid.*, 'Vain Questioning' [*sic*], p. 41.

9 – *Ibid.*, 'Eyes', p. 36; 'Life', p. 37.

10 – For both quotations, *ibid.*, 'Vain Questioning', p. 40, which has: 'An endless war'.

11 – *Ibid.*, 'Life', p. 37: 'Still out of ecstasy turn trembling back/ To earth's same empty track/ Of leaden day by day, and hour by hour, and be/ Of all things lovely the cold mortuary.'

12 – *Ibid.*, 'Fare Well', p. 75.

The Claim of the Living

Mr George[2] is one of those writers for whom we could wish, in all kindness of heart, some slight accident to the fingers of the right hand, some twinge or ache warning him that it is time to stop, some check making brevity more desirable than expansion. He has ideas and enthusiasms, prejudices and principles in abundance, but in his fluency he repeats himself, bolsters up good arguments with poor illustrations, and altogether uses more paper than the country can well afford. The following sentence shows how his ideas tend to overlap each other owing to the speed at which they are composed: 'Autobiography has had its way with him ⟨Mr E. M. Forster⟩ a little in *A Room with a View*, and very much more in that tale of schoolmasters *The Longest Journey*, but it was *Howards End*, that much criticised work, which achieved the distinction of being popular, though of high merit.'[3] Thus hooking one statement to another Mr George rambles over a great many ideas connected with novelists and their art, and abuses the public at great length for its insolent neglect of the artist. Proof is added to proof. When Lord Curzon, the Bishop of London, and Mr Conrad come into a room which of them causes 'a swirl in "the gilded throng"'?[4] 'The attitude of the State to the novelist defines itself most clearly when a royal commission is appointed.'[5] What novelist has ever been asked to sit upon a royal commission? What novelist has ever been welcomed as a son-in-law? To cut the matter short, if the present Lord Nelson owns 7,000 acres of land, what is the amount of pension enjoyed by Leigh Hunt's daughter?[6]

But Mr George's chief claim to attention lies not in this voluble and elementary satire, but in the courage with which he has faced his contemporaries. It is a courage that overshoots its mark, but still it needs considerable courage to declare that one has found 'more that is honest and hopeful in a single page of *Tono-Bungay* than in all the great Victorians put together'.[7] It needs, oddly enough, some quality rarer than courage and more desirable to have read all the novels mentioned in this book and to hold a serious opinion as to their merits. For it is extremely difficult to take the writings of one's contemporaries seriously. The spirit in which they are read is a strange compact of indifference and curiosity. On the one hand the assumption is that they are certainly bad, on the other the temptation assails us to find in them a queer and illicit fascination. Between these two extremes we vacillate, and the attention we grant them is at once furtive, intermittent and intense. In proof of this let anyone read over the list of seven young novelists accepted by Mr George as the most promising of their generation – Mr Beresford, Mr Cannan, Mr Forster, Mr Lawrence, Mr Compton Mackenzie, Mr Onions and Mr Swinnerton.[8] The list is fairly representative, but certainly if our income depended upon passing an examination in their works we should be sweeping the streets tomorrow. We feel sure that such a test would produce a large army of street-sweepers. It is not that we have neglected to order a certain number of their novels from the library. It is not that, on seeing them before us, we have neglected to read them. But our knowledge is perfectly haphazard and nebulous. To discuss the point of view, the growth, nature and development of any one of these writers in the same spirit that we discuss the dead proves impossible. The difficulty which lies at the root of this attitude affects Mr George too, in spite of his enthusiasm for modern fiction and his proud claim for the prose form. He does not find it at all easy to make out what is happening.

The literary tradition is changing and a new one is being made.[9] Perhaps we may divide these seven writers into three groups – self-exploiters, mirror-bearers and commentators ...[10] They stand midway between the expression of life and the expression of themselves ...[11] A new passion is born, and it is a complex of the old passions; the novelist ... needs to be more positive, to aspire to know what we are doing with the working class, with the Empire, the woman question, and the proper use of lentils. It is this aspiration towards truth that breaks up the old form: you cannot tell a story in a straightforward manner when you do but glimpse it through the veil of the future.[12]

Fiction is becoming chaotic and formless and omnivorous. But the attempt at a general survey, or at any grouping of tendencies, is very vague; and Mr George turns not without relief to the criticism of the novels in detail, to biographical sketches, and even to memories of garden parties on Campden Hill.[13] The criticism is not bad criticism, but it has too great an air of the personal and provisional to be accepted with conviction. There is no perspective, no security about it.

But the fault hardly lies with Mr George and scarcely at all with the novelists. They must live before they achieve the repose which is so much more ornamental than life. They must appear at garden parties and achieve, or fail to achieve, the 'swirl' which Mr George thinks a proper tribute to their powers. But they must be content to forgo authoritative criticism until they are long past the age at which they can profit by it. They must put up with the random patronage of people who subscribe to libraries and to the snapshots of reviewers. Meanwhile they enjoy a kind of homage which is not altogether to be despised. We should judge it an immense calamity if all the writers whom Mr George speaks of were destroyed in a single night. Yes, in our condescending, indolent way we are proud of them; we need them; we have a dim consciousness of a band of light upon the horizon which is due to their incessant imaginative fervour, and sometimes we seem to see that from all this agitation and confusion something of great importance is taking shape.

1 – A review in the *TLS*, 13 June 1918, (Kp CIII) of *A Novelist on Novels* (W. Collins Sons & Co. Ltd, 1918) by W. L. George. Reprinted: *CW*.

2 – Walter Lionel George (1882–1926) was the author of several novels and of other miscellaneous publications, including *Labour and Housing at Port Sunlight* (1909), *Anatole France* (1915) and *Further Notes on the Intelligence of Women* (1916).

3 – George, 'Who is the Man', pp. 86–7; E. M. Forster, *The Longest Journey* (1907), *A Room With a View* (1908), *Howards End* (1910).

4 – *Ibid.*, 'Litany of the Novelist', p. 38; George Nathaniel Curzon, Marquess Curzon of Kedleston (1859–1925), statesman, Viceroy of India, 1898–1905, spent the years from 1905 in the political wilderness, until, in 1916, he became a member of Lloyd George's War Cabinet. Joseph Conrad (1857–1924).

5 – *Ibid.*, p. 39.

6 – For the unwelcome son-in-law, *ibid.*, p. 26; and for Lord Nelson and the daughter of Leigh Hunt (1784–1859), essayist, critic and poet, *ibid.*, p. 44.

7 – *Ibid.*, p. 60; H. G. Wells (1866–1946), *Tono Bungay* (1909).

8 – J. D. Beresford (1873–1947); for VW on his works, see 'Freudian Fiction' and 'Revolution', *III VW Essays*. Gilbert Cannan (1884–1955); see 'Mummery' below. E. M. Forster (1879–1970); see '*A Room With a View*', *I VW Essays*, and 'The Art of Fiction' and 'The Novels of E. M. Forster', *IV VW Essays*. D. H. Lawrence (1885–1930); see 'Postscript or Prelude?', *III VW Essays*. Compton Mackenzie (1883–1972); see 'The "Movie" Novel' below and 'Sylvia and Michael', *III VW Essays*. Oliver Onions (1872–1961); see 'A Practical Utopia', below. Frank Swinnerton (1884–1982); see 'Honest Fiction', below and 'September', *III VW Essays*.

9 – *Ibid.*, 'Who is the Man?', p. 67.

10 – *Ibid.*, p. 69, which has: 'If we wish to measure these dangers, then we must analyse the men one by one, and it will serve us best to divide them into three groups:'.

11 – *Ibid.*, p. 68, from a longer sentence.

12 – *Ibid.*, 'Form and the Novel', pp. 122–3.

13 – *Ibid.*, 'Three Young Novelists', pp. 101–2; the party-goer at the centre of George's account is the novelist Amber Reeves, a graduate of Newnham College, Cambridge, lover of H. G. Wells, and author of *The Reward of Virtue* (1911), *A Lady and Her Husband* (1914) and *Helen in Love* (1916). (The other two young novelists discussed are D. H. Lawrence and Sheila Kaye-Smith (1887–1956), author of *Starbrace* (1909), *Sussex Gorse* (1916) and other works.)

Loud Laughter

We have seen Mr Leacock[2] described both as Doctor and Professor; and his industry and success in making people laugh seem to entitle him to the brass plate, the variegated letters, and the consulting room of the specialist. If when Mr Leacock has applied all the batteries and tests of the most improved humorous science upon you you still remain grave and careworn in his hands, it is probable that you are hopelessly deficient – a chronic invalid. Upon us, we admit at once, his verdict was grave; he said that he had only been able to produce hearty laughter nine or ten times in the course of two hundred and forty pages; that our risible faculties were far too easily exhausted; and from the alert condition of the critical faculty under the process he could detect signs of premature decay. Possibly this was due to the enervating influence of an ancient civilisation; possibly the American climate might even now work wonders.

That is the worst that we have to say about Mr Leacock; he is a specialist in laughter. He is one of those people with an abnormal gift such as brings its possessor to celebrity upon the music-hall stage. His skill in producing the comic reminds us of the gentleman who whips off the tablecloth and turns it into Napoleon's hat; so Mr Leacock seems to delight in showing how he can make funniness out of anything. Humour, to judge by the reviewers' chorus of praise, is the right term to apply to his production; but to our thinking it is no more humour than the tablecloth is Napoleon's hat. It is a specialised product which, like a pug dog or a garden plant, has been bred so carefully that it no longer resembles the common stock. We have the hardihood to declare that the common stock flourishes naturally and profusely in these islands. With Falstaff and Mrs Gamp for parents it could not well be otherwise; but leaving them, as fairness requires, out of account, what we call humour in England seems to us a very different thing from the humour of *Frenzied Fiction*. Mr Leacock's method is probably too well known for it to be necessary to describe these fresh examples in great detail. They are almost without exception funny stories; and the fun consists in turning some foible or craze upside down by heaping exaggeration upon exaggeration, so that you laugh both at the absurdities of Mr Leacock's fancy and at the wretched ghost of reality thus nimbly travestied. A skit upon amateur agriculture opens in the following way:

I have hung up my hoe in my study; my spade is put away behind the piano; I have with me seven pounds of Paris Green that I had over. Anybody who wants it may have it. I didn't like to bury it for fear of its poisoning the ground. I didn't like to throw it away for fear of its destroying cattle. I was afraid to leave it in my summer place for fear that it might poison the tramps who generally break in in November. I have it with me now. I move it from room to room, as I hate to turn my back upon it. Anybody who wants it, I repeat, can have it.[3]

And so he goes on piling it up, one fantasy on top of another, until we hold our breath and wonder with what final perversion of sense he will cap the towering pyramid. The effect is cumulative, and fragmentary quotations give no true impression of the intensity and unreality which make this humour so different from the English variety. In candour we must admit that in certain of these skits, such as 'The Prophet in our Midst' and 'To Nature and Back Again',[4] Mr Leacock makes points a great deal quicker than we are used to take them. His lively sense of satire is never too deeply sunk in extravagances to cease to sting. But if laughter, if the degree in which we are soothed and expanded and persuaded into a mood of tolerant joviality are the tests of humour, we have no hesitation in bestowing our palm elsewhere. Ruling out the immortals, let us consider the claims of Mr Briggs[5] of Victorian *Punch*. Let us put in a word, too, for the humour that flourishes every night among a tangle of rubbish in the music halls. This humour is much slower and more cumbrous than anything in *Frenzied Fiction*; it can scarcely be said to have a point; but it has breadth, it has character; in its primitive way it has a good deal of human nature in it. It takes hold of the audience; it shakes them and seizes them and settles them down again in a mood of immense good temper. And then, quite slowly and deliberately and with an odd mixture of emotions, we begin to laugh.

Perhaps, after all, when we call Mr Leacock a specialist we mean that his emotions are not sufficiently mixed. He has isolated one from the rest, and each time he takes up his pen he goes straight for it, as if the human mind were a target with a golden bull's-eye in the centre and neat circles of different colours surrounding it. In truth, the book of humour is something of a prodigy, although custom has brought us to see nothing unnatural in it. But turn it the other way round; suppose that Mr Leacock had written, instead of *Frenzied Fiction, Funereal Fiction*. Suppose we began with a sob, went on to a tear, developed into a roar, and culminated in a paroxysm of uncontrollable lamentation – should we think that a desirable form of art? Would the critics be so eager then to acclaim him a master of tears?

1 – A review in the *TLS*, 20 June 1918, (Kp c112) of *Frenzied Fiction* (John Lane, The Bodley Head, 1918) by Stephen Leacock.
2 – Stephen Butler Leacock (1869–1944), English-born, Canadian-educated professor of political economy at McGill University, Montreal, author of *Elements of Political Science* (1906) and of several highly popular humorous works, including

Literary Lapses (1910), *Nonsense Novels* (1911) and *Sunshine Sketches of a Little Town* (1912).

3 – Leacock, xiv, 'Back from the Land', p. 178.

4 – *Ibid.*, iii, 'The Prophet in Our Midst', pp. 34–42; vi, 'To Nature and Back Again', pp. 76–90.

5 – The character created by the artist John Leech (1817–64) and based in part upon Leech's friend Millais. Mr Briggs's adventures were the inspiration for VW's juvenile serial story 'A Cockney's Farming Experiences' (see I QB, p. 30).

A Victorian Socialist

The reminiscences and reflections of Mr Belfort Bax[2] are distinguished from most of their kind by the conception which the writer has formed of his task. His aim has been to 'offer data and suggestions ... for the due appreciation, now or hereafter, of the particular period of historic time in which my life has been cast – to wit, roughly speaking, the last third of the nineteenth and the opening years of the twentieth century'. The 'personal note' has been rigorously 'damped down',[3] whether from shyness on the writer's part or because such matters do not seem to him likely to interest the historian of the future. However this may be, the method certainly produces a curious sense that the mid and late Victorian age, so near ours in point of time, is already distant and different enough to be summed up and judged as we sum up and judge the lives of the dead. As we read we feel ourselves exalted almost to the rank of that impartial observer to whom the England of the nineteenth century will appear as the Rome of the year 116 appears to an observer of the present day.[4] Bating a certain unnecessary sensitiveness to possible disagreements and one or two beliefs whose fervour seems rather personal than universal, Mr Bax's book might very well stand for the book of the average thinking man of middle-class origin and socialist persuasion born in or about the year 1854. It is very sincere, very plain spoken, and very much in earnest.

An aged American gentleman[5] who revisited England in 1901 told Mr Bax that he was astonished at the change between the English of that day and the English of 1848. When he compared the men and women he met in the Strand with their forebears they seemed to him to belong to a different race. Not only dress, but faces, ways, and manners had completely changed. In what the change consisted he unfortunately omitted to say; but the reader of Mr Bax's book will find a great deal to help him in framing an opinion upon that point. When, for example, Mr Bax was a boy the main topic of conversation in the family was religious dogma. Not only in his family but in most families of the Evangelical set Romanism and Latitudinarianism, preachers and the quality of their orthodoxy, were the staple of discussion, and upon all brooded equally the shadow of Sunday and the ban of social enjoyment. The theatres were especially condemned, save indeed as convenient signposts of destruction; for had not a lady, seeing the words 'To the Pit' emblazoned on the theatre door, read into them their right meaning and immediately sought salvation elsewhere?[6] The only permissible form of art, according to Mr Bax, was the oratorio. The *Messiah* and the *Elijah* were the only legitimate channels for aesthetic emotions, and the one piece of music that resounded from church, chapel and parlour indiscriminately was Mendelssohn's 'O rest in the Lord'.[7] How far this religious fervour was genuine, and how far it was the result of what Mr Bax calls 'unconscious hypocrisy'[8] it is hard to determine; but it is certain that those who were young enough to be coerced and sensitive enough to revolt 'preserved enduringly unpleasant reminiscences of that time'. Worse still, the memories of those who had held these 'morally repulsive and intellectually foolish beliefs', were held in no respect by their descendants, for 'their characters were poisoned and warped by the foulness and follies of their creed'.[9]

From such unpleasant reminiscences and early impressions sprang, no doubt, the drastic moral tone of Mr Bax's generation. No words seem to have been more often upon their lips than 'humbug', 'cant', 'sentimentalism' and 'superstition'. No generation has ever put more trust in reason, or rated more highly the powers of pure intellect. In an interesting passage Mr Bax traces the decline and death of his own belief in the supernatural, and is so sanguine as to suppose that reason has so far permeated the race that the modern child goes to bed without any fear of the dark. It seems probable that each generation of children will have its own fear of the dark, but we may certainly cede to Mr Bax's generation the credit of having marked out the boundary where light ends and darkness begins. This temper is notable in his remarks upon the Society for Psychical Research.[10] After examining some of the claims put forward by the Society, he comes to the conclusion that his own attitude may be described as 'an "agnostic" one, with a bias in favour of the negative opinion'.[11] The conclusion seems to us highly characteristic of his generation. With fairness, with honesty, with a display of reason before which emotion must shrink abashed, they tested the common objects of belief and proved them for the most part baseless, or, if judgment was suspended, they had a distinct 'bias in favour of the negative opinion'. Whether it is due to this spirit or to some temperamental quality of his own, the pervading atmosphere of this book would lead us to judge the mid and late Victorian period a dry, if wholesome, stage in our mental history. The moral earnestness which replaces and demolishes a too-easy credulity is bound in retrospect to seem a little excessive. Even when they took upon them to chide prigs or to denounce asceticism, one feels that the ghosts of the Evangelicals have inspired them rather than a pure delight in the joys of the senses. Mr Bax supports his advocacy of drink in moderation, or rather his attack upon the asceticism of doctors, by the statement that it 'is a noteworthy fact that the physical degeneration of the Scotchman of today is coincident with an increasing abstemiousness as regards whisky'.[12] It is hardly necessary to tell us that he has never 'gloried and drunk deep'.[13] One of the very few stories in the book of the great men with whom he has associated leaves us with an added impression of the seriousness which might attend even a walk in the country. He was walking with William Morris by the side of a stream.

Suddenly Morris became morose and unsociable in manner. A little while after again coming upon the high road we turned into an inn for luncheon. Sitting after the meal, I asked Morris the reason of his grumpiness. He replied that he was much exercised in passing through those fields in that he saw bulls regarding us in a more or less menacing manner, and that, although he himself could have escaped by swimming across the little river, knowing that I could not swim, he was perplexed as to what course to pursue in the event of a bovine attack. Hence his surliness.[14]

But these, after all, are trifles, little eccentricities that strike the eye as it rests upon the surface of an age. It need scarcely be said that the age was one that brought about an important change, and that if Mr Bax and his friends did their work of destruction, they also sought to establish what he calls 'the only true religion for human beings', that which has for its object 'the devotion to the future social life of Humanity'.[15] In this crusade Mr Bax has fought valiantly; upon that cause he has lavished all his passion. The only tears recorded in his book were shed 'in secret and in my own room'[16] for the martyrs of the Commune; his deepest source of gratification lies in the enlightenment of the working classes. His hope for the future is so deeply founded that it bridges the gulf cut by the war. The Socialist ideal reaches beyond 'any mere material transformation';[17] and, believing in its attainment, he looks forward to a time when the working classes of the world will be united in such an international society that the struggle of race with race will be for ever impossible.

1 – A review in the *TLS*, 27 June 1918, (Kp C113) of *Reminiscences and Reflexions of a Mid and Late Victorian* (George Allen & Unwin Ltd, 1918) by Ernest Belfort Bax.

2 – Ernest Belfort Bax (1854–1926), socialist and barrister, was an active member of the Social Democratic Federation and, with William Morris, co-founder in 1885 of the Socialist League. His several works of history and socialist philosophy include *Socialism: Its Growth and Outcome* (1893) written jointly with Morris.

3 – For both aims and personal note, Bax, Pref., p. 5.

4 – *Ibid.*, ch. XII, pp. 279–80: 'What would the modern classical scholar not give to have such an imperfect set of reminiscences and reflexions even as those contained in the foregoing pages, written in the year 116 by an inhabitant (say) of Rome, Alexandria, or Antioch, born in the year 54.'

5 – *Ibid.*, ch. X, p. 222: 'This gentleman, whose name was Hinton, had been one of the friends and companions of John Brown in the Harper's Ferry incident of 1857.'

6 – For the story of the converted playgoer, *ibid.*, ch. I, pp. 13–14.

7 – For Handel's *Messiah* (1742) and Mendelssohn's *Elijah* (1846), *ibid.*, p. 16.

8 – *Ibid.*, pp. 17–18; 'By unconscious hypocrisy I understand an attitude of mind which succeeds in persuading itself that it believes or approves certain things as it professes to do, while really *in foro conscientiae* this profession is dictated by a sense of its own interests, real or supposed.'

9 – For all three preceding quotations, *ibid.*, p. 20.

10 – For Bax on the Society of Psychical Research, founded in 1882, *ibid.*, pp. 25–7.

11 – *Ibid.*, p. 26.

12 – *Ibid.*, ch. XII, p. 267fn.

13 – *Ibid.*, pp. 278–9, quoting *The Rubáiyát of Omar Khayyám*, and remarking: 'I would certainly much rather think that the lion and the lizard keep the Halls where I had "gloried and drunk deep" (not that I ever did so), than that their sites should be reserved, not for the roar of the lion, but for the shriek of the steam whistle. Such is sentiment!'

14 – *Ibid.*, ch. V, p. 120.

15 – *Ibid.*, ch. I, pp. 29–30.

16 – *Ibid.*, p. 29.

17 – *Ibid.*, ch. IV, p. 93.

Mr Merrick's Novels

Twelve distinguished authors 'have fallen over each other', says Sir James Barrie, 'in their desire to join in the honour of writing the prefaces'[2] to the edition of Mr Merrick's collected works. At the present moment only the first of the twelve, Sir James Barrie, has appeared in the capacity of introducer, and he is in charge of *Conrad in Quest of his Youth*. Sir James, we need not say, makes the introduction in the most graceful terms, and leaves us to become better acquainted with the genial assurance that we shall get on splendidly; but, should it fall out otherwise, it will make no difference to his opinion of Mr Merrick. 'For long he has been the novelist's novelist, and we give you again the chance to share him with us; you have been slow to take the previous chances, and you may turn away again, but in any case he will still remain our man.' To start us on the right track he gives it as his opinion that *Conrad in Quest of his Youth* 'is the best sentimental journey that has been written in this country since the publication of the other one'. To leave us in no possible doubt of his meaning he adds, 'I know scarcely a novel by any living Englishman, except a score or so of Mr Hardy's, that I would rather have written.'[3]

The reader, thus advised and admonished, bethinks him perhaps of the *Sentimental Journey*,[4] conjures up the name of any novel by a living author that he might choose to have written, and conjectures that Mr Merrick will be first and foremost an artist whose gift has a rarity that specially appeals to connoisseurs. We maintain that this is the wrong way of approaching Mr Merrick. When Sir James suggests Sterne, when he talks of Mr Hardy, he is challenging us to make comparisons which we would much rather make in silence. He is putting us into the ungrateful position of the critic whose main business it is to find fault. Now the interest and value of the art of criticism lie more than anything in the critic's ability to seize upon what is good and to expatiate upon that. The only criticism worth having, we sometimes think, is the criticism of praise; but to give praise its meaning the standard of the first rate must be present in the mind, unconfused and unlowered, though kept in the background unless the merit of the work makes open reference to it worth while. Rightly or wrongly we cannot see that there is anything to be gained by naming

the classics when we are discussing the interesting but unequal works
of Mr Merrick.

Conrad in Quest of his Youth is an extremely readable book. More
than that, it is sufficiently unlike other books to make you wish to take
its measure, to account for its failure or its success. Here, evidently, is a
novelist endowed with wit, with lightness of touch, with a sensitive
quick-darting intelligence, and with just that turn of mind that is needed
to give his work an unmistakable character of its own. Perhaps this last is
the quality that has endeared him to his fellow writers. It is very rare, and
yet, if unsupported by commoner gifts, it is apt to be thrown away, or at
least completely ignored by the public. Competence, completeness and a
dozen other virtues are negligible compared with the sensitive though
perhaps ineffective handling of the artist. Within his limits Mr Merrick
shows unmistakable traces of this endowment. Is not *Conrad in Quest
of his Youth* an undoubted proof of it? From a dozen different scenes,
precariously poised one on top of another, we get a charming irregular
whole; we get a sense of the past; of deserted piers, of bathing places out
of season, of barrel organs out of tune, of ladies past their prime. It has
an atmosphere of its own. Mr Merrick possesses the cynicism peculiar to
the sentimentalist; and in *Conrad* the mixture is extremely skilful, the
sweet turning bitter, the sunset merging surprisingly into the daylight of
three o'clock in the afternoon. His talent seems to lend itself peculiarly
well to the faded distinction of the year 1880, when Piccadilly was
blocked with hansom cabs and well-dressed people sat by Rotten Row
and offered each other nicely turned phrases which already sound a little
obsolete. Here is an example of this urbane dialogue; Conrad is talking
to the lady whom he loved in his youth:

'You hurt me,' said Conrad, 'because for the first time I realise you are different from
the girl I've looked for. Till now I've felt that I was with her again.' 'That's nice of
you, but it isn't true. Oh, I like you for saying it, of course . . . If you had felt it really –'
'Go on.' 'No; what for? I should only make you unhappier.' 'You want comedy?'
he demurred; 'you have said the saddest things a woman ever said to me!' She raised
a white shoulder – with a laugh. 'I never get what I want!' 'It should have taught you
to feel for me, but you are not "wondrous kind."' ' 'Oh, I am more to be pitied than
you are! 'What have I got in my life? Friends? Yes – to play bridge with. My
husband? He delivers speeches on local option, and climbs mountains. Both make
me deadly tired. I used to go in for music – God Save the King is the only tune he
knows when he hears it, and he only knows that because the men take their hats off. I
was interested in my house at the beginning – after you've quarrelled in your house
every day for years it doesn't absorb you to make the mantelpiece look pretty. I

wanted a child – well, my sister has seven! . . . Voilà my autobiography up to date.'
'There is tomorrow,' said Conrad, moved. 'Tomorrow you must give me the
comedy,' she smiled ⟨. . .⟩[5]

There is much that is up to that level, a good deal that is above it, and as
his books are full of dialogue you may accuse Mr Merrick of airiness,
perhaps of emptiness, but never of being a bore.

The success of *Conrad in Quest of his Youth* lies in the skilful balance
of sweetness and bitterness, of romance and reality. But in the other
novels the union is far more unequal, and in some of them the results
appear to us to be more interesting. We can guess that Mr Merrick has
tried, as most good novelists try, to shape a world bearing some
resemblance to the world of his vision. Failure, the loss of ideals, the
sacrifice of good to evil, and, above all, the degradation wrought upon
the character by poverty, were some of the aspects of life that claimed
Mr Merrick's attention. He did not master his theme, and perhaps he
spoilt a book or two in trying; but it is evident that he was not content
with a scene of brilliancy here, a character of vitality there, but aimed at
something more complete. If you choose, as this characteristic makes it
possible, to consider his books as one large composition, you must place
in the centre a blazing fire, a radiance that casts its fictitious splendour to
the furthest corners of the picture. This, of course, is the stage. Into that
fire, from distant and obscure sources, come running heroes and
heroines and other strange figures, who struggle to the light and pass out
again into the dreary twilight of failure or disillusion, or remain
hovering unsatisfied at a distance. And now we reach the dilemma by
which Mr Merrick seems so often to have been posed. He feels the
glamour of the stage in every nerve, he thrusts his men and women again
and again into the furnace, but then at the last moment he repents and
saves them alive. He bestows all sorts of gifts upon them. This one turns
out to be a successful dramatist; that one earns £4,000 a year by painting
pictures which are, incredibly enough, works of the highest merit. We do
not believe with Sir James Barrie that Mr Merrick has frightened the
public by his pessimism; we think it more probable that he has puzzled it
by his compromises. His mediocrity is so strangely combined with his
excellence. We have always to reckon with a lapse into melodrama as in
the ending to *The Man Who Was Good*, or with the commonplace and
conventional as in the climax of *The House of Lynch*.[6]

But we own to a grudge against the influence that has tried to spoil
Peggy Harper or *The Quaint Companions*,[7] because, pruned of certain

weaknesses, each of these books contains first-hand truth seized and set down with extraordinary vivacity. The proximity of the stage always revives Mr Merrick, and a second-rate actress never fails to put him on his mettle. Her cheap prettiness, her artistic incompetence, her vanity, her courage, her poverty, her makeshifts and artifices and endurance, together with the seduction of the theatre, are described not with mere truth of detail, though we guess that to be considerable, but with the rarer truth of sympathy. The description of Peggy Harper's home and of her mother, the decayed actress who has taken to drink but preserves the artistic instincts and passions, makes you feel that you have learned the truth about that section of humanity once for all. From each of Mr Merrick's books one could select a chapter or two possessing, often among second-rate surroundings, this stamp of first-hand quality. We find it most often when he has to deal with the seamy side of the stage; we find it oddly often in some minor character or in some little scene dashed off apparently by an afterthought. A touring company comes to grief, a girl stumbling through her part before the author, a troupe of actors trailing their draggled feathers and cheap tinsel across the windy parade of a seaside resort at Christmas time – into such scenes he puts so much spirit, so many quick touches of insight, that the precarious, flaring, tenth-rate life of the provincial stage has not only glamour and bustle, but beauty into the bargain. These are the scenes that we shall wish to read again.

The last of Mr Merrick's books, *While Paris Laughed,* should win a greater popularity than the others. Nothing in it is so good as certain passages that we should have liked to quote, from *Peggy Harper* in particular, but the quality is far more equal. It has all the quickness, lightness, and dexterity which scarcely ever fail him, and, in addition, the balance of this uneven talent is more successfully maintained. In recording the adventures of the poet Tricortin in Paris he is never quite serious, but he never laughs aloud; he hints at disagreeables and glances at delights; he suggests the divinity of art and the obtuseness of the public, but never for an instant does he pass from raillery to satire, or from suggestion to statement. It is a very skilful and craftsmanlike piece of work, and, if Mr Merrick still remains unpopular, we confess ourselves unable to guess the reason.

1 – A review in the *TLS,* 4 July 1918, (Kp c114) of *While Paris Laughed. Being Pranks and Passions of the Poet Tricortin* and of *Conrad in Quest of His Youth. An*

Extravagance of Temperament. With an introduction by J. M. Barrie (Hodder & Stoughton, 1918) by Leonard Merrick (1864–1939); the second work was originally published in 1903. 'Still, the classics *are* very pleasant, and even, I must confess, the mortals. I found great consolation during the influenza in the works of Leonard Merrick,' VW had written as early as 25 February 1918 to Saxon Sydney-Turner (*II VW Letters*, no. 910), 'a poor unappreciated second rate pot-boiling writer of stories about the stage, whom I deduce to be a negro, mulatto or quadroon; at any rate he has a grudge against the world, and might have done much better if he hadn't at the age of 20 married a chorus girl, had by her 15 coffee coloured brats and lived for the rest of the time in a villa in Brixton, where he ekes out his living by giving lessons on elocution to the natives – Now if this were about a Greek writer, it would be what is called constructive criticism, wouldn't it?' On Tuesday, 7 May, she noted in her diary that she had 'a rush of books' hanging over her, including Merrick; and on Thursday, 27 June, she wrote, 'I still find it difficult to make head or tail of Labour Party politics, or indeed of any other; but with practice I suppose it wouldn't be harder than reviewing Mr Merrick'.

See also 'Mr Howells on Form', below. Reprinted: CW.

2 – *Conrad*, intro., p. viii; J. M. Barrie (1860–1937).

3 – For all three quotations, *ibid.*

4 – Laurence Sterne, *A Sentimental Journey Through France and Italy* (1768).

5 – *Conrad*, ch., XII, pp. 159–60, which has: 'you *are* different'.

6 – *The Man Who Was Good.* With an introduction by J. K. Prothero, and *The House of Lynch.* With an introduction by G. K. Chesterton (Hodder & Stoughton, 1918), originally published in 1892 and 1907 respectively.

7 – *The Position of Peggy Harper.* With an introduction by Sir Arthur Pinero, and *The Quaint Companions.* With an introduction by H. G. Wells (Hodder & Stoughton, 1918), originally published in 1907 and 1903 respectively.

Two Soldier-Poets

It is natural to feel an impulse of charity towards the poems written by young men who have fought or are still fighting; but in the case of Mr Sassoon[2] there is no temptation to indulge in this form of leniency, because he is so evidently able-bodied in his poetic capacity and requires no excuses to be made for him. At the same time, it is difficult to judge him dispassionately as a poet, because it is impossible to overlook the fact that he writes as a soldier. It is a fact, indeed, that he forces upon you, as if it were a matter of indifference to him whether you called him poet or not. We know no other writer who has shown us as effectually as Mr Sassoon the terrible pictures which lie behind the colourless phrases of the newspapers. From the thousand horrors which in their sum compose one day of warfare he selects, as if by chance, now this of the counter-attack, now that of mending the front-line wires, or this again of suicide in the trenches. 'The General' is as good an example of his method as another:

> 'Good-morning: good-morning!' the General said
> When we met him last week on our way to the line.
> Now the soldiers he smiled at are most of 'em dead,
> And we're cursing his staff for incompetent swine.
> 'He's a cheery old card,' grunted Harry to Jack,
> As they slogged up to Arras with rifle and pack.
>
> * * * * * *
>
> But he did for them both by his plan of attack.[3]

The vision of that 'hell where youth and laughter go'[4] has been branded upon him too deeply to allow him to tolerate consolation or explanation. He can only state a little of what he has seen, a very little one guesses, and turn away with a stoical shrug as if a superficial cynicism were the best mask to wear in the face of such incredible experiences. His farewell to the dead is spoken in this fashion:

> Good-bye, old lad! Remember me to God,
>   And tell him that our politicians swear
> They won't give in till Prussian Rule's been trod
>   Under the heel of England ... Are you there? ...
> Yes ... and the war won't end for at least two years;
> But we've got stacks of men ... I'm blind with tears,
>   Staring into the dark. Cheero!
> I wish they'd killed you in a decent show.[5]

There is a stage of suffering, so these poems seem to show us, where any expression save the barest is intolerable; where beauty and art have something too universal about them to meet our particular case. Mr Sassoon sums up that point of view in his 'Dead Musicians'. Not Bach or Beethoven or Mozart brings back the memory of his friends, but the gramophone does it bawling out 'Another little drink won't do us any harm.'[6] Mr Sassoon's poems are too much in the key of the gramophone at present, too fiercely suspicious of any comfort or compromise, to be read as poetry; but his contempt for palliative or subterfuge gives us the raw stuff of poetry.

No two poets could be more different than Mr Sassoon and Mr Dearmer;[7] the difference in point of view is unimportant, but the difference in expression is very interesting. Mr Dearmer writes of soldiers waiting in the trenches:

> We waited, like a storm-bespattered ship
> That flutters sail to free her grounded keel,[8]

and from that image it is at once evident that Mr Dearmer is trying to make a kind of poetry so different that the comparison with Mr Sassoon will serve us no longer. Reality is an accident that passes across the mirror of his mind and makes images that interest him far more than the object that caused them. While he unfolds his metaphor the scene that he is describing is over and done with. The cavalry and the batteries and the mules are tramping down the street, 'but all is dim' —

> Only my dreams are still aglow, a throng
> Of scenes that crowded through a waiting mind.
> A myriad scenes: For I have swept along
> To foam ashriek with gulls, and rowed behind
> Brown oarsmen swinging to an ocean song
> Where stately galleons bowed before the wind.[9]

Some of the loveliest poems in the language have been produced in the manner that Mr Dearmer attempts, and a young poet venturing once more as Keats[10] ventured commands our sympathy. But if the prize is of the greatest the undertaking is so perilous that it is no harsh criticism to say that Mr Dearmer's imagination is neither strong enough nor trained enough to do the work he asks of it. The romantic poet lays heavier tasks upon his imagination than any other. The vision alone is not enough; he must see it in detail as well as hold it in mass; he must know when to release and when to restrain the words which flock too fast and freely. Mr Dearmer has a wide range of language, but he trusts too much to chance, as if beauty could be captured by a random fling, and twenty words wide of the mark made no difference provided six or seven fall moderately near. He slips too often into the habit of imaginative inaccuracy; he compares men dashing to their holes to 'burrowing moles'; he says that gossamer clouds crossing the moon 'scurrying ran'; he makes glow-worms 'crawl excitedly'; he stuffs out his verse with such tags as 'glad tidings', 'laughter of the main', 'jewelled night'.[11] These instances may seem trivial, but they help to explain why it is that, though the effect of Mr Dearmer's longer poems is vaguely fine and vigorous, the whole seems to be slackly or numbly grasped, or, as in 'Gomme-court' to reel itself off into rhetoric. The war, perhaps, has brought these pieces forth before their time; for, where he is forced to concentrate, as in his 'Eight Sonnets', he comes much nearer to writing poetry.

1 – A review in the *TLS*, 11 July 1918, (Kp c115) of *Counter-Attack and Other Poems* (William Heinemann, 1918) by Siegfried Sassoon and of *Poems* (William Heinemann, 1918) by Geoffrey Dearmer. See also *I VW Diary*, 29 July 1918: 'a week end at Garsington . . . The string which united everything from first to last was Philip [Morrell]'s attack upon [J.M.] Murry in The Nation for his review of Sassoon . . . I was taxed with being on Murry's side . . .'; and see 'Mr Sassoon's Poems', above. Reprinted in part in 'Mr Sassoon's Poems', *B&P*.

2 – In May 1918, Captain Siegfried Sassoon (1886–1967) of the Royal Welch Fusiliers had rejoined his battalion in France. He was wounded in the head the following July and this brought his active military service to an end.

3 – Sassoon, 'The General', p. 26, the complete poem.

4 – *Ibid.*, 'Suicide in the Trenches', p. 31.

5 – *Ibid.*, 'To Any Dead Officer', p. 42.

6 – *Ibid.*, 'Dead Musicians', p. 59, italicised in the original.

7 – Geoffrey Dearmer was the son of the divine, Percy Dearmer. His brother Christopher had been killed at Gallipoli in 1915. Dearmer survived the war and later published a number of dramatic works.

8 – Dearmer, 'A Trench Incident', p. 54, which has 'keel;'.

9 – *Ibid.*, 'Reality', p. 55.

10 – Dearmer not only emulated Keats but wrote poems about him, e.g., 'Keats, Before Action' (*ibid.*, p. 41) and 'Keats' (*ibid.*, p. 74), in the last line of which he declares: 'Dear Keats your name is Paradise to me!'

11 – For the dashing moles *ibid.*, 'The Sentinel', p. 9; for the gossamer clouds, *ibid.*, 'Gommecourt', p. 28; for the excited glow worms, *ibid.*, 'Everychild', p. 63; for the three tags, *ibid.*, 'Resurrection', p. 23: e.g. 'Glad tidings to each clod, each particle of earth'; and 'Spring in the Trenches', p. 37: 'Glad tidings thrill the re-awakened earth'; *ibid.*, 'Eight Sonnets', V, p. 70; and 'The Strolling Singer', p. 86.

On Re-reading Meredith

This new study of Meredith is not a text-book to be held in one hand while in the other you hold *The Shaving of Shagpat* or *Modern Love*;[2] it is addressed to those who have so far solved the difficulties of the Master that they wish to make up their minds as to his final position in English literature. The book should do much to crystallise opinion upon

Meredith, if only because it will induce many people to read him again. For Mr Crees has written in a spirit of enthusiasm which makes it easy to do so. He summons Diana and Willoughby Patterne and Richard Feverel[3] from the shelves where they have fallen a little silent lately and in a moment the air is full of high-pitched, resonant voices, speaking the unmistakable language of metaphor, epigram, and fantastic poetic dialogue. Some readers, to judge from our own case, will feel a momentary qualm, as at meeting after the lapse of years some hero so ardently admired once that his eccentricities and foibles are now scarcely tolerable; they seem to preserve too well the faults of our own youth. Further, in the presence of so faithful an admirer as Mr Crees we may be reminded of some intervening disloyalties. It was not Thackeray or Dickens or George Eliot[4] who seriously tempted us from our allegiance; but can we say the same of the great Russians? Oddly enough, when Mr Crees is taking Meredith's measure by comparing him with his contemporaries he makes no mention of Turgenev, Tolstoy, or Dostoevsky. But it was *Fathers and Sons, War and Peace, Crime and Punishment*[5] that seduced multitudes of the faithful and, worse still, seemed for the time to reduce Meredith to an insular hero bred and cherished for the delight of connoisseurs in some sheltered corner of a Victorian hothouse.

The Russians might well overcome us, for they seemed to possess an entirely new conception of the novel and one that was larger, saner, and much more profound than ours. It was one that allowed human life in all its width and depth, with every shade of feeling and subtlety of thought, to flow into their pages without the distortion of personal eccentricity or mannerism. Life was too serious to be juggled with. It was too important to be manipulated. Could any English novel survive in the furnace of that overpowering sincerity? For some time the verdict seemed to go tacitly against Meredith. His fine phrases, his perpetual imagery, the superabundant individuality which so much resembled an overweening egotism seemed to be the very stuff to perish in that uncompromising flame. Perhaps some of us went as far as to believe that the process had already been accomplished and that it was useless to open books in which you would find nothing but charred bones and masses of contorted wire. The poems, *Modern Love, Love in the Valley*,[6] and some of the shorter pieces survived the ordeal more successfully and did perhaps keep alive that latent enthusiasm upon which Mr Crees now blows with the highest praise that it is possible to bestow upon literature.

He does not scruple to compare Meredith with Shakespeare. Shakespeare alone, he says, could have written the 'Diversion Played upon a Penny Whistle' in *Richard Feverel*.[7] Meredith 'illustrates better than any since Shakespeare that impetuous mental energy which Matthew Arnold deemed the source of our literary greatness'.[8] One might even infer from some statements that Meredith was the undisputed equal of the greatest of poets. 'No man has ever been endowed with richer gifts.'[9] He was the possessor of 'in some ways the most consummate intellect that has ever been devoted to literature'.[10] These, moreover, are not the irresponsible flings of a momentary enthusiasm but the considered opinion of a man who writes with ability and critical insight and has reached his superlatives by intelligible degrees of appreciation. We should perhaps alter his scale by putting Donne in the place of Shakespeare;[11] but however we may regulate our superlatives he creates the right mood for reading Meredith again.

The right mood for reading Meredith should have a large proportion of enthusiasm in it, for Meredith aims at, and when he is successful has his dwelling in, the very heart of the emotions. There, indeed, we have one of the chief differences between him and the Russians. They accumulate; they accept ugliness; they seek to understand; they penetrate further and further into the human soul with their terrible power of sustained insight and their undeviating reverence for truth. But Meredith takes truth by storm; he takes it with a phrase, and his best phrases are not mere phrases but are compact of many different observations, fused into one and flashed out in a line of brilliant light. It is by such phrases that we get to know his characters. They come to mind at once in thinking of them. Sir Willoughby 'has a leg'. Clara Middleton 'carries youth like a flag'. Vernon Whitford is 'Phoebus Apollo turned fasting Friar';[12] everyone who has read the novels holds a store of such phrases in his memory. But the same process is applied not only to single characters but to large and complicated situations where a number of different states of mind are represented. Here, too, he wishes to crush the truth out in a series of metaphors or a string of epigrams with as little resort to dull fact as may be. Then, indeed, the effort is prodigious, and the confusion often chaotic. But the failure arises from the enormous scope of his ambition. Let us suppose that he has to describe a tea party; he will begin by destroying everything by which it is easy to recognise a tea party – chairs, tables, cups, and the rest; he will represent the scene merely by a ring on a finger and a plume passing the window. But into the ring and plume he puts such passion and character and such penetrating rays of vision play about the denuded room that we seem to be in possession of all the details as if a painstaking realist had described each one of them separately. To have produced this effect as often as Meredith has done so is an enormous feat. That is the way, as one trusts at such moments, that the art of fiction will develop. For such beauty and such high emotional excitement it is well worth while to exchange the solidity which is the result of knowing the day of the week, how the ladies are dressed, and by what series of credible events the great crisis was accomplished. But the doubt will suggest itself whether we are not sacrificing something of greater importance than mere solidity. We have gained moments of astonishing intensity; we have gained a high level of sustained beauty; but perhaps the beauty is lacking in some quality that makes it a satisfying beauty? 'My love,' Meredith wrote, 'is for epical subjects – not for cobwebs in a putrid corner, though I know the fascination of unravelling them.' He avoids ugliness as he avoids dullness. 'Sheer realism,' he wrote, 'is at best the breeder of the dungfly.'[13] Sheer romance breeds an insect more diaphanous, but it tends perhaps to be even more heartless than the dungfly. A touch of realism – or is it a touch of something more akin to sympathy? – would have kept the Meredith hero from being the honourable but tedious gentleman that, with deference to Mr Crees, we have always found him. It would have charged the high mountain air of his books with the greater variety of clouds.

But, for good or for ill, Meredith has the habit of nobleness ingrained in him. No modern writer, for example, has so completely ignored the colloquial turns of speech and cast his dialogue in sentences that could without impropriety have been spoken by Queen Elizabeth in person. 'Out of my sight, I say!' 'I went to him of my own will to run from your heartlessness, mother – that I call mother!'[14] are two examples found upon turning two pages of *The Tragic Comedians*. That is his natural pitch, although we may guess that the long indifference of the public increased his tendency to the strained and the artificial. For this, among other reasons, it is easy to complain that this world is an aristocratic world, strictly bounded, thinly populated, a little hard-hearted, and not to be entered by the poor, the vulgar, the stupid, or that very common and interesting individual who is a mixture of all three.

And yet there can be no doubt that, even judged by his novels alone, Meredith remains a great writer. The doubt is rather whether he can be called a great novelist; whether, indeed, anyone to whom the technique of novel-writing had so much that was repulsive in it can excel compared with those who are writing, not against the grain, but with it. He struggles to escape, and the chapters of amazing but fruitless energy which he produces in his struggle to escape are the true obstacles to the enjoyment of Meredith. What, we ask, is he struggling against? What is he striving for? Was he, perhaps, a dramatist born out of due time – an Elizabethan sometimes, and sometimes, as the last chapters of *The Egoist* suggest, a dramatist of the Restoration? Like a dramatist, he flouts probability, disdains coherency, and lives from one high moment to the next. His dialogue often seems to crave the relief of blank verse. And for all his analytic industry in the dissection of character, he creates not the living men and women who justify modern fiction, but superb conceptions who have more of the general than of the particular in them. There is a large and beautiful conception of womanhood in Diana rather than a single woman; there is the fervour of romantic love in Richard Feverel, but the faces of the lovers are dim in the rosy light. In this lies both the strength and the weakness of his books, but, if the weakness is at all of the kind we have indicated, the strength is of a nature to counterbalance it. His English power of imagination, with its immense audacity and fertility, his superb mastery of the great emotions of courage and love, his power of summoning nature into sympathy with man and of merging him in her vastness, his glory in all fine living and thinking – these are the qualities that give his conceptions their size and universality. In these respects we must recognise his true descent from the greatest of English writers and his enjoyment of qualities that are expressed nowhere save in the masterpieces of our literature.

1 – A review in the *TLS*, 25 July 1918, (Kp C116) of *George Meredith. A Study of his Works and Personality* (B. H. Blackwell, 1918) by J. H. R. Crees, headmaster of the Crypt Grammar School, Gloucester.

See also 'Small Talk About Meredith' and 'Memories of Meredith', *III VW Essays*, and 'The Novels of George Meredith', *V VW Essays* and CR2. Reprinted: *G&R, CE.*

2 – George Meredith (1828–1909); *The Shaving of Shagpat, an Arabian Entertainment* (1856), *Modern Love* (1862).

3 – The references are to: Diana Warwick, heroine of *Diana of the Crossways* (1885); Sir Willoughby Patterne, a character in *The Egoist* (1879); and the hero of *The Ordeal of Richard Feverel* (1859).

4 – W. M. Thackeray (1811–63); Charles Dickens (1812–70); George Eliot (1819–80).

5 – Ivan Turgenev (1818–83), *Fathers and Sons* (1862); L. N. Tolstoy (1828–1910), *War and Peace* (1865–72); Fyodor Dostoevsky (1821–81), *Crime and Punishment* (1866).

6 – 'Love in the Valley', 1851 and 1878.

7 – Crees, ch. III, p. 40: 'In a pastoral modestly styled "a diversion on a penny whistle" we have a passionate outburst of soaring poetry which in the fervour of its impulse perhaps none else but Shakespeare could have written, and which in its appeal to natural beauty recalls us to Theocritus.'

8 – *Ibid.*, ch. VII, p. 183.

9 – *Ibid.*

10 – *Ibid.*, p. 190.

11 – Cf. 'Donne After Three Centuries', *V VW Essays* and *CR2*: 'He [Donne] is one of those nonconformists, like Browning and Meredith, who cannot resist glorifying their nonconformity by a dash of wilful and gratuitous eccentricity'; and 'The Novels of George Meredith', *ibid.*: 'Meredith's flamboyancy has a great ancestry behind it; we cannot avoid all memory of Shakespeare.'

12 – For Sir Willoughby, Crees, ch. II, p. 19; *The Egoist* (1879), ch. 2 (ed. George Woodcock, Penguin, 1968, p. 43). For Clara Middleton, Crees, ch. II, p. 31, and ch. VI, p. 138; *The Egoist*, ch. 4, p. 66: 'The young lady was outlined to Laetitia as tall, elegant, lively; and painted as carrying youth like a flag.' For Vernon Whitford, Crees, ch. II, p. 19; *The Egoist*, ch. 2, p. 42: 'And that [Mrs Mountstuart Jenkinson's portrait] of Vernon Whitford: "He is Phoebus Apollo turned fasting friar", painted the sunken brilliancy of the lean long-walker and scholar at a stroke.' The model for Whitford was VW's father, Leslie Stephen, leading figure in that fraternity of 'long-walkers' known as the Sunday Tramps, to which Meredith also belonged.

13 – For both quotations, Crees, ch. V, p. 107, Meredith writing to Frederick A. Maxse, 28 December 1865. Crees misquotes 'sheer Realism, breeder at best of the dung-fly!', according to *Letters of George Meredith* (2 vols, Constable, 1912).

14 – *The Tragic Comedians. A Study in a Well-known Story* (1880), ch. VIII (Memorial ed., Constable & Co., 1910, p. 95; p. 96).

Rupert Brooke

This memoir of Rupert Brooke has been delayed, in Mrs Brooke's words, because of 'my great desire to obtain the collaboration of some of his contemporaries at Cambridge and during his young manhood, for I strongly believe that they knew the largest part of him.'[2] But his contemporaries are for the most part scattered or dead; and though Mr Marsh has done all that ability or care can do, the memoir which now appears is 'of necessity incomplete'.[3] It is inevitably incomplete, as Mr Marsh, we are sure, would be the first to agree, if for no other reason because it is the work of an older man. A single sentence brings this clearly before us. No undergraduate of Rupert Brooke's own age would have seen 'his radiant youthful figure in gold and vivid red and blue, like a page in the Riccardi Chapel';[4] that is the impression of an older man. The contemporary version would have been less pictorial and lacking in the half-humorous tenderness which is so natural an element in the mature vision of beautiful and gifted youth. There would have been less of the vivid red and blue and gold, more that was mixed, parti-coloured, and matter for serious debate. In addition Mr Marsh has had to face the enormous difficulties which beset the biographers of those who have died with undeveloped powers, tragically, and in the glory of public gratitude. They leave so little behind them that can serve to recall them with any exactitude. A few letters, written from school and college, a fragment of a diary – that is all. The power of expressing oneself naturally in letters comes to most people late in life. Rupert Brooke wrote freely, but not altogether without self-consciousness, and it is evident that his friends have not cared to publish the more intimate passages in his letters to them. Inevitably, too, they have not been willing to tell the public the informal things by which they remember him best. With these serious and necessary drawbacks Mr Marsh has done his best to present a general survey of Rupert Brooke's life which those who knew him will be able to fill in here and there more fully, perhaps a little to the detriment of the composition as a whole. But they will be left, we believe, to reflect rather sadly upon the incomplete version which must in future represent Rupert Brooke to those who never knew him.

Nothing, it is true, but his own life prolonged to the usual term, and the work that he would have done, could have expressed all that was latent in the crowded years of his youth – years crowded beyond the measure that is usual even with the young. To have seen a little of him at that time was to have seen enough to be made sceptical of the possibility of any biography of a man dying, as he died, at the age of twenty-eight. The remembrance of a week spent in his company,[5] of a few meetings in London and the country, offers a tantalising fund of memories at once very definite, very little related to the Rupert Brooke of legend, present-ing each one an extremely clear sense of his presence, but depending so much upon that presence and upon other circumstances inextricably involved with it, that one may well despair of rendering a clear account to a third person, let alone to a multiple of many people such as the general public.

But the outline at least is clear enough. So much has been written of his personal beauty that to state one's own first impression of him in that respect needs some audacity, since the first impression was of a type so conventionally handsome and English as to make it inexpressive or expressive only of something that one might be inclined half-humorously to disparage. He was the type of English young manhood at its healthiest and most vigorous. Perhaps at the particular stage he had then reached, following upon the decadent phase of his first Cambridge days, he emphasised this purposely; he was consciously and defiantly pagan.[6] He was living at Grantchester; his feet were permanently bare; he disdained tobacco and butcher's meat; and he lived all day, and perhaps slept all night, in the open air. You might judge him extreme, and from the pinnacle of superior age assure him that the return to Nature was as sophisticated as any other pose, but you could not from the first moment of speech with him doubt that, whatever he might do, he was an originator, one of those leaders who spring up from time to time and show their power most clearly by subjugating their own generation. Under his influence the country near Cambridge was full of young men and women walking barefoot, sharing his passion for bathing and fish diet, disdaining book learning, and proclaiming that there was something deep and wonderful in the man who brought the milk and in the woman who watched the cows. One may trace some of the effects of this belief in the tone of his letters at this time; their slap-dash method, their hasty scrawled appearance upon the paper, the exclamations and abbreviations were all, in part at least, a means of exorcising the devils of the literary and the cultured. But there was too much vigour in his attitude in this respect, as in all others, to lend it the appearance of affectation. It was an amusing disguise; it was in part, like many of his attitudes, a game played for the fun of it, an experiment in living by one keenly inquisitive and incessantly fastidious; and in part it was the expression of a profound and true sympathy which had to live side by side with highly sophisticated tastes and to be reported upon by a nature that was self-conscious in the highest degree. Analyse it as one may, the whole effect of Rupert Brooke in these days was a compound of vigour and of great sensitiveness. Like most sensitive people, he had his methods of self-protection; his pretence now to be this and now to be that. But, however sunburnt and slap-dash he might choose to appear at any particular moment, no one could know him even slightly without seeing that he was not only very sincere, but passionately in earnest about the things he cared for. In particular, he cared for literature and the art of writing as seriously as it is possible to care for them. He had read everything and he had read it from the point of view of a working writer. As Mrs Cornford says, 'I can't imagine him using a word of that emotional jargon in which people usually talk or write of poetry. He made it feel more like carpentering.'[7] In discussing the work of living writers he gave you the impression that he had the poem or the story before his eyes in a concrete shape, and his judgments were not only very definite but had a freedom and a reality which mark the criticism of those who are themselves working in the same art. You felt that to him literature was not dead nor of the past, but a thing now in process of construction by people many of whom were his friends; and that knowledge, skill, and, above all, unceasing hard work were required of those who attempt to make it. To work hard, much harder than most writers think it necessary, was an injunction of his that remains in memory from a chaos of such discussions.

The proofs of his first book of poems were lying about that summer on the grass. There were also the manuscripts of poems that were in process of composition. It seemed natural to turn his poetry over and say nothing about it, save perhaps to remark upon his habit of leaving spaces for unforthcoming words which gave his manuscript the look of a puzzle with a number of pieces missing. On one occasion he wished to know what was the brightest thing in nature? and then, deciding with a glance round him that the brightest thing was a leaf in the sun, a blank space towards the end of 'Town and Country' was filled in immediately.

Cloud-like we lean and stare as bright leaves stare.[8]

But instead of framing any opinion as to the merit of his verses we recall merely the curiosity of watching him finding his adjectives, and a vague conception that he was somehow a mixture of scholar and man of action, and that his poetry was the brilliant by-product of energies not yet turned upon their object. It may seem strange, now that he is famous as a poet, how little it seemed to matter in those days whether he wrote poetry or not. It is proof perhaps of the exciting variety of his gifts and of the immediate impression he made of a being so complete and remarkable in himself that it was sufficient to think of him merely as Rupert Brooke. It was not necessary to imagine him dedicated to any particular pursuit. If one traced a career for him many different paths seemed the proper channels for his store of vitality; but clearly he must find scope for his extraordinary gift of being on good terms with his fellow-creatures. For though it is true to say that 'he never "put himself forward" and seldom took the lead in conversation',[9] his manner shed a friendliness wherever he happened to be that fell upon all kinds of different people, and seemed to foretell that he would find his outlet in leading varieties of men as he had led his own circle of Cambridge friends. His practical ability, which was often a support to his friends, was one of the gifts that seemed to mark him for success in active life. He was keenly aware of the state of public affairs, and if you chanced to meet him when there was talk of a strike or an industrial dispute he was evidently as well versed in the complications of social questions as in the obscurities of the poetry of Donne. There, too, he showed his power of being in sympathy with the present. Nothing of this is in the least destructive of his possession of poetic power. No breadth of sympathy or keenness of susceptibility could come amiss to the writer; but perhaps if one feared for him at all it was lest the pull of all his gifts in their different directions might somehow rend him asunder. He was, as he said of himself, 'forty times as sensitive as anybody else,'[10] and apt, as he wrote, to begin 'poking at his own soul, examining it, cutting the soft and rotten parts away'.[11] It needed no special intimacy to guess that beneath 'an appearance almost of placidity'[12] he was the most restless, complex, and analytic of human beings. It was impossible to think of him withdrawn, abstracted, or indifferent. Whether or not it was for the good of his poetry he would be in the thick of things, and one fancies that he would in the end have framed a speech that came very close to the modern point of view – a subtle analytic poetry, or prose perhaps, full of intellect, and full of his keen unsentimental curiosity.

No one could have doubted that as soon as war broke out he would go without hesitation to enlist. His death and burial on the Greek island, which 'must ever be shining with his glory that we buried there',[13] was in harmony with his physical splendour and with the generous warmth of his spirit. But to imagine him entombed, however nobly and fitly, apart from our interests and passions still seems impossibly incongruous with what we remember of his inquisitive eagerness about life, his response to every side of it, and his complex power, at once so appreciative and so sceptical, of testing and enjoying, of suffering and taking with the utmost sharpness the impression of everything that came his way. One turns from the thought of him not with a sense of completeness and finality, but rather to wonder and to question still: what would he have been, what would he have done?

1 – A review in the *TLS*, 8 August 1918, (Kp C117) of *The Collected Poems of Rupert Brooke: With a Memoir* [by Edward Marsh] (Sidgwick & Jackson Ltd, 1918).

Rupert Chawnor Brooke (1887–1915), son of William Parker Brooke, a master at Rugby School, and Ruth Mary Cotterill, was educated at Rugby and King's College, Cambridge, where he read classics and English, 1906–9, and in 1913 became a fellow. Brooke was elected a member of the exclusive Conversazione Society (the Apostles) in 1908, and the following year became president of the University Fabian Society. On the outbreak of war he enlisted in the Royal Naval Division. He died of blood poisoning on active service in the Aegean on 23 April 1915. His published works include *Poems* (1911), the posthumous collection *1914 and Other Poems* (1915), and *John Webster and the Elizabethan Drama* (1916).

'[Bruce] Richmond rang up to offer me Rupert's Life for next week,' VW wrote in her diary on Thursday, 18 July 1918, 'I told him that I should like to explain Rupert to the public. He agreed that there was much misunderstanding. "He was a very jolly sort of fellow" . . .' VW had already remarked upon the 'peculiar irony', to his friends, of Brooke's 'canonisation', in the *TLS*, 27 December 1917 (see 'The New Crusade', above), and there expressed the hope that 'some of those who knew him when scholarship or public life seemed even more his bent than poetry will put their view on record and relieve his ghost of an unmerited and undesired burden of adulation.'

The Stephens had known Rupert Brooke as a child on holiday at St Ives in Cornwall. In later years he and VW were to have many friends in common and for a time they enjoyed an intimate acquaintance. She felt strongly that the memoir by Edward Marsh (1872–1953), now published with the poems, again failed to do Brooke justice. Private Secretary to Winston Churchill, and Brooke's literary executor, Marsh was a classical scholar, a patron of painters and poets, and editor of *Georgian Poetry*. He was a graduate of Trinity College, Cambridge, and, like Brooke, an Apostle. Marsh introduced Brooke to Lady Ottoline Morrell's circle and later drew him into more mundane London society, as frequented by the Asquiths and similar luminaries. His memoir, one hundred and fifty-nine pages in length, was written in August 1915.

'The book is a disgraceful sloppy sentimental rhapsody, leaving Rupert rather tarnished,' she wrote (*ibid.*, 23 July), after a 'great deal of talk' about Brooke with Lytton Strachey. She also consulted James Strachey who had been at preparatory school and afterwards at Cambridge with Brooke and knew him intimately. But as Strachey 'had a medical examination, we couldn't say much about Rupert, save that he was jealous, moody, ill-balanced, all of which I knew, but can hardly say in writing' (*ibid.*, 27 July).

In 1912, much to their unhappy incomprehension, Brooke had abruptly broken with his Bloomsbury friends – 'Spit on Bloomsbury for me' he was to urge his Old Rugbeian and Cambridge friend Geoffrey Keynes in 1913 – following a rift (for which, irrationally, he held Lytton Strachey responsible) in his troubled affair with Katherine Cox.

On 13 August 1918, we find VW writing about her review to Katherine Cox (*II VW Letters*, no. 959): '*I* wrote the article on Rupert in the Times. Bruce Richmond sent the book to me; but when I came to do it I felt that to say out loud what even I knew of Rupert was utterly repulsive, so I merely trod out my 2 columns as decorously as possible. It seemed useless to pitch into Eddy [Marsh]. James [Strachey] meant to try, but gave it up. I think it was one of the most repulsive biographies I've ever read (this, of course, is a little overstated!). He contrived to make the [Brooke] letters as superficial and affected as his own account of Rupert. We're now suggesting that James should write something for us to print. He's sending us the letters to look at. But if you tell Mrs Brooke would you ask her not to tell anyone else, as Richmond is always anxious it shouldn't get out who has done reviews.'

VW next heard from Mrs Brooke herself, on 21 August, and on the same day replied: 'It was a great pleasure to get your letter this morning. I had rather hoped that you would *not* see my review, as I felt that I had not been able to say what I wanted to say about Rupert. Also I am afraid that I gave the impression that I disliked Mr Marsh's memoir much more than I meant to. If I was at all disappointed it was that he gave of course rather his impression of Rupert than the impression which one had always had of him partly from the Stracheys and other friends of his own age. But then Mr Marsh could not have done otherwise, and one is very glad to have the Memoir as it is. Rupert was so great a figure in his friends' eyes that no memoir could possibly be good enough. Indeed, I felt it to be useless to try to write about him. One couldn't get near to his extraordinary charm and goodness. I was 5 years older than he was, and I saw him as one knows one's own family. I stayed a week with him at Grantchester and then he came down here [at Little Talland House, Firle, in Sussex], and we met sometimes in London. He was a wonderful friend. I married in 1912, and was ill for a long time afterwards and never saw him after he went to America [in 1913].'

See also 'The Intellectual Imagination', *III VW Essays*. Reprinted: *B&P*.

2 – *Collected Poems*, intro., p. ix.

3 – *Ibid*.

4 – *Ibid*., Memoir, p. xxiv, a description of Brooke, as Marsh saw him for the first time, in the role of the Herald in a Cambridge undergraduate production of the Greek play *Eumenides*, in 1906.

5 – VW stayed with Rupert Brooke at The Old Vicarage, Grantchester, 14–19 August 1911, and the two had swum naked in the river together.

6 – Or *Neo-pagan*, as Bloomsbury dubbed the younger generation of mainly Cambridge friends – Katherine Cox, Gwen Darwin, Jacques Raverat, Justin Brooke, Dudley Ward, Gerald Shove, Geoffrey Keynes, David Garnett, the Olivier sisters – among whom Brooke was the leading spirit.

7 – *Collected Poems*, Memoir, p. xlii; Frances Crofts Cornford, *née* Darwin (1886–1960), poet, wife of the classical scholar and fellow of Trinity College, Cambridge, Francis Cornford, was one of Brooke's closest friends. Her first book, *Poems*, was published in 1910.

8 – *Ibid.*, p. 90, from the poem's penultimate stanza:

> Unconscious and unpassionate and still,
>   Cloud-like we lean and stare as bright leaves stare,
> And gradually along the stranger hill
>   Our unwalled loves thin out on vacuous air.

See also, *IV VW Diary*, 4 August 1934: 'Certainly bright leaves do glare [sic] as Rupert said'. And see Leonard Woolf, *II LW*, p. 8: 'Before his [Brooke's] quarrel with Lytton he was friendly both to me and to Virginia. He had a considerable respect for her, I think. He once stayed with her in Firle over a weekend and on Sunday morning they went and sat in Firle Park. He began to write a poem, his method being to put the last word of each line in rhyming quatrains down the sheet of paper and then complete the lines and so the poem. At one moment he said: "Virginia, what is the brightest thing you can think of?" "A leaf with the light on it," was Virginia's instant reply, and it completed the poem.'

9 – *Ibid.*, Memoir, p. xliii.

10 – *Ibid.*, p. cxv, Brooke writing to Marsh from Tahiti, in March 1914: 'The Game is Up, Eddie. If I've gained facts through knocking about with Conrad characters in a Gauguin *entourage*, – I've lost a dream or two. I tried to be a poet. And because I'm a clever writer, and because I was forty times as sensitive as anybody else, I succeeded a little . . . I am what I came out here to be. Hard, quite quite hard. I have become merely a minor character in a Kipling story.

'I'll never be able to write anything more, I think . . .'

11 – *Ibid.*, p. lvii, from a letter to Frances Cornford, February 1911.

12 – *Ibid.*, p. xlii.

13 – *Ibid.*, p. clix, from a description by Brooke's friend and fellow naval officer Denis Browne of 'Rupert's island [Skyros] at sunset'.

A Practical Utopia

Mr Onions has undertaken a much more difficult task than that of making a Utopia. It is much easier to forecast what will happen in a hundred years' time than in ten years' time. A century gives you space in which to remould the world to your liking, but in ten years' time England will be much the same as she is now – or only a little different.

Leaving the exact date undetermined Mr Onions supposes that the war is over; the period of reconstruction is in full swing. Dick Helme, who was wounded in the war, is now a member of the Canals and Water Power Section of the Imperial Transport Service. He is taking a convoy of motor lorries to their headquarters on the Severn, when Miss Betty

Lygard, of the Sixth District of the Western Agricultural Area, asks him to give her a lift with her patent beehives and grindstones and bill-hooks. They have never met before, but by the time she is set down with her cases they have arranged to marry each other. You get the impression that these questions will be dispatched very plainly and efficiently in ten years' time, as, indeed, there is not a minute to spare and not a farthing to waste. For the same reason each individual seems to be badged, numbered, and graded in the service of the State. The period of the blood-letting had exhausted England so far that new fabric had to be made from the very beginning. Every living creature was put to use. Every yard of land was turned to advantage. The power of electricity threaded the whole country. A picture of the scene on one of the main roads will serve to show the activity of the hive:

Half the population seemed to have become mobile. The towns were being eviscerated of their slums . . . And wherever there was a settlement or the nucleus of one or the site for one, there was traffic. Steam tractors drew the wagons loaded with building materials, six, and eight, and ten at a time. Lorries followed them with separators and churns, egg crates, and cheese wrings for the dairy services. Reapers and binders and cultivators followed these again drawn by horses. Along the main road, bands of workmen and labourers walked on foot, splitting into detachments, and scattering as they went. Then there was the furniture, the chars-à-bancs with families, loaded with bedding and birdcages . . .[2]

It is a fascinating little model, but, as tends to be the case with all forecasts of this kind, too much stress seems to be laid upon the development of electricity and too little upon the development of humanity. The real triumph for the imagination would be to reveal the end that has been produced by these improved means. A conversation, for example, between a group of people in ten years' time might show us more of the condition of England, than any enumeration of mechanical changes. What things do they take for granted? What startling announcements fall from them naturally? It is comparatively easy to imagine a town clear of smoke, or dinner raised by touching a switch, or an entire house run by a competent engineer in the basement. Perhaps we are meant to infer that the ancient stuff of human nature changes with extreme slowness, and that ten years (if we choose that period) even of such prodigious surface development as we have beheld can do but little to modify the natures of men. If we are to take Mr Onions for a prophet the change is in the direction of briefness, bluntness, and efficiency, as if more than half the attention of the race still went to control the machinery they have devised for saving time. And, clogging the free sweep of every reformer's imagination are the masses of the uneducated upon whom no swift conjuring tricks of change can be performed. The form is necessarily rough and vague, but we can guess how Mr Onions intends his model to shape out. In the world of business there is to be the Amity, a confederation of business interests in alliance instead of competition; in the world of politics the machine is to be worked frankly by newspaper men as a business concern. We are to reach no Utopia in our time. We are to become more clear-sighted, more unselfish, and necessarily more hard-working. Those who find an absorbing interest in making models of the future will find a much greater store of raw material for their industry in *The New Moon* than we have been able to indicate. The solidity of the work is shown by the resentment with which in the last chapter we see the whole structure tumble down and dissolve into a dream.

1 – A review in the *TLS*, 15 August 1918, (Kp C118) of *The New Moon. A Romance of Reconstruction* (Hodder & Stoughton, 1918) by (George) Oliver Onions (1872–1961), author of several novels, including the semi-autobiographical *Little Devil Doubt* (1909) and *Good Boy Seldom* (1911). He was the husband of the popular novelist Berta Ruck, whose name VW was by chance to reproduce on a tombstone in *Jacob's Room* (1922), much to Onions's vexation (see *II QB*, pp. 91–2).
2 – Onions, pt ii, p. 124, which differs from VW's version in several minor points of punctuation.

'The Sad Years'

More than half of the poetry which flowers in England seems to be grown from the same seed – the desire for self-expression. The seed, happily, is as various as the self. But through the screen of language and metre one can see plainly enough that the origin of the poem was a personal experience, too personal and disconnected from other experiences to be projected into a story or wrought into an argument. The presence of this element is one reason for finding most poetry, even most bad poetry, worth reading, and for reading it with a confusion of spirit such as the narrative of the writer's experience if told in person would inspire. Nevertheless, we are inclined to attribute the unimportance of most verse to the same cause. There are the seeds of two poems, for instance, in the two statements that so-and-so was unhappy on Friday because it rained, and happy on Saturday because the sun was out; but unless our fount of sympathy is inexhaustible we get tired of a volume composed of these simple experiences of sunshine and rain. The mere fact of rhyming and scanning, like the fact of being in a confessional, somehow hallows what is written and said; so that all platitudes and confessions naturally seek the sanctuary of verse. Women are more prone than men to take refuge in this form of simple egotism, though for reasons, perhaps, that have more in common with modesty than conceit. They appear to be more shy of using their brains and of displaying their love of language in poetry than men of the same poetic gift. A simple statement, a mere cry, is enough, the argument seems to be, if you are writing poetry, and with luck it may turn out that you have written a masterpiece.

Something of this kind applies to Mrs Shorter's work, although she was frequently almost lucky enough to make it seem a wise policy. 'The gifts came to her out of the air, so to speak,' writes Katharine Tynan, 'real gifts and nothing acquired.'[2] We need not quarrel with the statement that her gifts were real. Every page of her book goes to prove it. The most severe of critics if asked for advice could only have advised her to go on writing poetry; and, indeed, it is likely that the woman who wrote the following verses would have written verses against all the dissuasion in the world:

> I saw children playing, dancing in a ring,
>   Till a voice came calling, calling one away;
> With sad backward glances she went loitering,
>   Hoping they would miss her and so cease to play.
>
> Pettishly and pouting, ''Tis not time to sleep,'
>   Sobbing and protesting, slowly she did go;
> But her merry comrades they all run and leap,
>   Feeling not her absence, heeding not her woe.[3]

The line that the critic might have taken would have been to urge her to concentrate, to enrich, to perfect, not to trust merely to 'passionate emotion to give it wings'.[4] For to arrive at art without any apprenticeship may, as Mrs Tynan says, make the word genius not inapplicable to those who so arrive; but the difficulty is to name these fortunate people. Mrs Shorter, moreover, interests us partly because she was not content with her gift for singing songs that seem to sing themselves. The ideas behind several of her poems are subtle and difficult, and have evidently broken through her powers of expression so that they remain sketches rather than completed poems. One need not grudge an occasional stumble caused by an honest inability to get the meaning into words. But this faultiness of technique helps to make her verse seem unduly personal; she cannot give her melancholy or her indignation the impersonal stamp which perfect expression bestows, so that we forget the particular grief and the particular writer.

With these reservations one must give her a high place among those writers whose gift is such that one is almost afraid to advise them to concentrate, to finish or to perfect, lest in so doing they should spoil. They have virtues which seem to give their work the charm and intimacy of the living voice. To their own contemporaries they often seem more sympathetic, because they are more on our level of feeling, than the aloof and the contemplative. In reading Mrs Shorter's poetry, for instance, we are almost as much interested by her personality as we are by her poetry. We hardly know whether we like the verses we have quoted because they make us sympathise with her emotion or because we find them beautiful in themselves. The future of work marked by this twofold appeal is precarious, because its accent will scarcely be understood by a later age; but from that very reason arises much of its significance to us.

1 – A review in the *TLS*, 29 August 1918, (Kp C119) of *The Sad Years* (Constable & Co. Ltd, 1918) by Dora Sigerson (Mrs Clement Shorter). In a prefatory tribute to the author, who had died on 6 January 1918, Katharine Tynan relates that Dora Sigerson, daughter of an eminent Dublin doctor of medicine, had suffered a sudden breakdown in 1916 over the events that followed the Easter Rising and had died broken-hearted 'as she would have chosen to die, for the love of the Dark Rosaleen'.
2 – Sigerson, 'A Tribute and Some Memories' by Katharine Tynan, p. ix.
3 – *Ibid.*, 'I Saw Children Playing', p. 52, the first two of five stanzas.
4 – *Ibid.*, Tynan, p. xi.

The 'Movie' Novel

When we say that the adventures of Sylvia Scarlett are much more interesting than Sylvia Scarlett herself, we are recommending the book to half the reading public and condemning it in the eyes of the other half. There are people who require the heroines of their novels to be interesting, and they know by experience that the adventurous heroine is apt to be as dull in fiction as she is in life. It is true that adventurers are not dull in the ordinary sense of the word; they are monotonous, self-centred, serious, rather than dull. They have spun all their substance into adventure, and nothing remains of them but a frail shell inhabited by a very small creature with an enormous egotism and an overweening vanity. The charge may be just, yet there is a great deal to be said in praise of adventures themselves, and not a little relief in finding occasionally that people are not quite so interesting as writers are in the habit of insisting, in novels, that we shall find them. Perhaps Sylvia might have been interesting if she had ever had the time to set about it. She had her moments of introspection, as upon that occasion when she announced 'I represent the original conception of the Hetaera – the companion. I don't want to be made love to, and every man who makes love to me I dislike. If I ever do fall in love, I'll be a man's slave.'² But perhaps she was aware that being interesting was not in her line, as we are inclined to agree with her that it was not. At any rate, this reflection occurs in a momentary lull, and directly Mr Mackenzie catches her in the lazy pose of self analysis he gives a crack of his whip and sends her flying, as merrily as if she had never heard the word Hetaera, through the next hoop.

We cannot begin even to count those hoops. They are so many and so variously designed that a bare programme of the entertainment or a catalogue of the actors' names would fill perhaps a score of columns. In very early youth Sylvia came to England dressed as a boy and christened Sylvester to share the shifts and adventures of her father, an absconding clerk, in the shadier suburbs of London. From the addresses of their lodgings and the names of their friends the experienced reader who has read, among other books, the novels of Dickens will gather what sort of life they led, and will even be able to improvise a certain amount of the conversation of Mrs Bullwinkle, Mrs Gowndry, Mr Monkley; and General Dashwood of Tinderbox Lane. But it is better and simpler to rely entirely upon Mr Mackenzie. He does it so fast and so deftly that merely to keep up with him is quite enough strain upon the faculties. He not only finds names for landladies, cabmen, mountebanks, actresses, tenors, managers, schoolmistresses, barons, clergymen, natives of Brazil, and maiden ladies living in villas appropriately named too, but he provides them with queer occupations, and clever things to say, let alone a number of surprising things to do. You can scarcely open the book anywhere without finding a cab bolting down Haverstock Hill with an eloping couple inside it, or a baboon escaping from Earl's Court Exhibition, or an actor dropping dead, or a curtain going up, or a landlady being funny. Here is a shop incident to show how quickly it rattles along:

The confusion in the shop became general: Mr Gonner cut his thumb, and the sight of the blood caused a woman who was eating a sausage to choke; another customer took advantage of the row to snatch a side of bacon and try to escape, but another customer with a finer moral sense prevented him; a dog, who was sniffing in the entrance, saw the bacon on the floor and tried to seize it, but, getting his tail trodden upon by somebody, he took fright and bit a small boy who was waiting to change a shilling into coppers. Meanwhile Sylvia ... jumped on to the first omnibus, ⟨&c., &c.⟩[3]

When we reached this point we seized the opportunity, not so much of being bored as of being out of breath, to reflect upon the propriety after all of using the word adventure. It is true that Sylvia is left on top of an omnibus bound for West Kensington without a penny in the world; she is young, beautiful, and friendless into the bargain; we have no idea what is going to become of her; why then do we refuse to call it an adventure? The obvious way to settle the question is to bring to mind Tom Jones, Moll Flanders, Isopel Berners, or the Flaming Tinman.[4] These people may not be interesting either, but when any one of them has not a penny in the world it is a serious matter. Compared with Mr Mackenzie's characters they are a slow-moving race – awkward, ungainly and simple-minded. But consider how many things we know about them, how much we guess, what scenes of beauty and romance we set them in, how much of England is their background – without a word of description perhaps, but merely because they are themselves. We can think about them when we are no longer reading the book. But we cannot do this with Mr Mackenzie's characters; and the reason is, we fancy, that though Mr Mackenzie can see them once he can never see them twice, and, as in a cinema, one picture must follow another without stopping, for if it stopped and we had to look at it we should be bored. Now, it is a strange thing that no one has yet been seen to leave a cinema in tears. The cab horse bolts down Haverstock Hill and we think it a good joke; the cyclist runs over a hen, knocks an old woman into the gutter, and has a hose turned upon him. But we never care whether he is wet or hurt or dead. So it is with Sylvia Scarlett and her troupe. Up they get and off they go, and as for minding what becomes of them, all we hope is that they will, if possible, do something funnier next time. No, it is not a book of adventures; it is a book of cinema.

1 – A review in the *TLS*, 29 August 1918, (Kp c120) of *The Early Life and Adventures of Sylvia Scarlett* (Martin Secker, 1918) by Compton Mackenzie (1883–1972) whose works at this date included *Sinister Street* (1913–14) and *Guy and Pauline* (1915). Mackenzie served in military intelligence during the war, chiefly in Greece, where he set part of his next novel *Sylvia and Michael* (1919), the sequel to the book reviewed here. See 'Sylvia and Michael', *III VW Essays*. Reprinted: *CW*.
2 – Mackenzie, bk II, ch. I, pp. 270–1.
3 – *Ibid.*, bk I, ch. v, pp. 151–2.
4 – Characters respectively in: Henry Fielding, *Tom Jones, a Foundling* (1749); Daniel Defoe, *The Fortunes and Misfortunes of the famous Moll Flanders* (1722); George Borrow, *Lavengro and the Romany Rye* (1858), and *Lavengro, the Scholar – the Gypsy – the Priest* (1851).

War in the Village

Nowadays many whose minds have not been used to turn that way must stop and ponder what thoughts the country people carry with them to their work in the fields, or cogitate as they scrub the cottage floor. It is a matter for speculation and shyness since the gulf between the articulate and inarticulate is not to be crossed by facile questioning, and silence may seem after all the best we can offer by way of sympathy to people whose lives seem so mysteriously and for such ages steeped in silence. Thus Mr Hewlett[2] has chosen one of the most difficult of tasks when he tries to think himself into the mind of the village wife, and to express thoughts 'which she may never have formulated, but which, I am very sure, lie in her heart too deep for any utterance save that of tears'.[3] He has succeeded, beyond doubt, in writing a terse, moving, and very sincere poem; but that it is the lament of a village woman for her shepherd husband killed in France, and for the baby whose death followed upon his death, we are not so sure.

Yet it would be difficult to say what quality we seek for in Mr Hewlett's poem and find lacking. Where it would have been easy to offend there is no ground for offence; the conception is very dignified and as completely without a touch of the sentimentality, which the theme invites, as the language is almost equally free from the taint of the professional writer. The village wife has nothing idyllic about her. From her birth upwards she takes her share in what Mr Hewlett calls 'the unending war'[4] waged from one generation to another by the sons and daughters of the poor. She scrubs and rinses and milks the cows year in and year out.

> On winter mornings dark and hard,
>> White from aching bed,
> There were the huddled fowls in yard
>> All to be fed.
> My frozen breath stream'd from my lips,
>> The cows were hid in steam;
> I lost sense of my finger-tips
>> And milkt in a dream.[5]

Very finely and truly Mr Hewlett bases her life deep down among the roots of the earth; she grows among the other growing things, and the hills and woods of her parish are England and the world to her, and she has inherited from generations of village women who lived this life and knew its perils the morality upon which their lives were founded.

> I learned at home the laws of Earth;
>> The nest-law that says,
> Stray not too far beyond the hearth,
>> Keep truth always;
> And then the law of sip and bite:
>> Work, that there may be some
> For you who crowd the board this night,
>> And the one that is to come.
> The laws are so for bird and beast,
>> And so we must live:
> They give the most who have the least,
>> And gain of what they give.
> For working women 'tis the luck,
>> A child on the lap;
> And when a crust he learn to suck,
>> Another's for the pap.[6]

This hard natural life scarcely shares in the changes of the self-conscious world. It has grown so close to the earth and so shaped itself to the laws of nature that it might well remain unshaken for ever. But one summer evening the village wife hears one stranger say to another as he passes, 'Then that means war'.[7] From that moment her security is troubled, and by November, to her inexpressible bewilderment, her own house and happiness are at the mercy of a force so remote that, though it has power to take her husband from her, she can hardly figure to herself what the nature of it is. Her husband feels it, and goes; more strangely it takes not only his body, but makes unfamiliar all that she knew in his spirit. She hears that he is missing, and exclaims:

Missing! My man had been dead
Before he went away.[8]

What, then, remains for her? Nothing but to ask perpetually those questions as to the reason and justice of these events which in the mind of a woman who has placed her trust in the rightness of the natural order have an extreme bitterness mixed with their bewilderment. She must puzzle out why the world has deceived her; why her right was not right after all.

The verses, as our quotations show, are plain, deeply felt, and often beautiful. But, for all their scrupulous care and regard for the truth, they strike us not so much as the thoughts and laments of the woman herself as the words of a very sympathetic spectator who is doing his best to express what he supposes must be there beneath the silence and at the heart of the tears. The argument has too much cogency, the thoughts follow each other in too orderly a fashion to be the cry of a woman bereft of husband and son. Perhaps it is coarseness – the quality that is the most difficult of all for the educated to come by – that is lacking. By coarseness we mean something as far removed from vulgarity as can be. We mean something vehement, full throated, carrying down in its rush sticks and stones and fragments of human nature pell-mell. That is what we miss in Mr Hewlett's poem, fine though it is.

1 – A review in the TLS, 12 September 1918, (Kp C121) of *The Village Wife's Lament* (Martin Secker, 1918) by Maurice Hewlett. Reprinted: *CW*.
2 – Maurice Henry Hewlett (1861–1923) regarded himself primarily as a poet – in 1916 he had published an epic poem *The Song of the Plow* – but he was far more successful as an author of romantic and historical fiction and had found fame and fortune overnight with his first book *The Forest Lovers* (1898). Early in her career as a reviewer, VW had referred to Hewlett, in a letter to Madge Vaughan, mid-December 1904, as an 'affected Dandy' and expressed a wish to give him his due (*I VW Letters*, no. 202).
3 – Hewlett, Note, p. 62.
4 – *Ibid.*, p. 16: 'Watch you the same unending war/ Ontaken by your son.'
5 – *Ibid.*, p. 26.
6 – *Ibid.*, p. 15, which begins a new stanza at 'The laws are so for bird and beast'.
7 – *Ibid.*, p. 36.   8 – *Ibid.*, p. 55.

The Rights of Youth

The moralists of the nursery used to denounce a sin which went by the name of 'talking at', and was rendered the more expressive by the little stress which always fell upon the 'at', as if to signify the stabbing, jabbing, pinpricking nature of the sin itself. The essence of 'talking at' was that you vented your irritation in an oblique fashion which it was difficult for your victim to meet otherwise than by violence. This old crime of the nursery is very apt to blossom afresh in people of mature age when they sit down to write a novel. It blossoms often as unconsciously as we may suppose that the pearl blossoms in the breast of the oyster. Unfortunately for art, though providentially for the moralist, the pearl that is produced by this little grain of rancour is almost invariably a sham one.

In the early chapters of *Joan and Peter* there are a great many scenes and characters which seem to have been secreted round some sharp-edged grain which fate has lodged in the sensitive substance of Mr Wells's brain. Lady Charlotte Sydenham had some such origin; so, too, had Miss Phoebe Stubland; the sketch of Arthur Stubland was due to a disturbance of the kind, and certainly the schoolmistresses of St George and the Venerable Bede had no other begetter. We catch ourselves wondering whether Mr Wells is any longer aware of the grotesque aspect of these figures of his, burdened as they are with the most pernicious or typical views of their decade, humped and loaded with them so that they can hardly waddle across the stage without coming painfully to grief. The conscientious reader will try to refer these burlesques to some such abstraction as the Anglican Church, or the vagaries of aimless and impulsive modernism in the eighteen-nineties; but if you are indolent you will be inclined to give up playing your part in the game of illusion, and to trifle with idle speculations as to the idiosyncrasies of Mr Wells. But soon the very crudeness of the satire leads us to make a distinction, and directly we are satisfied of its truth our irritation is spent and our interest aroused. Mr Wells is not irritated with these people personally, or he would have taken more pains to annoy them; he is irritated with the things they represent. Indeed, he has been so much irritated that he has almost forgotten the individual. He is sore and angry and exaggerated and abusive because the waste, the stupidity, the senility of our educational system have afflicted him as men are, for the most part, afflicted only by their personal calamities. He possesses the queer power of understanding that 'the only wrongs that really matter to mankind are the undramatic general wrongs',[2] and of feeling them dramatically, as if they had wronged him individually. Here, he says, we have two children endowed with everything that the world most needs, and let us see what the world will make of them. What education have we to offer them? What are we able to teach them about the three great questions of sex and state and religion? First, he gluts his rage upon Lady Charlotte and Miss Phoebe Stubland, much to the detriment of the book, and then the matter is seriously taken in hand by Mr Oswald Stubland, V.C., a gallant gentleman with imaginative views upon the British Empire. He had believed that the Empire was the instrument of world civilisation, and that his duty in Central Africa was the duty of an enlightened schoolmaster. But when his health broke down he returned to the far more difficult task of educating two of the children of the Empire in the very metropolis of civilisation. He started off upon a pilgrimage to the schools and colleges of England, asking imaginative questions, and getting more and more dismayed at the answers he received.

Don't you *know* that education is building up an imagination? I thought everybody knew that ... Why is he to *do* Latin? Why is he to *do* Greek? ... What will my ward know about Africa when you have done with him? ... Will he know anything about the way the Royal Exchange affects the Empire? ... But why shouldn't he understand the elementary facts of finance?[3]

This is a mere thimbleful from the Niagara which Mr Wells pours out when his blood is up. He throws off the trammels of fiction as lightly as he would throw off a coat in running a race. The ideas come pouring in whether he speaks them in his own person or lets Oswald have them, or quotes them from real books and living authorities, or invents and derides some who are not altogether imaginary. He does not mind what material he uses so long as it will stick in its place and is roughly of the shape and colour he wants. Fiction, you can imagine him saying, must take care of itself; and to some extent fiction does take care of itself. No one, at any rate, can make an inquiry of this sort so vivid, so pressing, so teeming and sprouting with suggestions and ideas and possibilities as he does; indeed, when he checks himself and exclaims, 'But it is high time that Joan and Peter came back into the narrative,'[4] we want to cry out,

'Don't bother about Joan and Peter. Go on talking about education.' We have an uneasy suspicion that Joan and Peter will not be nearly so interesting as Mr Wells's ideas about their education and their destiny. But, after all, we know that Mr Wells is quite right when he says that it is time to bring them in. He would be shirking the most difficult part of his task if he left them out.

Like his own Oswald Stubland, Mr Wells 'belongs to that minority of Englishmen who think systematically, whose ideas join on'. He has 'built up a sort of philosophy for himself',[5] by which he does try his problems and with which he fits in such new ideas as come to him. He is not writing about education, but about the education of Joan and Peter. He is not isolating one of the nerves of our existence and tracing its course separately, but he is trying to give that nerve its place in the whole system and to show us the working of the entire body of human life. That is why his book attains its enormous bulk; and that is why, with all its sketchiness and crudeness and redundancy, its vast soft, billowing mass is united by a kind of coherency and has some relation to a work of art. If you could isolate the seed from which the whole fabric has sprung you would find it, we believe, to consist of a fiery passion for the rights of youth – a passion for courage, vitality, initiative, inventiveness, and all the qualities that Mr Wells likes best. And as Mr Wells can never think without making a picture of his thought, we do not have youth in the abstract, but Joan and Peter, Wilmington and Troop, Huntley and Hetty Reinhart. We have Christmas parties and dressings-up and dances and night clubs and Cambridge and London and real people disguised under fictitious names, and very bright covers on the chairs and Post-Impressionist[6] pictures on the walls and advanced books upon the tables. This power of visualising a whole world for his latest idea to grow in is the power that gives these hybrid books their continuity and vitality.

But because Mr Wells's ideas put on flesh and blood so instinctively and admirably we are able to come up close to them and look them in the face; and the result of seeing them near at hand is, as our suspicions assured us that it would be, curiously disappointing. Flesh and blood have been lavished upon them, but in crude lumps and unmodelled masses, as if the creator's hand, after moulding empires and sketching deities, had grown too large and slack and insensitive to shape the fine clay of men and women. It is curious to observe, for example, what play Mr Wells is now constrained to make with the trick of modernity. It is as if he suspected some defect in the constitution of his characters and sought to remedy it with rouge and flaxen wigs and dabs of powder, which he is in too great a hurry nowadays to fix on securely or plaster in the right places. But if Joan and Peter are merely masquerading rather clumsily at being the heirs of the ages, Mr Wells's passion for youth is no make-believe. The sacrifice, if we choose to regard it so, of his career as a novelist has been a sacrifice to the rights of youth, to the needs of the present moment, to the lives of the rising generation. He has run up his buildings to house temporary departments of the Government. But if he is one of those writers who snap their fingers in the face of the future, the roar of genuine applause which salutes every new work of his more than makes up, we are sure, for the dubious silence, and possibly the unconcealed boredom, of posterity.

1 – A review in the *TLS*, 19 September 1918, (Kp C122) of *Joan and Peter. The Story of an Education* (Cassell & Co. Ltd., 1918) by H. G. Wells (1866–1946). As VW noted in her diary on Wednesday, 18 September 1918, Sidney and Beatrice Webb, who, like H. G. Wells, were founding members of the Fabian Society, had come to visit the Woolfs at Asheham House, Sussex, the previous Saturday, 'a pouring wet day . . . Next day, which was said to begin for the W[ebb]s at 5.30, when they begin tea-drinking in their bedrooms, I had to withdraw in order to do battle with a very obstinate review of Wells' "Joan & Peter". My ideas were struck stiff by the tap of Mrs W.s foot, up & down the terrace, & the sound of her rather high, a rather mocking voice, discoursing to L[eonard Woolf] while she waited either for W[ebb] to come or the rain to stop.' See also 'Character in Fiction', *III VW Essays*. Reprinted: *CW*.

2 – Wells, ch. XIV, p. 698: 'The country was at sixes and sevens because its education by school and college, by book and speech and newspaper, was confused and superficial and incomplete because its institutions were a patched-up system of traditions, compromises, and interests, devoid of any clear and single guiding idea of a national purpose. The only wrongs that really matter to mankind are the undramatic general wrongs; but the only wrongs that appeal to the uneducated imagination are individual wrongs.'

3 – *Ibid.*, ch. X, pp. 322–3, adapted.

4 – *Ibid.*, ch. IX, p. 284, which has: 'this narrative'.

5 – For both quotations, *ibid.*, ch. XII, p. 500.

6 – Post-Impressionism makes an early and, to students of Bloomsbury, an interesting appearance in *Joan and Peter*, as does Roger Fry, organiser of the Post-Impressionist Exhibitions at the Grafton Galleries in 1910 and 1912, in the character of Stubland, e.g., *ibid.*, ch. I, p. 6: 'From the last stage of Quakerism to the last extremity of decoration is but a step. Quite an important section of the art world in Britain owes itself to the Quakers and Plymouth Brethren, and to the drab and grey disposition of the sterner evangelicals. It is as if that elect strain in the race had

shut its eyes for a generation or so, merely in order to open them again and see brighter. The reaction of the revolting generation has always been toward colour; the pyrotechnic display of the Omega workshops in London is but the last violent outbreak of the Quaker spirit. Young Stubland, a quarter of a century before the Omega enterprise, was already slaking a thirst for chromatic richness behind the lead of William Morris and the Pre-Raphaelites. It took a year or so and several teachers and much friendly frankness to persuade him he could neither draw nor paint, and then he relapsed into decoration and craftsmanship.'

Mr Hudson's Childhood

Since in this account of his childhood Mr Hudson[2] speculates as to the origin of certain childish instincts, one may perhaps suitably begin what one has to say of his book by recalling a childish impression which his writing has brought to mind. Between or behind the dense and involved confusion which grown-up life presented there appeared for moments chinks of pure daylight in which the simple, unmistakable truth, the underlying reason, otherwise so overlaid and befogged, was revealed. Such seasons, or more probably seconds, were of so intense a revelation that the wonder came to be how the truth could ever again be overcast, as it certainly would be overcast directly this lantern-like illumination went out.[3] Somehow or other Mr Hudson writes as if he held his lantern steadily upon this simple, unmistakable truth, and had never been deluded or puzzled or put off by the confusions which overlay it. It is an effect that the great Russian writers produce far more commonly than the English, and may perhaps be connected with the surroundings of their childhood, so different both for Mr Hudson and for the Russians from the surroundings of the ordinary English childhood. Therefore one is reluctant to apply to Mr Hudson's book those terms of praise which are bestowed upon literary and artistic merit, though needless to say it possesses both. One does not want to recommend it as a book so much as to greet it as a person, and not the clipped and imperfect person of ordinary autobiography, but the whole and complete person whom we meet rarely enough in life or in literature.

But Mr Hudson himself provides one clue to the secret which we have clumsily tried to prise open. He has been saying that it is difficult not 'to retouch, and colour, and shade, and falsify' the picture of childhood by the light of what we have since become. Serge Aksakoff, he goes on to say, in his *History of My Childhood*, was an exception 'simply because the temper and tastes and passions of his early boyhood – his intense love of his mother, of nature, of all wildness, and of sport – endured unchanged in him to the end and kept him a boy in heart, able after long years to revive the past mentally and picture it in its true, fresh, and original colours'.[4] That is true also of Mr Hudson. When he writes of himself as a little boy he does not get out of his large body into a small different one, or fall into that vein of half-humorous and romantic reverie which the recollection of our small predecessor usually inspires. The little boy whom he remembers was already set with even fresher passion upon the same objects that Mr Hudson has sought all his life. Therefore he has not to reconstruct himself, but only to intensify. It seems, too, as if it must be the easiest thing in the world to remember clearly such a childhood as his was, spent not in some cranny, artificially scooped out of the grown-up world, but in a place naturally fitted and arranged for it. His father lived in a vast house on 'the illimitable grassy plain of South America',[5] at a little distance from a plantation of various kinds of trees which were the nesting-place of many different birds. A man upon horseback raised three or four feet above the surrounding level would see all round

a flat land, its horizon a perfect ring of misty blue colour, where the crystal blue dome of the sky rests on the level green world . . .[6] On all this visible world there were no fences and no trees excepting those which had been planted at the old estancia houses, and these being far apart the groves and plantations looked like small islands of trees, or mounds, blue in the distance, on the great plain or pampa . . .[7] The picture that most often presents itself is of the cattle coming home in the evening; the green quiet plain extending away from the gate to the horizon; the western sky flushed with sunset hues, and the herd of four or five hundred cattle trotting homewards with loud lowings and bellowings, raising a great cloud of dust with their hoofs, while behind gallop the herdsmen urging them on with wild cries.[8]

One is inclined to hold the view, indeed, that parents of children have no business to live anywhere except on the pampas of South America. For beyond the daily ecstasy of living out of doors, fate seems to have seen to it that the few human beings who wandered into the large house as guests, beggars or tutors summed up in their persons the most marked characteristics of humanity. There was Captain Scott, captain of what is unknown, but an Englishman of immense bulk, 'with a great round face of a purplish red colour', dressed always in a light blue suit, who would arrive with his pockets bulging with sweets from the distant land where sweets were made, and stand, 'looking [...] like a vast blue pillar,'[9] motionless upon the bank, rod in hand. Unknown in origin, he disappeared to an unknown fate, 'yet in my mind how beautiful his gigantic image looks!'[10] Then every seven or eight weeks the Hermit arrived, to beg not money but food, which he would take only in the form of flawless biscuits, for should they be chipped or cracked he would have none of them. He was supposed to have committed some terrible crime, which he expiated by wearing a very thick mattress stuffed with sticks, stones, lumps of clay, horns, and other heavy objects, enough to weigh down two men, which he dragged about with him, in penance for what no one knew, since he could speak no intelligible language and died under his mattress alone on the plains without confessing the nature of his crime. The supply of tutors in the pampas was also limited to men who had mysterious reasons of their own, whether it was a devotion to white Brazilian rum or difficulties with the Roman Catholic Church, for choosing a nomadic life and being unable to retain their employment for long. Mr Trigg, for example, 'followed teaching because all work was excessively irksome to him',[11] and was hired by the month, like the shepherd or the cowman, to teach children their letters, until his failing found him out, and in spite of his delightful social gifts and his passion for reading Dickens[12] aloud, he had to take his horse again and ride off with a bag containing all his possessions over the plains.

With reluctance one must resist the temptation of transcribing one such character sketch after another, not only because the transcription damages the pleasure of coming upon the page itself, but also because to give the impression that the book is mainly composed of such sketches would not be true. The remarkably handsome young gentleman with a wash-leather bag attached to his wrist who threw pebbles at small birds on the Parade at Buenos Aires, the immensely fat lady who sat perpetually on a cane chair attended by four hairless dogs, the three on the floor 'ever patiently waiting for their respective turns to occupy the broad warm lap',[13] the stranger who played divinely on the guitar but could not go on playing for thinking of his own family in Spain, Don Gregorio with his passion for breeding piebald horses and his rage against anyone possessed of such an animal who refused to sell it – all these figures met the eyes of the observant little boy, and are faithfully presented as the sort of thing that you saw if you looked up in South America from the absorbing business of life. For he was a child, almost a baby, when he discovered instinctively what was the business, or rather the spirit, of life, the string upon which all sights and thoughts and adventures were hereafter to be threaded. He begins as a small child who notices things in the bulk to gaze at the trees in the plantation. It was a 'wonderful experience to be among them, to feel and smell their rough, moist, bark, stained green with moss, and to look up at the blue sky through the network of interlacing twigs'.[14] Then those trees became full of birds, and Mr Hudson is constantly tempted to make 'this sketch of my first years a book about birds and little else'.[15] He resists the temptation, but, like all writers of strong individuality, a colour gets into his pages apart from the actual words, and even when they are not mentioned we seem to see the bird flying, settling, feeding, soaring through every page of the book. There are the immensely tall white-and-rose-coloured birds of earliest memory who stand feeding in the river and then shake out their wings, which are of a glorious crimson colour; then the resounding screams of the travelling parrots are heard, and they appear, flying at a moderate height, 'with long pointed wings and long graduated tails, in their sombre green plumage touched with yellow, blue, and crimson colour'.[16] These are the birds of earliest childhood, and from them his dreams spring and by them his images are coloured in later life. Riding at first seemed to him like flying. When he is first among a crowd of well-dressed people in Buenos Aires he compares them at once to a flock of military starlings. From watching birds comes his lifelong desire to fly – but it is a desire which no airship or balloon but the wings of a bird alone will satisfy. Later these first impressions were intensified by his habit of rambling off alone and standing motionless, staring at vacancy as his mother, following him in anxiety for his state of mind, supposed; but to her joy she found that he was not staring at vacancy, but observing 'an insect perhaps, but oftener a bird'.[17]

And yet if we were to say that on this account Mr Hudson's book is written chiefly for naturalists it would not be true. The naturalist will see the bird accurately enough, but he will not see it in relation to the tree, to the small boy, to the strange characters of the plain; nor will the bodies of birds represent for him that mysterious spirit which Mr Hudson, for some reason that psychologists must explain, finds in all nature, but in birds particularly. Because Mr Hudson is able to do all this, to read his book is to read another chapter in that enormous book which is written from time to time by Rousseau and Borrow and George Sand[18] and

Aksakoff among other people – a book which we can never read enough of; and therefore we must beg Mr Hudson not to stop here, but to carry the story on to the farthest possible limits.

1 – A review in the *TLS*, 26 September 1918, (Kp C123) of *Far Away and Long Ago. A History of my Early Life* (J. M. Dent & Sons Ltd., 1918) by W. H. Hudson. 'I went over to Charleston last Tuesday,' VW wrote in her diary on Monday, 23 September 1918, '& . . . sat with Nessa & laid bare my sorrows, which she can more than match . . . I walked home shoving my bicycle, too badly punctured to ride.

'Well then, the Times began to shower books upon me, & I was reduced at one point to writing my review in the afternoon, nor can I discover any reason why one's brains should be unavailable between 3 & 5. When the telegraph girl rode up with a telegram from Clive to put us off, owing to some disease of Mary's, we were both immensely relieved, & I threw down my pen, as they say, & ate a large tea, & found my load of writing much lessened. When I have to review at command of a telegram, & Mr Geal has to ride off in a shower to fetch the book at Glynde, & comes & taps at the window about 10 at night to receive his shilling & hand in the parcel, I feel pressed & important & even excited a little. For a wonder, the book, Hudson, was worth reading.'

Shortly after Hudson's death, on 18 August 1922, VW was to remark, in a letter to Katherine Arnold-Forster, dated 23 August (*II VW Letters*, no. 1276): 'I was to have been taken to see Mr Hudson this winter by [Dorothy] Brett, who adored him . . . Parts of his books are very good – only others are very bad; isn't that so? Anyhow, I wish I had seen him'. Later, in 'How It Strikes a Contemporary', *IV VW Essays* and *CR1*, she wrote: 'Passages in *Far Away and Long Ago* will undoubtedly go to posterity entire.' See also '*A Russian Schoolboy*', above. Reprinted: *CW*.

2 – William Henry Hudson (1841–1922), naturalist and writer, was born at Quilmes, some ten miles from Buenos Aires, and came to England in 1869. His works include *The Purple Land* (1885), *A Naturalist in La Plata* (1892), *Green Mansions* (1904), and the classic *A Shepherd's Life* (1910), set in the downlands of Wiltshire.

3 – Compare 'A Sketch of the Past', *MoB*.

4 – Hudson, ch. VII, p. 226. Serge Aksakoff (1791–1850), *Years of Childhood* – published originally as part of *Family Chronicle*, 1856 – had appeared in English translation in 1916. See also 'A Russian Schoolboy', above.

5 – *Ibid.*, ch. IV, p. 45, which has: 'I remember – better than any orchard, grove or wood I have ever entered or seen, do I remember that shady oasis of trees at my new home on the illimitable grassy plain.'

6 – *Ibid.*, ch. V, p. 63, which begins: 'We see all round us'.

7 – *Ibid.*, p. 64, which has: 'On this visible earth'.

8 – *Ibid.*, ch. I, p. 10.

9 – *Ibid.*, p. 12.

10 – *Ibid.*, p. 13.

11 – *Ibid.*, ch. II, p. 26.

12 – Charles Dickens (1812–70).

13 – Hudson, ch. XI, p. 158.
14 – *Ibid.*, ch. IV, p. 45.
15 – *Ibid.*, p. 62.
16 – *Ibid.*, ch. VI, p. 86, which has: 'crimson colour!'.
17 – *Ibid.*, ch. VII, p. 93.
18 – Jean-Jacques Rousseau (1712–78); George Borrow (1803–81); George Sand (1804–76).

Caution and Criticism

One is inclined to say that if Mr Williams[2] had been less impartial and less conscientious he would have written a better, at least a more readable, book. If, like most historians of modern literature, he had written to prove a theory or impose a view of art, the 360-odd writers whose works he examines in these pages would have merged themselves magically in an orderly pattern, which, whether fallacious or not, we should have taken in at a glance. As it is each of these writers stands obstinately a little apart from his fellow; and when Mr Williams, drawing back and half closing his eyes, tries to resolve them into schools or tendencies he is forced to confess, being an honest man, that he can see nothing but individuals. That he set out in the hope of reducing them to some kind of order is obvious from the opening pages of his book. The year 1890, he does his best to insist, was the year in which the Victorianism of the Victorian age virtually, or practically, or to some extent, passed away; but as it was not of one texture, nor disappeared all at once, owing to the longevity of George Meredith[3] and other causes, nothing so dramatic as a fresh age could immediately succeed it. It was replaced gradually by a patchwork of influences – the significance of Oscar Wilde's aestheticism,[4] the aims of the *Yellow Book*, and the *Savoy*;[5] the influence of W. E. Henley;[6] and the ideals of the Celtic revival in Ireland. Under these banners we have with qualifications and exceptions, and, of course, with innumerable inter-alliances and reactions, fought until that other convenient date – August 1914.

This general statement being very guardedly and tentatively laid down, Mr Williams proceeds to examine into the cases of particular writers and finds before very long that it is impossible to keep them even within these sufficiently elastic boundaries. As early as page 68 he finds it necessary to content himself with the study of separate writers whose aims become increasingly individual and disconnected. Then a rough chronological order is attempted, and at one point it seems as if the novelists were to be grouped, not according to their age, but according to their worthlessness. It becomes, indeed, more and more evident, as Mr Williams says, that 'we are reading with our eyes too close to the book to see the print distinctly'.[7] Hampered by this drawback, and having no ulterior reward to offer himself in the shape of an aesthetic theory, Mr Williams is indefatigable and undaunted. His zeal is comparable to the zeal of the scientist who examines innumerable specimens and yet allows himself to draw no conclusions. The examination, too, seems to be equally thorough, whether the specimen is as rare and curious as Mr Conrad,[8] or as commonplace and abundant as writers whom we refrain from mentioning. His singular lack or disregard of personal preferences leads him to pronounce carefully balanced judgments upon books which, so far as we can see, no more deserve description than the dandelions of the year before last.

A forgotten writer called Henry Dawson Lowry[9] was once apparently compared by his admirers to Keats and Heine. Mr Williams in his careful way finds space to assure us that he has nothing 'of Heine's wayward strength, nothing of Keats's wealth of language and picturesque decorativeness,'[10] as if we were still in danger of wrecking ourselves upon that obsolete rock. Books whose writers alone can have any interest in their fate are carefully compared, their plots often analysed, and their final worth summed up in phrases which, if they censure, are generally moderately encouraging at the same time. 'Mr O'Sullivan has no affectation of startling originality, but he is rarely wholly commonplace.'[11] '*Auguries* (1913) contains grave and regular verse embodying the not too eager musings and emotions of a cultivated, thoughtful, but not original, mind.'[12] 'Her verse is never enhanced by those sudden and illuminating felicities of phrase and thought which mark greater poetry . . . but, on the other hand, she is not frequently disconcertingly empty of matter, and her sentiment rarely degenerates to insipidity.'[13] Such things have no doubt to be said in the world we live in, but we have always been sanguine enough to hope that the succeeding week strewed oblivion upon them.

But, making allowance for a certain formal remoteness of manner, which is, no doubt, inevitable considering the numbers to be surveyed, Mr Williams's judgment is uniformly fair and his mind singularly open.

He finds a good word not only for Mr Bennett and Mr Wells, but for Mr Tirebuck and Miss Milligan.[14] Most writers, again, set upon a task of such labour would by some means have deluded themselves into the belief that a good number of their vast flock of geese were swans. But Mr Williams is singularly without illusions. He reminds us that 'at the beginning of the twenty-first century, in all probability, the great number of the poets named in this book, with all their poems, will only be matter for comparative study by the literary expert'.[15]

As to the novelists, 'Of those who find a place here the greater number will be forgotten in a few decades.'[16] In a mood of intelligible pessimism he tells us indeed that it is better 'to read contemporary verse for the joy and inspiration it may afford us individually, untroubled by any desire to speak or write of it'.[17] Nevertheless, Mr Williams has been troubled to write, and to some purpose, for though the lack of complete bibliographies and the insufficiency of the biographies will not suit students who seek exact information, a foreigner wishing to take a bird's-eye view of modern English literature will find Mr Williams a safe guide.

1 – A review in the TLS, 3 October 1918, (Kp C124) of Modern English Writers: Being a Study of Imaginative Literature 1890–1914 (Sidgwick & Jackson Ltd, 1918) by Harold Williams. Reprinted: CW.

2 – Rev. Harold Herbert Williams (1880–1964), a graduate of Christ's College, Cambridge, was a devoted university extension lecturer. His previous publications included a volume of poetry, a novel, and Two Centuries of the English Novel (1911). He joined the Royal Army Service Corps during the war and, according to the DNB, 'presumably' wrote the present work while on active service.

3 – Williams, p. xiii; George Meredith (1828–1909).

4 – Ibid., p. xvi, discusses the aesthetic theories of Oscar Wilde (1854–1900) as expounded in the Preface to The Picture of Dorian Gray (1891) – in which Wilde asserted that 'All Art is quite useless' – and in the essay 'The Decay of Lying'.

5 – Ibid., pp. xviii–xx; the Yellow Book (1894–7), a self-consciously 'new' and 'bizarre' little magazine, was edited originally by Henry Harland and Aubrey Beardsley. It soon became commercialised and was never as consistent as Arthur Symons's short-lived Savoy (1896), in which the public were given the purest distillation of Nineties decadence.

6 – Ibid., pp. xxvi–xxvii; William Ernest Henley (1849–1903), poet, journalist and critic, a close friend of R. L. Stevenson, exerted considerable influence as the editor of the Magazine of Art, 1882–6, the Scots (later National) Observer, 1889–94, and the New Review, 1894–8.

7 – Ibid., pt I, ch. III, p. 115.

8 – For Williams on Joseph Conrad (1857–1924), ibid., pt IV, ch. III, pp. 387–96.

9 – Henry Dawson Lowry (1869–1906), poet and novelist, 'little known at any time' (*ibid.*, p. 117).

10 – *Ibid.*, pt I, ch. III, p. 117; Heinrich Heine (1797–1856); John Keats (1795–1821).

11 – *Ibid.*, pt II, ch. II, p. 181; Seumas O'Sullivan (James Starkey, 1879–1958), poet, in both English and Irish, whose most recent volume, *Requiem and Other Poems*, had appeared in 1917.

12 – *Ibid.*, pt I, ch. III, p. 85, discussing Laurence Binyon (1869–1943).

13 – *Ibid.*, pt II, ch. III, p. 192, discussing Dora Sigerson Shorter (d. 1918); see '*The Sad Years*' above.

14 – Arnold Bennett (1867–1931); H. G. Wells (1866–1946). William Edwards Tirebuck (1854–1900), author of several novels, generally depicting the life of the poor, and for which Tolstoy once expressed his admiration; he began his working life as an errand boy in Liverpool and was for some years a journalist with the *Yorkshire Post*. Alice Milligan (1880–1953), Irish poet, author of *Hero Lays* (1908).

15 – Williams, pt I, ch. III, p. 103.

16 – *Ibid.*, pt IV, ch. I, p. 279.

17 – *Ibid.*, pt. I, ch. III, p. 116.

Adventurers All

Miss Stuart[2] comes very near to being a poet, and if she fails it is, we believe, because she cherishes some old superstitious belief about the sanctity of inspiration; her Muse is an inspired figure with wild locks and a bandage round her eyes. The power of feeling emotion quickly and strongly is a great one and Miss Stuart has, in addition to this, an unusual power of putting her emotions, and also, for she thinks as well as feels, her ideas, into words that express them both beautifully and freely. For example, we might quote, although it is scarcely fair to quote single passages from a long poem, this from 'The Cockpit of Idols':

> And while these gods in the great shambles die,
> Thrust on each other's spears,
> He, nameless and unchallenged, wanders by
> In every tree that peers
> Into the wizard darkness of the hill,
> And in each tarn most deeply contemplates
> The image of His beauty, lingers still
> To twist again the purfled clover's ears,

World-weary feet He cools
Where windless noons lie bathing in the pools,
    Or takes His solitude
Where, in the purple cloak of twilight, waits
The moon to pierce the solitary wood.[3]

But too often at the height of her mood, when the utmost discretion and vigilance are needed, she seems to resign herself merely to utter words, herself accepting no responsibility for the sense or beauty or fitness of what is said. The common notion that poetry is something wild, emphatic, uttered in a shriek rather than in a singing or speaking voice, has persuaded her to pitch her normal tone so loud that when she wishes to be specially emphatic there is nothing for it but to coin monstrous superlative superlatives such as 'this most unquietest heart' or these 'most forlornest shells',[4] to rely upon the fortifying effect of capital letters, or upon a violence of imagery which jerks the whole stanza out of perspective. But faults of taste are not the worst of faults, and Miss Stuart proves, in such a poem as the quiet and beautiful 'Heliodore',[5] that she can free herself from them completely and remarkably.

The connection beween Miss Stuart and Mr Huxley[6] is the obvious one that they have nothing in common. The one is strong precisely where the other is weak. Miss Stuart has too many ideas and emotions, and is too careless as to what she does with them. But after reading the first few poems in Mr Huxley's little book it is clear that any idea or emotion that comes to him has the best possible chance of surviving beautifully. The criticism implied is, of course, that he is better equipped with the vocabulary of a poet than with the inspiration of a poet. He writes about the things he has thought and seen rather than about things he has felt, and in rendering them he shows a facility which begins by charming, but ends, as verse that relies so much upon happy adjectives is always apt to end, by running fluently to waste. The advice that one is inclined to give to an urbane and cultivated writer of his quality is to cease to use poetry in the serious, traditional manner, and to use it instead to explore those fantastic, amusing, or ironical aspects of life which can only be expressed by people of high technical skill and great sensibility. Mr Huxley proves himself, in verses like 'Social Amenities', 'Topiary', or 'On the 'Bus', quite capable of doing this:

Sitting on the top of the 'bus,
I bite my pipe and look at the sky.
Over my shoulder the smoke streams out

> And my life with it.
> 'Conservation of energy,' you say.
> But I burn, I tell you, I burn;
> And the smoke of me streams out
> In a vanishing skein of grey.
> Crash and bump ... my poor bruised body!
> I'm a harp of twittering strings.
> An elegant instrument, but infinitely second-hand,
> And if I have got phthisis it is only an accident.
> Droll phenomena![7]

If by a chance, which is not so improbable as at first sight appears, Miss Sitwell's[8] teapot reminded her first of the Tower of London and then of Joan of Arc she would say so without hesitation or consistency. The moon in one poem reminds her of a milk-white unicorn; in the next 'nurse's white gown' shines through the trees like a unicorn of unspecified colour.[9] For the most part we believe that Miss Sitwell is trying her best to be honest with her own conceptions, and, that being so, she is of course perfectly right not to care whether they appear outlandish, farfetched, or startling upon the printed page. But honesty of imagery is, after all, only the groundwork of writing. When you are sure that the sea is 'sequined with noisy light' or that 'colours like a parokeet Shrill loudly to the chattering heat',[10] you still have to decide what whole you wish to build up with these vivid or remarkable or unexpected phrases. By themselves they are little more than bright colours. But at this stage of her career the chief thing that Miss Sitwell has to tell us about the world is that it is extremely bright and very noisy. The air is brittle and bright as glass; 'plush mantles seemed to purr';[11] people are bright sparks; sound becomes substance, and sight becomes sound. There is almost invariably a brass band playing in the sun and tight green parasols reflect the blare of the brass. Miss Sitwell owes a great deal to modern painters, and until her optic nerve has ceased to be dazzled it is difficult to say how interesting her vision is.

> Green apples dancing in a wash of sun —
> Ripples of sense and fun —
> A net of light that waves as it weaves
> The sunlight on the chattering leaves;
>
> The half-dazed sound of feet,
> And carriages that ripple in the heat.
> The parasols like shadows of the sun
> Cast wavering shades that run

Across the laughing faces and across
Hair with a bird-bright gloss.
The swinging greenery cast shadows dark,
Hides me that I may mark

How, buzzing in this dazzling mesh, my soul
Seems hardening it to flesh, and one bright whole.
O sudden feathers have a flashing sheen!

The sun's swift javelin
The bird-songs seem, that through the dark leaves pass;
And life itself is but a flashing glass.[12]

That is proof that she can make charming ornaments already; in imitation of her manner we might liken them to the stiff china dogs that stand on farmhouse mantelpieces. But manner in the young is a form of paralysis, and already Miss Sitwell repeats her favourite adjectives and similes so often as to suggest that she is becoming prematurely imprisoned within the walls of her own style. She is too vigorous a writer to rest content with making china dogs indefinitely.

If you should buy the little anthology of recent poetry edited by Mr Jones[13] in the expectation of being brought into touch with the youngest and most revolutionary of modern poets you will, according to your temperament, be disappointed or relieved. Here is nothing to surprise and nothing to shock. The general attitude which we should have tried to define is very well expressed for us by Mr Earp:

I have been reading books
For about twenty years;
I have laughed with other men's laughter,
Wept with their tears.

Life has been a cliché
All these years.

I would find a gesture of my own.[14]

Of course there are exceptions. Mr Betts in 'The Pawns'[15] writes not only very well, but with a good deal of meaning; Mr Jones has an imagination which is trying to express itself; Miss Bridges[16] does exquisitely what it is no disparagement to say that her father has done more exquisitely still; and we can see no reason to think that Miss Sitwell has spent even a fraction of Mr Earp's twenty years in reading other people's books. But, speaking generally; the poets here represented in such modest quantities seem to be dealing with emotions received from books in language learnt from books. We must wait a little longer for that 'gesture of my own'.

1 – A review in the *TLS*, 10 October 1918, (Kp C125) of *The Cockpit of Idols* (Methuen & Co. Ltd, 1918) by Muriel Stuart; *The Defeat of Youth and Other Poems* (B. H. Blackwell, 1918) by Aldous Huxley; *Clowns' Houses* (B. H. Blackwell, 1918) by Edith Sitwell; and of *Songs for Sale. An Anthology of Recent Poetry* (B. H. Blackwell, 1918) ed. E. B. C. Jones.

'Roger [Fry], Duncan [Grant], Maynard [Keynes], Nessa [Vanessa Bell] & I all crammed in & padded along slowly across London to Chelsea,' VW recorded in her diary on Saturday, 12 October 1918. 'Somehow we passed Ottoline [Morrell], brilliantly painted, as garish as a strumpet, displayed in the midst of omnibuses under an arc lamp; & she reappeared in the Sitwells' drawing room. I had made acquaintance with the two Sitwell brothers the day before [at 46 Gordon Square], & been invited to the party. That very morning a review by me of Edith Sitwell's poems had appeared in the Times ... This group to which Gertler & Mary H[utchinson] are attached was unknown to me a year ago. I surveyed them with considerable, almost disquieting calm ... Edith Sitwell is a very tall young woman, wearing a permanently startled expression, & curiously finished off with a high green silk headdress, concealing her hair, so that it is not known whether she has any. Otherwise, I was familiar with everyone, I think.'

See also 'Cleverness and Youth' (a review of Aldous Huxley's *Limbo, 1920*), *III VW Essays.*

2 – Muriel Stuart was also the author of *Christ at Carnival, and Other Poems* (1916).

3 – Stuart, p. 24.

4 – For the first hyperbolical superlative, *ibid.*, 'The Bastard', p. 9; and for the second, 'The Cockpit of Idols', p. 18.

5 – *Ibid.*, pp. 43–6.

6 – Aldous Leonard Huxley (1894–1963) had published one other collection of poems, *The Burning Wheel*, in 1916, in which year he was also an editor of the annual anthology *Oxford Poetry*. Huxley was a contributor to *Wheels*, the anti-Georgian verse anthology edited annually, from 1916, by Edith Sitwell. VW had met him for the first time in April 1917, at Garsington Manor, the home of Philip and Lady Ottoline Morrell. There Huxley, unfit for military service, spent part of the war working on the land. (His first novel, *Crome Yellow*, was published in 1921.)

7 – Huxley, 'On the Bus', p. 39, the entire poem; for 'Social Amenities' and 'Topiary', p. 38.

8 – Edith Louisa Sitwell (1887–1964) published her first collection of poems, *The Mother*, in 1915, and in the following year there appeared a further volume, *Twentieth-Century Harlequinade*, a collaboration with her brother Osbert.

9 – For the first quotation, Sitwell, 'The Old Nurse's Song', p. 21; and for the second, 'Rocking-Horses', *ibid.*

10 – *Ibid.*, 'Minstrels', p. 8:

> Beside the sea, metallic-bright
> And sequined with the noisy light,
> Duennas slowly promenade
> Each like a patch of sudden shade,
>
> While colours like a parokeet
> Shrill loudly to the chattering heat;
> And gowns as white as innocence
> With sudden sweetness take the sense.

11 – *Ibid.*, 'Myself on the Merry-Go-Round', p. 19, which has: 'seem to purr'.

12 – *Ibid.*, 'Déjeuner sur l'Herbe', pp. 9–10, the complete poem, which has no stanza divisions.

13 – I.e., Emily Beatrice Coursolles ('Topsy') Jones (1893–1966) who, in 1917, had published with Christopher Jonson the collection *Windows*. In 1921 she was to marry Frank Laurence ('Peter') Lucas, a classical scholar of Trinity College, Cambridge, an Apostle, and a friend of Bloomsbury. *Songs for Sale* contains three of her poems, as well as pieces by Edith Sitwell and Aldous Huxley. In c. 1920 she published *Quiet Interior*, the first of several novels.

14 – Jones, 'Departure', p. 19. Thomas Wade Earp, author, of *Contacts and Other Poems* (1916) and an editor, 1918–20, of *Oxford Poetry*, later wrote books about art and artists.

15 – *Ibid.*, p. 8. Frank Betts had published *The Iron Age* (1916) and *Saga Plays* (1917).

16 – Jane Bridges, daughter of the then poet laureate Robert Bridges, is represented in Jones by one poem, 'Orpheus'.

Honest Fiction

Shops and Houses is one of those books which by their health and robustness should confute those who hold that English fiction is in a languid or degenerate condition. There can be no reason for despondency or for disparaging comparisons when novels of such care and conscience and ability are produced, not of course in any quantity, but still by a small and undaunted band of writers, among whom we must now place Mr Swinnerton. He is among the group of honest observers of contemporary life who filter their impressions sedulously and uncompromisingly through the intellect and suffer nothing to pass save what possesses meaning and solidity.

It is not necessary that Mr Swinnerton should say anything very

strange or very unpleasant in *Shops and Houses*. He sets out to show us
the life in a suburb not far from London where the men work in the city
all day and the women spend their time ordering their households, going
to tea parties, and buying things in shops. Mr Swinnerton takes up his
position upon a little mound of intellectual honesty, from which he
observes and according to which he judges. Perhaps there once happened to him what happened to his hero Louis Vechantor at the
Hughes's tea party. '. . . He seemed for a moment to lose consciousness
[. . .] The tea-table chatter sounded like a confused roaring of a crowd
some distance away . . . Their laughter seemed to him like the grinning of
skulls . . . Louis had never fainted, or he would have known that a
curious sweet remoteness precedes the total loss of sensation. It was just
that feeling of being apart and contemplative that had assailed him.'²
Shops and Houses may well have had its origin in some such moment of
remoteness at a tea party, but, having seen his vision, Mr Swinnerton set
to work to search out and verify every detail that went to compose the
large effect; and as each was received it was tested by a standard which
we may roughly describe as the standard of intellectual honesty. How
did they live, what did they live for, what were these healthy unemployed
young women, these indolent elderly ladies, after? He has discovered an
astonishing number of very minute facts as to the manner in which the
ladies of Beckwith perform their chief occupation in life – the 'consumption of precious time'.³ He is with them when they wish to attract, and
when they cease to wish to attract; he observes their attempts to marry
or to prevent marriage; he sees them piecing together into interminable
romances little shreds of gossip picked from the dust-heap. He examines
the process by which the public opinion of Beckwith is formed, and
traces it in operation upon a case specially submitted to it. How would
Beckwith, he asks, deal with the case of a respectable resident's disreputable cousin who has the effrontery to set up a grocer's shop in Beckwith
itself? By means of details and fragments he has set working a model
Beckwith which performs all the functions of spending time with the
regularity of an ant-heap; or, since the activity of an ant-heap has some
direction, with the automatic accuracy of a decapitated duck. Moreover,
he has created what he dissects. He is not only the 'disembodied and
cruel spectator';⁴ he has enough sympathy to show us, at any rate
through the eyes of Louis Vechantor, that there were possibilities and
varieties among the people of Beckwith which make them momentarily
attractive and intermittently pathetic.

But although there are passages of hope, Beckwith does not pass the test; Beckwith is shown up; as Dorothy Vechantor, who is appointed to wind up the spiritual affairs of Beckwith, says, 'I've been thinking whether perhaps Beckwith ... that it isn't altogether a place at all. I mean whether it isn't a sort of disease'.[5] In saying this she lays her finger not only upon the deficiency of Beckwith, but upon the deficiency which *Shops and Houses* shares with so many other novels of the intellectual school. Beckwith is proved to be a disease: it has failed to pass any of the tests which Mr Swinnerton so honestly and acutely applies; it is snobbish and vulgar, cruel, stupid, without worth, rhyme, or reason. Nevertheless, with all these proofs of its spiritual bankruptcy before us, we still remain unconvinced. Our lack of conviction is not, as at first sight appears, because of the incredible meanness and insignificance of the crimes cited against the inhabitants, although their minuteness certainly diminishes their power to affect us; we cannot believe that Beckwith is merely a disease because we cannot accept Mr Swinnerton's view of what constitutes health. Louis Vechantor and Dorothy, the daughter of the grocer, the grocer William, and the grocer's family are the representatives of sincerity and humanity. They are capable of thought and capable of love. They are the martyrs whom Beckwith half succeeds in pelting to death with its grains of spite; it is to them that we look with confidence to champion the human cause. And it is precisely these characters who fail us. Those scenes which should show us the honesty and energy of life removed from the burden of false convention are the weakest in the book. It is by their failure that we are led to doubt whether honesty and intelligence will really do all that the intellectual novelist claims for them, and whether because of their absence we are entitled to blot a whole suburb from the map. Perhaps there are other qualities, other aims, other desires which make even Miss Lampe of Station Road a little more complex than an agitated ant or a decapitated duck? Perhaps there is more in marriage, love, friendship, beauty than Mr Swinnerton altogether conveys? But, we repeat, it is a great thing that Beckwith should be destroyed; it is a most valuable work.

1 – A review in the *TLS*, 10 October 1918, (Kp c126) of *Shops and Houses* (Methuen & Co. Ltd, 1918) by Frank Swinnerton (1884–1982), novelist, critic and publisher's reader. Swinnerton was later to write unfavourably of VW's own fiction, and of Bloomsbury, in *The Georgian Literary Scene* (1935). For her reactions to his 'sneers' see *IV VW Diary*, 16 and 18 March 1935. See also 'September', *III VW Essays*. Reprinted: CW.

2 – Swinnerton, ch. IV, p. 60–1, slightly adapted.
3 – *Ibid.*, ch. II, p. 23.
4 – *Ibid.*, ch. IV, p. 60.
5 – *Ibid.*, ch. XXIV, pp. 290–1; the ellipsis is Swinnerton's.

Women Novelists

By rights, or, more modestly, according to a theory of ours, Mr Brimley Johnson should have written a book amply calculated, according to the sex of the reader, to cause gratification or annoyance, but of no value from a critical point of view. Experience seems to prove that to criticise the work of a sex as a sex is merely to state with almost invariable acrimony prejudices derived from the fact that you are either a man or a woman. By some lucky balance of qualities Mr Brimley Johnson has delivered his opinion of women novelists without this fatal bias, so that, besides saying some very interesting things about literature, he says also many that are even more interesting about the peculiar qualities of the literature that is written by women.

Given this unusual absence of partisanship, the interest and also the complexity of the subject can scarcely be overstated. Mr Johnson, who has read more novels by women than most of us have heard of, is very cautious – more apt to suggest than to define, and much disposed to qualify his conclusions. Thus, though his book is not a mere study of the women novelists, but an attempt to prove that they have followed a certain course of development, we should be puzzled to state what his theory amounts to. The question is one not merely of literature, but to a large extent of social history. What, for example, was the origin of the extraordinary outburst in the eighteenth century of novel writing by women? Why did it begin then, and not in the time of the Elizabethan renaissance? Was the motive which finally determined them to write a desire to correct the current view of their sex expressed in so many volumes and for so many ages by male writers? If so, their art is at once possessed of an element which should be absent from the work of all previous writers. It is clear enough, however, that the work of Miss Burney,[2] the mother of English fiction, was not inspired by any single wish to redress a grievance: the richness of the human scene as Dr Burney's daughter had the chance of observing it provided a sufficient stimulus; but however strong the impulse to write had become, it had at the outset to meet opposition not only of circumstance but of opinion. Her first manuscripts were burnt by her stepmother's orders, and needlework was inflicted as a penance, much as, a few years later, Jane Austen would slip her writing beneath a book if anyone came in, and Charlotte Brontë[3] stopped in the middle of her work to pare the potatoes. But the domestic problem, being overcome or compromised with, there remained the moral one. Miss Burney had showed that it was 'possible for a woman to write novels and be respectable',[4] but the burden of proof still rested anew upon each authoress. Even so late as the mid-Victorian days George Eliot was accused of 'coarseness and immorality' in her attempt 'to familiarise the minds of our young women in the middle and higher ranks with matters on which their fathers and brothers would never venture to speak in their presence'.[5]

The effect of these repressions is still clearly to be traced in women's work, and the effect is wholly to the bad. The problem of art is sufficiently difficult in itself without having to respect the ignorance of young women's minds or to consider whether the public will think that the standard of moral purity displayed in your work is such as they have a right to expect from your sex. The attempt to conciliate, or more naturally to outrage, public opinion is equally a waste of energy and a sin against art. It may have been not only with a view to obtaining impartial criticism that George Eliot and Miss Brontë adopted male pseudonyms, but in order to free their own consciousness as they wrote from the tyranny of what was expected from their sex. No more than men, however, could they free themselves from a more fundamental tyranny – the tyranny of sex itself. The effort to free themselves, or rather to enjoy what appears, perhaps erroneously, to be the comparative freedom of the male sex from that tyranny, is another influence which has told disastrously upon the writing of women. When Mr Brimley Johnson says that 'imitation has not been, fortunately, the besetting sin of women novelists',[6] he has in mind no doubt the work of the exceptional women who imitated neither a sex nor any individual of either sex. But to take no more thought of their sex when they wrote than of the colour of their eyes was one of their conspicuous distinctions, and of itself a proof that they wrote at the bidding of a profound and imperious instinct. The women who wished to be taken for men in what they wrote were certainly common enough; and if they have given place to the women who wish to be taken for women the change is hardly for the better, since any emphasis, either of pride or of shame, laid consciously upon the sex of a writer is not only irritating but superfluous. As Mr Brimley Johnson again and again remarks, a woman's writing is always feminine; it cannot help being feminine; at its best it is most feminine: the only difficulty lies in defining what we mean by feminine. He shows his wisdom not only by advancing a great many suggestions, but also by accepting the fact, upsetting though it is, that women are apt to differ. Still, here are a few attempts: 'Women are born preachers and always work for an ideal.' 'Woman is the moral realist, and her realism is not inspired by any idle ideal of art, but of sympathy with life.'[7] For all her learning, 'George Eliot's outlook remains thoroughly emotional and feminine'.[8] Women are humorous and satirical rather than imaginative. They have a greater sense of emotional purity than men, but a less alert sense of honour.

No two people will accept without wishing to add to and qualify these attempts at a definition, and yet no one will admit that he can possibly mistake a novel written by a man for a novel written by a woman. There is the obvious and enormous difference of experience in the first place; but the essential difference lies in the fact not that men describe battles and women the birth of children, but that each sex describes itself. The first words in which either a man or a woman is described are generally enough to determine the sex of the writer; but though the absurdity of a woman's hero or of a man's heroine is universally recognised, the sexes show themselves extremely quick at detecting each other's faults. No one can deny the authenticity of a Becky Sharp or of a Mr Woodhouse.[9] No doubt the desire and the capacity to criticise the other sex had its share in deciding women to write novels, for indeed that particular vein of comedy has been but slightly worked, and promises great richness. Then again, though men are the best judges of men and women of women, there is a side of each sex which is known only to the other, nor does this refer solely to the relationship of love. And finally (as regards this review at least) there rises for consideration the very difficult question of the difference between the man's and the woman's view of what constitutes the importance of any subject. From this spring not only marked differences of plot and incident, but infinite differences in selection, method and style.

1 – A review in the *TLS*, 17 October 1918, (Kp C127) of *The Women Novelists* (W. Collins Sons & Co. Ltd, 1918) by R. Brimley Johnson. Reprinted: *CW*.

2 – Frances Burney (1752–1840), later Madame d'Arblay, author of *Evelina* (1778), *Cecilia* (1782), *Camilla* (1796), and *The Wanderer* (1814); she was the daughter of Dr Burney, the musician and historian of music. (See also 'Dr Burney's Evening Party', V *VW Essays* and *CR2*.)
3 – Jane Austen (1775–1817); Charlotte Brontë (1816–55).
4 – Brimley Johnson, 'A Study in Fine Art (Jane Austen ... 1775–1817)', p. 68.
5 – *Ibid.*, 'A Professional Woman (George Eliot 1819–1880)', p. 210; the source of these accusations is not given.
6 – *Ibid.*, 'A Picture of Youth', p. 53; the observation arises in a discussion of Dr Johnson's influence on Fanny Burney, who, he says, 'wrote Johnsonese fluently, and thereby mined her natural powers. We cannot estimate, by her foolishness, the influence of the Dictator.'
7 – *Ibid.*, 'A Professional Woman', p. 211; p. 207; both slightly adapted.
8 – *Ibid.*, p. 212.
9 – Becky Sharp and Mr Woodhouse, characters respectively in *Vanity Fair* (1847–8) by W. M. Thackeray and *Emma* (1816) by Jane Austen.

Valery Brussof

If we had no means of knowing that this book was the work of a Russian writer, should we guess from something indefinable in the quality of the writer's mind, from his style and his point of view, that he was at any rate not English? We think it very doubtful. Valery Brussof is, so Mr Graham tells us, 'a sort of Mediterraneanised Russian, with greater affinities in France and Italy than in his native land';[2] and besides, judging from this book of short stories, he is not a great writer: he does not hint at something more than he can state, or imply a whole of which he is only a part. Yet, though one could find his match for power within these islands, he has a quality which distinguishes him from the mass of good story-writers, in that he has a point of view. He has expressed his belief that 'there is no fixed boundary between the world of reality and that of the imagination, between the dreaming and the waking world, life and fantasy';[3] and the stories in the present volume all more or less give shape to his notion that the things commonly held to be visionary may be real, while the reality may equally well be a phantom. In England this train of thought is certainly not unknown in fiction; but we are apt to relegate it, a little nervously perhaps, to certain writers who make a study of the supernatural and by divorcing it from normal life envelop it in an atmosphere of emotional mysticism. Brussof's method is the exact opposite of this. As Mr Graham points out, he 'is not emotionally convinced of the truth of his writing, but wilfully persistent, affirming unreality intellectually and defending his conception with a sort of masculine impressionism'.[4]

Stated as he states it with hard intellectual power, there is no reason to question the truth of his assertion that the most vivid part of many lives is spent in a region invisible to the eyes of the rest of the world. The little Roman girl Maria, for instance, spent the greater part of her life dreaming that she was a reincarnation of Rhea Silvia, until she believed it so completely that she drowned herself in the Tiber; another woman lives her true life in communication with her own reflection in a mirror; a third endows the pens and papers in a stationer's shop with the qualities of living creatures, and loves them accordingly. In the literal and urgent way in which Brussof pursues his search through these shades there are signs that remind us that he comes of the race which approaches such subjects with magnificent seriousness and without sentimentality. Rather than invoke a supernatural power or any sensational agency, he explains these queer obsessions on the part of his characters by telling us that they were known to be weak-minded people or were actually confined to lunatic asylums. To doubt whether you are awake or dreaming, to be unable to decide whether you are real or a reflection, to get more pleasure from what you imagine than from what is true, is to be mad. But Brussof saw, of course, that this is no explanation at all. 'Is not our craziness,' he makes his Roman lovers ask, 'better than the reasonable life of other people?'[5] How does it differ, and who is to decide, after all, which things are real, which are unreal, what constitutes sanity and insanity?

But although it is interesting to find how firmly and even prosaically this creed is held by a mind which is neither emotional nor mystical, the theme has no special artistic merit, and easily becomes a formula which is not more interesting than any other. On the other hand, the stories which deal with the borderland between sanity and insanity are of far greater value, if only because they are more subtly graded and do not end in the convenient *cul-de-sac* of the mad house. They hint at least at the strange balancing and checking of dreams and realities that goes on in the minds of those who are able only by semi-conscious adjustments to behave in the same way as other people. There is the case of the old tramp who has stolen the bust of a woman's head because it reminded him of a woman he had once loved. He is asked whether he will not attempt to get an acquittal, and he answers, 'But why? . . . isn't it just the same where I shall think about Nina – in a doss-house or in a prison? . . . One thing worries me ⟨he adds⟩ What if Nina never existed?'⁶ That is a dilemma which is always being dealt with by the mind: what is reality, and why are we so eager about things that are created for the most part chiefly by our own imaginations? Brussof does no more, and perhaps is unable to do more, than hint at the irrational element which, when we come to examine them, is so profoundly mixed with the most rational desires of ordinary people. But the fact that he has chosen to shift the weight of interest from the beaten track to this obscure and nebulous region of the mind's territory certainly makes him very well worth reading.

1 – A review in the *TLS*, 24 October 1918, (Kp c128) of *The Republic of the Southern Cross and Other Stories* . . . with an introduction by Stephen Graham (Constable & Co. Ltd, 1918) by Valery Brussof (1873–1924).
2 – Brussof, intro. p. v.
3 – *Ibid.*, p. vi, quoting Brussof's preface to the second edition of his *The Axis of the Earth*, publication date untraced.
4 – *Ibid.*, p. xi.
5 – *Ibid.*, 'Rhea Silver', p. 128, which has: 'And is not . . .'
6 – *Ibid.*, 'The Marble Bust: a tramp's story', p. 40, which has: 'Only one thing . . .'; and continues: '. . . existed, and it was merely my poor mind, weakened by alcohol, which invented the whole story of this love whilst I was looking at the little marble head?'

'The Candle of Vision'

The reader may perhaps remember the experience of reading Thomas à Kempis, or *The Love Letters of a Portuguese Nun*² precociously before he was of an age to understand either religion or love. He will remember the inarticulate thunder of the words drumming so persistently and remorselessly upon the immature understanding that at length the book was thrown away not so much in boredom as a kind of exasperated humility. Occasionally *The Candle of Vision* produces the same desperate sense of obtuseness, as it reiterates passionately a belief which remains just beyond the doors of our perception. 'A. E.' has constant experience of certain spiritual states which are as remote from the ordinary person as the religious ecstasies of a saint are remote from a child. He is able by the exercise of his will to bring about some mental enlightenment in which perceptions and visions appear to him and dictate a different reading of life and a different relationship with other human beings. In the present book he desires, as he says, 'to be precise';[3] to analyse these experiences psychologically, and to induce others to make the same attempt.

All such revelations are at the present time bound to be inconclusive, to be contradictory, to make use of language which is highly metaphorical, and to be almost as unsatisfying as they are rich in suggestions. Where there is no argument and no proof one can only by quotation hint vaguely at the line 'A.E.' takes through the crowd of his spiritual experiences. At about the age of sixteen or seventeen 'the mysterious life quickening within my life'[4] began for him. Magical lights dawned and faded in him, as they do, he believes, in every one of us. He wished to obtain mastery over them, and for this purpose set himself the task of concentrating his mind upon some mental object, 'so that not for a moment, not for an instant, would the concentration slacken ... Five minutes of this effort will at first leave us trembling as at the close of a laborious day.'[5] The habit of concentration having been won, he found himself in possession of a power of immense force for good or for evil.

But the ancients who taught us to gain this intensity taught it but as a preliminary to a meditation ... The meditation they urged on us has been explained as 'the inexpressible yearning of the inner man to go out into the infinite'. But the Infinite we would enter is living. It is the ultimate being of us. Meditation is a fiery brooding on that majestical Self. We imagine ourselves into Its vastness. We conceive ourselves as mirroring Its infinitudes, as moving in all things, as living in all beings, in earth, water, air, fire, aether ... We have imagined ourselves into this pitiful dream of life. By imagination and will we re-enter true being, becoming that we conceive of. On that path of fiery brooding I entered.[6]

Then there follow the dreams and the visions, the sudden illuminations of the text of a book, the cathedral filled with ancient worshippers, the spectral airship with its crew of prehistoric voyagers, scenes from the unknown lives of strangers – dreams and visions without end, and yet to what purpose? 'A. E.' will have it that the professed psychologists have been drawn from the ranks of the naturally unimaginative, and that their visions are caused neither by memories nor by the suppressed impulses and desires to which modern writers so confidently ascribe them. They come from outside, because, to use the inevitable metaphors, our minds are leaky boats upon the deep sea, cloudy panes obscuring the light, imperfect instruments for the conveyance of divine harmony; and step by step we proceed to spin round in the Dervish dance of unintelligible communion with the essential, the divine, the spirit of the universe, or whatever we choose to call it. That dance may be to us unintelligible, but we can witness the gyrations of 'A. E.' not only without a smile, but with confidence that for him the ceremony is sacred as well as absorbing.

There lies the value of his book as a record of ardent though stumbling conviction. But 'A. E.' does not escape what appears to be the inevitable penalty of any psychic experience, whereby it seems to be better, higher, more enlightened than any other; so that the world must be altered in accordance with it, and other minds must share the same experiences and come to the same conclusions. But let us imagine ourselves in that gaslit office where 'A. E.' spent some years of his boyhood, 'little heaps of paper mounting up before me'[7] and quick people flitting about with feverish faces and voices. One of his trances would come upon him, and he would find himself on a remote steppe, or exalted into communion with the spirits in a region of clouds and stars. Suppose, however, that this excursion had been not into the remote and invisible, but into the mind of the clerk, with his wrinkled face and blinking eyes, who sat beside him. According to some of us, that would have been a more exalted, difficult and imaginative affair altogether, a method no less true than the other of taking one's way out 'into the infinite'.[8] The drawback, as these papers perhaps show, of indulging too unreservedly in contact with the disembodied spirit is that it tends to become a monotonous process, lacking the humour and passion that diversify human intercourse, and too apt to end in a rapture of egotistic exaltation. 'A. E.'s' book helps to explain the curious transparency of modern Irish literature. But it is a mistake to read 'A.E's' book as if it were merely literature, and not to recognise the fact that in spite of difficulty and obscurity he has conveyed to us a fresh sense of the illimitable and inexplicable faculties which lie undisciplined and only half realised within the human mind.

1 – A review in the TLS, 31 October 1918, (Kp c129) of *The Candle of Vision* (Macmillan & Co., Ltd, 1918) by A. E., pseudonym of George William Russell (1867–1935), Irish poet, painter and mystic – also a man of more mundane affairs, who edited the *Irish Homestead*, 1904–23, and worked for the Irish Agricultural Society.

2 – Thomas à Kempis (1380–1471), German Augustinian monk, traditionally considered the author of the great devotional work on the soul's progress to perfection, *De Imitatione Christi*. Marianna Alcofcorado (1640–1723), the Portuguese nun whose letters have been published in numerous editions.
3 – A.E., 'The Many-Coloured Land', p. 27, which has: 'Spiritual moods are difficult to express and cannot be argued over, but the workings of the imagination may well be spoken of, and need precise and minute investigation.'
4 – *Ibid.*, 'Retrospect', p. 4.
5 – *Ibid.*, 'Meditation', p. 21.
6 – *Ibid.*, p. 23, which has: 'But that Infinite'.
7 – *Ibid.*, 'The Earth Breath', p. 10.
8 – See n. 6.

'Abraham Lincoln'

When upon page 57 of this play, Mr Drinkwater quotes Shakespeare,[2] a curious thing happens – or happened in one particular case. Instead of straining itself to visualise deal tables and top hats the mind begins with alacrity to conjure up cloud-capp'd towers and gorgeous palaces; as if a top hat were harder to imagine than a palace, as if clouds were our natural element. We are not therefore so foolish as to draw the conclusion that Shakespeare is a better dramatist than Mr Drinkwater, but only that Shakespeare's plays can be read, and we believe that *Abraham Lincoln* needs to be seen upon the stage to be seen at its best.

The first act represents the parlour of Lincoln's house at Springfield in the year 1860. Abraham Lincoln comes in wearing a 'greenish and crumpled top hat';[3] his pockets are stuffed with documents; a map of the United States hangs upon the wall; there is a cupboard which, when he looks to find a bottle in it, is found choked with papers instead. The mind is uncomfortably split up into perceiving that all this would tell upon the stage, and in realising that for some reason it is an obstacle to imagination upon the printed page. These cupboards and top hats are too real and prominent for their importance, just as we cannot help feeling that the dialogue is too thin and spare for its importance. The realistic dramatist is always faced with the difficulty that he can only allow his characters to say the barest abstract of what is in their minds; and for the dialogue to be further denuded of its scenery, deprived of its actors, and read as we read a book, with a mind hungry for a thousand details and comments which cannot possibly be put into the dialogue, is a test that, perhaps, Ibsen and Tchehov[4] alone of the moderns survive.

Mr Drinkwater is of course too serious and honest a writer for nothing to survive; a readable and interesting statement of the Northern case survives; but it is much like hearing played by one instrument – and that a piano – a piece which demands a whole orchestra of brass and strings. One seems to perceive long empty spaces when the piano keeps on strumming its homely chords in the bass and the melody is absent. President Lincoln comes out speaking good sense, good morality, and tolerable prose, but we wait in vain for any proof that besides the simplicity of genius he also possessed the inspiration. He is shown to be a very homely, uncouth, plain-spoken, sensible man; and when the great moments – such as the pardon of the boy sentry, or the last speech from the box at the theatre – arrive, they read, at least, with marked flatness. 'There, there; I believe you when you tell me that you couldn't keep awake. I'm going to trust you and send you back to your regiment.'[5] That sounds as if Mr Drinkwater were determined to prove that one of the remarkable things about Lincoln was that where smaller men said something striking he said something dull. But in the theatre the cumulative effect of sense, truth, honesty, and courage may have lent these speeches a force which it is impossible to perceive when we read them.

1 – A review in the *TLS*, 31 October 1918, (Kp C130) of *Abraham Lincoln: A Play* (Sidgwick & Jackson, 1918) by John Drinkwater (1882–1937). First produced in 1918 at the Birmingham Repertory Theatre, of which Drinkwater was the original manager, the play transferred in 1919 to the Lyric Theatre, Hammersmith. There it ran for over a year and, according to the *DNB*, 'established Drinkwater's fame at a blow'.
2 – Drinkwater, sc. iv, p. 57; Lincoln asks Slaney to read from *The Tempest*, IV, i, ll. 148ff: Prospero: 'Our revels now are ended . . .;' and himself concludes the extract speaking ll. 156–8: 'We are such stuff/ As dreams are made on . . .'
3 – *Ibid.*, sc. i, p. 11, stage directions.
4 – Henrik Ibsen (1828–1906); Anton Chekhov (1860–1904).
5 – Drinkwater, sc. v, p. 63, Lincoln addressing the sentry William Scott, 'a boy of twenty', court-martialled for sleeping on duty.

Mr Howells on Form

When Mr Howells[2] says that he is not going to define what he means by form in fiction, since it is 'one of those elusive things which you can feel much better than you can say',[3] we applaud his wisdom, and accept his decision. There may be truth as well as indolence in the remark that the less we seek to define art the more chance there is that we shall be able to produce it. At any rate let us leave these questions to be settled once in a generation, and meanwhile let us flatter ourselves that by continuing to frame tentative outlines of belief, always shifting and modifying their terms as we read, we are providing material for the great critic to build with when he comes.

Form, Mr Howells goes on to say, is very rare in English fiction, so that the public will probably not understand what he means when he singles out this quality in the novels of Mr Merrick for special praise. 'Our public might very well enjoy form,' he adds, 'if it could once be made to imagine it.'[4] Here we think he does us some injustice. We need neither persuasion nor force to make us enjoy the form of Pope or Peacock, Jane Austen or Gray;[5] one might go farther and say that half our pleasure in reading the writers of the eighteenth century comes from the delight we take in their sense of form. In the case of the Victorians it is more difficult; in the case of our own generation it is almost impossible to see that such a thing as form exists. But it seems likely that this is in part the result of trying to squeeze our voluminous moderns into the finely shaped mould of *The Rape of the Lock*, or of the *Princesse de Clèves*.[6] When we talk of form in the loose fashion confessed above we probably mean more than anything the form not of the Elizabethans but of the eighteenth century. It is very natural. Who, after all, can resist the fascination of their writers or refuse at some time or another to make such sacrifices as may enable him to attempt at least to write what would have satisfied their ears? For perhaps the most striking of their qualities is one that seems to demand some sacrifice: it is their power to omit. Take down, for instance, the letters of Gray, freely written to intimate friends, and you will be struck by the way in which almost nothing is said and almost everything is suggested. He has to write a letter of condolence:

I break in upon you at a moment, when we least of all are permitted to disturb our friends, only to say, that you are daily and hourly present to my thoughts. If the worst be not yet past, you will neglect and pardon me: but if the last struggle be over; if the poor object of your long anxieties be no longer sensible to your kindness, or to her own sufferings, allow me (at least in idea, for what could I do, were I present, more than this?) to sit by you in silence, and pity from my heart not her, who is at rest, but you, who lose her. May He, who made us, the Master of our pleasures and of our pains, preserve and support you! Adieu.[7]

Eloquence might embellish that theme for page upon page and yet in the end the few formal words would still say more. In contemplating them one is led to imagine an art of suggestion, a shorter, denser, richer form of literature refusing to waste itself in repetition or explanation, an art recognising the ludicrous incapacity of words to repeat even a simple emotion exactly, but the magical power of the right words to do more – to abstract and exalt it.

But the sense of form which seems to have prevailed in the eighteenth century may be much more perceptible to us than to them. It may be that they stand at precisely the right degree of distance from us to appear in the light most becoming to their peculiar qualities. The repose, the distinction, the reserve of their manner are precious to us – enviable, almost incredible. Perhaps we endow them with more of substance than really belongs to them; perhaps we admire them partly because we find them so easy to understand, so definite, so assured that their version of life and of art is the right one. Such admiration on our part is a tribute to the completeness with which they triumphed, imposing shape upon the tumult of their material, so that after more than a century their masterpieces appear to us shaped with a flawless simplicity, as if the task had been easier then, the material less complex and stubborn.

But, granting them every grace and perfection of art, did they not perhaps leave out too much, and sacrifice so devoutly at the shrine of form that some very important qualities were excluded along with those that they rightly judged to be superfluous? Perhaps we feel the form of the eighteenth century so sharply because it is not merely beyond our reach but utterly opposed to our temper. When Mr Howells speaks of the neglect or absence of form in modern fiction we should more hopefully assert that it is everywhere scattered about us but that we are as yet unable to see it. Whether this particular quality is ever visible to the generation that is engaged in creating it seems very doubtful. We cannot recognise among ourselves a conception of the art of fiction such as Jane Austen seems to have held so surely and unquestioningly; we are only now beginning to make out with hesitation and difficulty the form concealed in what still appears to many the formlessness of Mr Hardy's novels.[8] It is not that life is more complex or difficult now than at any other period, but that for each generation the point of interest shifts, the old form puts the emphasis on the wrong places, and in searching out the severed and submerged parts of what to us constitutes form we seem to be throwing fragments together at random and disdaining the very thing that we are trying our best to win from chaos.

1 – A review in the *TLS*, 14 November 1918, (Kp C131) of *The Actor-Manager . . .* With an Introduction by W. D. Howells (Hodder & Stoughton, 1918) by Leonard Merrick (1864–1939). The work was originally published in 1898. See also 'Mr Merrick's Novels' above.

2 – William Dean Howells (1837–1920), American novelist, playwright, critic and editor. See also '*The Son of Royal Langbrith*', *I VW Essays*.

3 – Merrick, intro., p. v, which continues: 'better than you can say; to define it would be like defining charm in a woman, or poetry in a verse'.

4 – *Ibid.*, from a longer sentence.

5 – Alexander Pope (1688–1744); Thomas Love Peacock (1785–1866); Jane Austen (1775–1817); Thomas Gray (1716–71).

6 – Alexander Pope, *The Rape of the Lock* (1714); Mme La Fayette, *La Princesse de Clèves* (1678).

7 – Thomas Gray to William Mason, 28 March 1767, no. ccxcvi in vol. iii of *The Letters of Thomas Gray. Including the correspondence of Gray and Mason*. Ed. Duncan C. Tovey (3 vols., G. Bell & Sons Ltd, 1900–12), which has 'you. Adieu!' William Mason (1724–97) was a poet and a fellow of Pembroke College, Cambridge; his wife Mary, *née* Sherman, had died of consumption at Clifton on the previous day.

8 – Thomas Hardy (1840–1928); for VW's views on his novels, see 'Half of Thomas Hardy', *IV VW Essays*, and 'The Novels of Thomas Hardy', *V VW Essays* and CR 2.

Bad Writers

Perhaps it is unnecessary to feel a slight pang of commiseration for Solomon Eagle when he talks of papers 'contributed weekly, without intermission, to the *New Statesman* since April, 1913'.[2] But it is difficult when a writer hopes that he has produced a book to read in 'without tedium, for ten minutes before one goes to sleep'[3] not to feel slightly ashamed of oneself, as a single head of the many-headed beast, for not having gone to sleep hours ago. Here we have kept him at it, flattering us, wheedling us, telling us funny stories, never boring us, or making us think, or making us cry, for five years and a half; and we are still awake, and as exacting and capricious as a pampered Sultan sunk among cushions on a divan. Books of essays somehow have a tendency to make us feel autocratic and oriental. We are conscious of retinues of slaves. Numbers of them have had their heads cut off and been thrown into the moat for failing to please us already; but Solomon Eagle amuses the Sultan; he has made the Sultan laugh; therefore we grant him permission to go on living on condition that he makes us laugh every night before we go to sleep for ever and ever.

Solomon Eagle has made a discovery which bids fair to enable him to fulfil this condition very easily: he has discovered that English literature is funny. On hearing this, the well-read reader runs over the scale from Chaucer to Robert Bridges in the space of a second or two and raps out something about Falstaff or Mrs Gamp. Anyone can do that. But who save Solomon Eagle, can begin the scale with John Lyly and end it with Mrs Barclay?[4] Have you any conception of what he calls 'the beauties of badness'? Are you aware that 'peculiar poetic treasures'[5] lie uncollected and unappreciated in every bookshop in the Charing Cross Road? Do you, in short, know the look of literature the wrong side out? From a brief and increasingly anxious inspection of one's bookcase the probability seems to be that one knows nothing whatever about it. There are Shakespeare and Shelley and Keats and Matthew Arnold and Gibbon and Walter Pater – a rabbit-run through the ages – a path absolutely dusty with the traffic of culture. The sole possibility of badness is provided by the works of one's friends, and that hope fades soon enough. Which of them would have the imaginative abandonment to write —

> I have found thee there, in a world of rest,
> In the fair sweet gardens of sunlit bliss,
> Where the sibilant sound of an Angel's kiss
> Is the sanctioned seal of a Holy quest?[6]

Which of them has sufficient passion to make his hero speak thus over the telephone to an unknown lady? 'Speak to me again,' he said, 'you, who spoke to me last night. Speak to me again. What wait I for? I wait for you! Just now – in my utter loneliness, in my empty solitude – I wait for you.'[7] They lack passion; they lack abandonment.

These are by no means the best of Solomon Eagle's discoveries; for the best bad writers often take a page at a stride, but even from them you can judge, perhaps, the sort of quality that bad literature possesses. It is the quality of unfettered imagination. Bad books are written in a state of boiling passion, with a complete certainty of inspiration. Language and grammar are impediments which are disregarded if they become troublesome; and thus you get in the best bad writers that sense of quickly following the half-articulate words of nightmare which is so exciting or so bewildering, as the case may be. The process is not one of thought but one of intuition, and as in this they seem to follow such great examples as Scott, if we are afraid to claim Shakespeare also, let us inquire into the reason of their badness. Why do they invariably suggest not only the incoherence but the unreality of nightmare? The bad writer seems to possess a predominance of the day-dreaming power, he lives all day long in that region of artificial light where every factory girl becomes a duchess, where, if the truth be told, most people spend a few moments every day revenging themselves upon reality. The bad books are not the mirrors but the vast distorted shadows of life; they are a refuge, a form of revenge. Should you feel, however, that these reflections are tending to become melancholy or dull, you have only to shuffle Solomon Eagle's pages and make your choice of something more pleasant to think about. Shall we consider whether Wordsworth, the divine poet, was a dull man?[8] Shall we ask who wrote the worst sentence in the English language? Shall we re-write it in the manner of Henry James,[9] and so dreaming fall asleep?

1 – A review in the *TLS*, 21 November 1918, (Kp C132) of *Books in General* (Martin Secker, 1918) by Solomon Eagle (i.e. J. C. Squire). For VW's private opinion of the 'omnivorous & callous throated Eagle . . . that cheap & thin blooded creature, (I speak of his journalism) & his methods of running the paper, his lack of power judgment & competence', see *I VW Diary*, 5 April 1918. She did not herself contribute to the literary pages of the *New Statesman* under Squire's editorship, but LW did.

See also 'Parodies' and 'Imitative Essays', above.

2 – Squire, Pref., p. 7; John Collings Squire (1884–1958), poet and critic, was literary editor of the *New Statesman* from 1913 to 1919, when he left to found the *London Mercury*; he was succeeded at the *New Statesman* by Desmond MacCarthy ('Affable Hawk'). Squire issued two further selections from his 'Books in General' column, in 1919 and in 1921.

3 – *Ibid.*, p. 7.

4 – For Squire on John Lyly (1554?–1606), author of *Euphues: the Anatomy of Wit*

(1578) and *Euphues and his England* (1580), *ibid.*, 'The Worst Style in the World', pp. 214–20; and for Mrs (Florence Louisa) Barclay (1862–1921), author of romances, including *The Rosary* (1909), and *The White Ladies of Worcester* (1917), *ibid.*, 'Mrs Barclay Sees It Through', pp. 79–85.
5 – *Ibid.*, 'The Beauties of Badness', p. 48.
6 – *Ibid.*, p. 45; the author is unidentified.
7 – *Ibid.*, 'Mrs Barclay Sees It Through', p. 82.
8 – *Ibid.*, 'Wordsworth's Personal Dullness', pp. 174–9.
9 – *Ibid.*, 'Henry James's Obscurity', pp. 179–84.

Trafficks and Discoveries

Most people have only time to ask whether history is readable, not to seek further whether it is true. But in one sense the most readable histories are also the most true, in so far as their vivid and spirited qualities arise from the force with which the historian himself has believed in his narrative; and perhaps no one can write with fire and conviction unless he has got hold of some form of the truth. It is partly this sense of conviction, partly the great artistic skill with which, having decided upon his interpretation, he shapes his narrative in conformity with it that makes Froude among the most readable of historians. His history was, as he said that it ought to be, 'as interesting as a novel'.[2] His account of the English seamen of the sixteenth century tells itself rather than is told. The knots of the narrative dissolve in his fingers as he touches them. The figures of the Queen, of Philip of Spain, of Drake, of Medina Sidonia[3] and the rest, stand out as clear-cut in feature and as inevitably placed in relation to each other as if Froude spun the story from his own imagination. It has the force and directness of fiction. He was helped, of course, by those famous prejudices and opinions which colour all his writing. He believed fervently in the English Reformation; he believed that the English seamen were its most sturdy disciples; he believed emphatically that Drake, Hawkins,[4] and their fellows were the best and bravest of mankind; and he came forth not as an apologist for their deeds, but as the champion of heroes who needed a Homer to sing them in strains befitting their merit. For all these reasons the story, as he told it, would have been a good one, had it not been intrinsically one of the best in the world. Nothing is lacking that poet, novelist, or historian could desire. In the first place, there is the sea, washing the shores of unknown lands; then, for adversary, there is the pride of the Spaniard, his mastery still undisputed; the prize itself is virgin land of untold capacity, or caraques heavy with bars of silver and gold; the spirit which inspires the whole is love of religious freedom and love of country; and the catastrophe, as Froude develops it with superb dramatic power, is the complete overthrow of the usurper by a handful of private gentlemen on the threshold of victory. The very titles of his lectures might serve for the books of an epic poem, as grand, so Froude declared, as the *Odyssey*.[5]

The heroic figures which Froude has extracted and shaped are not, however, in the least visionary. Indeed, in the shaping process they lose inevitably something of the humanity which we discern in them obscurely engaged with their forgotten comrades upon those trafficks and discoveries which are recorded in the volumes of Hakluyt.[6] Their destiny was not always by any means so patently to the glory of God and the confusion of the Spaniard as would appear from the vantage-ground of the historian. They had, as we have, a mixture of motives in their undertakings, among which the desire to justify the Protestant faith was not always to the fore. But what they lose in symmetry, when studied in the rough, they gain in richness, depth and variety. They gain to such an extent, indeed, that it seems worthwhile to exhort those who have not read to read, those who do not possess to buy, the principal navigations, trafficks and discoveries of the English nation made by sea or overland to the remote and farthest distant quarters of the earth, as Richard Hakluyt, preacher and some-time student of Christ Church, in Oxford, collected and set them forth.

As good a starting-place as another is provided by the letter which Hakluyt drew up in the year 1582, and gave to a friend 'that was sent into Turkey'.[7] Here we have set forth in urgent and eloquent language the great need of establishing a trade between England and the East. The chief English commodity was wool. The English wool is the most fine, most soft, most strong, most durable of any wool in the world, and the least subject of any to the moth, as the old Parliament robes of the king and noble peers plainly testify. If he can find a market for wool, he will give 'an infinite sort of the poor people occasion to pray' for him, since through their misery they were forced to crime and 'daily consumed with the gallows'.[8] Next, the English traveller is to look about him curiously, and, in particular, to make inquiry whether 'Anile that coloureth blue be a "natural commodity of those parts" . . . and if it be compounded of an herb to send the same into this realm by seed or by root in barrels of earth, with all the whole order of sowing, setting, planting, replanting, and with the compounding of the same.'⁹ Needless to say, immortal fame would be his if he could discover a method of producing oil in England, since the method of making it from radish seed has failed. He is reminded how the stock of English commodities has been gradually improved by the adventure and generosity of bygone travellers. Dr Linaker, in the time of Henry VII, brought the damask rose, and lately 'flowers called tulipas' have been introduced from Austria, to say nothing of bull, cow, sheep, swine, horse, mare, cock, hen, and a thousand other beasts and plants, without which 'our life were to be said barbarous'.¹⁰ In short, this journey is not only to bring profit to himself, but to increase knowledge, and, in particular, to benefit the poor 'ready to starve for relief'¹¹ more than by building them almshouses or by giving them lands and goods. Many voices at that time were urging the same plea; and nothing more strikes the imagination than the readiness with which some gentleman from the West Country, perhaps, hears the summons, lays his case before the rich men of his acquaintance, fits out his little band of ships, collects his company, and sets sail, 'having saluted their acquaintance, one his wife, another his children, another his kinsfolk, and another his friends dearer than his kinsfolk'.¹² At Greenwich the courtiers come running out at the news that the ships are in the river; 'the Privy Council looked out of the windows of the Court . . . the ships thereupon discharge their ordnance . . . and the mariners they shouted in such sort that the sky rang again with the noise thereof'.¹³ Considering that the ship in which Drake sailed round the world was no bigger than 'a second-rate yacht of a modern noble lord',¹⁴ and that the voyage was generally a voyage to an unknown land, over seas made dangerous by hostile Spaniards, Portuguese, and French, the solemn leave-taking is accounted for. Well might the mariners walk upon the hatches, climb the shrouds, stand upon the mainyard to wave their friends a last farewell. Many would come back no more; let alone the risk that a wave would swamp the little ship, as happened to Sir Humfrey Gilbert, or that they might be 'congealed and frozen to death', like Sir Hugh Willoughby, or hung up by adverse winds off the coast of Cornwall for a fortnight, until, in their thirst, they licked the muddy water off the deck, as happened to the Earl of Cumberland.¹⁵

There was also the terror of the supernatural. The spiritual atmosphere was very cloudy, though pierced in a manful way by the sense and piety of the sailors. Sea lions, sea serpents, evaporations of fire and whirlpools that cast ships upon shore, 'as Richard Chancellor told me that he had heard Sebastian Cabot report',[16] were at all times possible, and might well be the disguise of the Devil himself. The survivors of some of these early voyages came home to England in such a state that 'Sir William, his father, and my Lady, his mother, knew him not to be their son, until they found a secret mark, which was a wart upon one of his knees'.[17] Significantly, the articles and orders to be observed by the ships often begin with the injunction to lead a holy life on board, and 'serve God twice a day'.[18] Encompassed with such perils and obscurities, they might well have cause to call upon Divine help before the voyage was out. The Divinity may be addressed much as if He were a temporal prince scarcely hidden by the clouds; but their piety is real enough. Down they fall upon their knees before doing battle with the Turkish galleys; the owner of the vessel preaches his sermon, bidding them not repine, nor do as 'the citizens of Bethulia did';[19] after which drums, flutes, and trumpets sound, and the *Three Half Moons* engages eight of the enemies' vessels.

Then stood up one Grove the master, being a comely man, with his sword and target, holding them up in defiance against his enemies ... But chiefly the boatswain showed himself valiant above the rest; for he fared among the Turks like a wood lion; for there was none of them that either could nor durst stand in his face, till at the last there came a shot from the Turks, which brake his whistle asunder, and smote him on the breast, so that he fell down, bidding them farewell and to be of good comfort.[20]

For thirteen years John Fox and his companions served in captivity to the Turks, until, being weary thereof, 'he lift up his bright, shining sword of ten years' rust,'[21] and struck his keeper such a blow that his head clave asunder, the sword which did the deed being claimed by the abbot and monks of Gallipoli and hung for a monument upon their convent walls.

But the hopes and expectations of these adventurers more than counterbalanced their sufferings. There was the chance of the North-West Passage, and gold, perhaps, in the commonest black stone. They went not only to dispose of merchandise, but as ambassadors from the Queen of England, taking a present with them to the sovereign of the land, 'three fair mastiffs', perhaps, 'in coats of red cloth', together with a sonorous letter, 'the paper whereof did smell most fragrantly of camphor and ambergris, and the ink of perfect musk'[22] from Elizabeth herself. Strange and splendid were the ceremonies that the English sailors newly landed from their voyage were invited to behold. They saw the Emperor at Moscow 'sitting in his chair of estate, with his crown on his head and a staff of goldsmith work in his left hand', and beheld 'the great Turk where he sumptuously sate alone'.²³ Marvellous was the richness of the earth and the shapes of the creatures seen, as John Locke saw the elephant, 'not only with my bodily eyes, but much more with the eyes of my mind and spirit'.²⁴

So the different companies established themselves in different quarters of the globe, and lonely little groups of Englishmen began doing trade with the natives, bartering their wool and cloth for wax and tallow in Russia, tempting the African savages to give them ivory and gold in exchange for hawks' bells, horses' tails, hats, and unwrought iron. The letters of instructions sent by merchants in London to their agents, and the agents' replies, abounding in detail and preserving the names of many forgotten adventurers, make as good reading as the more heroic passages which have become famous. But to abstract is idle. The only possible course to take with Hakluyt's voyages, whether you own them in the convenient Everyman edition or in the five quarto volumes published about 1810,²⁵ is to read them through; to read dedications, ambassages, letters, privileges, discourses, advertisements; for only thus will you become possessed of the unity of the whole. Different people write the book, but they have the same outlook, the same manner of speech. Beauty of phrase, astonishing and scattered impartially, is frequent enough; the average of their writing is full of freedom and melody; but beyond that lies what is more difficult to define, something common to them all – an attitude of mind, large, imaginative, unsated. There is a sort of nobleness about them; seen through their eyes, the world appears fresh and flowing, unexplored, and of infinite richness.

1 – A review in the *TLS*, 12 December 1918, (Kp C133) based on *English Seamen in the Sixteenth Century* (Longmans, Green & Co., 1895), and, as stated at the head of the article, 'The Hakluyt's Voyages, Travels, and Discoveries of the English Nation', for which VW used *Hakluyt's Collection of the Early Voyages, Travels and Discoveries of the English Nation. A New Edition, with Additions* (5 vols., R. H. Evans, 1809–12), making certain modifications to the original spelling.

On Saturday, 7 December 1918, she wrote in her diary: 'For some reason, not connected with my virtues I think, I get 2 or even 3 books weekly from the Times, & thus breast one short choppy wave after another. It fills up the time while Night & Day lies dormant . . . I have spent the week (but I was interrupted 2 days, & one cut short by a lunch with Roger) over Hakluyt: who turns out on mature inspection to justify over & over again my youthful discrimination. I write & write; I am rung up & told to stop writing; review must be had on Friday; I typewrite till the messenger from the Times appears; I correct the pages in my bedroom with him sitting over the fire'.

See 'Sir Walter Raleigh' above; 'Trafficks and Discoveries', *I VW Essays*; '*Richard Hakluyt*', *III VW Essays*; 'The Elizabethan Lumber Room', *IV VW Essays* and *CR1*. Reading Notes (MHP, B.2d), reproduced in Appendix I.

2 – The origin of this phrase has not been discovered. James Anthony Froude (1818–94), historian and man of letters, whose *English Seamen* ... consists of lectures originally given at Oxford, where, in 1892, he was appointed regius professor of modern history.

3 – Elizabeth I (1533–1603); Philip II of Spain (1527–98); Sir Francis Drake (1540?–96); Alonso Pérez de Guzmán, duque de Medina Sidonia (1550–1615), who commanded the Spanish Armada.

4 – Sir John Hawkins (1532–95).

5 – Froude, Lecture iv, 'Drake's Voyage Round the World', p. 80. The other lectures are: 'The Sea Cradle of the Reformation'; 'John Hawkins and the African Slave Trade'; 'Sir John Hawkins and Philip the Second'; 'Parties in the State'; 'The Great Expedition to the West Indies'; 'Attack on Cadiz'; 'Sailing of the Armada'; 'Defeat of the Armada'.

6 – Richard Hakluyt (1552?–1616), geographer, educated at Christ Church, Oxford, 1570–4, actively promoted English discovery and colonisation and became a member of the London or South Virginian Company. A one-volume version of *The Principal Navigations* ... first appeared in 1589, and a three-volume edition in 1598–1600.

7 – Evans, vol. ii, 'A brief Remembrance of things to be indevoured at Constantinople, and in other places in Turkie ... drawn by M. Richard Hakluyt of the Middle Temple, and given to a friend that was sent into Turkie 1582', p. 279.

8 – For both quotations, *ibid.*, vol. iii, 'A discourse written by Sir Humphrey Gilbert Knight, to prove a passage by the Northwest to Cathaia and the East Indies', p. 45.

9 – *Ibid.*, vol. ii, 'What you shall do in Turkie, besides the businesse of your Factorship', p. 282, which has: 'And in any wise, if Anile that coloureth blew be a naturall commodity of those parts, and if it be compounded of an herbe, to send the same to this realme by seed or by root in barrell of earth ... compounding of the same, that it may become a naturall commodity in this realme as Woad is, to this end that the high price of forreine Woad (which devoureth yeerely great treasure) may be brought downe.'

10 – For both quotations, *ibid.*, 'Other some things to be remembered', p. 284. Dr Thomas Linacre (1460?–1524), English humanist and physician, founder of the Royal College of Physicians.

11 – *Ibid.*, p. 285.

12 – *Ibid.*, vol. i, 'The booke of the great and mighty Emperor of Russia, and Duke of Muscovia, and of the dominions orders and commodities thereunto belonging; drawn by Richard Chancelour', p. 272.

13–*Ibid.*

14–Froude, 'Drake's Voyage Round the Worlde', p. 107.

15–Sir Humfrey Gilbert (1539?–83). For the quotation regarding Sir Hugh Willoughby (d. 1554), Evans, vol. iii, 'Certaine other reasons, or arguments to proove a passage by the Northwest, learnedly written by M. Richard Willes Gentleman', p. 47. George Clifford, 3rd Earl of Cumberland (1558–1605).

16 – Evans, vol. ii, 'The second voyage to Guinea . . .', p. 478.

17 – *Ibid.*, vol. iii, 'The voyage of M. Hore and divers other gentlemen, to Newfoundland, and Cape Briton, in the yeere 1536 and in the 28 yere of king Henry the 8', p. 169: 'They arrived at S. Ives in Cornewall about the ende of October. From thence they departed unto a certaine castle belonging to Sir John Luttrell, where M. Thomas Buts, and M. Rastall and other Gentlemen of the voyage were very friendly entertained: after that they came to the Earle of Bathe at Bathe, and thence to Bristoll, so to London. M. Buts was so changed in the voyage with hunger and miserie, that Sir William his father and my Lady his mother knew him not to be their sonne, untill they found a secret marke which was a wart upon one of his knees, as hee told me Richard Hakluyt of Oxford himselfe . . .'

18 – E.g., *ibid.*, 'Articles and orders to be observed for the Fleete . . .', p. 106: 'Inprimis, to banish swearing, dice, and card-playing, and filthy conmunication [sic], and to serve God twice a day, with the ordinary service usuall in Churches of England, and to clear the glasse, according to the old order of England.'

19 – *Ibid.*, vol. ii, 'The woorthy enterprise of John Foxe an Englishman in delivering 266. Christians out of captivity of the Turkes at Alexandria, the 3. of Januarie 1577', p. 246.

20 – *Ibid.*, which concludes: 'encouraging them likewise to winne praise by death, rather then to live captives in misery and shame.'

21 – *Ibid.*, p. 248.

22 – For the three mastiffs, *ibid.*, vol. ii, 'The voyage of the Susan of London . . .', p. 291; and for the fragrant letter, *ibid.*, 'A letter written by the most high and mighty Empresse the wife of the Grand Signior Sultan Murad Can to the Queenes Majesty of England, in the yeere of our Lord, 1594', p. 453.

23 – For the Emperor, *ibid.*, vol. i, 'The voyage, wherein Osep Napea the Moscovite Ambassadour returned home . . .', p. 352, which has 'goldsmiths worke'; and for the Turk, *ibid.*, vol. ii, 'The Voyage of the Susan . . .', p. 291.

24 – *Ibid.*, vol. ii, 'The second voyage to Guinea set out by Sir George Barne, Sir John Yorke, Thomas Lok, Anthonie Hickman and Edward Castelin, in the yeere 1554. The Captaine whereof was M. John Lok', p. 474: 'At this last voyage was brought from Guinea the head of an Elephant, of such huge bignesse, that onely the bones or cranew thereof, beside the nether jaw and great tusks, weighed about two hundred weight, and was as much as I could well lift from the ground . . . This head divers have seene in the house of the worthy marchant Sir Andrew Judde, where also I saw it, and beheld it, not only with my bodily eyes, but much more with the eyes of my mind and spirit, considering the worke, the cunning and wisedome of the workemaister: without which consideration, the sight of such strange

and wonderfull things may rather seeme curiosities, then profitable contemplations.'
25 – *The Principal Navigations, Voyages, Traffiques and Discoveries of the English Nation* ... With an introduction by John Masefield (8 vols., Everyman's Library, 1907).

'The Three Black Pennys'

The obvious thing to say about Mr Joseph Hergesheimer's novel *The Three Black Pennys* is that it possesses form as undoubtedly as a precious stone shaped to fit exactly into a band of gold possesses form. The comparison with something hard, lustrous and concrete is not altogether fanciful. In recollection, the last sentence being read, the reader's impression of the book as a whole assumes something of the smooth solidity of a well-fashioned gem. When the last sentence is finished nothing vague or superfluous is left to blur the outline; the substance is all neatly packed into the form, rounded off, disposed of, completed. The sense of conclusiveness is so satisfactory, and also so rare, that we could enjoy it separately from any feeling of pity or pleasure aroused by the fortunes of the characters, as a blind man might enjoy the shape of a stone though unable to see its colour.

Mr Hergesheimer's story, the story of a family owning a great ironworks in Pennsylvania from the middle of the eighteenth century to modern times, had need of this shaping if only to compress it within a volume of moderate size. Each of the Pennys whom he has selected to represent his theme stands out from the rest of his family because the Welsh blood mixed with the English blood centuries ago asserts itself in him. It produces, Howat's father says, 'a solitary living, dark lot. Unamenable to influence, reflect their country, I suppose, but lovers of music ... it sinks entirely out of sight for two or three and sometimes four generations; and then appears solid, in one individual, as unslacked as the pure, original thing.'[2] It appears in Howat; in his grandson Jasper; in Jasper's grandson Howat, the last of the Pennys. The black Pennys did not take to life easily; there was something unmalleable in their composition which stayed unmelted in the common furnace. They did not run into the ordinary social mould. In their obdurate ways of impressing themselves upon other people they more resembled the great hammer at Myrtle Forge, persistently and relentlessly beating out iron, than the iron itself. 'If the hammer stops,' Howat told his wife in the eighteenth century, 'all this, the Pennys, stop, too.'[3] The last Penny was unable even to make one of those marriages which his ancestors had achieved with so much difficulty; the hammer had stopped in his father's time; the Pennys made iron no longer.

But the story cannot, as this summary might suggest, be read as a discourse upon heredity with a satiric motive; Mr Hergesheimer is too much of an artist to insist that human life is capable of any such forced solution. If, curiously enough, a certain type of character occurs at intervals in the same family, it occurs as a blue or a green might repeat itself beautifully in a pattern. The beat of the great hammer recurs too; when it stops we know that something more important has ceased; the raccoon hunt repeats itself; for, as we began by saying, Mr Hergesheimer has a strong sense of form, and these are some of the more obvious devices used by him to hold his story together, to secure continuity, to bind his gem in a circle of gold. An attentive reader will discover others less obvious. Whether he has succeeded equally in another direction is more open to doubt. The entrances and exits of the Pennys and of the women allotted them as partners are so carefully timed and regulated that they would tend to be mechanical were they not more obviously pictorial. There is no room here for license or for the larger sweep and expressiveness of human character. Perhaps Mr Hergesheimer is a little hampered in this direction by his keen susceptibility to material objects. He handles, for the concrete term is justified, his blue decanters and cut-glass decanters, holds them to the light, relishes their grain and texture with a gusto which is sometimes excessive. He cannot resist observing. We can remember no novel in which women's dresses are more frequently and carefully described. This is not done, however, to give atmosphere or local colour, but because the beauty of still life makes part of the writer's vision. We owe to this individual gift some remarkable scenes at the forge and descriptions of American landscape. It is one of the qualities that make the *Black Pennys* an unusual novel, to be read slowly, thoughtfully and with a sense of luxury.

1 – A review in the *TLS*, 12 December 1918, (Kp C134) of *The Three Black Pennys. A Novel* (William Heinemann, 1918) by Joseph Hergesheimer (1880–1954). On 7 December 1918, VW wrote in her diary: 'No sooner had I done a little type setting,

& ruled off the hour & a half before dinner in which to read my distinguished American novelist [Hergesheimer] recommended by Mr Galsworthy [unelucidated], than Lottie admitted Sydney Waterlow.'

See also '*Java Head*', '*Gold and Iron*', 'The Pursuit of Beauty' and 'Pleasant Stories', *III VW Essays*. Reprinted: *CW*.

2 – Hergesheimer, I, 'The Furnace', ch. III, pp. 30–1.

3 – *Ibid.*, ch. VII, p. 92; Howat Penny to Mrs Ludowika Winscombe, whom, at this stage in the story, he has yet to marry, her husband being still alive.

A View of the Russian Revolution

Mr Hugh Walpole[2] in his short foreword to this volume seems to us to be doing its writer rather a disservice than a service. Invoking that blessed word 'atmosphere', he sets out a claim which, we think, Miss Buchanan could hardly wish to put forward on her own behalf. 'I believe,' says Mr Walpole, 'that I am speaking without any exaggeration when I say that this book of Miss Buchanan's is the first attempt of any writer in any language to give to the world a sense of the *atmosphere* of Russia under the shock and terror of those world-shaking events', the war and the Revolution. Mr Walpole explains that by 'atmosphere' he means in this connection the general outlook upon events of the sort of people whom in English we should refer to as 'the man in the street'.[3] In our opinion this frank and vivacious diary of 'Sir Buchanan's'[4] daughter cannot claim to represent this outlook. The book sets out to be an account of Petrograd in the last four years as it appeared to a young lady moving in the diplomatic 'set', and the result does not pass beyond this modest aim.

At the outbreak of the war Miss Buchanan volunteered as a nurse in one of the Petrograd hospitals; in order to discharge her duties more efficiently she set to work to learn Russian – a study in which, we gather from the few sentences quoted in this book, she is not yet very proficient. The first half of her book describes in vivid fashion the outbreak of the war and Miss Buchanan's and her friends' experiences with the wounded, the refugees and their children – '"Meriel, his head was absolutely alive," she said, with a little gasp'[5] – and there are also descriptions of the Russian Court and its ceremonies as Miss Buchanan saw them. The following passage is a typical example of her method; it has the merits and defects of descriptions which rest wholly upon shrewd but sympathetic personal observation:

Looking back at my diary, I see that it was this winter also that I met General Polivanov, the new Minister of War. We dined yesterday evening with the Sazonoffs, and I sat next to Polivanov. Politically I know really nothing about him, but personally I immediately took a great sympathy to him. He is one of those grand old Russians, enormously tall, with a wonderfully commanding, imposing presence. A rugged face framed in a short dark beard, and deep-set grey eyes, keen and very bright and yet unspeakably kind. He asked me all about the hospital and my work, and when I said I loved the soldiers beamed on me delightedly, and promised me very soon to come and visit them himself.[6]

Miss Buchanan leads up to the outbreak of the Revolution with one of the more particularly fearsome accounts of Rasputin's death. After drinking nearly a whole bottle of poisoned wine and eating a dish of poisoned cakes and being shot through the heart, the 'priest'[7] (as Miss Buchanan inaccurately calls him) still recovers consciousness, hurls himself at Prince Yusupov, and tries to escape through the garden. Three months later Miss Buchanan returned to Petrograd from a holiday just in time for the outbreak of the Revolution. 'Shut up now in the house and forbidden to go out, I think I spent most of my time that morning sitting on the big staircase of the Embassy, gleaning what information I could from the various people who came and went.'[8] Her account of the summer and winter of 1917 follows the usual path; like so many other observers, she notices the indiscriminate enthusiasm of the Russian soldiery and peasants for even the most contradictory doctrines, and the facility with which skilful orators were able to manipulate the sympathy of the crowds they addressed. The British Embassy was faced across the river by Lenin's stronghold, and whenever there was a prospect of a Bolshevist rising the members of the Embassy staff were pressed either to leave the building altogether or to take safety in the more protected part of it. Miss Buchanan's desire not to miss any of the excitement led to General Knox's assuring her that she 'was more trouble than all the Russian Army'.[9] Her descriptions of the Bolshevist *émeutes*, as seen from the Embassy windows, are the best thing in the book.

It is unfortunate that the writer has allowed herself to enter upon the troubled sea of the Russian revolutionary politics of last year. Certainly she does not profess to be qualified to pass final judgments, but even in the vague outline of events which she gives there are too many traces of gossip accepted as fact. In the Kornilov affair, for example, it is hardly fair to M. Kerensky, for whose intentions Miss Buchanan expresses her admiration, to say that 'the papers published a telegram of Kerensky's proclaiming himself Dictator and commanding Kornilov to resign at once'.[10] It was not Kerensky himself, but the Provisional Government which gave him special powers to deal with the liquidation of the Kornilov affair, and he was not thus or otherwise invested with dictatorial powers. When, again, Miss Buchanan says, 'What seems, however, certain is that, fearing a Bolshevik rising, the Government negotiated with Kornilov to send troops up to Petrograd to quell the insurrection under the command of General Krimov',[11] she should remember that one of the Government's main accusations against General Kornilov was not that he sent the troops to Petrograd, but that he sent them, as he had been particularly requested not to do, under the command of General Krimov. When Miss Buchanan assumes that her statement 'seems certain', she is unintentionally begging one of the most vexed questions of an intensely complicated business. Unlike personalities, politics cannot always be elucidated by the clever intuition which Miss Buchanan in her purely descriptive chapters shows herself well able to command.

1 – A review in the TLS, 19 December 1918, (Kp C135) of Petrograd. The City of Trouble 1914–1918 by Meriel Buchanan. Daughter of the British Ambassador (W. Collins Sons & Co. Ltd, 1918).

2 – Hugh Walpole (1884–1941), the popular novelist, had served during the war with the Russian Red Cross and was head of Anglo-Russian propaganda in Petrograd during the February Revolution of 1917. His experiences in Russia inform a number of his works, including The Green Mirror (1918) – see 'The Green Mirror', above – from which Buchanan quotes, ch. XXXII, pp. 251–2.

3 – Buchanan, Foreword, p. 1.

4 – Sir George William Buchanan (1854–1924) was ambassador at St Petersburg, 1910–18. (The misappellation does not occur in Petrograd.)

5 – Buchanan, ch. VII, p. 49.

6 – Ibid., p. 51, which has quotation marks round 'We dined . . . himself.'; and also has 'gray' eyes.

7 – Ibid., ch. XI, p. 82; p. 83. Grigori Yefimovich Rasputin (b. 1872) was killed in December 1916.

8 – Ibid., ch. XIII, p. 97.

9 – Ibid., ch. XX, p. 152.

10 – Ibid., ch. XXII, p. 165. Alexander Fordorovich Kerensky (1881–1970), head of the provisional government from July 1917, in September ordered the arrest of the army's commander-in-chief, General Lavr Georgyevich Kornilov (1870–1918), who had attempted to seize Petrograd and establish a military dictatorship.

11 – Ibid., ch. XII, p. 169.

The Russian View

When, in one of Mr Galsworthy's latest stories one of the characters addresses a stranger as 'Brother'[2] you rub your eyes and wonder whether it is possible that you are reading a translation from the Russian. It is true that both the characters are at the moment in a condition of great misery, but in a book about English people written by an Englishman such a word seems out of keeping. 'Mate', perhaps, would be the English equivalent; but mate does not mean brother, and it would be wisest to accept the fact that, however much we may wish to follow the Russian example, we cannot say 'brother' to a stranger in England. Turning to the pages of Elena Militsina and Mikhail Saltikov[3] in the belief that we have met the word over and over again, we do not, as a matter of fact, find a single example of it. We have found it in the atmosphere, then; it is the word which expresses, not only the attitude of the characters to each other, but the writer's attitude towards the world. Saltikov died in the year 1889; Elena Militsina is still apparently a young woman. Half a century lies between the appearance of the first book of the one and the first book of the other; but, as Dr Wright notes, 'the unity of outlook and the kindred sympathies shared by these two writers of successive generations show that the aspirations uttered in 1847 were still unfulfilled in the first decades of the twentieth century . . .[4] ⟨The stories⟩ should help us to realise ⟨he adds⟩ that a change in the government of Russia was inevitable.'[5] But the unity which we feel in both writers lies deeper than that – it will outlive a change of government; roughly stated, it seems to consist in their sense of brotherhood. It is for the sake of the outlook which they have in common that we translate and publish and read with interest stories which are not of themselves of great artistic importance.

Call it what we like, the quality which we recognise at once as the Russian quality in the stories before us is hardly to be found in English literature. The impulse to write has come to us from a different direction – from so many different directions, indeed, that it is impossible to say that there is any one quality supremely characteristic of English literature. The impulse which urges the Russians to express themselves seems more simple, and is more easily detected in the lesser writers than in the great; they have been driven to write by their deep sense of human suffering and their unwavering sympathy with it. An able English writer treating the theme which Elena Militsina has treated in *The Village Priest*, would have shown his knowledge of different social classes, his intellectual grasp of the religious problem. His story would have been well constructed and made to appear probable. All this seems irrelevant to the Russian writer. She asks herself only about the soul of the priest, and tries to imagine what was in the hearts of the peasants when they prayed or came to die. As for the story, there is none; there is no close observation of manners; her work shows very little sense of form; she leaves off anywhere, as it seems, without troubling to finish. And yet, in spite of its formlessness and flatness, she produces an effect of spirituality. It is as if she had tried to light a lamp behind her characters, making them transparent rather than solid, letting the large and permanent things show through the details of dress and body. She is not a writer of remarkable gift, so that, having produced this sense of transparency, with its strange power to make us imagine that we are on the threshold of something else, she stops short; she cannot show us what goes on in the souls thus unveiled. Saltikov is more penetrating and more masterly; but he, too, approaches his work in the same spirit of sympathy with suffering rather than in a spirit of curiosity, or amusement, or intellectual interest. It is sympathy that enables him to draw in so short a space so remarkable a picture of the Russian peasant toiling in the immense field of Russia.

There is no end to the field; you cannot get out of it anywhere. Konyaga has drawn the plough afar and across it, yet he never reached the boundary of this land. Whether it is bare or flowery, or benumbed under a snowy winding sheet, it stretches far and wide in its might; it does not provoke to strife with itself but straightway leads captive. It is not possible to guess its secret, nor to overcome, nor to exhaust it; as soon as it dies, it is alive again ... The land crushes him, takes away his last powers, and yet will not confess itself satisfied.[6]

Both writers seem to be saying to us constantly, in the words of Militsina's priest:

Learn to make yourself akin to people. I would even like to add: Make yourself indispensable to them. But let this sympathy be not with the mind – for it is easy with the mind – but with the heart, with love towards them.[7]

In some such words one might sketch roughly the nature of the gift made us by the Russian writers. More than any others they seem impressed with the profound suffering of human beings; and perhaps it is common

suffering rather than common happiness or effort or desire that produces the feeling of brotherhood. 'Deep sadness,'[8] says Dr Wright, is
typical of the Russian people. Whether or not they are more sad than
other people, it is certain that they never attempt to conceal their
sadness. There is none of that effort so common in England to appear
better off than you are; there is no disgrace in poverty and failure; the
feeble-minded are called with reverence 'the Slaves of God'.[9] On the
other hand there is none of that instinct to rebel against sorrow, to make
something brave, gay, romantic, intellectual, out of life, which the
literatures of France and England so splendidly express. The gulf
between us and them is clearly shown by the difficulty with which we
produce even a tolerable imitation of the Russians. We become awkward and self-conscious, or worse, denying our own qualities, we write
with an affectation of simplicity and goodness which soon turns to
mawkish sentimentality. The truth is that if you say 'brother' you must
say it with conviction, and it is not easy to say it with conviction. The
Russians themselves produce this sense of conviction not because they
acquiesce or tolerate indiscriminately or despair, but because they
believe so passionately in the existence of the soul. Konyaga, the worn-
out horse who typifies the Russian peasant, may be beaten, harassed,
hardly alive, 'but a sound core lives in him, neither dying, nor dismem-
bered, nor destroyed. There is no end of this living core, that alone is
clear.'[10] And that alone is important; that living core which suffers and
toils is what we all have in common. We tend to disguise or to decorate
it; but the Russians believe in it, seek it out, interpret it, and, following its
agonies and intricacies, have produced not only the most spiritual of
modern books but also the most profound.

1 – A review in the *TLS*, 19 December 1918, (Kp c136) of *The Village Priest and
Other Stories* from the Russian of Militsina & Saltikov. Translated by Beatrix L.
Tollemache. With an introduction by C. Hagberg Wright (Fisher Unwin Ltd, 1918).
VW later adapted and made use of part of this review when writing 'The Russian
Point of View', *IV. VW Essays* and *CR1*.
2 – John Galsworthy (1867–1933), 'The First and the Last', in the collection *Five
Tales* (Heinemann, 1918), p. 18: 'A surge of feeling came up in Laurence for this
creature, more unfortunate than himself ... "Well, brother," he said, "*you* don't
look too prosperous!"'
3 – Elena Dmietrievna Militsina, dates untraced, is represented in the present
volume by the title story and by 'The Old Nurse'. Mikhail Evgrafovich Saltikov
(1826–89), better known under his pseudonym Schédrin, author of *Provincial*

Sketches (1857–8) and editor of the *Fatherland Review* from 1878, until its suppression by the authorities in 1884. The present volume contains three of his stories: 'Konyaga', 'A Visit to a Russian Prison' and 'The Governor'.

4 – *Village Priest*, intro., p. viii; Sir Charles Hagberg Wright (1862–1940), librarian and specialist in Russian literature, educated privately in Russia, France and Germany, and at the Royal Academical Institution, Belfast, and Trinity College, Dublin. From 1893 until his death he was secretary and librarian of the London Library.

5 – *Ibid.*, p. xxii; see also n. 9 below.

6 – *Ibid.*, 'Konyaga', p. 75; the ellipsis marks the omission of: 'You cannot grasp which is death and which is life. But in life or in death the first and unchangeable eye-witness is Konyaga. For others these fields represent abundance, poetry, and vast spaces; but for Konyaga – they mean servitude.'

7 – *Ibid.*, 'The Village Priest', p. 34.

8 – *Ibid.*, intro., p. xxii: 'They [Saltikov's sketches] reveal his love of humanity and his greatness of heart, while giving us a typical picture of the Russian people, their deep sadness, their inherent simplicity and kindliness. They should help us to realise that a change in the government of Russia was inevitable.'

9 – *Ibid.*, 'The Village Priest', pp. 8–9: 'Beside her were the two old maids – Slaves of God she called them – the foolish, simple-minded Theckla and the crazy Mokrena. They were winding thread, or else knitting or sewing something.'

10 – *Ibid.*, 'Konyaga', p. 77, which has: 'A sound core'.

'Mummery'

Mummery, which is apparently the nineteenth volume from Mr Cannan's[2] pen, is a clever readable novel, as we have some reason to expect that an author's nineteenth book should be. Nineteen volumes cannot be brought from start to finish without learning whatever you are capable of learning about writing books; but the risk of learning your lesson so thoroughly is that you may become in the process not an artist, but a professional writer. You may learn to write so easily that writing becomes a habit. Mr Cannan has to tell the story of two men of genius, one a painter, the other a dramatist; both would reform the stage, one by his designs, the other by his plays; but they are both frustrated, so far as the present is concerned, by the British public and by Sir Henry Butcher, the actor-manager, who serves that public faithfully or with only an occasional disloyalty. The theatrical world is very vivaciously and very literally represented by Mr Cannan, so that many of the characters in it seem to belong as much to the actual world as to the world of fiction. But whether or not he has his counterpart in life, Sir Henry Butcher is certainly the most imaginative character in the book. One can believe that actor-managers famed for their sumptuous representations of Shakespeare, as illustrious in society as upon the stage, in whom strangely enough the dramatic genius burns up by fits and starts, are much as Mr Cannan depicts them. The wealthy peer who supports the higher drama, the manager's wife who regards the theatre 'as a kind of salon' and hates any attempt 'to divert Sir Henry from the social to the professional aspect of the theatre',[3] the atmosphere of the Imperium behind the scenes and in the boxes, are all done skilfully and with humour.

So long as Mr Cannan is noting down what he has observed he shows himself a shrewd though not a very subtle observer. But when he draws conclusions from what he has seen and becomes the intellectual satirist, he writes as if from habit, repeating what he has learnt by heart from writers of what he calls 'the Sturm and Drang period'[4] in whom the intellect was often very keen and the satiric gift very fine. Mr Adnor Rodd is their representative. The name is sufficient to show us that, let alone the distinguished appearance and the abrupt manner. But Mr Adnor Rodd, though he is a very conscientious man and writes plays which no one will produce, is not, so far as our experience goes, a very clever man. 'Money!' he exclaims. 'That is the secret of the whole criminal business. Money controls art. Money rejects art. Money's a sensitive thing too. It rejects force, spontaneity, originality. It wants repetition, immutability, things calculable. Money . . . '[5] He is, in short, what the conventional idea of an artist is supposed to be, 'demoniac and challenging';[6] just as Charles Mann, the painter, is the irresponsible and non-moral variety of the same type. Sir Henry Butcher and the Imperium theatre are quite proof against attacks levelled at them by people of this calibre, and deserve to be so. But it is a misfortune from the point of view of the book, in so far as it is a book of criticism and ideas. Mr Cannan has every right to criticise society in his books, but, like everything else in a novel criticism must be the expression of a writer's own convictions; the conventions of the intellectual are at least as sterile as the conventions of the bourgeois. Mr Cannan seems to be falling into the habit of being intellectual in a perfectly conventional way, so that his criticism is more and more a stereotyped complaint and his remedy more and more a nostrum made up for him by other people. If he had thought out his position afresh and for himself, he would scarcely have spoilt Clara Day by making her half a natural nice woman and half the embodiment of somebody's theory upon the function of the female sex in human society. 'Her childish detestation of her womanhood was gone. She accepted it, gloried in it as her instrument, and knew that she could never be lost in it. For ever in her mind that crisis was associated with Kropotkin's escape from prison [. . .]'⁷ On the advice, no doubt, of some distinguished writer, she saw 'that being a woman, she must work through a man's imagination before she could become a person fit to dwell on the earth with her fellows',⁸ and married Rodd; but a marriage so cordially vouched for by the best authorities has no need of our commendation. It is in Mr Cannan's interest, and not in Mr and Mrs Rodd's, that we recommend him to find some means of destroying the careful selection of books, including six volumes of Ibsen, which they took with them on their honeymoon.

1–A review in the TLS, 19 December 1918, (Kp c137) of *Mummery. A Tale of Three Idealists* (W. Collins Sons & Co. Ltd, 1918) by Gilbert Cannan. Reprinted: CW.

2 – Gilbert Cannan (1884–1955), novelist, dramatist and dramatic critic; his works include the *roman à clef Mendel* (1916), based on the life of the painter Mark Gertler (1891–1938) and dedicated to (Dora) Carrington (1892–1932), a book that VW had thought 'rather interesting' (*II VW Letters*, no. 805, to Saxon Sydney-Turner).

3 – Cannan, ch. X, p. 127.

4 – *Ibid.*, ch. XI, p. 142; the writers are listed as: 'Shaw, Barker, Galsworthy, Ibsen, Schnitzler, Hauptmann, Tschekov, Andreev, Claudel, Strindberg, Wedekind'.

5 – *Ibid.*, ch. XII, p. 160, which has: 'You! You talk of money! That is the secret', and 'a sensitive thing, too'.

6 – *Ibid.*

7 – *Ibid.*, ch. VIII, pp. 103–4, which has a paragraph at 'For ever'.

8 – *Ibid.*, ch. XVIII, p. 243, which has: 'and being a woman'.

'The Method of Henry James'

Henry James² is much at present in the air – a portentous figure looming large and undefined in the consciousness of writers, to some an oppression, to others an obsession, but undeniably present to all. In either case, whether you suffer from the consciousness of Henry James or rejoice in it, you can scarcely do better than read what Mr Beach has to say about him. He has seen we will not say the, but certainly a, figure in the carpet, which, considering the width of the fabric and the complexity of the pattern, is something of an achievement. But further and more remarkably, considering his race, it is not to Mr Beach a mere diagram to be committed to memory in order to win the prize, whatever that may be, of accurate culture. You will not come out top through reading Mr Beach, but you will be made to enjoy thinking about Henry James and stimulated to frame theories to account for him; you may in the end find yourself with a pattern of your own.

Mr Beach is far too fruitful and cogent a writer to lend himself to summary, nor can we develop a fraction of the things which tempted us to amplify them as we read; but we may perhaps brood for a moment upon the question in general. It is a commonplace to say that no other writer causes his readers to ask so many questions or has a following more sharply divided among themselves than Henry James. Mr Beach is a Jacobean – that is to say he believes that in *The Wings of the Dove*, *The Ambassadors*, and *The Golden Bowl* Mr James produced 'the beautiful fruits'[3] of a method which he had invented and perfected through a long series of failures and experiments. Other admirers cease to admire at or about the year 1889 – the year of *The Tragic Muse*.[4] Both these sects can make out a good case for their beliefs, and are happy in their convictions. But more difficult to define and less enviable is the position of a third group, which cannot accommodate itself to either camp. The trouble with them is that they admire both periods, but with inexplicable lapses, almost unknown in the case of other writers, when from the extreme of admiration they turn to something like contempt. A sudden chill in an atmosphere of cordiality, a hint of callousness beneath the show of affection – by some such figures alone can they describe the insidious sensation which converts them from enthusiasts to outcasts. The worst of it is that they scarcely dare formulate their meaning, since any plain statement seems so grievously an over-statement. If you woke in the night and found yourself saying, 'Henry James is vulgar – Henry James is a snob', you would annihilate these words, lest the very darkness should overhear them. In the light of day the utmost you can bring yourself to murmur is that Henry James is an American. He had the American love of old furniture. Why these characteristics should at moments appear capable of such devastating effects is one of those puzzles that so often destroy the peace of mind of the fickle Jacobeans. His characters, so they say, are somehow tainted with the determination not to be vulgar; they are, as exiles tend to be, slightly parasitic; they have an enormous appetite for afternoon tea; their attitude not only to furniture but to life is more that of the appreciative collector than of the undoubting possessor.

But somehow none of this seems of importance compared with the other fact, which becomes increasingly clear, that Henry James, whatever else he may have been, was a great writer – a great artist. A priest of the art of writing in his lifetime, he is now among the saints to whom every writer, in particular every novelist, must do homage. His pursuit of his method was religious in its seriousness, religious in its sacrifices, and productive, as we see from his prefaces and sketches, of a solemn rejoicing such as one can imagine in a priest to whom a vision of the divinity has been vouchsafed at last. A glimpse of the possibilities which in his view gather round every story and stretch away into the distance beyond any sight save his own makes other people's achievements seem empty and childish. One had almost rather read what he meant to do than read what he actually did do. Merely as the writer who could make words follow his bidding, take his inflection, say what he wished them to say until the limit of what can be expressed seems to be surpassed, he is a source of perpetual wonder and delight. That is one side of him which is of perennial fascination, but perhaps it is not the most important side. The important side is suggested by the design which he made in order to explain his conception of *The Awkward Age.* He drew on a sheet of paper

the neat figure of a circle consisting of a number of small rounds disposed at equal distances about a central object. The central object was my situation, my subject in itself, to which the thing would owe its title, and the small rounds represented so many distinct lamps, as I liked to call them, the function of each of which would be to light with all due intensity one of its aspects.[5]

One has to look for something like that in the later books – not a plot, or a collection of characters, or a view of life, but something more abstract, more difficult to grasp, the weaving together of many themes into one theme, the making out of a design.

1 – A review in the *TLS*, 26 December 1918, (Kp c138) of *The Method of Henry James* (Yale University Press, 1918) by Joseph Warren Beach, Associate Professor of English, University of Minnesota. 'For some reason, not connected with my virtues I think,' VW wrote in her diary on 7 December 1918, 'I get 2 or even 3 books weekly

from the Times, & thus breast one short choppy wave after another. It fills up the time while Night & Day lies dormant; it gives me distinct pleasure I own to formulate rapid views of Henry James & Mr Hergesheimer [see '*The Three Black Pennys*' above]; chiefly because I slip in some ancient crank of mine.'

See also 'Mr Henry James's Latest Novel', *I VW Essays*; 'The Old Order', above; 'Within the Rim', 'The Letters of Henry James', 'Henry James's Ghost Stories', *III VW Essays*.

2 – Henry James (1843–1916).

3 – Beach, pt II, p. 255; *The Wings of the Dove* (1902), *The Ambassadors* (1903), *The Golden Bowl* (1904).

4 – *Ibid.*, 'Explanations', p. 4.

5 – *Ibid.*, pt I, pp. 19–20, quoting *Harper's Weekly*, vol. ix, 1898, pp. xvi–xvii.

Appendices

APPENDIX I

Reading Notes

The reading notes reproduced here relate to the articles 'Coleridge as Critic' and 'Trafficks and Discoveries'. They are the only such notes from the period 1913–18 known to have survived. Those on Coleridge were originally made, with others, at the opposite end of a notebook later used by Virginia Woolf as part of her diary for 1918 and 1919 (Reading notes: Berg, xxx, 4pp. numbered 7–10). They are based upon two works: *Omniana* in vol. i of *The Literary Remains*, ed. H. N. Coleridge (2 vols., Pickering, 1836); and: *The Table Talk and Omniana of Samuel Taylor Coleridge. With a note on Coleridge by Coventry Patmore* (OUP, 1917).

The notes for 'Trafficks and Discoveries' are transcribed from MHP (B. 2d., 7pp and 2pp.). They are based upon two works: vols. i–iii of *Hakluyt's Collection of the Early Voyages, Travels and Discoveries of the English Nation. A new edition, with additions* (5 vols., R. H. Evans, 1809–12); and: *English Seamen in the Sixteenth Century* (Longmans, Green, & Co., 1895) by J. A. Froude.

The transcriptions retain the original haphazard punctuation, with two exceptions: single rather than double quotation marks are used and have been supplied, with the help of the texts concerned, wherever Virginia Woolf has failed either to close or to open these; a full point has been inserted in two or three instances after page references. Virginia Woolf's insertions are indicated by ⟨angled brackets⟩; her cancellations are marked through with a fine line. Dubious readings have been enclosed in square brackets and queried [thus?].

Coleridges Table Talk & Omniana

OMNIANA (in my edition) _____

Reading this through, I was struck by C's greater than ⟨remembered⟩ humanity & ~~subtlety~~ humour. His discrimination of course very subtle, but often fine into the bargain:

335. a good passage upon the falseness of sympathy: how it comes from insincerity. No doubt he saw much into character —— more than one has come to think, owing to his character. always heard of as a spout of words, not as a person with insight.

343. 'in every face a history or a prophecy.'

356. It is unworthy to do nothing but enjoy poetry.

369. Evils of procrastination.

385. The handsome hypocricies that spring from the desire of distinction.

Table Talk – Oxford Edition. 1918.

C. thought Old Mortality, Guy Mannering the best of Scott.

41. Euripides like a modern Frenchman – never so happy as when giving a slap at the Gods altogether.

41. Snuff the final cause of the human nose.

56. 'If you take from Virgil his diction & metre, what do you leave him'?

65. 'I have a smack of Hamlet myself.'

73. definition of prose & poetry: prose = words in their best order; poetry = best words in best order.

74. genius can't exist with envy.

86. liked Jane A's novels.

91. 'poetry must be good sense.'

93. 'no subjectivity in Homeric authors' – argument for their being many authors.

103. had been flogged into being a Christian.

106. Mrs Barbaulds criticism of the A.M. lacked a moral.

108. works of imagination should be written in very plain language.

115. on Rabelais (good). Swift compared with R.

117. C. a post Imp: 'th overcoming difficulties the way of decadence.'
118. Everyone born an Aristotelian or a platonist.
132. 'I have no ear whatever; – but intensest delight in music, & can detect good from bad.'
135. Col. in favour of adult suffrage.
141. C. at pictures.
163. on Home rule.
166. Children graceful before they have learnt to dance.
182. Old Greek & Latin same order as English: Virgil & Tibullus not.
184. on beauty of Greek language.
185. America. slang.
189. W.^th greatest phil. poet since Milton.
190. great things done by individuals, not Acts of Parl.
194. English habit of praising foreigners to their own cost.
195. Milton's love of music greater than of painting.
198. Keats. 'The school is your father &c'.
201. Great minds androgynous.
209. Home rule to be an absolute division.
213. one can't imitate Sh^re: has no manner.
239. The Sonnets written to a woman: in So^y.
252. As a boy Aeschylus; youth & middle age Euripides; now in declining years Sophocles, the most perfect.
256. when Johnson's talk the bow-wow manner.
258. Coleridge seems to have been a mass of sensibilities. I love Purcell —— the effect of music in helping him to write poetry.
260. no pleasure from associations with places – living collaterally.
261. philanthropists hostile to the individual but benevolent to the race.
262. C^llhad memory for words.
263. against Gibbon.
267. greatest pleasure in Milton's poetry comes from his egoism. M: himself that you see.
269. Tristram Shandy scarcely readable by women – higher powers can only act with help of lower.
284. Scotts novels the only books he could *read* when ill.
286. Landor cd. not make his poetry into a whole. Chronological order best for poems.
293. I take no interest in facts —— they must refer to something else.
~~261. philanthropists always wrong; in heart hostile to individuals, but benevolent to the race.~~

293. Sh<u>res.</u> way of creating sentences – not seeing them entire first.

293. & Crabbe gives one little or no pleasure.

295. Sh<u>re</u> not more intelligible to his own time than to ours.

318. Excellence of verse to be untranslatable – 'printers devils personifications' (Gray).

344. 'The impossibility of any man's being a great poet without being first a ~~grea~~ good man' Ben Jonson. Dedict Volpone.
(*Allsops recollections*).

416. on Scotts novels. less indecent than Sterne, but none of his characters so good: in all subjects there is a struggle between opposites.

421. Lamb essentially a Xtian, tho' a sceptic.

430. good description of Cobbett.

437. Works written upon 'Scraps of Sibylline leaves, including margins of books & blank pages.'

440. – strange that no great poet has come from the lower classes except Burns.

441. Crashaw & St Theresa perhaps suggested the first thought of Christabel.

445. his discrimination between one's feelings for poor & rich.

447. Greater part of L.B. sold to seafaring men, who thought that A.M. must have relation to Nautical matters.

452. Shelleys wish to consult Co.

470. Wordsworth <u>all</u> man: least femininity in his mind.

Hakluyt. Vol. I.

how H. looked at maps when a boy.

v. Strange that natives of Japan &c. shd. be seen here.

xii. Records lie recklessly hidden in misty darkness.

258. Sir H. Willoughby frozen to death in 1553 'for pickerie ducked at the yards arm & so discharged.' Thomas Nash. Queer names rescued.

271. Sir H.W. of goodly personage (for he was of tall stature).

271. Master Sidney's discourse – all shareholds in the discovery of Muscovy. Chancelor did it 1553.

272. The ships leave; crew in watchet; privy council on the towers to see; men ran up the masts.

273. if the cruelty of death hath taken hold of them God send them a Christian grave & sepulchre.
list of native words given – all directions for finding

326. your way. Ambassador wrecked off Scotland; how he was treated by the Lord Mayor in London.

323. & sent back with a male & female lion for the Czar.

306. Cabot comes to Greenwich to say goodbye to Burrough.

330. little companies of ships setting fourth to trade with Muscovy.

332. coloured cloths sent to Russia; cables & rope & furs bought wax flax tallow & train oils.

323. gifts sent by King & Queen to Russia:

347. whales ingendering time. superstitions & habits of natives.

356. merchants 'dining' with Emperor.

415. what the merchant adventurers have discovered, & hope to discover. 'not commonly by seas frequented'

416. English merchants for discovery of new trades – monopolies

<u>vol.2.</u>

the great wealth of good reading in H: even dedications & addresses worth something

ix. wollen [sic] cloth the natural commodity of the realm

216. the vermin of Cyprus. Takes note of religious practises.

210. man had hold of cable by his teeth; 217. the cat wh. swam.

219. how the natives charm away the water spout

222. fine [leisured?] reading: the Vulture.

246. John Fox meets the eight gallies of Turks: his address to his sailors.

246. Then stood up John Grove the master .. with his sword & target (being a comely man) beauty held in esteem. 'fared among the Turks like wood lion'.

247. Fox 13 years prisoner to the Turks.

250. the Christian God helpful: Turk God very dull. howsoever their God behaved himself, our God showed himself a very God indeed.

250. The sword ⟨248⟩ with wh. Fox killed the keeper hung up by the Monk of Gallipoli.

253. Elizabeth 'Cloud of most pleasant rain & sweetest fountain of noblenesse & virtue.'
256. Certain of our subjects slaves in your gallies
261. E. apologises for evil doers.
268. Their sense of wonder unexhausted: canary birds.
268. The women of Venice rather monsters than women.
270. Protestant brings bad luck to the ship.
272. trusting gallies of Turks
279. to sell knit socks of Norwich yarn in Con.ple
280. The special virtue of English wool, testified by condition of old Parliament robes. no moth in them
 — 'turning to hag & wallet' of the poor people.
281. 'apt young men' always sent out.
282. passion for Anile: to grow it in England. The Turkish dies [sic].
 — They cd. dye yellow & green. Anile made blue.
282. if any man cd. discover oil in England he wd. have immortal fame. oil from radish seed.
284. What discoveries of plants & fruits a m traveller may make for his country — Dr Linaker brought in the damask rose, & tulipas from Vienna; seed of Sabacco from West indies 'many have been eased of the rheumes'. the good of the poor.
287. trumpets drum & flute on board.
291. present of dogs made to the Turk. magnificence with wh. the English sailors are entertained.
 — the prophet'(a fool) who cried Hough!
307. falsehood seldom known among merchants.
422. ships setting out together because of Spanish threats. Turkish flowers of speech.
452. a garden of nightingales — a flock of phasant birds
453. The Queen's letter smelt of camphor & ambergris. ink of musk
474. saw the elephant not only with bodily eyes but with the eyes of my sy spirit. admiring the workmaster.
475. habits of the elephant: debate with dragon: mixture of their blood produces vermilion.
478. what Chancellor said that Cabot reported about whirlpools.
479. worms & shells on the ships.
595. to observe the daily order of Common Prayer.
607. the nature of the prize: sugar, phants teeth &c.

620. commodities include horsetails hats; brought back pepper, phants teeth, oil

656. Sailors imagining what running at tilt there wd. be at Whitehall on the Queen's day.

656. how they lay off Cornwall for 14 days without drink. Good account of rain caught.

657. how they gave the T^rk to drink, to teach them humanity

659. talks of Irish habits as of a completely strange country.

662. The leaders of the gallies dressed in silk, with silver whistles & plumes of feathers.

676. whole key covered with silver & gems.

682. Sir R.G. very unquiet in his mind [is?] greatly affected to war.

Hakluyt vol. 3.

9. E. withdraws her consent to R's going: he misunderstands

14. the cargoe of spices & calicoes. Her majesty chief among adventurers.

28. Cabot came to London as a merchant 'to sail by the West into the East where spices grow .. more divine than human.'

31. desire of discovery inherited like sickness.

45. Egg in moonshine – need makes the old wife to trot.

47. Sir HW. congealed & frozen to death.

45. one of the reasons for the N.W. passage: 'needy people of our country wh. now trouble the commonwealth & through want here at home are inforced to commit outrageous offences, whereby they are daily consumed with the gallowes'.

53. the Queen waving her hand to Frobisher.

59. Frobishers Prayer. natives to be made Xtian.

94. unicorns horn given to the Queen.

106. articles & orders drawn up by Frobisher.

98. how the captive savages met each other.

168. desirous to see the strange things of the world.

169. The men eat each other – How Mr Buts was only known by a mark on his arm.

189. music, morris dancers, hobby horses, & maylike concerts to delight the savage people–

Froude. English Seamen.

10. Cabot looked for passage to Cathay. Henry 7[th.]
12. Henry 8[th.] Hawkins went to Guinea.
12. Thorne (H.8th) went for NW passage.
12. Hore – to Newfoundland.
22. Spirit of enterprise grew with reformation.
24. the privateers a force to put down the Inquisition
28. how the west country families took to the sea.
46. Stukeley.
54. An African co. formed by Hawkins.
55. Got slaves in Sierra Leone & sold them at St Domingo
64. Drake comes in.
65. reasons of Philips dislike.
70. Drakes 3[rd.] voyage 1567.
84. Very good story teller – impossible to re-tell Froude.
95. the story reads like a chapter from Monte Christo.
104. shd. be an epic as grand as the Odyssey.
117. how they were puritans. Drake taking communion with Doughty.
122. her ballast was silver, her cargo gold, – emeralds & rubies
123. Capture of the Cacafuego.
124. Drake dined alone with music.
⟨[Pelican]⟩
138. vessel no larger than a second-rate yacht of a modern noble lord.
178. Drakes largest expedition starts 1585 to revenge the corn ships taken by Spain. Froude spins out a fine coherent story from the mass of H.
224. Drake sent to Cadiz on the Bonaventura.
236. takes the San Philip.
241. Safety of England rested on adventurers.

APPENDIX II

Notes on the Journals

All but one of the articles in this volume appeared in the *Times Literary Supplement*, which continued to be edited by Bruce Lyttelton Richmond (1871–1964), who had taken over the newly-founded paper in 1902. The exception is the essay 'Heard on the Downs: The Genesis of Myth', contributed to *The Times*, 15 August 1916.

The *TLS* articles are listed here by year and date of publication.

1912: '*Frances Willard*' (28 November); *1913*: 'Chinese Stories' (1 May); '*Jane Austen*' (8 May); '*Les Copains*' (7 August); *1916*: 'Queen Adelaide' (13 January); 'A Scribbling Dame' (17 February); 'Charlotte Brontë' (13 April); '*Past and Present at the English Lakes*' (29 June); 'A Man With a View' (20 July); '*The Park Wall*' (31 August); 'The Fighting Nineties' (12 October); 'Among the Poets' (2 November); '*London Revisited*' (9 November); 'In a Library' (23 November); 'Hours in a Library' (30 November); 'Old and Young' (14 December); '*Social Life in England*' (21 December); 'Mr Symons's Essays' (21 December); *1917*: '*Romance*' (18 January); 'Tolstoy's *The Cossacks*' (1 February); 'Melodious Meditations' (8 February); 'More Dostoevsky' (22 February); '*Before Midnight*' (1 March); 'Parodies' (8 March); '*Sir Walter Raleigh*' (15 March); '*The House of Lyme*' (29 March); '*Poe's Helen*' (5 April); 'A Talker' (12 April); '*In Good Company*' (12 April); 'A Cambridge V.A.D.' (10 May); 'The Perfect Language' (24 May); 'Mr Sassoon's Poems' (31 May); '*Creative Criticism*' (7 June); '*South Wind*' (14 June); '*Books and Persons*' (5 July); 'Thoreau' (12 July); '*Lord Jim*' (26 July); '*John Davidson*' (16 August); 'A Victorian Echo' (23 August); 'Mr Galsworthy's Novel' (30 August); 'To Read Or Not To Read' (6 September); 'Mr Conrad's *Youth*' (20 September); '*Flumina Amem Silvasque*' (11 October); 'A Minor Dostoevsky' (11 October); 'The Old Order' (18 October); '*Hearts of Controversy*' (25 October); 'A Russian Schoolboy' (8 November); 'Stopford Brooke' (29 November); 'Mr Gladstone's Daughter' (6 December); '*Charlotte Brontë*' (13 December); '*Rebels and Reformers*' (20 December); 'Sunset Reflections' (20 December); 'The New Crusade' (27 December); *1918*: '*Visits to Walt Whitman*' (3 January); 'Philosophy in Fiction' (10 January); 'A Book of Essays' (17 January); '*The Green Mirror*' (24

January); 'Across the Border' (31 January); 'Coleridge as Critic' (7 February); 'Mr Conrad's Crisis' (14 March); 'Swinburne letters' (21 March) 'Papers on Pepys' (4 April); *Second Marriage* (25 April); 'Two Irish Poets' (2 May); 'Tchehov's Questions' (16 May); 'Imitative Essays' (23 May); 'Moments of Vision' (23 May); 'Dreams and Realities' (30 May); 'The Claim of the Living' (13 June); 'Loud Laughter' (20 June); 'A Victorian Socialist' (27 June); 'Mr Merrick's Novels' (4 July); 'Two Soldier-Poets' (11 July); 'On Re-reading Meredith' (25 July); 'Rupert Brooke' (8 August); 'A Practical Utopia' (15 August); *The Sad Years* (29 August); 'The "Movie" Novel' (29 August); 'War in the Village' (12 September); 'The Rights of Youth' (19 December); 'Mr Hudson's Childhood' (26 September); 'Caution and Criticism' (3 October); 'Adventurers All' (10 October); 'Honest Fiction' (10 October); 'Women Novelists' (17 October); 'Valery Brussof' (24 October); *The Candle of Vision* (31 October); *Abraham Lincoln* (31 October); 'Mr Howells on Form' (14 November); 'Bad Writers' (21 November); 'Trafficks and Discoveries' (12 December); *The Three Black Pennys* (12 December); 'A View of the Russian Revolution' (19 December); 'The Russian View' (19 December); *Mummery* (19 December); *The Method of Henry James* (26 December).

Bibliography

This list does not include information about the several collections of Virginia Woolf's writings to which reference is made in the annotations. For this information, and for certain other bibliographical references, the reader should consult the list of Abbreviations at p. xxv

ESSAYS

The Moment and Other Essays, ed. Leonard Woolf (Hogarth Press, London, 1947; Harcourt Brace & Co., New York, 1948)

The Captain's Death Bed and Other Essays, ed. Leonard Woolf (Hogarth Press, London, and Harcourt Brace & Co., New York, 1950)

The London Scene (Frank Hallman, New York, 1975; Hogarth Press, London, and Random House, New York, 1982)

OTHER WORKS

The Complete Shorter Fiction of Virginia Woolf, ed. Susan Dick (Hogarth Press, London, and Harcourt Brace Jovanovich, New York, 1985)

WORKS OF REFERENCE

Virginia Woolf's Reading Notebooks (Princeton University Press, Princeton, New York, 1983) by Brenda R. Silver

Virginia Woolf's Literary Sources and Allusions. A Guide to the Essays (Garland, New York, 1983) by Elizabeth Steele

CRITICAL STUDIES

Victorian Bloomsbury. The Early Literary History of the Bloomsbury Group. Volume One (Macmillan Press, London, St Martin's Press, New York, 1987) by S. P. Rosenbaum

INDEX

This index is not exhaustive: references to fictional characters in the ephemeral popular novels which VW reviewed are not entered and minor characters in other works are also omitted, unless the reference has been judged to be of special interest; fictional characters are otherwise identified in this way: 'Quint, Peter, H. James's character . . .' Place names are indexed on a selective basis, according to the frequency of reference and also to their significance to VW. Works are indexed under their author and in the case of biographies, their subject. The notes are indexed selectively, generally only in relation to references in the text. Thematic entries have been included under the following heads: American Literature; Aristocracy; Biography; Character; Contemporaries; Criticism; Democracy; Drama; Eighteenth Century, the; Essay, the; Elizabethans, the; Greek; Latin; Letters; Literary Pilgrimage; Moment, the; Novel, the (and fiction); Poetry; Post-Impressionism; Prose; Reader, the (and reading); Realism; Romance; Russian Literature; Victorian Era; War, the; Women. General references under a given subject are cited last, unless written works are involved, in which case these conclude the entry concerned.

*By Virginia Woolf and available
from Harcourt Brace Jovanovich, Publishers,
in Harvest/HBJ paperback editions*

BETWEEN THE ACTS
BOOKS AND PORTRAITS
THE CAPTAIN'S DEATH BED AND OTHER ESSAYS
THE COMMON READER: *FIRST SERIES ANNOTATED EDITION*
THE COMMON READER: *SECOND SERIES ANNOTATED EDITION*
THE COMPLETE SHORTER FICTION OF VIRGINIA WOOLF
CONTEMPORARY WRITERS
THE DIARY OF VIRGINIA WOOLF, VOLUMES I–V
THE DEATH OF THE MOTH AND OTHER ESSAYS
THE ESSAYS OF VIRGINIA WOOLF, VOLUME I
THE ESSAYS OF VIRGINIA WOOLF, VOLUME II
FLUSH: *A BIOGRAPHY*
FRESHWATER: *A COMEDY*
GRANITE AND RAINBOW
A HAUNTED HOUSE AND OTHER STORIES
JACOB'S ROOM
THE LETTERS OF VIRGINIA WOOLF, VOLUMES I–VI
THE MOMENT AND OTHER ESSAYS
MOMENTS OF BEING
MRS. DALLOWAY
MRS. DALLOWAY'S PARTY
NIGHT AND DAY
ORLANDO: *A BIOGRAPHY*
THE PARGITERS: *THE NOVEL-ESSAY PORTION OF* THE YEARS
ROGER FRY
A ROOM OF ONE'S OWN
THREE GUINEAS
TO THE LIGHTHOUSE
THE VIRGINIA WOOLF READER
THE VOYAGE OUT
THE WAVES
WOMEN AND WRITING
A WRITER'S DIARY
THE YEARS